LANDS, LAWS, & GODS

STUDIES IN THE HISTORY OF GREECE & ROME

P. J. Rhodes & Richard J. A. Talbert, editors

LANDS, LAWS, & GODS

MAGISTRATES & CEREMONY IN THE REGULATION
OF PUBLIC LANDS IN REPUBLICAN ROME

DANIEL J. GARGOLA

THE UNIVERSITY OF NORTH CAROLINA PRESS · CHAPEL HILL & LONDON

© 1995 The University of North Carolina Press
All rights reserved
Manufactured in the United States of America

The paper in this book meets the guidelines for permanence and durability of the Committee on Production Guidelines for Book Longevity of the Council on Library Resources.

Library of Congress Cataloging-in-Publication Data
Gargola, Daniel J.
Lands, laws, and gods : magistrates and ceremony in the regulation of public lands in Republican Rome / by Daniel J. Gargola.
   p. cm. — (Studies in the history of Greece and Rome)
  Includes bibliographical references and index.
    ISBN 0-8078-5705-X
   1. Public lands — Rome. 2. Agricultural laws and legislation (Roman law) I. Title. II. Series.
HD137.G37   1995   95-3406
333.1'0937 — dc20   CIP

99 98 97 96 95 5 4 3 2 1

THIS BOOK WAS DIGITALLY MANUFACTURED.

CONTENTS

ACKNOWLEDGMENTS vii

INTRODUCTION 1
    I. The Laws and the Government 2
    II. Government, Religion, and Ritual in Rome 4
    III. The Evidence and the Limits of the Study 7
    IV. The Plan of the Work 10

1. THE ROMAN GOVERNMENT IN ACTION 12
    I. Magistrates, Priests, Senate, and People 12
    II. The Location and Form of Official Action 16
    III. Conclusion 24

2. RITUAL, LAW, & SPACE 25
    I. Lands and Laws 25
    II. Boundary Markers 31
    III. Magistrates and the Definition of Spaces 33
    IV. Ritual and Ceremony in the Definition of Spaces 35
    V. Roman Surveying 39
    VI. Religion, Ritual, and Centuriation 41
    VII. Conclusion 50

3. COLONIAL LAWS, COLONIAL COMMISSIONERS, & COLONISTS 51
    I. Colonial Legislation 52
    II. Colonial Commissions 58
    III. The Enlistment of Colonists 64
    IV. The Departure for the Site 67
    V. Conclusion 70

4. AS IF SMALL IMAGES OF THE ROMAN PEOPLE 71
    I. The Formation of City and Citizenry 72
    II. The Spaces Necessary for Public Life 82
    III. Territorial Subdivisions Intended for Private Use 87
    IV. The Assignment of Plots 95
    V. After the Foundation 98
    VI. Conclusion 100

5. VIRITANE ASSIGNMENTS & AGRARIAN COMMISSIONS 102
   I. The Laws 103
   II. The Commissioners 106
   III. The Installation of Settlers 107
   IV. Conclusion 112

6. THE SALE & LEASE OF PUBLIC LANDS 114
   I. Public Lands as a Source of Revenue 115
   II. The Auction 116
   III. The Establishment of Boundaries 119
   IV. Conclusion 127

7. *LEGES DE MODO AGRORUM* 129
   I. Laws and Their Implementation 130
   II. The History of Laws *de modo agrorum* 136
   III. The Law's Purpose in the Literary Sources 138
   IV. Laws *de modo agrorum* as a Kind of Sumptuary Legislation 143
   V. Conclusion 145

8. THE GRACCHAN REFORM 147
   I. The *lex Sempronia agraria* 148
   II. The Implementation of the Law 155
   III. The Agrarian Legislation of C. Gracchus 163
   IV. The Triumvirs *lege Sempronia* 167
   V. Conclusion 174

9. TOWARD THE PRINCIPATE 175
   I. The Projects of the First Century 176
   II. Administrative Procedures 179
   III. The "Rationalization" of the Process 184
   IV. Conclusion 188

CONCLUSION 190

NOTES 195

BIBLIOGRAPHY 253

INDEX 265

ACKNOWLEDGMENTS

I began work on this project as part of my doctoral dissertation at the University of North Carolina at Chapel Hill spurred by an interest in the Gracchan reform as well as some dissatisfaction with modern studies of this land law and others, which often postulated broad effects without indicating how they were achieved. Behind these immediate concerns, I had other, broader questions. How did Roman government actually function? In what ways did Roman religion influence law and government? More generally, I was interested in government, in governmental intervention in social and economic processes, and in the cultural limits on both.

Chapel Hill was a good place to pursue such a study. Henry Boren, my dissertation advisor, shared his time and his understanding of Roman history and of the Gracchi. Jerzy Linderski, George Houston, and T. R. S. Broughton clarified many points of Roman politics, administration, law, and religion for me. Others provided ideas and comments at a later stage: Richard Talbert, T. J. Cornell, and my colleagues at the University of Kentucky, Alice Christ, Thomas Cogswell, Bruce Holle, David Olster, and Mark Summers. All deserve my gratitude. Finally, I would like to acknowledge the assistance of the University of Kentucky and the University of Kentucky Research Foundation, which contributed fellowships and grants.

Daniel J. Gargola
Lexington, Kentucky
November 1994

LANDS, LAWS, & GODS

INTRODUCTION

Soon after entering office as tribune of the plebs for 133, Tiberius Sempronius Gracchus proposed a law intended to reclaim public land from those unofficially occupying it, a group that included many of the wealthiest and most powerful Romans, and distribute it among poorer citizens.[1] That act quickly led to confrontation, and over the following months the struggle between Ti. Gracchus and his opponents increased in intensity, ending in violence which cost the sacrosanct tribune his life. Those events opened a cycle of political turmoil, which ultimately led to the end of the republic. Ti. Gracchus's measure was not the first intended to govern the exploitation of public lands, nor would it be the last; agrarian laws can be found throughout the history of the Roman republic, and they form one of the most common categories of legislation. In the fourth, third, and second centuries, such measures occupied a prominent place among the means by which the Romans organized their conquests over much of Italy. In the last republican century, the great dynasts—Marius, Sulla, Pompey, Caesar, Mark Antony, and Octavian—or their agents also put forward laws to divide public lands, often in times of open civil war.

Such an important body of legislation has necessarily received much attention, with scholars using the laws to clarify a range of social, political, legal, and constitutional issues. Through such laws, historians have sought to establish the programs of major political figures or to find the roots of the political methods of the late republican *optimates* and *populares*. Others have attempted to use the legislation as evidence for the core concepts of Roman law and especially for the development of property rights and the means for defending them. Many have focused on the relationship between agrarian laws and Roman society at large, seeing in certain measures responses to broad social and economic developments.[2]

But legislation, to be effective, must be both enforceable and enforced, and for that reason some studies have a certain aura of unreality about them, for their authors have often made implicit, and occasionally explicit, assumptions about the range and the effectiveness of government, derived at least in part from the practices of modern states, where, as a result of extensive bureaucracies, policies can be implemented broadly. But the Roman state did not possess such an organization, and public lands, the target of the legislation, often lay far from the centers of power and the law. The means by which Roman officials sought to implement agrarian laws, therefore, must be a matter of concern to those seeking to assess their significance.

The administration of agrarian legislation, then, is the subject of this study. The chief aim is not to examine in depth the substantive provisions of the laws, the fundamental principles behind the regulations, their evolution, or the personal and political motives of the legislators—all important in their own right. Instead, the investigation will focus on the processes by which officially determined goals for the use of public lands were set and the ways those charged with achieving them proceeded. Certain matters will be emphasized: the position in state and society of those who first proposed laws, the range of publicly set goals deemed appropriate, the manner in which projects were framed, the procedures by which proponents gained authorization, the rank of those charged with implementation and the ways they were chosen, the administrative stages through which they proceeded, the principles, concepts, and categories that governed their operations, the context in which individuals occupying a range of statuses interacted, and the manner in which these practices evolved. These aspects of the laws have not yet been the subject of systematic study.

The project necessarily goes beyond that limited goal, for the manner in which ends are defined and the ways intentions are turned into actions reveals much about the political culture of a society. It is the very basis of the organization of power. Important members of the governing elite occupied a central role in framing laws and in implementing their provisions, and their actions involved the central institutions of the Roman state. An examination of the administration of agrarian legislation, then, shows some of the governing principles, practices, and assumptions of the republican order.

I. THE LAWS AND THE GOVERNMENT

In Rome, public land could be exploited in many ways, some more regular than others. Magistrates occasionally made ad hoc arrangements for the use of such land, assigning portions to subordinate communities, settling deported populations, and rewarding helpful individuals in allied communities or hostile states. In other cases, those seeking to turn public lands to public ends used more regular forms, ones that bulk large in the history of the consolidation of Rome's conquests and in the political struggles of the late republic. These projects began in formal legislation, put forward by magistrates of the Roman people, often acting on the advice of the senate, and passed by assemblies of citizens.

Although such laws were enacted over several centuries, those who framed individual proposals conformed to a few basic patterns, which long preserved their features. The laws can be divided into two broad categories, each with different goals. The first, far more common than the second, includes those positive rules intended to turn tracts of land to a definite and specific use. Such measures, bound to particular places and circumstances, generally required the division of cultivatable or potentially cultivatable land into plots of varying sizes, which were then transferred to individuals. Laws of this type formed two separate subcategories. In one, the framers intended that prospective farmers be organized into semiautonomous communities, *coloniae*, each with a civic organization mimicking in many ways that of Rome itself. In the other, the author of the measure instructed that allotments be distributed to individuals (*viritim*); farmers in a "viritane" assignment did not become part of a new urban order. Laws authorizing the sale and lease of public land exhibit many of the same defining features legally and administratively. In colonies, viritane assignments, sales, and leases, moreover, those receiving land were expected to fulfill various conditions that remained in force long after the original arrangements had been made.

Laws *de modo agrorum* form the second category of agrarian laws. A *lex de modo agrorum* placed restrictions on the temporary and unofficial use of public land by setting limits to the amounts individuals could cultivate and to the size of the herds they could pasture on it—the law applied to land used for pasture as well as that used for crops. Legislation of this type, then, did not ordain any particular use for land, nor was it bound to a specific set of circumstances. Instead, the laws established broad norms, applicable over all the public land of the Roman people, and valid whenever similar circumstances obtained.

The government responsible for implementing those laws, however, was not bureaucratic in a modern sense, and its ability to act on a large scale was limited. Bureaucracy, as a form of administration, has been defined as a rational organization of power with offices established and their occupants chosen according to specific requirements fitting the position. The term also can refer more narrowly to governments characterized by professionalization, regular use of written records, and delegation of authority resulting in a chain of command, the last a necessity for the broad implementation of centrally defined policies.[3] Studies of the Roman state framed in such terms exclude with reason the republican period. Detailed investigations of the imperial administration and of specific elements within it begin with the reign of Claudius, the fourth emperor.[4] Indeed, the government of the middle republic and to a considerable extent also that of the late republic can be characterized as relatively undifferentiated with its leadership acting in military, civilian, religious, executive, and legal spheres without regard to special qualifications or abilities.[5]

Students of the Roman imperial government have begun to question the degree to which its administration fits such a definition of a bureaucratic order, and some have come to view the central government as passive in areas considered crucial in many modern states, to challenge the "rationality" of many of its actions, to doubt the existence of regular, formal administrative hierarchies, and to see personal patronage and other factors as more important than ostensibly job-related criteria in gaining certain positions.[6] On closer inspection, then, the government of the Empire to many does not appear all that rational or efficient. Whatever the nature of the imperial administration, however, the republic clearly lacked those ideal bureaucratic features, even to the extent that they may be found in the Empire. Indeed, despite its increase in size and in power throughout the republican period, Rome preserved much of its origins as a city-state in its administrative structure. Its government consisted of a relatively small number of officials, elected for fixed terms, who acted directly in all areas in which they had responsibilities, for governmental practices emphasized face-to-face encounters between the governed and their governors over action at a distance through intermediaries, and the spoken word took precedence over the written.

II. GOVERNMENT, RELIGION, AND RITUAL IN ROME

The nature of the administrative operations magistrates performed and the manner in which they interacted with citizens are of special importance for this study. Any examination of Roman government in action leads immediately to the practices, concepts, and terms of the state religion and to a wide variety of ritual. Both permeated public life. The Greek historian Polybius (6.56.6–15) expressed puzzlement over the degree to which the Romans had turned their religious observances into rites and the extent to which these formalities entered into public and private life. These same formal attributes, moreover, also characterized many seemingly secular operations. An investigation into the concrete processes of administration, therefore, is also a study of the place of ritual and of religion in Rome's public life.

This study does not purport to be an investigation of either the totality of Roman ceremonial or of state ritual. Instead, a narrower group of rites will receive the most attention. The definition of ritual has long been the subject of dispute. Wishing to maintain a dichotomy between the sacred and the profane, some limit the use of the term "ritual" only to matters of religion and characterize as ceremony similar behavior forming part of apparently secular activities.[7] This sharp distinction, essentially modern in origin, has often proven unsatisfactory in practice. Others widen their definitions to include all types of formal behavior, but this blurs distinctions between the range of fields in which such behavior can be found—etiquette, drama, the many formalities of family life, and the great ceremonies of the state—for in one way or another it touches on virtually all human activities.[8] In this work, the words "ritual," "rite," and "ceremony" will be used interchangeably to signify a mode of action characterized by formalized behavior, special settings, fixity of word or of gesture, and regular repetition whenever similar circumstances again arose, without regard to their religious or secular nature, as defined either from a modern perspective or that of the Romans themselves. Within the wide range of events that fit this broad definition, the primary focus will be on those occasions when magistrates of the Roman people seeking to pass or to implement agrarian legislation acted in a ritualized manner.

Both the religious and the ceremonial aspects of Roman political culture have caused difficulties for modern interpreters, who often bring to their studies rationalizing attitudes and modernizing assumptions about the nature of religion and the relationship between religious beliefs and the life of the individual and the community. Roman public cult does not easily fit a pattern familiar to the modern world. It had no clear, fixed, and systematic theology. There was no certain body of beliefs to which individuals were to adhere. Instead, religion focused on ritual performances that emphasized the exact replication of a traditional pattern. Because of this tendency to interpret those practices in a modern light, observers often see Roman religion as without serious content, and they often assume that in the middle and late republic, when the underlying beliefs had supposedly been weakened by changing circumstances and by the influx of foreign (especially Greek) ideas, the Roman upper classes must have seen matters in the same way.[9] The necessary conclusion is that members of the elite in the second and especially in the first century did not take their traditional religion seriously and were not guided by its requirements to any significant extent. Surviving practices, then, were but the fossilized remnants of a more primitive period, the monarchy or the early republic, preserved beyond their time as a consequence of the basic conservatism of Roman public life and of antiquarian interests among the elite.[10] Although the secular ceremonies of the state have received much less attention, the same basic attitudes govern their interpretation.

Students of ritual practices in other societies often have given them greater significance. Public rites can be seen as a form of symbolic communication, disseminating an idealized representation of the community, its leadership, its constituent units, the necessary relationships between them, and the place of all in the larger world.[11] Performances are highly charged public occasions in which participants bring to life for themselves and for others the social roles and the groups thought necessary to communal life and act out their imagined interrelationships. Ritualized events, then, serve to strengthen ties among the participants, building at least the appearance of group solidarity through common action and reinforcing patterns of superordination and subordination. Rites, in other words, define membership and status for those taking part—and for those observing—and ideally exhibit leaders leading and followers following, show those in charge making the proper arrangements for the participants in the proper way, and present to the crowds others obeying and to the leaders the masses acquiescing.

Roman citizens of all classes, as will be shown in the following chapters, must have experienced their government largely as a sequence of rituals, religious or secular. The ceremonies performed by the leaders of the political order as they went about public business would have set the ways power was exercised, visualized, and perhaps actually perceived, both by the governed and those who governed them. Viewed in such a fashion, Roman state ceremonial and the religious conceptions associated with it can be seen as retaining their centrality throughout the republican period. In the words of one scholar, "the gods and the rituals addressed to those gods enter into every institution and every transaction of public life; into the whole of the Romans' system of orienting themselves in time and space; it provided them with an essential point of reference in their organization of society and in particular their organization of power."[12] Despite attempts at manipulation for political purposes and proclamations of doubt on specific points by individual Romans, these conceptions and practices permeated communal activities and were largely inescapable.[13]

One feature of ritual in the Roman context is of central importance to this study. A sharp distinction between rituals (which carry symbols) and the administrative structures of government (which involve technical operations) may be problematic in other societies, but it is especially so in

Rome. Roman magistrates were both the primary officiants in state ceremonial and the chief actors in the implementation of policies. Certain rites formed necessary elements in a range of administrative operations and ritualized occasions often included the targets of particular governmental projects, required specific actions from them, and were observed by witnesses deemed essential to larger processes. Indeed, some public rites included elements that would be considered useful even by those with the most utilitarian of sensibilities. In addition to being viewed as a form of symbolic communication, as a means of reinforcing lines of authority, and as a method of increasing at least the appearance of group solidarity, then, rites and the necessary preparations for performances can also be seen as essential elements of administration in a nonbureaucratic state.

The Roman science of government, it will be argued, was in large part a matter of rites. At one level, a ritualized occasion served as a way to organize people under the leadership of a public official, communicate decisions and commands to them, and lead them through necessary steps. At another, rituals are manifestations of a body of knowledge that guided and limited officials in fulfilling their responsibilities. A wide variety of rules, rites, and principles, peculiar to the Roman state, its history and traditions, and its civic spaces, clustered around magistracies, determining not only the proper actors, but also the necessary actions, the appropriate locations, and the required forms. The reconstruction of a portion of that body of knowledge and the determination of the ways it directed official activity are among the chief aims of the study.

III. THE EVIDENCE AND THE LIMITS OF THE STUDY

The broad chronological sweep of the series of agrarian laws, ostensibly coextensive with the republic itself, creates problems for any investigation. Authors writing at the end of the republic placed such measures in the early years of the republic and even during the monarchy. But the legal forms through which the Roman state sought to maintain its control over subordinate communities and to govern captured territory—and the necessary processes and defining procedures needed to establish certain of those forms on the scene—apparently began to take the shape so important in later periods only in the middle and late fourth century, early in the process of expansion that would eventually extend Roman power throughout Italy and the Mediterranean world.[14] In this work, the emphasis will be on the middle republic, the years between the middle of the fourth and the middle of the second centuries. Many of the sources for the fourth and early third centuries, however, are of questionable reliability, for they lie beyond the easy reach of our sources, since the writing of history itself did not begin in Rome until the end of the third century.[15] As a practical matter, then, the discussion will emphasize the late third and early second centuries. In the last chapters, the laws and administration of the late second and first centuries will be examined to determine the ways the Roman leadership adapted these patterns and forms to fit new situations.

The evidence for this project is extensive and allows the subject to be addressed at a number of levels, providing a fuller picture than for other areas of republican administration. Various authors presented brief descriptions of laws, noted the names, offices, and powers of those responsible for administration, and provided occasional anecdotes about their activities. Inscriptions add to the quantity and the quality of our evidence. Beginning in the second half of the second century, official boundary markers record the acts of magistrates, their titles, and their legal authority. The texts of laws surviving on bronze — the most notable are the fragments of the agrarian law of 111 and the *lex coloniae Iuliae Genetivae* of the colony at Urso in Spain — provide definitions of projects, establish the powers of magistrates, and order or reveal specific administrative actions.

Certain aspects of the sources allow the construction of a picture of Roman magistrates in action. To fill out their accounts, Roman historians often described officials acting in various customary ways, and while the accuracy of such a description may be doubted for a specific case, such passages do indicate the way the writer visualized the official as proceeding. Furthermore, notices of the performance of certain rites, often with the names of the magistrates who performed them, form a regular part of histories. Indeed, when affecting the annalistic style, authors regularly noted the completion of essential governmental tasks such as the census or the foundation of colonies by recording the performance of the censors' purification ceremony or *lustrum* or the foundation ceremony of a colony.[16]

Some ancient authors included detailed accounts of ritual events in their works. By the end of the second century, a tradition of antiquarian scholarship had emerged, to some extent separate from historical writing but influencing and influenced by it. Ancient antiquarians set forth such matters as the origins of cities and magistracies, provided explanations of cults and of customs, and determined the meanings of obsolete words (often preserved in rites), and antiquarians and historians often used such accounts to illustrate technical points of law or to add color to a narrative.[17] To be used as evidence, the events they described must be located chronologically and in the context of the magistrates' other responsibilities. Many are clearly datable, explicitly or on internal evidence, to the late third and second centuries, the period of our primary focus. Such accounts and the contexts in which they are placed will be accepted unless there are clear reasons in individual cases to do otherwise.

Rituals assigned to an earlier date present greater difficulties. Here, one feature of historical and antiquarian literature is especially significant: the authors of both usually presented the republic as unchanging in its essentials and saw it as functioning in the fifth century much as it did in later years. Thus, writers often provided detailed accounts of the actions of officials of the early republic and even of the kings by projecting practices of their own day or of the recent past, or perhaps antiquarian reconstructions based on such practices, into the remote past.[18] Use will be made of those descriptions and their contexts when the overall practice (such as divination by observation of the flight of birds) is known to have existed in the third, second, and first centuries.

Aspects of the administration of agrarian legislation have left physical traces. To implement some laws, Roman officials and their assistants developed a distinctive system of surveying known as centuriation or limitation, and on occasion this process permanently marked the land. In most cases, the remains cannot be dated by purely archaeological means, but when found in areas of colonization and of viritane assignments, the dates of which are preserved in literary sources, they may be connected with specific projects.[19]

A specialized technical literature described the techniques of centuriation; its surviving representatives are gathered in the collection known as the *Corpus Agrimensorum Romanorum* or the *Gromatici veteres*.[20] The origins of this literature lie in the last years of the republic, but the authors of the surviving works, the *gromatici* or *agrimensores*, are later. Frontinus (probably the governor of Britain under the Flavians), Siculus Flaccus, Hyginus, and Hyginus Gromaticus wrote the most important works during the late first and second centuries A.D.[21] They defined technical terms, noted regional peculiarities of land law, and gave directions to magistrates and surveyors engaged in dividing public land. In the process, they regularly cited republican examples, especially the colonies of Julius Caesar, Mark Antony, and Augustus, and they occasionally gave older instances, some from the fourth and third centuries; physical traces of many have been identified. The method of centuriation they described reached its full development in the late third century and, in that form, was used in many projects of the second and first centuries. In matters of surveying, then, there was considerable continuity over several centuries. The *agrimensores'* descriptions of the ways a field system was established, the crucial stages in the process, and the terminology will be regarded as valid for the entire period — the substantive rules of law, on the other hand, were influenced over time by non-Roman systems of land tenure and are less useful for our purposes.

The range of evidence, then, permits the broad reconstruction of laws, the identification of the officials who proposed and implemented them, their typical ways of proceeding, the rituals and ceremonies that accompanied their activity, the ends those rites were to achieve, and the essential technical operations needed to prepare lands for distribution. The result is necessarily an idealized portrait, from the perspective of the elite, that makes administration of laws seem more regular than it probably was, slighting differences between specific projects and the various problems resolved, more or less, by the magistrates on the scene and making the forms of the governing ceremonies and the conceptual framework into which they were placed appear more fixed than perhaps they were. Much of importance, moreover, is a matter for speculation: the social status and motivation of those Romans who decided to leave their homes and seek others elsewhere; the place, if any, of their families in the settlement process; the extent to which they maintained arrangements as intended after Roman officials had departed; the fate of the previous inhabitants; the reactions of natives to newcomers in their midst. Nevertheless, such a reconstruction of Roman government in action addresses more aspects of government as it actually functioned than is possible in most other areas of official activity.

IV. THE PLAN OF THE WORK

The remainder of the work consists of nine chapters organized into two broad parts. The first seven chapters address the basic principles of Roman government in action and the ways they are reflected in the implementation of each category of agrarian legislation. In Chapter 1, the features of Roman government will be outlined. In Chapter 2, the rules and procedures governing the treatment of land for public purposes will be set forth. The next four focus on ways public land could be exploited: Chapters 3 and 4 examine colonization; Chapter 5, viritane assignments; and Chapter 6, the sale and lease of lands. *Leges de modo agrorum* are the subject of Chapter 7. In those five chapters, each type of law will be examined from the manner of its formulation to the completion of implementation. In the process, the crucial stages will be distinguished, the leading actors and the other participants identified, the place, time, and form of actions determined, and their place in the Roman scheme set forth.

In their essentials, these legal forms remained relatively constant over the period covered by the investigation, as did the basic processes and defining administrative stages. When discussing those aspects, therefore, no substantial chronological distinctions will be made. But other features of agrarian legislation underwent considerable change from the middle to the late republic. At the most basic level, in the earlier period, colonies, viritane assignments, and the sale and lease of land formed entirely separate categories with their own magistrates, while in the late republic they were grouped in laws crossing several of the boundaries and with magistracies defined in new ways. In these matters, Chapters 3 through 7 will focus on the middle republic, when each category was essentially independent.

In the last two chapters, the emphasis will shift from the general principles that governed the framing of all laws of a particular type and the processes necessary to implement them to the programs of specific legislators in the last century of the republic. Starting with Ti. Gracchus, the framers of agrarian laws combined traditionally separate tasks in larger projects and, while maintaining the same overall processes, they made adjustments in the definition of magisterial powers and in the range of actors who could implement the laws, an important step toward a more bureaucratic order. In Chapter 8, the Gracchan reform will be surveyed. Chapter 9 will examine certain broad lines of development in the first century.

THE ROMAN GOVERNMENT IN ACTION

The central institutions of the Roman state produced laws regulating the use of public lands, and administrators chosen and based in Rome itself had primary responsibility for implementing their provisions. Bound by a need to act directly and surrounded by rules and practices limiting the time, place, and form of their activities, Roman officials going about their business generally operated in well-defined situations and settings. As a necessary preliminary to more detailed investigations, the basic organization of this government, its main actors, the spatial limits on their actions, and their typical ways of proceeding will be set forth.

I. MAGISTRATES, PRIESTS, SENATE, AND PEOPLE

The administrative apparatus of the Roman state was neither very large nor very specialized. In outline, government was simple, resting on a small group of officials who served for fixed terms, generally of one year. The Romans elected individuals to fill a few offices, each with its own powers and spheres of activity. Each position was collegial: two censors, two consuls, praetors varying in number from one in 367 to eight in the time of Sulla, two curule and two plebeian aediles, ten tribunes of the plebs, and a varying number of quaestors. Beginning early in the second century, these offices increasingly were organized into a formal *cursus honorum*, with prospective magistrates expected to hold certain posts in a more or less fixed order.[1] Despite the hierarchical arrangement, lesser officials rarely faced interference from higher ones.

The total number of magistrates was small — in the first century, after several centuries of steady growth, less than fifty filled the regular positions. The number of officials available for assignment could be increased temporarily by a number of expedients. Some magistrates, generally those whose responsibilities took them away from Rome, were instructed to continue in their assignment beyond their term and serve as promagistrates; after 200, the Romans increasingly turned to the promagistracy, especially to extend the number of governors for the extra-Italian provinces. In addition, for certain projects, the Romans elected special colleges of magistrates, usually numbering two (*duumviri*), three (*triumviri*), five (*quinqueviri*), seven (*septemviri*), or ten (*decemviri*), to manage a single, limited task for a fixed period of time. Such colleges occupied a prominent place in the implementation of agrarian legislation. Because of the restricted number of officials, many governmental tasks requiring consistent effort over time were directed by private contractors, the *publicani*.[2] Those who successfully bid for contracts are found collecting regular revenues of the state, leasing public lands, building roads and temples, and providing the state with essential goods and services.

Elected officials did not act with complete independence. The senate, a council formed primarily from former officeholders, played an important role as the repository of knowledge and experience in government, advising and to a certain extent instructing officials and providing what consistent direction over time could be found in the Roman state.[3] For much of the republic, it numbered around three hundred, perhaps doubling only toward the end of this period. In addition to their service as members of a formally constituted body, individual senators also accompanied magistrates in the field as assistants and advisors, served as messengers between generals and the senate, and acted as ambassadors to foreign states.

Ultimately Roman government rested on the popular assemblies, composed of adult male citizens, which elected officials and passed laws. Roman voting assemblies possessed strong internal structures based on the major categories thought to divide the citizenry. Depending on the circumstances, citizens could be organized in different ways: the centuriate assembly (*comitia centuriata*), the citizen body formed as an army in centuries on the basis of wealth and age; the tribal assembly (*comitia tributa*), the same citizens arranged in tribes based on place of residence; and the plebeian assembly (*concilium plebis*), the tribal assembly without its patrician members. Each form of assembly had its own meeting places and was closely associated with specific officials and tasks.[4]

Despite the centrality of the assemblies, a small group of men dominated Roman public life. Magistracies, and thus places in the senate, were not open to all. Only the wealthy could seek office. Among those who possessed sufficient property, moreover, certain families tended to predominate in the highest posts and to lead in the senate. In the last two centuries of the republic, 40 percent of all consuls had consular fathers; 20 percent had both a consular father and a consular grandfather.[5] The framers of legislation, the magistrates who put laws into practice, and many of the experts who advised them regularly came from the same restricted segment of the citizenry. Indeed, the knowledge of elements essential to the drafting of legislation and to the proper structuring of official action was the possession not only of this group, but more strictly of an even smaller body within it.

The role of central figures in the governing class was not limited to strictly political matters in the modern sense. The state religion formed a crucial element in the public life of the city, and its terms, concepts, and activities permeated government. This official religion possessed its own organization with a complicated array of priesthoods, each with different areas of responsibility and each interacting with senate and magistrates.[6] Two of the major colleges, the *pontifices* and the *augures*, were especially important in politics and government.[7] Only a few individuals filled the places on these colleges—the number of both pontiffs and augurs apparently reached nine in 300 and increased to fifteen under Sulla—and they served for life. Originally the members of each priesthood co-opted new priests, but in 104, as a result of a plebiscite, the *lex Domitia*, they came to be elected by a vote of seventeen of the thirty-five tribes. New priests were not chosen because of any specifically religious qualifications. The holders of the major sacred offices often had political careers in magistracies and in the senate, and they tended to be chosen from the families that led this body. The identity of the religious and political leadership, as Cicero (*Dom.* 1.1) made clear, could be seen as a source of strength.

Pontiffs and augurs were central to much of Roman public life, and their expertise, as priests, extended beyond purely religious matters. Knowledge of the provisions of private law and of the exact formulas needed to proceed in legal actions was originally the possession of members of the great priestly colleges, the *pontifices* especially. Although this knowledge did not remain entirely in the priestly sphere, most of the known jurists up to the end of the second century were pontiffs or augurs, and some held the office of *pontifex maximus*. Those jurists not known to have been priests were members of the senatorial elite and were closely related to those who did hold priesthoods.[8]

Despite the lack of differentiation in the personnel managing politics, administration, religion, and law at the highest levels, Roman public life was in theory compartmentalized to a considerable degree, with the activities of private citizens, magistrates, and priests divided into categories and subcategories, each with its own sphere of action, its own procedures, and its own substantive rules.[9] At one level — important if one is concerned with matters of administration — Roman public and religious law defined classes of actors, with each having its own proper responsibilities, powers, and the procedures for using those powers. At different times and under differing circumstances, a well-placed individual could adopt the role of magistrate, priest, senator, legal advisor to magistrates and private citizens, and, indeed, mere private citizen. Much of the complexity of Roman public life stems from the interaction of these roles.[10]

In practice, the elaborate system of division and definition came together around the figure of the magistrate and the body of the senate. Magistrates, not priests or jurists, were the chief actors of public life. They not only supervised seemingly secular governmental operations and presided over the courts handling private law disputes, but they also took a central role in the practices of the state religion, supervising sacrifices, festivals, games, processions, and rites of divination. The role of experts simply was to advise and assist the magistrate, the organizer and officiant of major religious observances and the implementer of policy, and to coach him in the proper procedures.[11] Documents, *commentarii*, describing in detail what to do on certain occasions could also assist all parties.[12] Behind magistrate and priest stood the senate. Ostensibly only advisory, this body in practice directed much of public life, especially during the middle republic. Not only were magistrates expected to consult it and act on its recommendations, but the senate's formal authorization was required for those official actions the priestly colleges thought necessary on the basis of religious law.

That concentration of religious responsibilities around the figure of the magistrate determined much of an official's activities. Certain magistracies had their own well-defined religious programs, which required those holding them to stage games and processions and perform sacrifices at fixed times.[13] Seemingly secular operations also included religious elements.

Officials conducting trials before the people and consuls who intended to preside over the centuriate assembly both performed divinatory rites before proceeding.[14] Furthermore, large-scale projects, whether sacred or secular, often included substantial segments from both spheres. Thus, magistrates raising armies ritually purified the assembled soldiers in the ceremony of the *lustrum*, the same rite used in the quinquennial census of the Roman people.[15] Similarly, strictly religious projects could include secular operations: the process of establishing a temple required an auction to place the contract for its construction.[16]

Thus, although Roman theorists made clear distinctions between categories of actors and of actions, in practice the various spheres were intertwined. A major political figure could function during his career both as a priest and a magistrate. An official's term in office included various religious rituals interspersed with other actions. Substantial projects included specifically religious elements, and seemingly secular meetings between magistrates and those who were the targets of their action were preceded by rites of divination. One could expect, therefore, that despite the formal distinction between public, private, and religious, in practice the rules and procedures applying to each would exhibit many similarities.

II. THE LOCATION AND FORM OF OFFICIAL ACTION

Roman officials acted in well-defined circumstances and often at places and times determined by rules of a religious nature. The administration of the republic largely was based in Rome itself. Officials were elected and instructed by assemblies of citizens that only gathered there, they were advised and directed by a council that only met in the city, and many of these officials exercised their powers exclusively at Rome. Within the city itself, moreover, magistrates performed many of their necessary functions in the major public spaces of Rome, locations sanctified by tradition and the practices of the augurs and dominated by many of the most important and impressive temples and public buildings.[17] Yet despite the emphasis on direct contact between governors and governed, the Roman state of the middle and late republic was able to dominate a large territory, a feat that was possible because Roman officials, away from Rome, sought to act directly in only a limited range of cases, thus preserving a considerable degree of local autonomy.

The basic practices the Roman elite used to organize the territory it dominated appeared early in the process of steady expansion that characterized the history of the middle and late republic.[18] Although probably the largest polity in its region in land and in population, throughout most of the fourth century Rome was a relatively small state surrounded by others. In the middle of the century, Roman territory extended no more than about forty kilometers from the city in any single direction, and in some the frontiers were much closer. Around the fringes clustered other states. Some were allies. Of these, the Latin city-states were especially important, for they shared with Rome elements of language and culture and certain privileges of citizenship and they had cooperated with the Romans in war for many years, although not necessarily in a one-sided alliance under Roman leadership as Roman authors later claimed. Other neighboring states were regularly or intermittently hostile.

In the decades following the middle of the century, Rome began to expand dramatically, changing the nature of its relationship with its former allies and its old enemies and eventually affecting communities too distant to have been significant factors in Roman life earlier. Building on traditional practices in ways that are obscure, the Roman leadership began to develop a hierarchical system of legal statuses in which lesser states and their citizens were assigned a place that defined more or less precisely their relationship with Rome. The arrangements made in these years to secure Rome's domination of its neighbors, to extend the boundaries of its own territory, and to render more secure its possessions served as the pattern for the organization of further conquests. In the process, the formalized relationships, legal categories, and the necessary procedures would probably have become more abstract, more standardized, and more elaborate over time.

The Latin War, traditionally placed in the years 340 to 338, marked the first dramatic change. Probably as a reaction against the increasing predominance of Rome, many old allies revolted against that city, but were quickly defeated. Certain communities were incorporated into the Roman state, for their territories became part of Roman territory and their citizens became Roman citizens, although some did not obtain the right to vote in Rome. Cities treated in this fashion gained the special status of a *municipium*, but all *municipia* continued to function as city-states with their own magistrates, priesthoods, assemblies, cults, and laws and the customs and practices necessary to their proper functioning, for the Roman government possessed neither the resources nor the institutions to govern these places directly. Less urbanized regions received their own organization of villages and rural districts, each with its own government, less elaborate than those of cities, and cultic practices. Other subjected communities, however, remained ostensibly independent allies and some were permitted to retain the old status of the Latin allies, now probably more carefully defined and restricted. All followed Roman leadership in war.

At the same time, the Romans also attempted to secure control over that network of subordinate polities by creating new settlements to guard crucial points on the frontier and essential lines of communication and to act as advance posts against hostile or potentially hostile states even farther away. Perhaps making more systematic earlier practices, the Romans installed new communities or colonies, drawn from their citizenry and possessing a civic organization patterned after Rome. In some, the settlers received the remains of the privileges of the old Latins, while in others they remained Roman citizens. In segments of land adjacent to their core territory and protected by colonies, moreover, the Romans assigned possession of confiscated lands to individuals in viritane assignments, giving them only the most rudimentary form of communal organization and government.[19]

As a result of that network of settlements, each of which managed its own local affairs, Roman officials away from Rome were responsible primarily for the conduct of war, and they were usually present only in areas where fighting was taking place or threatening to take place. Otherwise, Roman magistrates acted only when order appeared to be threatened or when specific tasks, such as the foundation of a colony or the assignment of lands *viritim*, required their presence for a limited period of time. In certain extra-Italian regions, the regular presence of Roman officials was institutionalized through the formation of provinces, areas to which Roman magistrates were sent regularly: the first appeared as a result of Rome's victory in the First Punic War and others were steadily added after the Second Punic War. There, the Roman governor, usually a consul or a praetor or a former consul or a former praetor serving as a promagistrate, commanded armies when necessary and, when not leading in war, toured his province with a small staff resolving disputes between communities and hearing legal cases. Colonies and viritane assignments, the objects of much of our attention, are not found outside of Italy until the last quarter of the second century.

Wherever they acted and for whatever end, Roman officials had to arrange the necessary contacts between themselves and the targets of their activities. Certain lesser-ranking members of the magistrate's entourage had essential roles in facilitating and managing such matters, summoning individuals and groups to the official's presence, making announcements to them, and maintaining order. Paid attendants or *apparitores*, having little ability to act independently and a markedly lower social status, regularly accompanied magistrates, and each magistrate received those *apparitores* appropriate to his office.[20] Apparitorial posts formed a hierarchical sequence of ranks, each with its own separate organization, responsibilities, and status. The *praeco* or herald functioned as a public crier; through him, the magistrate summoned the people to meetings, called the senators to sessions of the senate, and made declarations to those assembled in his presence. *Viatores* served as messengers, often summoning specific individuals, such as those accused in court cases and senators who had delayed attending meetings of the senate, rather than larger groups as was often the case with heralds. Finally, the *lictores*, who served consuls and praetors among others, maintained order in official gatherings and punished those designated by the official to whom they were attached.

Ceremonial settings, colorful costumes, and formal language and behavior characterized a wide range of meetings between magistrates and citizens. In Rome, most public activity was concentrated in open spaces—the *forum*, the adjacent *comitium*, the *area Capitolina*, the *circus Flaminia*, and the *campus Martius*—and in the temples and other public buildings in and around them. In such places, magistrates typically took position on a platform that elevated them over those who were to witness their actions, often using for such a purpose the high podium of a temple or less permanent wooden stages; from an early date, temples with permanent and often highly decorated speakers' platforms clustered along the sides of the major places of assembly.[21] Elevated above the crowd in such a fashion, officials addressed the citizens in assemblies or soldiers in the camps, supervised voting, presided over sacrifices, listened to citizens' complaints, heard testimony and rendered judicial decisions, paid soldiers, directed executions, and guided auctions of public property or state contracts.[22]

Costumes and ritual paraphernalia signaled the rank of the official and the importance of the occasion. Curule magistrates—censors, consuls, praetors, and curule aediles—wore in public the special purple-bordered toga of a magistrate, the *toga praetexta*, and when presiding they sat in a special chair inlaid with ivory, the *sella curulis*.[23] Lictors bearing the *fasces*, an Etruscan symbol of kingship in a republican setting, accompanied consuls and praetors. In contrast, tribunes and plebeian aediles wore an ordinary citizen's *toga* and sat on a bench, the *subsellium*; they were accompanied neither by lictors nor by *fasces*. Outside of the city and on certain occasions within it, high officials wore specialized costumes. When leaving Rome, generals put on a red cloak, the *paludamentum*, and had their lictors add the ax to the *fasces* (indicating the official's now virtually unlimited power), and, if granted a triumph on their return, they entered the city wearing the *toga purpurea* and the *tunica palmata*. In some rites and sacrifices, moreover, the officiant wore his *toga* bound in the special pattern known as the *cinctus Gabinus*.

The ceremonial aspects of an official's public appearances often extended beyond setting and costume, for formalism in word and deed characterized many of his activities. Public cult consisted of a range of rituals in which the exact performance of seemingly trivial details and the recitation of customary formulas formed a crucial element. Alongside the rites of the state religion, there also existed an elaborate body of ritual, less well known today, covering the secular aspects of government.

Official actions often were divided into segments to which experts assigned specific rules and formal practices. As a necessary first step, magistrates contemplating public action first consulted Jupiter through the proper rites of divination. The act of calling together groups or individuals, an *inlicium*, had its own formalities. Quoting consular *commentarii*, Varro (*LL* 6.88) preserved a ritual dialogue between a consul summoning the centuriate assembly and his *accensus*, an *apparitor* who served consuls and praetors:[24]

> he who is about to call the army shall say this to his *accensus*: "Calpurnius, call all citizens to an *inlicium* here before me." The *accensus* says thus: "All citizens, come to an *inlicium* here before the judges." "C. Calpurnius," the consul says, "call to an assembly [*conventionem*] all citizens here before me." The *accensus* says thus: "All citizens, come to an assembly here before the judges." Then the consul speaks to the army: "I order you to form a centuriate assembly by the way it is assembled."

Censors in summoning the people to a *lustrum* and quaestors in calling the accused to his trial used other sequences of words and actions to achieve these ends.[25]

Ceremony and formula also permeated the gatherings themselves, where such behavior reinforced the image provided by the impressive setting of the official on his tribunal. Formal appearances of magistrates often were aimed toward the completion of a single task. When the course of action was predictable and liable to be regularly repeated, meetings often had well-defined identities, possessing distinctive procedures and terminology and special audiences: when consulting the senate, an official called it to meet in one of its customary places; when supervising elections or the passage of legislation, magistrates called together assemblies of citizens, *comitia* or *concilia*; when conscripting soldiers, they summoned those at Rome liable for military service to the *campus Martius* or the *area Capitolina* for the *dilectus*; when placing a public contract or arranging for the sale of public property, they notified those *publicani* interested in bidding that an auction would be held; and when investigating crimes or suspicious occurrences, they ordered witnesses and the accused to appear for a hearing or trial. The practice of consulting the gods by divination emphasized this feature of government, since a successful answer to these rites authorized a single action at a specific time and place.

Meetings could be dominated by their formalities. The lawcourts, where the concerns of private individuals and of magistrates intersected, provide a good example, one often paralleled in later chapters. Accompanied by two lictors bearing *fasces*, the urban praetors placed their curule chairs on a tribunal in the *comitium* or the adjacent *forum*, where they received the petitions of citizens.[26] A trial in two parts characterized the proceedings.[27] In the first, citizens approached with their dispute and the praetor, if he decided to allow the case to proceed, assigned as judge (*iudex*) a private citizen; that judge heard the case in the second phase and made the ruling.

The first segment — the one that involved more directly an elected official — was characterized by formal language and gestures. One prohibition illustrates the importance of those forms and demonstrates one of the ways religious regulations could affect more secular aspects of government. On the fifty-eight days classed as *nefas* on the ritual calendar of the republic, actions at law were prohibited. The grounds for the ban are straightforward: on those days the praetor was forbidden to speak the words "I give" (*do*), "I say" (*dico*), and "I award" (*addico*), necessary to the essential formulas. Q. Mucius Scaevola, the first-century jurist and pontiff, held that praetors who unknowingly had conducted proceedings on such a day must sacrifice to expiate the fault, but those who had done so knowingly could not expiate the offense.[28]

That emphasis on form carried over into the actions of the other participants. *Legis actiones*, the dominant republican court procedure, required the rigid delivery in the proper circumstances of fixed formulas.[29] In a dispute pursued as a *legis actio per sacramento in rem*, Gaius (4.16) preserved what amounts to a ritual dialogue between the claimants of a property; when the proper words had been spoken and the necessary gestures made, the praetor assigned a judge who ultimately would issue the verdict. The process did not allow much space for variation, and the consequences of error could be severe. Gaius (4.11) noted that a man who had brought a suit because another had cut down his vines lost his case because he had used the word "vine" rather than the "trees" included in the action provided by the Twelve Tables. In essence, a ritual flaw negated the process. In private law proceedings, then, magistrate and citizens did not interact outside of the context of a ritualized meeting.

In that ceremonial confrontation, the central administrative act, the granting of a judge, took place entirely within a single meeting. Governmental activities also could involve more complicated actions, often extending over a considerable amount of time and taking place at a number of locations. Essential portions of these larger processes were accomplished in series of ritual acts, often with different audiences and participants, and sequences of especially prominent ceremonies could serve as a way to record and represent the entire operation. Here, the establishment of a temple or altar to fulfill a vow provides a good illustration. Livy, the chief source for mid-republican practice, regularly represented the establishment of a temple as a process with three stages — the vow (*votum*), the placing of the contract for construction (*locatio*), and the dedication (*dedicatio*) — each taking place under the leadership of a magistrate at one place and time.[30] Although the sequence of acts apparently was fixed, the duration of the entire task was not, for the intervals between the stages varied considerably. The magistrate who made the vow often placed the contract and dedicated the temple while holding further offices. In such cases, the timing may well have been largely determined by the progress of the magistrate's career.

Each element centered on ritual and formal rules. Magistrates customarily made vows to Jupiter and to other gods before setting out to their armies and provinces, and they often did so at crucial moments on campaign. The verbal forms of vows were fixed and their construction involved much priestly learning; the same peculiarities of vocabulary and phrasing were also a feature of laws.[31] Contracts to build the necessary structures were placed in a formal auction held in one of the public spaces of Rome.[32] Magistrate and pontiff dedicated the structure and from the moment the rite was completed the land and the building were turned to their intended purpose;[33] the foundation day of the temple was often observed with ceremonies in the following years.

These three stages did not encompass all necessary official actions. Other events, some also ritualized, were reported much less frequently. When no regular magistrate was available for the task, special commissions, *IIviri aedis locandi* and *IIviri aedis dedicandi*, were elected in formal assemblies of citizens to place the contract or dedicate the shrine;[34] these titles describe the magistrates' responsibilities as the management of a single act, although more probably was involved. Before the dedication, moreover, magistrate and augur inaugurated the temple enclosure, defining its limits and freeing it from undesirable influences, and after it, the dedicator put on special games or *ludi*.[35] Some parts of the magistrate's task, however, were much less structured, especially when they involved actions that could not be mapped out clearly in advance and would not have been often repeated: Q. Fulvius Flaccus, who had vowed a temple to Fortuna Equestris as praetor in 182, as censor eight years later took marble tiles for its roof from the temple of Hera Lacinia at Croton, resulting in a public controversy that came to involve the senate.[36] Roman authors noted such actions only occasionally, generally when something unusual had occurred.[37]

In a system that operated in such a manner, members of the elite and citizens at large would regularly have encountered government in the form of ritualized occasions of one kind or another, and this feature of public life would have influenced perceptions about the nature of government and magistracies and clearly identified the proper sort of activity conducted in the appropriate way. On one level, these ceremonial events emphasized the distance between officials and common citizens. Unauthorized actions by spectators and lesser-ranking participants were not encouraged, and acts of disrespect could assume special importance: tribunes could be considered "reduced to the ranks" for the day if citizens reviled them and interfered with necessary procedures, while the authority of a consul or a praetor could be temporarily nullified if a mob smashed the official's *fasces*.[38]

On another level, formal occasions could serve as a means of validation for larger processes and as an arena for conflict between members of the governing elite. Participants in rites or the opponents of the leading magistrate could use flaws, or the claim that flaws had occurred, to call into question entire operations. In a religious performance, failure to follow exactly prescribed patterns could require the supervising magistrate to repeat it.[39] Similar faults in the religious ritual accompanying secular activity could jeopardize major governmental actions. The failure of Ti. Sempronius Gracchus (cos. 163) to consult the gods at the appropriate moment resulted in the augurs advising and the senate agreeing that the elections he had supervised were invalid, while those who wished to overturn the census of 89 apparently did so by finding flaws in the purification rite that both closed and symbolized it.[40]

Ritual faults could also explain failure, and the fates of those willful individuals who chose to ignore the proper procedures could serve as cautionary tales to encourage others to follow the right path. Thus, some attributed the defeat and death of Q. Petilius Spurinus (cos. 176) to the difficulties he had in obtaining the proper signs when entering office and to the improper way he cast lots when dividing responsibilities with his colleague, while others blamed the defeat of C. Flaminius (cos. 217) at Lake Trasimene on his failure to perform the Latin festival or to give the proper vows to Jupiter Best and Greatest on the Capitol before departing.[41]

III. CONCLUSION

Roman government, then, possessed relatively few major actors, who were chosen from a restricted social group and who operated in a relatively few places and according to well-established rules. In the following chapters, attempts will be made to reconstruct the way officials conceived, formulated, and proposed projects dealing with public lands, the steps magistrates found necessary to implement the measures and to validate the process, the concepts and categories that guided both, and the goals these actions were thought to achieve. Some operations took place in Rome itself, according to the rules appropriate for public action in the city. Others were staged at the site of the project, and they were governed by their own procedures. Before examining the individual forms of exploitation, however, the principles behind the use of lands for public purposes will be set forth.

RITUAL, LAW, & SPACE

By its very nature, agrarian legislation involved the categorization and regulation of space. The rules that governed these efforts, however, formed part of a much larger body of practices that occupied a central place in the Roman vision of a civic order. The city's leadership possessed an elaborate body of definitions, rules, and procedures governing a variety of areas with differing governmental, sacred, and legal characteristics. Laws, sometimes of great complexity, governed those spaces, and rituals defined new ones. These principles, places, and formal practices, moreover, served to guide and limit magistrates and priests as they went about their business. The outlines of that body of knowledge and the requirements it placed on Roman officials are the subjects of this chapter.

I. LANDS AND LAWS

Roman public and religious law firmly linked specific tracts of land to their own rules, rituals, proper actors, and permissible activities. Most basically, experts made a distinction between the territory of Rome itself and those of foreign states; the former was subject to Roman law, while the latter were not. Thus, Roman citizens could escape legal penalties by leaving Roman territory for residence elsewhere, and that right of exile was mirrored by another apparently old practice, *postliminium*, giving Roman citizens abroad a right to reclaim their positions in the city on their return.[1] The boundaries of Roman territory also marked the limits of Roman religious practices; according to the younger Pliny (*Ep.* 10. 50), the emperor Trajan maintained that dedications of temples in accordance with Roman procedures were not valid in the territory of non-Roman cities.

Augural procedures illustrate some of the complexity. The augurs, one of the most important of the priestly colleges, had a central role in the categorization and the definition of space for political as well as religious ends. Their area of expertise included the interpretation of the auspices, certain divine signs through which Jupiter signified his approval or disapproval of all impending actions by public officials, and those rituals by which persons and places were inaugurated.[2] The classification of land formed an important element in augural law. At one level, the augurs distinguished between Roman territory and that of other states. Varro (*LL* 5.33) reported that they recognized five broad types of land: *ager Romanus*, *ager Gabinus*, *ager peregrinus*, *ager hosticus*, and *ager incertus*. The date at which the system reached this form remains uncertain, but some elements certainly are old.[3] The *ager Romanus*, in its augural sense, remained unchanged from the early years of the republic; perhaps for this reason its early boundaries were preserved in ritual.[4] As a result, regions such as the *ager Veiens* and the *ager Crustuminus* remained to a certain degree religiously distinct after their incorporation into the Roman state. The augural distinction between *ager Romanus* and *ager Gabinus*, therefore, could well date back to the end of the sixth century, when Gabii became a dependent ally of Rome.[5] The process of categorization continued within Roman territory. There, the most prominent of the divisions was between the city of Rome itself, the *urbs*, and the surrounding *ager*; the *pomerium*, the line of separation, set the spheres of *domi* and *militiae*, central to a determination of the powers of officials and the rights of citizens.[6]

The augurs also preserved ritually the lines that separated certain kinds of land. Himself an augur, Cicero (*Leg.* 2.8.21) described this as "keeping free and unobstructed the city, the fields, and the *templa*." This task involved two activities, the *liberatio* and the *effatio*. The aim of the latter was to separate places by drawing their outer limits or *fines*; the action *effari*, then, signified the process of setting the augural lines that separated the *ager effatus* from the surrounding lands. The *liberatio* of an area meant the removal of all unwanted supernatural and human influences from the area enclosed within the outer boundaries.[7]

The augurs did not merely recognize and reinforce existing conditions; they also possessed the knowledge needed to separate and establish new places. The goal of such a process of inauguration, the result of a *liberatio* and an *effatio*, was to institute a ritually defined space or zone, a *locus inauguratus*. The *pomerium* itself, the zone separating the *urbs* from the surrounding *ager*, was such a place, but the most common form of inaugurated location was the rectangular enclosure known as a *templum*.[8] When subjected to further rites of consecration and dedication, a *templum* became the site of a temple (*aedes*), altar, or shrine.[9] To end the special character of such a place, a ceremony of *exauguratio* was required.

The augurs' system occupied a central place in Roman government. Varro claimed that each of the five augural categories of land had its own form of the auspices and within the *urbs* itself magistrates took the urban auspices (*auspicia urbana*).[10] Augurs and magistrates clearly would have found it useful and necessary to know the boundaries between different *agri*, and, indeed, the lines of separation themselves often had ritual significance. Thus, magistrates crossing the *pomerium* and leaving the sphere of the urban auspices were expected to auspicate. Ti. Sempronius Gracchus (cos. 163), having returned to the city to consult the senate, forgot to take the auspices again when he crossed the *pomerium* on the way back to the *campus Martius* to supervise the election of his successors, and for this reason the augurs recommended to the senate that the elections be held to be invalid.[11] Officials performed another form of auspices, the *auspicium pertermine*, when they left Roman territory and entered peregrine lands.[12] Augural boundaries also affected the powers of magistrates and the rights of citizens. Higher magistrates could not cross the *pomerium* to enter the city without laying down their military *imperium*, and they had to hold meetings of the centuriate assembly outside its circuit. The rights of citizens and lesser magistrates also were connected with that limit; the citizens' right of appeal for protection against magistrates (*provocatio*) and the tribunes' ability to block official actions were restricted to the area within the *pomerium* and up to one Roman mile outside.[13]

Augural procedures also set the place in which certain operations or portions of operations should be performed. *Templa* were essential to the functioning of officials and priests, for they served as places from which the auspices could be taken and also were regularly used for a variety of religious and political actions: in general, priests accomplished consecrations *in templo*, magistrates conducted meetings of popular assemblies, administered oaths, and made sortitions and dedications all while standing in *templa* (and sometimes on a temple platform), and decrees of the senate were not considered valid unless they had been given not only in a *templum* but under the roofs of an *aedes*.[14] *Templa* served not only as places in which certain activities were staged but also as the starting points for larger tasks. Thus, censors performing the *lustrum* first took the auspices in one *templum* and then cast lots in another to determine which of them would preside over the ceremony, while an official about to begin a criminal trial before the people auspicated in a *templum* before summoning the defendant.[15] Failure to use such an enclosure at the appropriate moment could call the entire action into question: Livy (45.12.9–12) reported that a consul of 168 issued an edict setting a day for his soldiers to assemble but failed to enter a *templum* to auspicate before doing so; the augurs declared the day wrongfully set and the legions remained in Rome.

Away from Rome, magistrates acted in a similar setting whenever possible. The camps, where officials most frequently interacted with Roman citizens away from the city, were provided with spaces analogous to those at Rome itself. On campaign, generals regularly made camp according to a fixed pattern that may date back to the period of the Samnite wars.[16] According to Polybius (6.27), who provided a detailed description of the process, surveyors first determined the future site of the *praetorium*, chosen to have the best view and to be most suitable for issuing orders. Around that point the surveyors then laid out an open square, part of which Polybius (6.31) elsewhere called an *agora*. Hyginus, an author of the second or early third centuries A.D., provides the clearest and most detailed account of the layout of the central square:[17] "altars having been instituted in the lowest part of the *forum*, we shall assign an *auguratorium* in the right part of the *praetorium* toward the *via principalis*, so that the general will be able to take the auspices correctly in it; the tribunal is placed in the left part, so that, the *auguria* having been taken, he may ascend above and address the army auspiciously." Tacitus (*Ann.* 15.30) and Livy (41.18.6–10) confirm that the camp contained an altar for sacrifices and a place for taking the auspices and making sortitions—Livy called the latter a *templum*.

The powers of magistrates and their ability to act, then, were closely connected to certain well-defined places that had been established according to the proper routine. But the connection of actors and rules for acting with specific locations is not only a characteristic of augural law. When a magistrate acting with the assistance of a *pontifex* consecrated and dedicated a *templum* to a particular god in the form of a temple or altar, it also came to be governed by fixed rules and practices, some of which could be peculiar to it.[18] Turning a formula into a narrative, Livy (1.10.5–7) outlined the procedure in his account of Romulus's consecration of a shrine and of the armor he had personally taken from the enemy leader.[19] Romulus, both king and augur, marked off the boundaries of the temple while saying: "Jupiter Feretrius, I, the victorious king Romulus, bear royal arms to you here, and I dedicate the *templum* here . . . which I am measuring off in my mind by these boundaries [*regiones*] to be the seat for the *spolia opima*, which those following after me, having killed the kings and leaders of the enemy, shall bear following my example." The king identified himself and the deity to whom the dedication was to be made, established in his mind the area of the *templum* to be dedicated (probably already inaugurated), and set forth in the form of a promise a rule governing the area's future use.

A number of surviving inscriptions give a virtually identical procedure. A local official of the *colonia Martia Iulia Salonae* in Dalmatia dedicated with the assistance of a colonial *pontifex* an altar to Jupiter Best and Greatest in A.D. 137 as follows:[20]

> Jupiter Best and Greatest, when I give and dedicate this altar to you today, I will give and dedicate by these rules and by these boundaries, which I will say here publicly. . . . Let there be those other laws for this altar which are given for the altar of Diana on the Aventine. By these rules and by these boundaries in this way I have given this altar to you, Jupiter Best and Greatest, I give, I speak, I dedicate, so that you wish favorable things for me, my colleagues, the decurions, colonists and inhabitants of the *colonia Martia Iulia Salonae*, and for our wives and children.

This text illustrates clearly the close connection between a defined space and a particular body of rules. The governing law of that temple was not exceptional, for the crucial phrase — "When I give and I dedicate this altar to you today, I will give and I will dedicate by these rules and by these boundaries" — is paralleled in a number of other inscriptions recording the dedications of other shrines.[21] Indeed, such a law (a *lex templi*) was an expected part of the process.[22] The rules covering such a place could be detailed, defining the rites, identifying those in charge of the rites, setting out financial arrangements, prohibiting a range of activities, establishing penalties for violating the rules, and identifying the magistrates responsible for punishing infractions. At the *vicus* of Furfo, for example, the *lex* established in 58 for the temple of Jupiter Liber provided for the leasing of temple land by the aediles of the community and ordained that the skins and hides of all animals sacrificed there belonged to the temple.[23] There could be a marked tralatician element in such laws; several are known to have followed the pattern of the law of the temple of Diana on the Aventine.[24]

Other spaces could be regulated in a similar manner. At the colony of Luceria (founded in 314), an inscription, probably dating to the second half of the third century, preserves a law governing a sacred grove (*lex luci*) that proclaimed that no one should throw dung, cast dead bodies, or perform sacrifices for his ancestors in the grove and authorized a magistrate to fine anyone who did so.[25] Another late third-century inscription, from the colony of Spoletium (founded in 241), announced that no one was permitted to damage the grove, cut wood in it, or cart anything away from it, and that anyone who violated the law was to be fined.[26] In a space on the Esquiline Hill with a different legal character, L. Sentius, an urban praetor early in the first century, set forth restrictions on the disposal of corpses and dung to apply within boundary markers, perhaps defining and regulating again the place where bodies of criminals had been deposited in the third century and those of slaves in the first;[27] in the same area, an inscription visible in the late first century proclaimed the dimensions of a seemingly rectangular space one thousand Roman feet by three hundred and announced that the land could not be inherited—a place for burials legally was *res nullius*.[28]

Such a connection between a specific body of rules and a defined area was not just a feature of relatively small spaces. Scipio Aemilianus, having performed at Carthage in 146 the rite of *evocatio* through which a Roman general called on the protecting gods of a besieged city to abandon the place in return for later benefits from the Roman state, next vowed to certain Roman gods the city, its fields, places, and regions according to those laws used whenever enemy cities were devoted.[29] Founders of colonies, moreover, proclaimed formally at the moment the settlement was created in law and religion both the charter of the settlement and the area over which it applied, often identifying the boundaries of the latter in some detail.[30]

Thus, efforts to turn certain public lands to specific uses, a category that includes agrarian laws, required a magistrate to define the area in question and set forth the rules that were to govern it. Such laws were called *leges datae* or *leges dictae*, measures established by a magistrate competent to do so and intended to govern a well-defined place or a specific group of people, such as a *collegium*.[31] Although each category of land had its own body of rules and practices, this course of action was followed whether the final result was to be a religious space, a secular public space, land that was to form a new community, or land turned over to private citizens. The implementation of these regulations, it should be noted, was not the responsibility of the magistrate who established them.

II. BOUNDARY MARKERS

Lands governed by different rules and possessing different characters were often adjacent: *urbs* and *ager*, Roman territory and non-Roman, sacred and profane, public and private, and the private property of one owner and that of another. Visible boundaries, therefore, would have been a necessity. The establishment of dividers such as fences, stone *cippi* or *termini*, and boundary paths (*limites*) was recommended, ordained, or expected in a variety of circumstances. Thus, every *templum* was to be fenced, officials set rules to govern "within the *termini*," and even Romulus could be pictured as establishing the *pomerium* of Rome itself with fixed *termini*.[32] The establishment of such boundaries was not limited to public and sacred land. Private landowners, eager to avoid difficulties with their neighbors, were urged to make their boundaries more visible and more permanent. The Elder Cato (*Agr.* 6.3) and Varro (*R.* 1.14–15) advocated that their readers plant trees or build stone fences along the edges of their estates, and Varro explicitly stated that one advantage of doing so was to make unnecessary the fixing of *limites* through lawsuits. According to Cicero (*Leg.* 1.21.55), the Twelve Tables, the oldest codification of Roman law, contained a clause barring ownership of a strip or *limes* of five Roman feet between properties.

Physical boundaries defined the limits of land set aside for a particular use, but they were more than this. In the absence of an elaborate system of record keeping, the markers themselves served such a purpose. Thus, when a private estate was sold, the vendor, at the moment when the sale was completed, defined the land in question by pointing out its boundaries in the presence of the purchaser and other witnesses.[33] The removal or the obliteration of the boundary markers, moreover, had the practical (although not the legal) result that public land sold to private citizens returned to its original status.[34]

Defending markers against the effects of time and of human activity, then, was a matter of some significance. Disturbing such signs, *terminus motus* or the *crimen termini moti*, was among the oldest offenses in Roman law — some Roman authors attributed the origins of the regulations to Numa Pompilius;[35] it remained a subject for legal treatment throughout the history of Roman law. Private citizens protected their bounds against others through the regular processes of private law. According to Cicero

(*Leg.* 1.21.55), the *legis actio finium regundorum*, which supposedly went back to the Twelve Tables, allowed landowners to seek private *arbitri* to resolve boundary disputes.

The defense of public ownership or of the boundaries of public and sacred spaces was another matter. Magistrates of the Roman people were responsible for this task, but their numbers were limited and officials certainly would not have been regularly present in all areas where public land could have been found. Indeed, boundary markers on public land away from Rome and its environs must have been especially vulnerable, since they often would have been located among defeated populations. When the boundaries were lost, much of the task of restoring the area to its intended use involved reestablishing its defining limits, which required that the original procedure be at least partially repeated.[36] In this regard, it should be noted that the right of private citizens to acquire ownership of private land through *ususcapio*—that is, after two years of uncontested possession—did not apply to public land or to land set aside for sacred purposes;[37] private action could not turn public property into private.

Boundary markers, therefore, were necessary for a well-ordered society. Numa Pompilius, the second of the kings of Rome and traditionally the founder of Rome's domestic order, was thought to have ordained the establishment of boundaries, public as well as private, and instituted punishments for their transgression:[38] Dionysius of Halicarnassus (*Ant. Rom.* 2.74.2–5) claimed that the king instructed landowners to mark their boundaries with stones consecrated to Jupiter Terminus and held that anyone who took away these signs was also to be consecrated to the god. The author of a text preserved in the *Corpus Agrimensorum Romanorum* (pp. 350– 51L) also gave great significance to boundaries. Purportedly a prophecy of Vegoia, the deity who gave to the Etruscans the secrets of the *disciplina Etrusca*, the document probably dates to the early years of the first century, after years of turmoil engendered in part by a long series of agrarian laws.[39] In it, Vegoia, having declared that Jupiter had established boundary markers in order to limit greed, predicted that these divinely established signs would be moved or destroyed resulting in natural disasters and civil disorder.

Control over markers could symbolize control over the territory itself and, indeed, over the entire civic and religious order. In what may have been the formula for such an act, Livy (1.38.1–2) presented the citizens of Collatio, in their formal surrender or *deditio* to Tarquinius Priscus, as giving up their land, their city, their temples, and their boundary markers (*terminos*). Later, in a speech placed in the fourth century, he (9.9.5) had a speaker urge the Romans to reject the peace made at the Caudine Forks, complaining that the Samnites "had compelled us to pronounce the solemn form of words of those who surrender cities" and asking those who urged acceptance of the peace if they would "say that the Roman people had been surrendered, and that this city, temples, shrines, boundaries [*fines*], and waters had become the property of the Samnites."

It is no surprise, then, to find that boundary stones had their own protective deity. In the Roman calendar, February 23 was set aside for the *Terminalia*, given to the worship of Terminus, the god of boundaries.[40] The festival formed part of the religious life of individual households, for during it landowners, their families, and their neighbors performed the associated rites. Just as the original, restricted sense of *ager Romanus* was preserved in Roman religious thought, so also were certain archaic boundaries preserved in ritual. Priests and officials made a sacrifice on this day at the sixth milestone from Rome along the *via Laurentina*, probably the early frontier between the *ager Romanus* and the territory of the Laurentes.[41]

Terminus was a tenacious god. One account, known to the Elder Cato and recounted by others, holds that the last king of Rome, L. Tarquinius Superbus, wishing to build the temple of Jupiter Optimus Maximus on the Capitol, had to remove a number of shrines to other gods in order to make way for the new structure.[42] In most cases, the *exauguratio* was successful. One deity, however, refused to move; the shrine to Terminus remained and the temple of the greater god was built around it, leaving open the roof over the boundary stone. Immobility is a desirable trait in boundary markers and in gods of boundaries.

III. MAGISTRATES AND THE DEFINITION OF SPACES

When public land was turned to public purposes, the linked process of defining and physically marking a territory—the *terminatio* or *determinatio*—and subjecting it to a set of rules was crucial. Dionysius of Halicarnassus (*Ant. Rom.* 8.73.3), in a passage probably owing more to the practices of the late republic than to the fifth century where he placed it, illustrated clearly the procedure when he had a speaker during a debate over a proposed agrarian law recommend that ten of the leading senators be chosen to fix the limits of public land, mark them with inscribed stones, and then lease a portion and sell the rest.

Various actors possessed the legal right to define limits in different situations. Private landowners marked the bounds of their lands. Magistrates performed the task in cases involving public land, whether it was to be used for a secular or a sacred purpose; only magistrates, therefore, could determine the lines separating public or sacred places from private. During the late third and early second centuries, holders of specific magistracies generally were charged with defining land intended for certain ends, although that became less regular from the time of the Gracchi.[43] Thus, plebiscites instructed special commissions of three (*triumviri coloniae deducendae*) to mark out the land for a colony and assign portions to individuals and colleges of ten (*decemviri agro dando*) to perform the equivalent operations for viritane assignments.[44] In the same period, censors, consuls, and praetors possessed the *ius publicorum privatorum locorum*, enabling them to define the limits of public spaces.[45] When properly instructed, officials could change the legal status of the enclosed land. Thus, the senate sent L. Postumius Albinus (cos. 173) to demarcate public land in Campania, while a tribune carried a plebiscite in the following year instructing the censors to lease the enclosed territory.[46] A range of magistrates defined the locations for temples, altars, and shrines and dedicated them to a god: censors, consuls, praetors, aediles, and special colleges of two (*duumviri aedibus dedicandae*).[47] In 304, the senate and assembly reportedly ordered that no official dedicate a temple or altar against the will of the senate and a majority of the tribunes of the plebs, while a *lex Papiria*, probably passed between 174 and 154, limited the ability of certain officials to consecrate a temple or altar against the will of the plebs.[48]

Away from Roman territory, nonmagistrates could be involved in the marking of boundaries. In disputes between allied cities, the senate often assigned a consul, a praetor, a proconsul, or a propraetor to arbitrate, but it could also give the task to groups of senatorial legates, not technically magistrates of the Roman people. Thus, the senate in 168 sent five legates to resolve a dispute between Pisa and the colony of Luna, established only nine years earlier; it instructed Sex. Atilius Sarranus (cos. 135), as proconsul, to establish and mark the boundary between the cities of Ateste and Vicetia; and it sent two brothers, M. and Q. Minucius Rufus, as legates to fix the limits between the people of Genoa and the Veturii in 117.[49] Outside of Italy and in the first century, legates also resolved boundary disputes between allied cities and Roman *publicani* over which lands within the cities' territories were subject to tribute.[50]

A number of inscribed public boundary stones survive. The texts often are simple and their basic contents apparently were consistent over time. Gracchan *termini*, among the earliest if not actually the earliest surviving examples, record the officials and their office: according to one, "C. Sempronius, the son of Tiberius, Ap. Claudius Pulcher, the son of Gaius, and

P. Licinius Crassus, the son of Publius, triumvirs *agris iudicandis adsignandis*."[51] On other markers, some nearly contemporary, the same basic information was expanded by noting whether the official operated under the authority of a senatorial decree or a plebiscite.[52] Information about the exact legal status of the land or the purpose for the act of definition appears less often. Clearly the emphasis was on the magistrate and his action first, his authorization second, and the status of the land third. The process received more attention than the result.

IV. RITUAL AND CEREMONY IN THE DEFINITION OF SPACES

Magistrates, priests, and private citizens, when creating new spaces or changing the status of old ones, proceeded in a formal manner. Their task involved three basic actions: a verbal identification of the space at the moment of creation, the indication of the defining limits by gesture at the same time, and the establishment of permanent markers.

The augurs again provide a clear illustration of the core features. When seeking to determine the will of Jupiter as revealed through the observation of birds, an augur stood on the *arx* and, looking down over the city and the fields toward the distant hills, defined a temporary field of vision, also called a *templum*, existing only while the auspices were being taken. In the course of its construction, the auspiciant defined its limits with the appropriate phrases and gestures. In Livy's description (1.18.6–10) of the inauguration of the second of the kings of Rome, Numa Pompilius sat facing south on a stone in the *auguraculum* on the *arx* near the temple of Jupiter, a location offering a clear view of the sky and of the surrounding countryside, while the augur, who actually would take the auspices, sat to the king's left and faced east.[53] The priest then looked out over the city and the fields, and, taking his curved staff or *lituus* in his right hand, established (*determinavit*) the lines or *regiones*, thus separating the areas to be searched for signs.[54] At the same time, he pronounced a prayer to Jupiter asking the god to send definite signs (*signa certa*) "within these boundaries which I have made," if it was proper (*fas*) for Numa to be king. In Livy's view, the augur designated a visual field with gestures and ritual words and then, in a *legum dictio*, called upon Jupiter to send a fixed sign inside that space. The *lex dicta*, then, governed the use of that imaginary and temporary *templum* in a way analogous to that in which the *lex* given at the time of dedication governed a temple.

Priests and officials of cities organized in the Roman manner were expected to perform the same operations, although each town would have had its own special forms. Varro (*LL* 7.8–9) noted that such *templa* were defined by ritual words that were not fixed for all occasions but were tailored to a specific location, where they would be unchanging.[55] To illustrate that point, Varro gave the formula by which the augurs defined a *templum* from the vantage point of the *auguraculum* on the *arx* at Rome. The text was apparently quite old: the words are obscure and archaic and the formula is now corrupt, apparently having caused difficulties to copyists.[56] Varro himself explained the words as establishing the outer limits or *fines* of the *templum* by means of trees and subdividing it by lines or *regiones* (*conregiones* in the formula itself) created by a glance. When Bantia became a *municipium* after the Social War, an *auguraculum* was built to take the auspices in the Roman manner, and stone markers or *cippi* were installed to assist in the construction of the *templum*.[57]

Such *templa* were temporary spaces defined in the imagination for the purposes of auspication, but the same word also signifies a permanent enclosure on the ground, a *templum inauguratum* or *templum terrestre*. Here again, a rite defined the *fines*. While explaining the temporary enclosure known as a *templum minus*, Festus (p. 146L), probably following the Augustan antiquarian Verrius Flaccus, noted that it was "defined by fixed words."[58] Magistrates seeking to use a *templum* for a temple or altar also identified the lines that were to define the place in their mind, by word, and probably by gesture. Livy (1.10.5–6) had Romulus show (*designavit*) the boundaries of the temple of Jupiter Feretrius while saying: "Jupiter Feretrius, I, the victorious king Romulus, . . . dedicate the *templum* here by these *regiones*, which I am measuring off in my mind." Operating in conjunction with a colonial *pontifex*, the magistrate who dedicated the temple at Salona announced publicly before reading out the words of the law: "I will give and dedicate by these rules and by these *regiones*, which I will say here publicly today."[59] Romulus and the other dedicators, then, in their prayers of dedication, defined the outer limits by establishing the *regiones* with the appropriate words and they probably also employed the proper gestures. One meaning of the verb *designare* is "to point out" and this interpretation is strengthened by the use of the demonstrative "these *regiones*."

An apocryphal story placed in the reign of the fifth king of Rome by an annalist of the Gracchan age, L. Calpurnius Piso Frugi (cos. 133), illustrates the importance of the linked actions of defining and identifying a place by word and by gesture while proclaiming its legal or religious qualities in fixing those characteristics to a specific spot.[60] While preparing a shrine in a *templum* on the Capitol, a human head was found. In order to determine the significance of the prodigy, L. Tarquinius Priscus sent envoys to the Etruscan expert Olenus Calenus, who recognized the importance of the sign and wished to gain the benefits it signaled for his own people. The Etruscan traced on the ground with his staff an outline of the *templum* and then announced: "Then are you saying this, Romans? Here will be the *templum* of Jupiter Optimus Maximus, here we found the head?" The Romans replied that the head was found at Rome, not within the limits marked off by the Etruscan, and thus preserved the sign for Rome.

In private law, those seeking to sell property had to make a clear demonstration of the limits of the land to be sold, and if a vendor wished to sell only part of his land, he was expected to indicate that portion on the scene by pointing out its *fines* and by this act create a new estate.[61] Indeed, Cicero (*Tul.* 7.17) indicated that the sale was not considered complete until this act had been performed. The procedure in private law for resolving boundary disputes between neighbors also required both parties to point out the boundaries they were claiming in front of the judge and other witnesses.[62] Such a formal demonstration of boundaries by word and by gesture may also have had a part in the procedure by which magistrates assigned plots to individuals. Hyginus Gromaticus (p. 204L) indicated that the founders of colonies led those about to receive land into the fields and "assigned" *fines*; a common meaning of *assignare* is "to point out" or "to show."

In many cases, the individual could create the space, define it by words and gestures, and give to it its rules from one position and at one time. But an official defining a larger space could not have defined its limits verbally and pointed out their locations from a single point. For certain boundaries, the person in charge made a circuit around the place. In a ritual that the Elder Cato thought old, the founder of a colony plowed a furrow around the site of the future city, while reciting the proper formula — an act that established the colonial *pomerium* and constituted the city's legal and religious foundation.[63] In the late republic, those magistrates who possessed the right to extend the *pomerium* of Rome itself, the *ius pomerii proferendi*, which belonged only to those who extended the *fines* of the Roman people, did so in a similar rite.[64]

In larger territories, such as that of a city, an official need not travel ritually around the circumference of its *ager* in such a fashion. Two legates sent by the senate in 117 to resolve a dispute between the people of Genua and the Veturii read aloud publicly a description of the boundaries at the scene (thus probably marking the end of the arbitration) and again at Rome;[65] in the text of that declaration, later preserved in an inscription, the ambassadors specified the location of the boundaries in great detail, identifying certain permanent features such as rivers, ridges, and crossroads. The founders of colonies identified the *fines* of the colonial territory in much the same manner, doing so at the moment the colony received its laws, just as the auspiciant or the dedicator of a temple proclaimed the *fines* at the moment he created the space legally and religiously.[66] Neither the legates nor the colonial commissioners, however, could have indicated by gesture these limits at this time.

For certain places, the creation of permanent signs of the frontiers was necessary. Before auspication, inauguration, dedication, or the transfer of land from one condition to another, temporary markers may have been erected to guide the ceremony; more permanent signs, if not already in place, would have come later. When an augur created a *templum in terra* for the purpose of auspication, he could use trees or *cippi* to guide in the creation of the defining *regiones*, but the *templum* itself, temporary and immaterial, was not marked.[67] At some point, *templa minora* were fenced either with planks and linen cloth or with stakes and spears.[68] In other spaces, sturdier signs would have been required. The legates of 117 noted in their verbal description places where the parties were to erect boundary markers; since those legates were not magistrates and the points in question were on foreign soil, they probably could not have performed the operation themselves. Here also ceremony, or rather a sequence of ceremonies, had a role. The founders of colonies marked points along the colonial *fines* by *termini* and at especially important places by altars, a practice similar to that by which the limits of the *ager Romanus antiquus* were preserved.[69] The dedication of altars certainly involved ritual and the establishment of *termini* probably also involved ceremony. In the private sphere, Siculus Flaccus (p. 141L) reported that, in the past, private landowners had placed stones with the appropriate ceremonies and sacrifices to Terminus, while Dionysius of Halicarnassus (*Ant. Rom.* 2.74) held that Numa Pompilius had instructed *privati* to place boundary markers with the appropriate rites to Jupiter Terminus. Dionysius, moreover, went on to claim that Numa had ordered that indicators of the limits of public land be established in the same way and that recurring rites at these places still were performed in his own day. Indeed, at points along the limits of a colonial territory, stakes known as *pali sacrificiales* were established, and their name alone implies ritual.[70]

Individuals constructing a space, then, established at the moment of creation its bounds by word and if possible by gesture, giving the place at the same time its laws and its legal existence. In some cases, the area could be defined in such a fashion at one time and from one location. For certain larger spaces, such as the city boundary of an *urbs*, a more elaborate procedure would have taken much of a day and required the official to traverse the outer limits of the area in question. In still larger territories, in the central ceremony the person in charge only defined the space and its rules verbally. The establishment of permanent markers was a separate operation that involved its own rites and practices.

V. ROMAN SURVEYING

Roman officials performed a *terminatio* to define the outer limits of a section of land, but on certain occasions they also had to divide an extensive tract into a large number of plots, equal in size.[71] While occasionally used to prepare land for sale or lease, magistrates most frequently performed such an operation to ready land for distribution to a large number of individuals. To achieve this end, the Romans first began to develop and deploy formal methods of surveying in the fourth century—when the Roman state first gained control over large amounts of captured land—primarily to assist in founding colonies and making viritane assignments. Over time these practices, *limitatio*, or as modern scholars often call it, centuriation, became ever more elaborate and regular.[72]

Roman surveying changed the shape of the landscape. Using simple implements, surveyors laid out an elaborate network of roads, paths (*limites*), and lines, in the process obliterating the boundaries of the previous inhabitants' properties, changing traffic patterns through the fields, and setting the form of the new settlers' use of the countryside. Roman methods created units on three different levels: the individual plots themselves, the overall arrangement of the fields, and certain intermediate formations which contained the plots and served to give structure to the entire system. Although there could be considerable variation in practice, especially in the earliest period, by the end of the century the most common method involved dividing land *per strigas et per scamna*, creating *ager scamnatus* or *ager strigatus*. The surveyors laid out parallel and equidistant roads known as *decumani*, thus dividing the land into strips. Then, they established at intervals paths or lines (*rigores*) transversing the land between the *decumani*. As a result, they created a number of rectangular modules, which could be subdivided again by *limites* and *rigores*. In scamnated land, the long side of each rectangle was parallel to the *decumani*, while in strigated land it was perpendicular. Frontinus (pp. 3–4L) identified this practice as the ancient custom, and traces of such systems have been found at a number of early colonies, such as Cales (334), Luceria (314), Alba Fucens (303), Cosa (273), and Ariminum (268); in areas of early viritane assignments, such as Privernum and the *ager Falernus*, settled after their conquest in 340; and in places such as Cures Sabini, where land apparently was sold shortly after its conquest in 290.[73]

Toward the end of the third century, the Romans made those practices much more regular.[74] Surveyors subdivided a tract of land by laying out two sets of parallel roads, separated by a standard interval. The *decumani* theoretically ran along an east-west course, while the *kardines* tended to run north-south. *Kardo* and *decumanus*, then, intersected at right angles, forming the basis for a clear and uniform grid. In the most regular form, parallel *limites* were separated by a distance of twenty *actus* (708 meters). Thus, the four lines made by two adjacent *kardines* and two adjacent *decumani* enclosed a square of twenty *actus* containing two hundred *iugera*; such a module was known as a *centuria*, giving to centuriation its name. Each *centuria*, in turn, could be subdivided by lesser *limites* or by lines (*rigores*) into a number of smaller plots to be given to individuals; here, however, the pattern was much less regular. The earliest certain use of the technique was at the foundation of the colony of Cremona in 219, and grids of this type were especially common in the land assignments of the second century:[75] at the colonies of Bononia (189), Luna (177), Mutina (183), and Parma (183), and perhaps at the Gracchan colony at Carthage in North Africa, in the viritane assignments along the *via Aemilia* (173), and in the land leased by the censors in the *ager Campanus* (165).[76]

Two main orthogonal axes organized the grid, and the point where the *kardo maximus* and the *decumanus maximus* intersected formed the system's center, conceptually if not physically. The layout allowed individual *centuriae* to be named and located. Thus, *centuriae* were either to the right (*dextra*) or left (*sinistra*) of the *decumanus maximus* and were either on this side (*citra*) or beyond (*ultra*) the *kardo maximus*. By counting the number of roads intervening between any given century and the main axes, the surveyors were able to identify the location of any square;[77] thus, a Gracchan boundary stone proclaimed that the place it occupied was the intersection of the eleventh *limes* this side (*kitra*) of the *kardo* with the first to the left (*sinistra*) of the *decumanus*.[78] Surveyors recorded the entire network on a schematic drawing or *forma*, which according to Siculus Flaccus (p. 154L) could be inscribed on wood, leather, or bronze, although only the last was to be trusted. The bronze *forma* connected with the centuriation of the *ager Campanus* in 165 is the earliest known.[79]

The construction of a network began at a single point—in a centuriation grid the place where the *kardo maximus* and the *decumanus maximus* were to meet. There, the surveyor set up the *groma*, the basic instrument, and from that point he measured out the defining lines. Although the amount of centuriated land could be large, the technology was simple. The best preserved example of a *groma*, found at Pompeii in 1912, had as its core an iron-covered cross, and plumb bobs apparently were attached to the end of each of the four arms.[80] This assembly of iron cross and plumb lines was placed horizontally on top of a wooden staff, and, to give a clear line of sight, the cross apparently was fixed off-center on the staff by means of a bracket. In addition to the *groma*, the Roman surveyor also depended on measuring rods, the *pertica* or the *decempeda* of ten Roman feet. With such instruments, the surveyor was able to lay out straight lines and right angles and measure distances with reasonable accuracy, which was all that was required of him.

The Romans, it should be noted, used the same instruments and basic techniques for other purposes beyond the division of land for assignment. Formal town planning, in which Roman practices can be traced back at least as far as those involved in the surveying of fields, parallel the various forms of land division: the plans of Alba Fucens (303) and Cosa (273) were based on longitudinal streets—the equivalent of *decumani*—crossed at regular intervals by lesser orthogonal transverse streets, enclosing blocks (like the *scamna* of fields) whose long side was parallel to the longitudinal streets, while Placentia, founded in the same year as Cremona, where regular centuriation may have made its first appearance, was laid out in square blocks.[81] A plan centered on two orthogonal main axes can be found in certain early settlements. At Ostia, the town founded toward the end of the fourth century was divided into four equal sections by two orthogonal axes, and the same basic arrangement may have been used in small (ca. three hundred *coloni*) citizen colonies in the same period.[82] Roman marching camps were established by a similar method. In a practice perhaps reaching back at least to the early third century, surveyors began the camp by placing the *groma* at the center, where the commander's tent would be erected, and from that point they laid out at regular intervals a system of orthogonal streets, establishing a grid of rectangular blocks (sometimes called *scamna* and *strigae*) dominated by two parallel roads, the *via principalis* and the *via quintana*.[83]

VI. RELIGION, RITUAL, AND CENTURIATION

Roman officials, then, used a very regular system of land division when preparing lands for distribution, and over time they made it even more regular. The precise forms of that fully developed process were not arbitrarily constructed, for centuriation had clear associations with ritual and religion, another instance of their power and of the degree to which they permeated public life.

Following Varro, Frontinus and Hyginus Gromaticus placed the roots of limitation in the divinatory practices of the Etruscan *haruspices*—both versions explain only the most regular form of Roman surveying. According to Frontinus (pp. 27–28L):

> The first origin of limitation, as Varro has described, is from the *Etrusca disciplina*, because the *haruspices* divided the world into two parts. They called that which lies toward the north the right part and that which lies toward the south the left from the east to the west, because the sun and the moon looked to that point.... The haruspices divided the earth by another line from the south to the north, and they named the part beyond the line *antica* and that on the near side *citra*.

Like Frontinus, Hyginus Gromaticus (pp. 166–67L) saw Roman practices as deriving from the Etruscan system of celestial orientation:[84] the *decumani* and the *kardines* were, he said, laid out according to the path of the sun, since the Etruscans first divided the world into two parts, calling the northern the right (*dextra*) and the southern the left (*sinistra*), and then drew a line from north to south, identifying the far side as *antica* and the near as *postica*.

That seemingly simple and straightforward attribution conceals difficulties. Some connection did exist between Roman and non-Roman practices, for certain of Rome's neighbors employed the same instruments and broadly similar techniques. The *groma* has clear Greek antecedents—the word itself apparently was derived, perhaps through Etruscan, from the Greek *gnoma*—and the simple surveyor's cross, sometimes known in Latin as the *stella*, had its roots in the Greek *asteriskos*.[85] Greeks and Etruscans, moreover, used such instruments to lay out the streets of newly founded cities and the fields associated with them by forming networks constructed from straight lines and right angles. Etruscan cities, such as Marzabotto, Spina, and Capua, show rectangular street plans in the fifth century, and a number of Greek cities of southern Italy and Sicily exhibit such an organization even earlier.[86] Traces of a number of non-Roman field systems, more or less rectangular in layout, have been found in central and southern Italy.[87] Roman practices, however, seemingly were more regular than those of the surrounding states and this regularity became more pronounced over time, for the rigid division of a field into squares arranged by orthogonal axes central to regular centuriation was apparently absent elsewhere.

That failure of Etruscans and Romans to survey in exactly the same manner does not prove Varro mistaken, for the antiquarian did not claim that the Etruscans themselves had used regular centuriation or that they had patterned their own surveying after a form of divination. Frontinus (p. 28L) continued Varro's description of Etruscan practices by noting: "From this foundation [the system of the *haruspices*] our ancestors are seen to have constituted the method of measuring fields. First, they led two *limites*: one from the east to the west, which they called the *decumanus*, and the other from the south to the north, which they called the *kardo*. Now the *decumanus* divided the land by left and right, and the *kardo* by *citra* and *ultra*."

Varro, then, saw the most regular form of centuriation as a Roman elaboration of a technique the Etruscans deployed in a different sphere. The Romans, that is, modified methods of surveying to conform to an existing religious system of orientation and of division. The nature of this process of adaption has proven contentious, but much of the difficulty lies in certain unjustified assumptions. Some reject any Etruscan connections since the Romans used limitation for ends the Etruscans did not, associated with it certain of their own practices, such as auspication, and developed it long after their religious practices supposedly had lost their force — claims that there was a connection, then, must have been the result of later speculation.[88] Others maintain that religion and technology are, or should be, distinct spheres of activity and that any attempt to find the former in the latter must be mistaken.[89] These positions, and others like them, assume that technology and religion — modern categories — necessarily must have been entirely distinct in republican Rome, that Roman religion was sterile in the third and second centuries, and that if the Romans had in fact borrowed a foreign technique, they must have used it for the same ends or have left it unchanged. All these assumptions are unlikely.

The techniques that served as a pattern for centuriation were deeply rooted in one of the central institutions of Roman public life. Like the systems of the *haruspices* and of surveyors, the science of the augurs also regularly divided spaces into quadrants oriented toward the cardinal directions and named these divisions from the perspective of a peripheral observer. Indeed, by Varro's time the Romans had so thoroughly adapted certain Etruscan practices to their own use that the original boundary between the two was unclear to them (and to us).[90]

In the definition of *templa*, the augurs, possibly proceeding by analogy, imposed a common terminology and a similar process of division on markedly different spaces. Varro (*LL* 7.6) identified three types of visual field: those in the heavens (*templum in caelo*), on the land (*in terra*), and under the land (*sub terra*). To assist with divination, the priests also acknowledged a variety of signs, each with its own rules and procedures. Festus (pp. 316–17L) gave five categories: *ex caelo, ex avibus, ex tripudis, ex quadripedibus*, and *ex diris*; the first two required the definition of fields of vision in which the hoped-for signs (certain celestial phenomena or the flight of birds) were to be sought. Although there is some uncertainty over the details, *templa in caelo* and *templa in terra* were associated with the different forms of divination.[91]

According to Varro (*LL* 7.6–7), the *templum in caelo* was defined by nature; the field of vision of an immobile observer formed its outer limits.[92] The antiquarian also noted that the person examining the heavens subdivided that space by projecting into it two intersecting imaginary lines, thus dividing the *templum* into four sections: "The four parts of this *templum* are called the left [*sinistra*] to the east, the right [*dextra*] to the west, the front [*antica*] to the south, the back [*postica*] to the north."

The *templum in terra*, created for the purpose of bird divination, contained a similar arrangement of its internal divisions, although its establishment required the auspiciant also to define the outer limits of the field.[93] The observer stood on a high place and looked down, defining his *templum* against the land. In Livy's description (1.18.6–10) of the inauguration of Numa Pompilius, the augur defined a line from east to west, calling the part to the south right and that to the north left; Varro's archaic formula (*LL* 7.8–9) used to create a *templum* from the *arx* confirms that the augurs did define interior *regiones* in their *templum*. In Livy's account, the officiant seemingly divided the enclosed space into only two parts, but the *pomerium* itself crossed the field of vision and apparently formed an upper and a lower section.[94] At Bantia, moreover, the *cippi* indicate that the *templum terrestre* there was divided into four parts, which may indicate a similar division of the field of view.[95] In other cases where divination through observation of the flight of birds was practiced, the auspiciant certainly established a fourfold division of the field of view. Cicero (*Div.* 1.17.31) reported that the legendary augur of the age of the Tarquins, Attus Navius, did so while performing the *augurium stativum* to identify the location in a vineyard of grapes he had vowed to a god.

The internal subdivisions created within those fields assisted in the observation and interpretation of signs, but permanent *templa* defined on the ground also possessed a fourfold division of their interiors, although the ritual function, if any, of these subspaces is unknown. This aspect of their construction need be no more than the result of the augurs imposing the organization of the field of vision on another form of *templum*. Dionysius of Halicarnassus (*Ant. Rom.* 4.60–61), when recording his version of the prodigy of the head found on the Capitol, had the wily Etruscan Olenus Calenus divide his image of the *templum* at Rome into four parts (east, west, north, and south). Festus (pp. 244L, 476L), following the authority of the late republican augur P. Servilius, used the term *posticum* to refer to part of an *aedes* and reported that a *stella* used to be placed on inaugurated places. Furthermore, Dolabella, one of the authors whose work is contained in the *Corpus Agrimensorum Romanorum* (p. 303L), claimed that the "ancients" placed a cross over the entrance to public temples and called portions of the temple *antica* and *postica*—a practice he explicitly linked to the way the Etruscan *haruspices* divided the world.

That process by which the augurs defined spaces according to the *ratio templi* bears obvious resemblances to centuriation in its most regular form.[96] Indeed, Festus (p. 262L), quoting the augur Ser. Sulpicius, Varro's contemporary, noted that a portion of the centuriation network was known as "*posticam*." The terminology of division is especially artificial in the case of centuriation: the surveyor began in the middle, and the entire space to be divided could not possibly stretch out before him.[97] Of the various kinds of *templa*, the closest analogy can be made between centuriation and the *templum in caelo*, which may have had some Etruscan associations since it was used to observe lightning, an Etruscan specialty, for neither required the formal definition of outer limits. In this regard, Varro's statement about the roots of centuriation makes sense.

One feature of that system of *haruspices* and augurs and probably also of surveyors is worthy of note. The use of those defining lines was not merely a technique for orientation and division: when associated with *templa*, it was an essential part of an involved body of ritual through which officials created spaces and turned them to their intended purpose. Now, the priests and magistrates who established and subdivided a *templum* indicated those lines by gesture, named each division as they created it, and announced the purpose of the rite. Thus, Livy (1.18.6–10) had the augur who inaugurated Numa Pompilius indicate with his staff a line in the *templum in terra* from east to west and call the parts right and left, while asking Jupiter to send a sign within those limits if it was *fas* that Numa be king. Dionysius of Halicarnassus (*Ant. Rom.* 4.59.2–61.4), moreover, presented the Etruscan *vates* Olenus Calenus as defining the image of the *templum* with his staff, identifying the place verbally and seeking confirmation of its status, pointing out the parts with his staff, and naming in a formulaic manner two pairs—east and west, north and south—each defined by placing a single line.

Ritual certainly was present when the process of building a limitation network began, although unlike the formation of a *templum*, the building of an entire centuriation system could not have been completed from a single point or on only one day. Yet the establishment of a grid certainly did begin at one place and at one time. To preserve the regular interval between parallel *limites* and to keep the crossing lines at right angles, the surveyors would necessarily have had to establish first a single line, marked out from a *groma* placed at one point, and then set the remaining lines in relation to it. Possibly following Varro, Hyginus Gromaticus (p. 170L) reported that surveyors first set up the *groma* in the presence of a magistrate who had just taken the auspices, an indication that this particular placement of the *groma* was seen as being especially significant and that those auspices authorized the entire project.[98] From that point, the surveyors then "sent out" (*emiserunt*) in both directions (*in utramque partem*) the *limites* that formed one of the defining axes of the system. This act, oriented toward the rising sun, established the *decumanus maximus*, the east-west axis of the system, and necessarily divided the field into two *partes*: right and left. The surveyors would next have created the other defining axis, the *kardo maximus*, by constructing a line through that starting point perpendicular to the *decumanus*, establishing the parts *antica* or *ultra* and *postica* or *citra*. While beginning the project, the supervising official probably indicated the direction of the *limites* and named the parts as did those creating *templa*, effectively announcing the location of the land to be divided, the place where the *kardo maximus* and the *decumanus maximus* were to intersect, and the orientation of the defining lines. Indeed, such a moment would have lent itself to the adoption of a pattern of ritual phrases and gestures similar to those used to define or govern *templa*.

Plautus may have preserved traces of such a ceremony. In the preface to his *Poenulus* (49–50), the playwright put himself into the role of a surveyor or *finitor* and announced his intention to begin to divide the play in the same manner that the surveyor divided the field:[99] "I will now mark out [*determinabo*] its *regiones, limites,* and *confinia*; in this matter I have been made *finitor*." In the preface, Plautus parodied certain formal actions by Roman officials, instructing the *praeco* to order the crowd to remain silent and issuing an edict (*edicta* is the word used) to *lictores* and the crowd; indeed, the playwright's opening instructions to *praeco, lictores,* and audience imitate the proper verbal forms of the magisterial edict which the audience doubtless would have heard many times.[100] Plautus probably also intended the parody of official action to continue into the portion where he likened himself to a surveyor beginning the process of definition — an indication that the *finitor* also began his task with some formal announcement. Indeed, the sequence of acts follows a clear ritual pattern. First, the playwright announced in the future tense his intention to define the appropriate limits of the play and proclaimed his intention to outline its plot, stating that he had been properly authorized to do so. The remainder of the preface is taken up with this plot summary. That series of events — formal definition of a space (the stage), followed by the announcement of the authority for the action, and then by the proclamation of the rules governing the space (the plot) — closely corresponds to the sequence of events through which a magistrate charged with dedicating a temple announced his intention, again in the future tense, to define the limits of the place and then proclaimed its governing *lex*.[101]

Those processes of orientation and division were matters of ritual, not of science in a modern sense, for the needs of the rite or the project, rather than the cardinal directions, determined the actual placement of the defining lines. The Augustan architect Vitruvius (4.5) recommended a western orientation for temples, but allowed this to be varied so that the structures could fit street plans or along riverbanks. Because of the topography of the area, moreover, augurs who defined a *templum in terra* from the Roman *arx* probably faced southeast in order to give the broadest view over the city, while priests at the colony of Cosa necessarily would have faced to the north for otherwise the city itself would not have lain in the field of view, prohibiting the division into *urbs* and *ager* by the colonial *pomerium* — the physical relationship of the *arx* to the *urbs* probably determined the actual orientation.[102]

Like temples and *templa*, centuriation networks often were oriented according to local conditions, rather than the actual course of the sun. The connection between *kardo* and *decumanus* and the cardinal directions, in other words, was contained in the conventions of the rite, rather than firmly and inevitably fixed by heavenly bodies. Surviving centuriation networks often vary from the strict rules: those constructed for the colonies and viritane assignments of the 180s and 170s in Cispadane Gaul, for example, are clearly oriented along the *via Aemilia*, while the *kardines* in the *ager Campanus* run east to west, rather than north and south.[103] Indeed, Frontinus (p. 29L) and Hyginus Gromaticus (p. 170L), after setting forth the ideal, both noted that the actual orientation of a grid could vary from the norm if circumstances warranted and that the *decumani* (which were to be longer than the *kardines*) were often located according to the nature of the territory.

Augurs and surveyors, then, possessed similar systems of division and of orientation to govern essential elements of their tasks, but the similarities between these two spheres were a matter of process, not of results, for the methods could be deployed over spaces in a variety of media and intended to serve a range of purposes.[104] The *templum ex caelo*, the *templum in terra*, and the *templum terrestre* shared terminology and aspects of construction, but they were in their ends quite distinct, for each served a different purpose and was governed by different rules. Although they involved the same broad processes, centuriation modules were not sacred space;[105] they did not serve as fields of vision for the auspices nor were they inaugurated like earthly *templa*—nor did any ancient author ever claim that they were. Other analogies in process certainly were made in similar situations without destroying distinctions between the ultimate natures of the spaces. The temple of Vesta, unlike other temples, was not rectangular but round, and although an *aedes*, again unlike other temples it was not located in a *templum*;[106] Hyginus (p. 117L) reported that the boundaries of land leased out to support the Vestal Virgins, land clearly used for profane purposes, should not have right angles in its defining limits.

The Romans, then, adjusted their techniques of surveying so that they followed as nearly as possible a ritual pattern, making them accord with certain customary practices in overall arrangement, in terminology, and in formal beginning. Now augury and its associated practices clearly were not innovations of the late first century, when Varro wrote—they certainly reached back farther in some form than did the techniques of surveying. While augural activities would have been very much alive among those who first developed regular centuriation toward the end of the third century, those same practices would also have been familiar to officials and scholars in later periods. When, then, was the connection between surveying and augury first made? Did those who developed Roman techniques follow a religious pattern or did later scholars or experts try to explain existing methods through perceived parallels to cultic practices?[107] Claims of antiquarian reconstruction and speculation imply attempts to explain a practice whose roots were lost in time or to elaborate on analogies seen in various customary practices. But thought about such matters can also result in the construction of new practices, or the modification of old, in ways that themselves will become customary.

The explicit analogy between the two spheres of activity probably already had been made by the time regular centuriation first appeared, exercising a strong influence over its development. Roman magistrates regularly pursued supposedly "pragmatic" goals in a manner that included religious and secular elements, and they began projects or elements of them in occasions permeated by ritual and formula. In such circumstances, analogies between centuriation and the *ratio templi* probably would have been made quickly. Indeed, Plautus expected members of his audience to recognize a parody of a rite that presented surveying in terms similar to the ritual definition of space for religious ends. Together, Plautus's and Varro's passages indicate that analogies between religion and land division were being drawn over a long period and that they were being made openly by near-contemporaries of the first appearance of regular centuriation.

Quite possibly links had been formed before regular centuriation first appeared. Just conceivably, earlier practices, scamnation and strigation, would have allowed the same analogy to have been made, although not necessarily in the same terms; even the shape of the simple surveyor's *stella* would have encouraged it. Like centuriation, scamnation and strigation had to begin at one definite point, for they too required parallel lines and standardized intervals. At Cosa, where the fields were divided into regular rectangles by *decumani*, these paths were aligned with the northeastern gate of the town, and the *groma* was probably first placed just outside that gate.[108] From this point, the surveyors apparently first laid out one *decumanus* and proceeded to place the others at fixed intervals to the right of the original. At this colony, surveyors would have found at the start the entire area to be divided included in just one of the quadrants defined by the four arms of their instrument and, looking into that space from this spot, they would not have been able to project the orthogonal lines characteristic of *templa* in any way that would have corresponded to the network of paths about to be constructed. In this circumstance, no analogies could easily have been drawn between the work of the surveyor and that of the augur.

But Cosa may not have been typical. The colony was placed on a high hill and hemmed in by others, and the suitable agricultural land lay to the east. A *decumanus* sent out toward the northeast from the northeastern gate would have marked the northwestern limit of the suitable terrain; movement to the left of this line would mostly have divided uncultivatable land. In other cases, a more central *decumanus* may have served as the starting point with surveyors moving first to adjacent *decumani* to the right and left. Then two of the four quadrants defined by the arms of the *groma* would have contained land to be divided and a single axis would clearly have run through the field dividing it into a right and a left.

In such a situation, magistrates and surveyors may well have recognized potential analogies with augural practice, especially if they began surveying with ceremony, if only the taking of the auspices. But the most obvious comparison would probably not have been with the *templum in caelo* associated with regular centuriation, but rather with the *templum in terra* used to observe the flights of birds from a high place, for the construction of that space required the projection of only a single line, dividing the field into right and left. Yet such a link may have proven suggestive but unsatisfactory, for while the *pomerium* itself provided a notable transverse axis in the *templum*, no prominent crossing line would have existed in the field. Roman surveyors made their systems more regular over time, and the potential to bring the layout of field systems more fully into line with perceived models may have existed long before the reality.[109]

VII. CONCLUSION

In Roman legal and religious thought, tracts of land, ideally with clearly defined limits, possessed their own, often highly individual characters. This organization of space determined the location of much official action and helped to give shape to a wide range of political and administrative processes. The number of such places was not fixed for all times. New spaces, governed by their own laws, could be created when need arose. These places were created in a formal and highly ritualized manner. Roman practice ordained the magistracies that could define boundaries in specific situations and set forward the operations that must be used to set certain boundaries. In the late third and second centuries, if not earlier, the procedures involved in turning a section of public land to a special purpose, sacred or secular, involved a standardized overall pattern, where actors in different circumstances went through the same broad sequence of stages. On the scene, an official marked the land and defined it verbally in a highly ritualized fashion, at the same time if possible, and if not, arranging them as separate events. If the project required a large number of subdivisions, the magistrate divided the land according to a highly formal process, having clear symbolic associations with some of the central practices of the Roman state. Finally, at the moment when those spaces became legal realities the officials turned them to their intended use or uses through a *lex data* or a *lex dicta*. The laws governing various types of spaces undoubtedly grew more complex over time, but the basic pattern probably is old. In the next four chapters, these principles will be applied to colonization, viritane assignments, and the sale or lease of land.

3

COLONIAL LAWS, COLONIAL COMMISSIONERS, & COLONISTS

Colonies were semiautonomous communities with their own governments, fighting forces, and religious observances. Although the Romans reportedly founded them under the kings and in the early republic, the legal aspects of colonization that characterized the better-known projects of the late third and early second centuries first appeared in the second half of the fourth century, at approximately the same time as the first traces of regular land division, the beginnings of what would become centuriation. Possessing many of the characteristics of self-supporting garrisons, colonies formed a crucial element in the consolidation of Roman control over Italy. In the late republic and the early Empire, they also could be used to provide land for poor citizens and for soldiers discharged from the proletarian armies of the late republic and from the professional armies of the Principate. The same form could serve a number of purposes.[1]

Members of the governing elite who advocated the foundation of such a settlement initiated a long and well-defined sequence of formal actions, involving many actors occupying a range of statuses. In this chapter, those aspects of the process that took place in Rome itself will be examined — the authorization and definition of projects, the selection of those responsible for installing the settlers, and the recruitment of the colonists. Here, there is an important chronological division. Although there was considerable continuity in the rules governing the status and the rights of colonies and colonists and in the ritual practices and technical processes associated with colonization at least from the late third century to the end of the republic, the content of the legislation authorizing individual projects and the rank and the range of responsibilities of those officials charged with essential tasks changed. The enabling legislation and the magistracies those laws created will be discussed in the form that was current in the middle republic; the late republican versions will be examined in a later chapter.

I. COLONIAL LEGISLATION

Although their identities are rarely known, those who initiated a colonization project and secured the necessary authorization belonged to that same small political elite that controlled so many aspects of Roman life. A successful proposal potentially could serve a number of purposes in such an individual's personal or political agenda. But the foundation of colonies was only thought appropriate in a limited range of circumstances; different forms would be more suitable for other public ends. From the late fourth to the early second centuries, during which they established at least fifty-three, the Romans regularly placed such settlements in locations open to enemy attack, in recently subjugated regions liable to revolt, at crucial river crossings and road junctions, and on vulnerable sections of coastline.

Informal discussion among magistrates and senators probably would have preceded any firm and binding decision, but its content and context are now largely lost. Much of the process of defining and gaining authorization for a project, however, followed well-defined rules and required formal meetings of bodies that followed their own highly formulaic procedures. These elements can be reconstructed in some detail. Livy provides the main evidence for the early second century, reporting the establishment of twenty new colonies, probably all that were founded in the period. His notices generally record one of two separate events, the beginning of a project (some combination of a senatorial decree, an authorizing plebiscite, and the election of the competent magistrates) or the formal foundation of a colony: for one colony, he gave only the former, for ten, only the latter, and for the remaining nine he provided both in separate notices in different years.[2] While doing so, Livy regularly identified the location of the settlement, its legal status, and the names of the magistrates who established or were to establish it, and he often provided the number of settlers and the size of the allotments they were given. These highly formulaic entries allow the broad outlines of individual projects to be determined, along with some of the stages through which each had to pass.

The effort to establish a new colony opened in a sequence of acts in the civic spaces of Rome, where senate, elected officials, and popular assemblies played well-defined but limited roles. Velleius Paterculus (1.14.1) claimed that the senate ordered the foundation of all colonies before the Gracchi, and in that period, no certain example is known of a colony founded without its approval. For the years from 200 to 167, when he referred at all to the authority underlying a foundation, Livy noted either a decree of the senate, a plebiscite, or in one case both, and a sequence of senatorial decree and plebiscite probably was the standard practice;[3] there is no certain trace of any other.[4]

Ritual and formula dominated the process of authorization. Like other formally constituted bodies in Rome, the senate had its own responsibilities, procedures, and customary meeting places.[5] It did not meet on its own initiative, for senators were summoned to discuss a specific matter by an official of the proper rank: dictator, consul, praetor, or tribune of the plebs.[6] Meetings were held only in a *templum* and only in those *templa* covered by a roof; the temple of Jupiter Optimus Maximus on the Capitol, the temples of Fides, Concord, and Castor and the *curia Hostilia* near the *forum* and *comitium*, and the temples of Apollo and Bellona on the *campus Martius* are among the known meeting places in the late third and early second centuries.[7] The session itself was governed by its own formalities. An official who called the senate had to sacrifice and auspicate before the session and then conduct the discussion and take the vote in the proper way, making certain that no decision was made before sunrise or after sunset.[8] As a result of a meeting, the senate issued a decree instructing, in the form of a recommendation, a magistrate or magistrates to perform certain tasks.

Like that first stage, the second also was highly formalized.[9] The first official expected to act in response to the decision of the senate would have been the tribune given the responsibility of making a proposal to the people.[10] Meetings of the plebeian assembly took place at a few well-defined places—in the third and second centuries, usually the *area Capitolina* and the *comitium*. Like other public occasions, ceremony and formula permeated the meetings of legislative assemblies. Joined by his *viatores* and by other tribunes ready to interpose their vetoes, the presiding tribune, wearing the citizen's *toga* and sitting on his tribune's bench or *subsellium*, took up the elevated position characteristic of officials in public. Procedures followed a fixed pattern and clearly emphasized the spoken word given directly to those concerned. The tribune ordered a *praeco* to read aloud the proposal (*rogatio*) and then informed the assembled crowd in a formulaic *carmen rogationis* of the rules governing the vote. Voting was by tribes, and in legislative meetings of the *comitia tributa* and the *concilium plebis* the tribes voted in succession. Before the passage of the ballot laws—the first of which was carried in 139—voting was oral, and each voter was asked by a *rogator*, a prominent person appointed by the president, for an affirmative or a negative vote on the matter at hand. Each tribe had but one vote, and when a majority was reached for or against the measure, voting ceased. The tribune formally announced the results, and, from that moment, his role, as tribune, ended.

Those procedures left no place for discussion: the voters simply responded positively or negatively to the proposal as it was presented to them. Assemblies that passed legislation, chose magistrates, and made judicial decisions were clearly differentiated from gatherings in which debate was permitted; the latter were known as *contiones*, while the former were the *comitia* or *concilia* in the proper sense of the terms. *Contiones*, like *comitia* and *concilia*, had their own formalities.[11] The presiding official summoned the people, either to the same locations as voting assemblies or to the *forum*, and there he began the proceedings with formal words.[12] Once under way, he kept strict control over those who were allowed to speak. The president could address the assembly himself, but he also chose others, instructing them to join him at the tribunal, where he could interrogate them on their positions. The speakers generally included other magistrates and some private citizens, usually members of the senate. It was expected that opponents would be allowed to express their disagreement; if the presiding official did not do so or did not grant them sufficient time, other officials could themselves summon a *contio* to discuss the matter.[13] Throughout the sequence of *contiones* and *concilium*, the tribune who proposed the law kept complete control over the text, for only he could make changes in it. In the late third and early second centuries, however, no colonial law is known to have inspired opposition.

A clear sequence of words and actions separated meetings where support and opposition were marshaled from the assembly that actually made the decision. The final *contio* took place immediately before the vote by the *concilium plebis*. After the last speech, the president began the series of acts that transformed the less structured *contio* into the more structured *concilium*. The urn and the lots used to determine the order of voting were brought onto the platform and the citizens were instructed to form their tribes with the proper words, and, at this point, those ineligible to vote were expected to leave.[14] The moment of transition from *contio* to *concilium* was the last opportunity for tribunes to cast their veto. Here, a series of ritual actions served to mark off one form of gathering from another, thus defining the context in which a valid and binding decision could be made.

Like the processes that authorized them, the laws that emerged from legislative assemblies were shaped and the range of variations limited by a strong concern for the appropriate forms. The text of a law conformed to a definite pattern and was framed in a language that was used only in a limited range of circumstances. In essence, a *lex* was a text spoken aloud ritually to those governed by it.[15] Basically a set of instructions on a specific matter, the law set forth the conditions to be achieved in phrases such as "would you wish and command that matters should be in such a manner" (*velitis, iubeatis, ut sit . . .*) and gave specific instructions to officials or private individuals in the future imperative, with passages such as "the praetor shall take an oath" (*praetor iurato*) or "the censor shall not take away his horse" (*censor ne equum adimito*).[16] Although much would have remained implicit, laws clearly set forth the manner in which they were to be implemented.

Surviving *leges* on various topics are often complex with convoluted wording and the regular use of verbal formulas—a characteristic of Roman public life in its public and sacred spheres—and the language itself is a clear indication that the presiding tribune constructed the proposal with the help of experts, either senatorial *iuris prudentes* or scribes.[17] Indeed, the regular use of instructions given in third-person imperatives ending in *-to* seems largely to have been limited to *leges* and may have been one of their defining marks.[18] That feature clearly distinguished the *lex* from the *senatus consultum* that may have preceded it: possessing their own linguistic peculiarities, senatorial decrees were not phrased as an order but as an opinion followed by a recommendation.[19] These linguistic aspects of laws and decrees point toward a well-established tradition. Indeed, the language, the formulas, and the many qualifications characteristic of legal texts are also found in documents of a religious nature—the *pontifices*, after all, traditionally had been the custodians of the forms of legal actions—and some of the specific linguistic features of *leges* are found in the wording of vows.[20]

The framers of proposals authorizing the foundation of colonies followed a clear and definite pattern, which included many standardized elements and left little room for creativity in the design of a project. Livy's notices again provide the bulk of the evidence for the early second century. Those recording the passage of the senatorial decree or plebiscite purport to include some of the provisions of the measure, regularly noting such features as the number of individual colonies it authorized, their intended size, their legal status, the region or regions to which the settlers were to be sent, and instructions to a regular magistrate to secure the election of a special college of magistrates for a fixed term. The same basic elements were present in the more complicated agrarian legislation of the late republic.[21] Those entries reporting the foundation by a special commission do not explicitly characterize the authorizing decrees or plebiscites in any way, but they do record the number of colonies the college founded, their legal status, and occasionally their size, all probably set by the underlying legislation.

Framers of laws could give their settlements one of only two legal statuses, and the range of possible sizes was closely linked to that choice. Mid-republican colonies fell into two categories, *coloniae civium Romanorum* and *coloniae Latinae*, a distinction involving clear differences in the number of settlers, in function, and in the legal rights of the communities, their citizens, and their governments. The nature of the distinction changed in the course of the second century, as citizen colonies grew larger and took over the duties of Latin colonies. In the first century, Latin status often was given to existing communities as a reward for their behavior.[22] Before the age of the Gracchi, in those cases where the number of colonists is known, citizen colonies received either 300 or 2,000 adult male settlers, but towns of the larger size may have appeared first in the second decade of the second century.[23] In the same period, known Latin colonies have 2,500, around 3,000, 4,000, or 6,000 adult male colonists.[24] Thus, the official who proposed a colony chose its size, and thus its legal status, from a restricted range of options, probably depending on the purpose of the new community, its location, and the mood of the surrounding population.

Special commissions actually managed the installation of settlers, and a colonial law instructed a consul or praetor to summon the *comitia tributa* for their election.[25] Colonial commissions invariably consisted of three members (special commissions of other sizes existed but their tasks in no way involved the foundation of colonies), and in the instances when terms in office were mentioned they were for three years.[26] In this, no distinction was made between colleges that were to found large colonies and those that were to settle small ones, between commissions that were to establish a number of settlements and those that were to found only one, or between boards instructed to establish new colonies and those that were to reinforce old ones.[27]

Laws varied only over a limited range in the number of settlements and colleges they authorized. Two of the five laws and decrees Livy recorded each commanded that one colony be founded, another two each instructed that two be installed, and the last approved five.[28] Four of the measures ordered the selection of only one commission to found all the settlements, but one, the *lex Aelia* of 194, instituted two colleges, each of which founded one colony.[29] Reports of the foundation of colonies by a specific triumvirate provide the only traces of the remaining projects: six boards founded one colony each, while three each instituted two.[30] Of the fifteen commissions known to have founded colonies in the late third and early second centuries, then, ten founded only one colony, four founded two, and only one set up five and those were of the smallest size possible.[31] Although a single law may have authorized more than one college, most commissions probably derived their powers and their assignments from a single law.[32] If that was the case, then the most frequent pattern would be for a legislator to construct a law authorizing the election of a single college that was to found but one colony. Despite the number of colonies it authorized, a plebiscite or a *senatus consultum* never crossed the boundary between citizen and Latin. The laws instructing the establishment of citizen or Latin colonies, then, may have contained special provisions and the triumvirates may have required special powers peculiar to that one form. It is possible, moreover, that all colonies authorized by a single law were to be of the same size. Placentia and Cremona (219) each had six thousand *coloni*, Volturnum, Liternum, Puteoli, Salernum, and Buxentum (197) all had three hundred *coloni*, and Mutina and Parma (183) each had two thousand.[33]

The relationship between laws and the number of colonies and colleges they authorized was not arbitrary. When a single commission founded more than one colony, the sites for those settlements generally were close. Thus, the pairs Placentia and Cremona and Mutina and Parma — each established by a single triumvirate, probably the result of a single law — were less than 50 kilometers apart, while Potentia and Pisaurum, also the products of a single college, were separated by less than 100 kilometers. But the two colonies authorized by the *lex Aelia* were not as closely grouped. Copia was to be placed in the territory of Thurii facing the Ionian Sea, while Vibo Valentia was to be located on the coast of Bruttium facing the Tyrrhenian Sea; the two sites, approximately 150 kilometers apart by air, are separated on the ground by mountains. But the Aelian law is the only one known to have established two commissions.[34] The concentration of a commission's responsibilities is clearly illustrated by the college chosen in 190 to lead new settlers to Placentia and Cremona. Shortly after its election, that triumvirate received the additional task of founding two new colonies, one of them

Bononia (the identity of the second is unknown and it may never have been established);[35] in order to lead reinforcements to the older settlements, the members of the college would have had to pass by the site of Bononia.

The evidence for colonization projects before 220 is too uncertain to allow for a similar discussion, since the list of colonies may be incomplete and the chronology is often confused. Still, what evidence there is reveals a similar pattern. Thus, Livy (8.16.14, 10.21.7–10) presented a single decision of the senate in 334 as authorizing the foundation of a single Latin colony, Cales, by a single triumvirate and a plebiscite in 296 as instructing that two small citizen colonies, Minturnae and Sinuessa, be settled by a single college of three on adjacent territories. Festus (p. 458L) preserved the membership of a triumvirate that founded the colony of Saticula in 313.

Individual laws, then, were constructed from elements that were themselves highly standardized: size, legal status, and founding commission. The choice made by the legislator in the first limited the range of possibilities available in the second. Beyond that bare outline, it is unclear how much more was needed. The rights and privileges of citizens of Latin colonies or citizen colonies, for example, may well have been traditional or defined by a reference to an earlier law, and the same may well have been the case with the magistracies.[36] The range of possible choices included in a single colonial law, then, may not have been large. Most laws merely authorized the establishment of a single colony by one triumvirate. A legislator could have built on that pattern in two simple ways, the more common of which would have been to add an additional colony of the same legal status and probably also size. Usually, the sites were close and a single commission was sufficient. Occasionally, however, they were far apart or separated by difficult terrain; then, the election of more than one college would have been authorized.[37]

II. COLONIAL COMMISSIONS

The consul or praetor instructed to supervise the election of the colonial commission by the *comitia tributa*, the tribes meeting under the auspices, was the first magistrate required to act as a result of the passage of a law.[38] He had a short and well-defined task of great formality. In elections, the president announced in advance the day and place of the meeting. Sessions of the tribal assembly took place only on those days of the calendar marked *comitiales* and on such days only when they did not conflict with a market day. In the third and second centuries, the usual places for meetings were the *comitium* next to the *forum* and the *area Capitolina*—Livy

(34.53.2) specifically noted that elections to fill two colonial commissions were held on the Capitol.[39] Unlike legislative and judicial *comitia*, electoral assemblies were not preceded by a series of *contiones*, for candidates campaigned privately.

Like the passage of the law, the election was a highly formal occasion. Having successfully taken the auspices at the appointed time and place, the consul or praetor, wearing the purple-bordered toga and accompanied by his *lictores* bearing the *fasces* that were a sign of his power, ascended a high platform and took his place on his curule chair.[40] With him were some of his *apparitores*, as well as other magistrates, the tribunes of the plebs, who must be present to interpose their vetoes, and an augur to assist in interpreting the lot and any signs from the gods; the candidates may also have attended. Like legislative meetings of the *concilium plebis*, electoral gatherings of the *comitia tributa* had their own procedures. The opening *contio* consisted only of a verbal formula and instructions to the voters, in which the magistrate asked the people to chose the new officeholders from names presented to them. After the vote, the official pronounced the formula of *renuntiatio*, and when it was given, the election was held to be valid. In the regular magistracies, the successful candidate took up the position on a fixed day, and his first official act was the taking of the auspices, the successful completion of which signaled Jupiter's acceptance of his right to auspicate. Special commissioners may well have entered office immediately, perhaps after similarly testing their auspices.

Now elections to fill regular offices, the most common arena of political competition, often were hotly contested, with candidates actively campaigning and seeking the support of those who had influence in the tribes and in the centuries. The resulting expenditure of time, money, and favors was worth the benefits that came to the successful candidates: the powers appropriate to the new office, access to the potential benefits that came from exercising those powers, and increased prestige among the people and in the senate. Elections to fill spaces on special commissions probably would not have been nearly as strongly contested—it is unlikely that they brought sufficient benefits to be worth the effort—and no reports of a contested election to any special commission survives.

The powers of the presiding magistrate and the influence and authority of the senate may have largely determined the membership. Certainly they could shape the result. Livy (24.7.12–9.1) noted that the consul of 215, Q. Fabius Maximus, displeased by the decision of the century that had just voted, ordered it to vote again. Those who wished to stand for election to one of the regular offices, moreover, presented their names to the presiding magistrate in a formal declaration known as a *professio*, and this official then ruled on the acceptability of candidacies, while the tribunes were permitted to challenge their suitability.[41] According to Livy (23.30.13–14), Q. Fabius Maximus wished to be chosen *IIvir* in 216 to dedicate a temple that he had vowed earlier as dictator, and the senate decreed that the consul who would hold the election should ask the people that they make Fabius a *duumvir*. The regular procedure in elections to fill special commissions, then, may well have been for the presiding magistrates to put forward only enough names to fill the slots or to allow competition only for some of the places.

Despite their ad hoc nature, colonial triumvirates formed a regular part of the mid-republican political order. In the fifty years between 219 and 169, at least nineteen colleges were active, some founding new colonies and others leading supplements to old ones; in the first twenty years of the second century, when most were concentrated, there would have been few years without such a commission in existence.[42] Many *IIIviri* were important members of the governing elite. The triumvirate that led *coloni* to Placentia and Cremona in 219 and 218 consisted of a former consular, C. Lutatius Catulus (cos. 220), and two former praetors, while one of the founders of Luna in 177, M. Aemilius Lepidus, had served as consul and censor and was *princeps senatus*. The names of fifty-six of the fifty-seven members of these colleges are known; the fifty-seventh's, one of the triumvirs who founded Tempsa in 194, is hopelessly corrupt in the manuscripts. Those triumvirs who had served as consul or praetor prior to their election to the commission can be identified with considerable confidence, for the consular and praetorian *fasti* are largely complete for the years in question.[43] The position in the senate, if any, of other commissioners is much less certain, for the *fasti* for the lesser offices are largely incomplete.[44]

Livy, it should be recalled, reported colonization projects in two forms: the passage of laws and election of the commissioners and the completion of the formal foundation by members of the college. For the years between the end of the Hannibalic war and 167, Livy noted the formation of ten colonial commissions and gave the names of thirty *IIIviri*. Fifteen had served either as consul or as praetor before joining the college and seven, almost half, had reached the higher office.[45]

The remaining nine boards present a slightly different picture, although the fact that Livy reported only the foundation makes its outlines more difficult to discern. At this time, four commissioners were consulars, one was actually serving as consul, eleven were praetorians, and one possibly was serving as praetor.[46] But the elections to fill the spots on those boards were held at an earlier time. When known, the interval between the sessions of the legislative and electoral assemblies and the completion of the foundation ranges from less than one year to more than two, but most are around one year.[47] If the elections to fill all the colleges took place in the consular year before that in which the settlements were founded, four triumvirs would have been consulars at the time of selection and twelve praetorians.[48] Putting the elections one year earlier would not change this greatly; there would be one less commissioner of praetorian rank.[49] In these boards, then, former consuls and praetors together held more than half of the positions, but consulars formed only one-quarter of the senior membership. Of all fifty-seven commissioners serving on the nineteen colleges, slightly more than half had previously served as consuls or praetors: eleven were consulars and nineteen or twenty praetorians. In this, the membership of colonial commissions did not differ greatly from the membership of the senate as a whole.[50]

Consulars and praetorians, however, were not evenly distributed across the commissions. Certain colleges contained two or even three former consuls or praetors, and the majority of those triumvirs who had previously reached the office of consul served on such boards. Ten triumvirates, slightly more than half of the total, contained nine consulars (almost all known to have served), and fourteen praetorians, more than half of those known to have been colonial commissioners.[51] In contrast, the membership of the eight remaining triumvirates certainly was considerably more junior. These twenty-four *IIIviri* included only two former consuls and five former praetors.[52] Of all eighteen commissions, three were entirely composed of consulars and praetorians: one had two consulars and a praetorian, another a consular and two praetorians, and a third three praetorians.[53] Seven included two former consuls and praetors: four triumvirates contained a consular, a praetorian, and a member of lesser rank; one had two consulars; and two each contained two praetorians.[54] Seven triumvirates had only one former consul or praetor, and in five that individual was a praetorian.[55] The remaining college included no consulars or praetorians.

An underlying principle to explain that variation is not immediately apparent. To some extent, the colleges that founded Latin colonies tended to include more consulars than those that founded citizen colonies, but the distinction is not strongly marked. The twenty-seven spaces on the colleges that dealt with citizen colonies contained four consulars and nine praetorians, while the same number of spaces on commissions concerned with Latin colonies had seven consulars and seven praetorians.[56]

A factor that may have influenced the choice of commissioners becomes clear upon examining two colleges entirely composed of consulars and praetorians. The triumvirate that established the colony at Aquileia in the years from 183 to 181 was the most senior of this period, with two consulars and a praetorian. The colony was to be founded in an especially dangerous area. The nearest Roman settlements, the citizen colonies at Mutina and Parma, founded in 183, the same year that the decision to found Aquileia was made, were both over 150 kilometers away. According to Livy (39.55.1–6), M. Claudius Marcellus (cos. 183) defeated in the region of the future colony some Gauls who had crossed the Alps, and the senate decided shortly afterward to plant a colony in order to prevent further immigration. The nearby Istrians were also a problem: Livy (40.26.2–3) noted that two years later they were preventing the settlement of the colonists and for that reason one of the praetors of 181 had begun a war against them.

The two former consuls and one former praetor who served on the colonial commission had all commanded armies successfully, two of them in the north of Italy. As consul, P. Cornelius Scipio Nasica (cos. 191) had fought the Boii and triumphed over them, and as praetor in 194, he also had won a victory in Spain and had his command extended.[57] The other consular, C. Flaminius (cos. 187), had campaigned against the Ligurians, defeating the Friniates and Apuani, and as praetor in 193 he had served in Spain, where his command was extended and he achieved some success.[58] The most junior member of the college was the only one never to have commanded an army in northern Italy. As praetor in 188, L. Manlius Acidinus served in Spain and his *imperium* apparently was also extended, since no successor was sent, but Manlius was one of the legates sent by the senate in 183 to the Transalpine Gauls to discourage further immigration.[59]

The college that founded Placentia and Cremona between 219 and 218 also included only consulars and praetorians. Both colonies were to be placed at some distance from other friendly settlements on land taken from the Boii and the Insubres, who were still strong and active, and the commissioners and their twelve thousand settlers apparently were protected by an army under a praetor.[60] This precaution proved to be inadequate, and the colony at Placentia was captured by the Gauls, who also besieged the praetor and his army at Tannetum. The consular commissioner, C. Lutatius Catulus (cos. 220), was experienced at warfare in the north, and as consul, he had campaigned as far as the Alps.[61] Due to the loss of Livy's second decade, the previous service of the two praetorians is unknown. These two commissions, slightly more that one-tenth of the triumvirates under examination, contained three of the eleven consulars known to have served on such boards in this period, slightly more than one-quarter of the total.

A tendency to include more experienced men on commissions intended to found settlements in unusually dangerous areas may have been mirrored by a similar inclination to construct less prominent colleges when those boards were to found settlements in stable, long-pacified regions. Of the seven colleges that had only one senior member—five included only a praetorian—almost all were in areas that had to be considered peaceful: one led a supplement to Venusia, another established five small colonies on the coast from Campania south, a third founded Sipontum on the coast of Apulia, the fourth founded Vibo Valentia, the fifth Copia in the *ager Thurinus*, and the sixth, Potentia and Pisaurum.[62] Indeed, the commission chosen in 180 to found Luca in territory provided by Pisa may be the only exception, for the settlement was to be placed near the Ligurians, but the board contained only a single praetorian.[63]

Colonial commissions of the late third and early second centuries, then, almost invariably contained at least one former consul or praetor.[64] The basic pattern probably was to have two of that rank, with at least one often a consular. Despite the apparent rigidity of the form, some adjustment to circumstances was possible. If the settlement was to be placed in an especially dangerous area, a more experienced commission may have been chosen, with all three consulars and praetorians. If, on the other hand, the area was long pacified with little likelihood that unexpected problems would develop, the founding commission could include only one senior member, most often a former praetor.

Such a pattern, at least in part, probably was a relatively recent development. In 242, the number of praetors was raised from one to two—equal, that is, to the number of consuls—and was increased again to four in 227, and to six in 197. Before the last third of the third century, then, consulars outnumbered praetorians in the senate and the same may have been true for the commissions. The members of only two triumvirates that served in the late fourth and early third centuries are known: the college that founded Cales in 334 probably contained three consulars, K. Duillius (cos. 336), T. Quinctius (dict. 361, cos. 354 and 353), and M. Fabius, either M. Fabius Ambustus (cos. 360, 356, and 354) or M. Fabius Dursuo (cos. 345), while the triumvirate that established Saticula in 313 included two former consuls, M. Valerius Corvus (cos. 348, 346, 343, 335, 300, and 299) and D. Iunius Brutus (cos. 325).[65] The membership of the first of those boards is even more senior than that of the commission that founded Aquileia, while the second is perhaps equal to it. Over the second half of the third century, then, praetorians gradually began to replace consulars in some of the positions on colonial triumvirates.

III. THE ENLISTMENT OF COLONISTS

The first major official responsibility of the commissioners probably was the enrollment of the colonists. No source directly describes the process, but there are indications that the crucial steps took place in face-to-face meetings, with the appropriate procedures, held in the public spaces of Rome. The central element in recruitment was the compilation of a written list of settlers.[66] Supervision of the construction of such a roster was a magisterial activity; indeed, Livy (39.23.4) characterized one triumvirate as having been chosen specifically for such a task, although it certainly would have had other responsibilities. The operation probably took place in one of the major public spaces of Rome and need not have lasted long; C. Laelius (cos. 190) enrolled six thousand *coloni* while supervising the election of his successors and persuading the senate to found new colonies.[67] Commissioners would have needed scribes to actually compile the lists and heralds to make the necessary announcements.[68]

Some of the phrases used to describe the process emphasize actions by the prospective colonists. The words *nomen dare* ("to give a name") regularly appear in the context of colonial recruitment and they seemingly imply some initiative on the part of would-be settlers, who probably were expected to come forward and submit their names to the commissioners.[69] Those who wished to be considered, then, came to those who compiled the lists.[70] At that point, some process of selection probably occurred, and at the end those who had successfully given their names, known as *adscripti*, were entered onto the roll of the colonists.[71]

Putting forward one's name involved certain claims of status and the inclusion of a name on the roster of colonists carried with it at least a provisional acceptance of the claim. Volunteers for Latin colonies faced a change in citizenship if successful. As a result, they were expected to be legally qualified to make such a decision—the jurist Gaius (1.131) maintained that Roman citizens who joined such colonies, if still *in patria potestate*, must enroll only at the command of their father.[72] Seeking a place also involved an assertion of one's status as a citizen or a Latin. Roman citizens could serve either in citizen colonies or in Latin ones; indeed, during the middle republic, most colonists were probably Roman citizens.[73] Latins could serve in Latin colonies, for in the middle republic Latins possessed the right of taking up citizenship in Rome as well as in other Latin communities, the *ius migrationis*.[74] The presence of non-Romans as full members of a citizen colony is more problematic: Latins traditionally may have possessed the right to enlist in such a settlement, but the privilege probably was eroded during the course of the second century.[75]

Colonial commissioners, then, assembled a list of colonists by accepting or rejecting prospective colonists who had put forward their names. To make possible an encounter between officials and would-be colonists, the responsible magistrates would have had to establish and proclaim a designated day or days and a specific location for them to gather; if, after all, volunteers were expected to submit their names, there must have been some place set aside for them to do so. In such gatherings, individuals implicitly or explicitly made certain declarations of status and those in charge made some process of selection, for all those who gave their names need not have become *adscripti*. No extant source describes such an event, but analogies with the procedures by which an army was enrolled at Rome, the *dilectus*, may prove instructive, for both operations aimed at constructing a list of adult males and both shared some of the same terminology and practices.[76]

The *dilectus*, like other major events in Roman public life, was conducted with its own formalities. Acting on a decree of the senate, the consuls proclaimed an edict summoning those of military age to assemble in Rome at a designated time and place.[77] When those citizens had gathered, the consuls, presiding from their curule chairs, subjected to penalties those absent and heard the claims of those who maintained that they were exempt from military service, received oaths in support of those claims, and ruled on their validity—colonial commissioners also would have had to accept declarations of status and any accompanying oaths.[78]

Polybius (6.19–21) preserves the most detailed description of the actual selection process after the supervising official had excluded those judged exempt, but his account presents certain difficulties.[79] He apparently followed closely a written account composed earlier, probably a military tribune's *commentarii*, since it emphasized the role of the twenty-four military tribunes assigned to the first four legions—officials who, like colonial commissioners, were elected by the *comitia tributa*—and ignored that of the consuls, who are known to have had a significant role.[80]

The twenty-four military tribunes, divided by lot into four groups, one for each of the legions, took up position on the Capitol where they summoned the citizens by tribes in an order determined by lot. As each tribal contingent came forward, the tribunes selected groups of four individuals, each of approximately the same age and physical condition, and assigned one to each of the legions, a process that went on until the four legions were filled. Festus (p. 108L) claimed that those bearing certain names were picked first because they were considered to be of good omen. The tribunes next administered the military oath to those chosen and then dismissed the soldiers, who were to reassemble later for actual service; no doubt the colonial commissioners could have handled selection much as the tribunes did. The closer that colonial recruitment approached the procedures of the *dilectus*, it should be noted, the more familiar it would have been to those participating, magistrates as well as prospective colonists, for all would probably have served in the army.

After selection had been completed and the oaths administered, Polybius represented the military tribunes as instructing the soldiers to gather later at a specific time and place. While tribunes may occasionally have performed that task immediately after the selection, consuls also issued those instructions, often some time after the formalities of the *dilectus*. Thus, L. Cornelius Scipio (cos. 190) issued an edict before a *contio* instructing that those he had enlisted earlier for his campaign in the East should assemble at Brundisium on the Ides of July, and the year before, M'. Acilius Glabrio (cos. 191) ordered his soldiers, enlisted by the outgoing consul L. Quinctius Flamininus, to meet again at Brundisium on the Ides of May where he would join them.[81] Livy (45.12.9–12) noted that the proclamation of such an edict required the taking of the auspices in a *templum* beforehand.

Colonial triumvirs certainly applied a similar procedure to the colonists after their enlistment. Polybius (3.40.3–10) claimed that after their recruitment the twelve thousand *coloni* to be sent to Placentia and Cremona in 219 were instructed to assemble on the scene in thirty days. Occasionally the colonists may have had to wait some time for orders. Some Latins who had enrolled in the citizen colonies authorized at the end of 197 were in Rome in 195;[82] the colonies were not founded until the following year.

Polybius claimed that the settlers for Placentia and Cremona were instructed to gather "on the scene." In this he was clearly mistaken. Both colonies were to be located among hostile and active populations, and a praetor and his army had to be assigned to protect the settlers.[83] Even in less hostile environments, without supervising magistrates and among populations that were to be displaced, the entry of settlers into land that was to be theirs held serious risk of leading to trouble. Just as the consuls used Brundisium as the assembly point for their armies headed east, so also colonial commissioners may have instructed their colonists to gather as close to the final destination as was practicable; that may have been the meaning of Polybius's "on the scene." The final stages of the approach to the colony, then, would have been as a group under the leadership of the colonial commissioners.

IV. THE DEPARTURE FOR THE SITE

Colonial commissioners and colonists performed the remaining operations at the site of the settlement and, for that purpose, the senate customarily provided officials with support. Livy (42.1.7–11) noted that magistrates who were to leave the city were provided with mules, tents, and the necessary equipment at public expense so that they would not be a burden to allies, and Plutarch (*TG* 13) reported that Ti. Gracchus sought the customary public tent and money from the senate for use while administering his land law. What the senate first gave was later provided by the authorizing law: Cicero (*Agr.* 2.13.32) held that the *rogatio Servilia* of 63 instructed that its commissioners receive mules, tents, and provisions.

Certain officials departed Rome according to a well-established procedure, for the official transition from the sphere *domi* to that of *militiae* was encompassed in ritual. A magistrate, when ready to leave the city to take up military command, was expected to take the auspices, make a public vow on the Capitol to be fulfilled upon returning successfully, proceed to the limits of the city in a procession formed by other officials, friends, and bystanders, and upon leaving the city change into the red cloak of the general in the field, the *paludamentum*, and instruct his lictors to put on their red cloaks and place the axes in the *fasces*.[84] Such a ceremonial departure is not attested for colonial commissioners, but it may not have been inappropriate, for, like generals, triumvirs operated away from the city and they could be leading their colonists into potentially dangerous areas.

The actual departure of commissioners and colonists need not always have followed closely the election or even the completion of enlistment. The commission instituted by the *lex Atinia* to found the citizen colonies of Volturnum, Liternum, Puteoli, Salernum, and Buxentum entered into office late in 197, but some, at least, of the colonists still were in Rome in 195, while the settlements were not actually founded until 194.[85] In this case, the reason for delay is clear. Two members of the founding triumvirate, Q. Minucius Thermus and Ti. Sempronius Longus, were also chosen to serve as praetors in 196 and were given provinces for the year: Thermus was assigned Nearer Spain, while Longus received Sardinia.[86] Neither returned to Rome immediately after completion of his term. Thermus was relieved by one of the praetors of 195, but he remained as proconsul until his replacement arrived and he probably returned to Rome no earlier than midsummer, since he celebrated his triumph two months after the *ovatio* of Cn. Cornelius Blasio whom M. Porcius Cato (cos. 195) had replaced on his arrival in Spain.[87] Longus's command in Sardinia was prorogued for the year 195, but on his return he was elected consul for 194 and was assigned the war against the Boii and the Ligures, in northern Italy rather than in the south where the colonies were to be located.[88]

In this triumvirate, then, one commissioner, M. Servilius Geminus (cos. 202), the sole consular, was available for the entire three-year duration of the project, a second was only available for the latter half of 195 and all of 194, while the third probably never really contributed to the efforts of the college. Geminus alone may have recruited the colonists—they were already enrolled in 195—although Thermus conceivably could have participated. The departure of officials and colonists to the site, then, was delayed until the entire college could be assembled, and the project went ahead only after it had become clear that one *IIIvir* could not participate during the board's three-year term.

In the late third and early second centuries, projects were organized around a single journey to the site and all three commissioners probably were expected to depart together—in this regard, mid-republican practice probably differed noticeably from that of later periods.[89] The triumvirs who founded Placentia and Cremona in 219 and 218 certainly operated together, and they may even have left Rome in this way. At any rate, the Gauls captured all three commissioners as they were surveying and dividing the land of Placentia. The same college also established the colony of Cremona nearby. Since the foundation rites at both were reportedly performed in the same year, 219, and since a praetor and his army were required for protection (when the commissioners were at Placentia, the praetor may have been guarding the recently founded Cremona), all three commissioners probably left the assembly point with the settlers of both colonies, joined the praetor and his army, and proceeded in a large body, founding the colonies in succession.[90] Commissioners of the middle republic certainly did not depart individually to work at separate sites.[91] Colleges founding more than one colony, moreover, probably founded all in a single journey, for if the triumvirs had made separate trips to the settlements, those colonies could just as easily have been widely scattered rather than in adjacent territories as was customary.

But at the Gracchan colony of Iunonia, the commissioners followed a different procedure. One went to the place to survey and mark the land,

and only after his return to Rome did a second triumvir lead the colonists to Africa, found the city ritually, and assign the land previously divided to settlers.[92] Here, two commissioners essentially operated independently during important portions of the operation, with two successive departures, each involving different individuals: in the first, one triumvir, the surveyors, and the necessary attendants, and in the second, another commissioner with his *apparitores* and the colonists. Although such an arrangement was common in the first century, the procedure employed by the colleges that founded Placentia and Cremona and the five colonies of Volturnum, Liternum, Puteoli, Salernum, and Buxentum probably was standard earlier, for the successive performance of segments of the colonizing process at the same site by different commissioners making separate journeys probably was a Gracchan innovation.

Certain other colonial projects give indirect support to such a conclusion, while explaining various delays in the process of foundation and emphasizing the importance of consulars and praetorians on the colleges. For several colonies established in the late third and early second centuries, Livy reported both the decision to found a community and the formal foundation of the settlement. The evidence, it should be noted, is found in annalistic passages isolated from the surrounding narrative, and, as a result, the years in which the two events took place are known, but the chronological position of the events within each year often is not. Of the six instances, the college and colonies authorized by the *lex Atinia* of 197, where foundation took place in the third year after authorization, have already been examined. Of the remaining five, two colleges (for Bononia and Copia) took a year or less to reach that stage, one (for Vibo Valentia) took between one and two years (although the interval need not have been much longer than the first group), and two (for Aquileia and Luca) took between two and three years.[93] In this regard, it should be noted that the *lex Atinia* and the *lex Aelia*, and possibly other colonial laws as well, set a three-year limit for the triumvirs' terms.[94]

Some members of those colleges that took more than a single year to arrange the actual establishment of their settlements were engaged in other activities at the same time, and thus the delay may indicate a desire to keep the college together, as was the case with the commission of 197. Q. Fabius Buteo (pr. 181), the only consular or praetorian on the triumvirate chosen in 180 to found Luca, served as proconsul in Gaul in that year and may also have done so in the following one;[95] the settlement probably was founded in 178.[96] In this regard, the two colleges authorized by the *lex Aelia* of late 194 provide a useful contrast. Both colleges were chosen at the end of 194.[97]

One member of the college that founded Copia had other responsibilities — Q. Aelius Tubero, the tribune who carried the law, was in office in 193 — but the triumvirs founded their settlement in the following consular year. But M. Minucius Rufus (pr. 197), the sole consular or praetorian on the other college, was sent as a legate to Africa after the college was formed to resolve a boundary dispute between Carthage and Masinissa, the king of Numidia;[98] Vibo Valentia was established in the second year. At Aquileia, which was founded in the third year, none of the commissioners is known to have had other tasks, but there conditions at the site probably were a factor, since the Istrians reportedly were interfering with the settlement.[99]

The commissions with the longest interval between passage of the law and performance of the rites of foundation tended to be those in which one or more commissioners were involved in other activities, especially if that number included the sole consular or praetorian. Such a conclusion should indicate that the usual mid-republican practice required the presence at the site at any one time of at least two members of the college, postponing any departure from Rome until that was possible.[100]

V. CONCLUSION

The process of founding a colony began in the civic spaces of Rome itself. An official raised the matter in the senate in the proper way and secured a decree in the appropriate form. A tribune then proposed and carried a law before the people, an operation with its own set of rules. The decree and the law were framed in ways that allowed little variation and followed closely an established pattern. Next, a consul or praetor supervised the election of three colonial commissioners by yet another formally constituted body. Again in the public spaces of the city, those triumvirs enlisted the necessary colonists and instructed them to meet at a designated time and place. Finally, the colonial commission departed the city, perhaps in ceremony, to meet the colonists and proceed to the site, where the most onerous portion of their task remained.

AS IF SMALL IMAGES OF
THE ROMAN PEOPLE

The remainder of the commissioners' task took place in the territory of the new colony. There, the triumvirs carried through operations that created a new community with all of its attributes, establishing a fortified center to protect the settlers, giving it its public institutions, and assigning lands to *coloni*. But a colony was more than a settlement of farmers with some self-government. For the Romans, it was an *urbs*, a complex organization of citizens, of magistracies, of ritualized practices, and of spaces. Within its territory, the founders sought to duplicate the *urbs Roma* and the *ager Romanus* in certain of their political, cultic, and legal aspects, instituting the equivalent of the Roman spheres of *domi* and *militiae*, placing the sacred spaces necessary for government, and creating the proper subdivisions in the citizen body. Aulus Gellius (16.13.9), after all, likened them to small images of the Roman people.

On the scene, the triumvirs dealt personally with colonists, natives of the area, and neighbors of the new settlement, some possibly unfriendly and uncooperative. Throughout the long process of installation, the commissioners probably kept the settlers together in a mass as long as possible, dispatching groups to secondary centers only when ready, and allowing colonists to disperse to their new houses and fields only toward the end. Such an arrangement would have been most suitable for defense, for maintaining control, and for avoiding unplanned incidents between colonists and the previous occupants. Indeed, to perform most of the major events of the foundation, the commissioners would have had to regularly assemble the settlers either in a body or in well-defined subgroups.

Ritual and formula dominated the interactions between the founders and those under their authority. Decisions and operations that would be considered "pragmatic" were confirmed and executed in the context of ritual, often versions of those rites that served the same purpose at Rome. Some of those ceremonial gatherings of commissioners and colonists, moreover, gave shape to the entire process, for the creation of an urban core with citizens, priests, and officials, the definition of the territory, the marking of lands for distribution, and the assignment of segments to individuals each focused on its own sequence of conventionalized actions, often with strong religious associations.

In this chapter, the task of establishing a colony will be examined in detail and the crucial stages identified: the first section will examine the creation of the categories of *urbs* and *ager*, the definition of the citizenry, and the establishment of public institutions; the second section will focus on the formation of the necessary public and sacred spaces within the city and its territory; the third, on the surveying of the lands to be given to private persons; and the fourth, on the assignment of lands to colonists. A fifth section will examine the possible installation of additional settlers at some time after the original foundation.

I. THE FORMATION OF CITY AND CITIZENRY

The triumvirs' central task was the creation of the urban core of the community, the future seat of its government and of many of the cults and spaces that organized its public life. The founders, leading the colonists through a series of ritual acts in and around the new city, separated the new *urbs* from other settlements in the territory of the colony, some of which were to be inhabited by colonists and others by the natives, formed the colonists into a ritually defined citizen body, and gave to the city its magistrates, priests, and civic institutions.

In some cases, commissioners may have had little freedom in locating the town itself. Livy (32.29.3–4) characterized the *lex Atinia* of 197 as authorizing the establishment of some small citizen colonies at three named places — Puteoli, the *castrum* of Salernum, and Buxentum — each already inhabited and used by the Romans as sites for garrisons during the Second Punic War;[1] the words *castrum Salerni* may indicate that the framers of the legislation had a specific place in mind. On other occasions, however, the choice may have been in the hands of the commissioners. The *lex Aelia* of 194 apparently specified only that its two Latin colonies be sent to the territories of Bruttium and the *ager Thurinus*.[2]

The immediate aim of the colony, concerns over its security, and the nature of the terrain probably were the determining factors in the location of that urban core. In some cases, the triumvirs placed the colony in relatively open territory. In others, especially when attack seemed likely, they chose more defensible locations, difficult of access. Indeed, Hyginus Gromaticus (pp. 178–79L) noted that the "ancients," because of the fear of sudden attack, often located the city on a high place; colonies such as Alba Fucens (303) and Cosa (273) are clear examples. Although the center of a new community, the site of the town itself need not have been previously uninhabited, for the Romans sent colonies to a number of long-settled places. Probably at first, and in exposed locations for a long time afterward, the fortified core of the settlement was intended to be largely free of foreigners, and it may be significant that the colony of Copia (193) was established at *castrum Frentinum* rather than the nearby Thurii, which was included in its territory.[3]

Legally and religiously the process of founding a colony culminated in the performance of a specific rite. In a practice dating back at least to the fourth century, the Romans conceived of colonies as beginning on a specific day, celebrated in the following years by the colonists and their descendants.[4] Three mid-republican foundation days are known: Saticula (313) on January 1, Brundisium (244) on August 5, Placentia (218) on May 31 or December 31, and Bononia (189) on December 28, and the foundation of Rome itself, ostensibly by the same procedures as colonies, was celebrated on the feast of the Parilia on April 21.[5] Yet the official activities of the founders, the *conditores* or *deductores*, did not end with the completion of the rite; although the colony legally existed from that date, much of the commissioners' task remained. Dionysius of Halicarnassus (*Ant. Rom.* 1.88) placed the construction of buildings at Rome after Romulus's formal foundation, and although the legal foundation of Placentia took place in the consular year of 219, the colonial commissioners were still measuring and dividing the land for the colonists in the next year.[6] A colony, then, could exist as a political entity before land was assigned to its citizens or the town itself was built.

The act most clearly associated with the foundation was the formal plowing of the *sulcus primigenius* or "primeval furrow" around the site of the new city.[7] Used for both citizen and Latin colonies, this rite was thought to be of great antiquity:[8] Romans of the first century (and probably those of a much earlier period) maintained that Romulus performed it at Rome itself, marking Rome's formal establishment as a city, and Dionysius of Halicarnassus (*Ant. Rom.* 1.88) held that Romulus's act served afterward as the pattern the Romans followed in all their colonies.

The plowing of the *sulcus primigenius* established one of the essential features of a civic order. According to Plutarch (*Rom.* 11), when Romulus performed the ceremony at Rome, he created the *pomerium* of the city, the limiting zone that not only defined the new *urbs* itself, but also its auspices, certain aspects of its religious life, and the powers of its officials. The course taken by a colonial commissioner when plowing the furrow also marked a *pomerium*, that of the colony. Varro (*LL* 5.143) noted that "The circle which was made behind this [i.e., the furrow] was the beginning of the city [*urbs*] ... and by it the urban auspices were bound." Varro then observed that older authors called all Roman colonies *urbes* because, like Rome, they had been surrounded by such a furrow and that colonies and cities were considered as founded [*conduntur*] because they were enclosed within a *pomerium*. The *pomerium* of Rome was a *locus inauguratus*, and Romulus was both king and augur; the founder of a colony in some fashion replicated that role.[9]

The outlines of that ritual are clear and its basic forms constant. Single magistrates supervised specific events, for only one individual at a time led ceremonial performances or took the auspices that began all public acts. The identity of the triumvir who would lead a specific rite could be determined in two ways: by casting lots (*sortitio*) or by agreement among colleagues (*comparatio*). The *deductor* began the actual definition of the limits of the city by taking the auspices, probably using the sacred chickens (*ex tripudiis*), an act that would have required the preliminary designation of a *templum*;[10] Cicero (*Agr.* 2.12.31) recorded the existence of special auspices for the founding of colonies. Then, the commissioner, using a plow with a bronze plowshare, made the furrow while reciting a formula of prayer.[11] The elder Cato, holding it to be customary, described the central feature of the rite in terms very similar to those the antiquarian Varro (*LL* 5.143) would use a century later:[12]

> The founders of cities yoked together a bull on the right and a cow on the inside and, having tied up the toga in the *cinctus Gabinus*, that is, having covered the head with part of the toga and with part girded

around the waist, they held the curved plow-handle so that all the clods fell inward, and in this fashion they marked out by the furrow they made the location of the walls, lifting up the plow around the places for the gates.

Romulus had assistants follow after him turning all the clods inward, and at the end of the ceremony he sacrificed the bull and the cow that had pulled the plow.[13] Varro's contemporaries, Julius Caesar, Mark Antony, and Octavian, used the rite in the foundation of their own colonies, and settlements recalled their foundation by minting coins showing their *conditor* with the plow well into the Principate.[14]

The formation of the *sulcus primigenius* need have required the presence only of the founder and a few attendants, but a closely associated rite certainly involved all or nearly all the colonists. Plutarch (*Rom.* 11) and Ovid (*Fast.* 4.820–24) reported that Romulus, before plowing the furrow around Rome, instructed the would-be citizens to go into the center of the proposed city and throw into a sacrificial pit the firstfruits of the land along with soil from their native territories; Plutarch called the pit the *mundus*—its nature and ritual functions are obscure. Ovid went on to note that the first king then erected an altar on the site and ignited a fire on it. According to Plutarch, that point served as the center around which Romulus later plowed the furrow that defined the city limits. After the foundation, the place maintained considerable significance. At the highest point, the *arx*, of the colony of Cosa (273), excavators have found traces of such a pit; a rectangular stone platform at first covered it and by the the middle of the second century that rectangle was incorporated into a large temple with the pit under its central axis.[15] The city, its limits, and one of its religious centers, then, were defined in closely linked rites by the founders in the presence of the settlers.

The formal establishment of the *urbs* through the creation of the *pomerium* was not the only ceremonial act needed to construct a city. Each colony required not only an urban core, but also citizens to inhabit it and magistrates and priests to govern it. Indeed, a city without all those elements was more than a mere anomaly. In a speech he attributed to a Greek ambassador, but which represents more closely Roman attitudes, Livy (31.29.11) described Capua, which had lost its civic organization of magistrates, senate, and citizenry in the Second Punic War, as mutilated (*urbs trunca*) and unnatural (*prodigium*).

The colonial commissioners gave the colonists their new status and when necessary formed them into tribes and classes in the *lustrum*, a ritual of purification and renewal in which all colonists probably participated. This ceremony closely resembled others performed at Rome itself and in the camps: Cicero (*Div.* 1.45.102) explicitly linked the colonial *lustrum* with those *lustra* by which the censors purified the Roman people and generals purified their armies. Here, then, the commissioners and the colonists followed a pattern broadly familiar to all the participants, who may have witnessed censors' purifications of the people and who certainly would have served in, or sometimes even commanded, armies. In a distant place, surrounded by natives who may have been unfriendly, that familiar rite would have defined the new citizenry to the colonists themselves and to outsiders and reinforced feelings of solidarity among the settlers.

At Rome, the censors' purification of the citizenry was the culmination of the regular census of citizens, for the ceremony closed the census and gave to it legally and ritually its validity.[16] The census was more than a mere listing of the names of those who held citizen status, for the Romans did not consider a citizen body to be an undifferentiated mass. Instead, the Roman leadership held that a properly ordered citizenry ought to be divided into a range of groups, which were to occupy important places in the political, administrative, and ritual order. At one level, Roman citizens were gathered into tribes by their place of residence; these served as the voting units in the tribal and plebeian assemblies and formed the basis for conscription. At another level, citizens were assigned to centuries that were grouped into a limited range of property classes. Some especially high ranking citizens, moreover, were formally separated from the bulk of the population: those who had received the public horse (*equites equo publico*)—originally the core of the cavalry—were placed in centuries of their own. These centuries formed the voting units in the *comitia centuriata* and, according to Dionysius of Halicarnassus (*Ant. Rom.* 4.19.1–4), served as the means to calculate the amount of each citizen's contribution when the payment of *tributum* was deemed necessary. Settlers in colonies established according to Roman rules were often or always arranged in similar groupings. Colonists installed in Latin colonies were placed in tribes and classified as either *equites* or *pedites*, a distinction that affected the amount of land each was to receive; the situation in mid-republican citizen colonies is less clear: all settlers in a colony received the same allotments, an indication that no distinctions on the basis of wealth were to be made, and settlements with only three hundred *coloni* were probably too small to require subdivisions, but the larger colonies of two thousand may have possessed some subunits—later citizen colonies certainly did.[17]

The rites that made up censorial *lustra* are fairly well known.[18] Having successfully taken the auspices, the censors summoned the people to gather, arranged in centuries, at dawn on the *campus Martius*, where the censors determined by lot which of them would actually perform the purification.[19] The assembly culminated in the *suovetaurilia*, a sacrifice of a bull, a boar, and a ram, also a feature of private lustral rites, for the Elder Cato (*Agr.* 141) recommended its regular performance to purify and protect the fields. The three victims were led around the assembled citizenry in a procession — in private rites, they were led around land to be protected;[20] Cicero (*Div.* 1.45.102) recommended that magistrates choose only those with names of good omen to lead the animals. Then, the presiding censor made a vow that a similar sacrifice would be performed at the end of the next *lustrum* if the state was preserved unharmed.[21] The censor completed the lustration by leading the people into the city in a procession behind a standard or *vexillum*.[22] C. Gracchus, triumvir for the colony of Iunonia at Carthage in 122, reportedly led such a procession, and Cicero, in one of his attacks against Mark Antony, characterized the latter as wishing to found a colony so that he might carry the standard and plow the furrow, thus clearly placing the procession among the most prominent features of colonial foundation.[23]

During the ceremony, the censors marshaled the assembled citizens in their centuries and tribes, constitutive units of the citizen body, and the *lustrum* fixed legally and religiously the groups that made up the citizenry. In the procedures of the census and in the ceremonies of the *lustrum* that confirmed it, therefore, the censors reestablished the citizen body of Rome and its necessary subdivisions.[24] Created in ritual, the units of the census continued to have an active ceremonial life: tribes and centuries were regularly summoned back into a clearly visible existence, recreating the social order in the formalities of the vote in legislative, electoral, and judicial assemblies and serving as the basis for administrative acts such as the *dilectus*, in which officials selected those who were to serve in armies. Just as the censors' *lustrum* constructed the citizen body and its necessary ritual and administrative units, so also did military *lustra* serve to form an army, for there was a close practical connection between the mustering of an army into its units and its sacral purification.[25]

Like the purifications of citizenry and armies, the colonial *lustrum* served a similar function in creating and organizing the citizen body of the settlement.[26] Prospective colonists did not receive their new status as citizens of the colony merely by being inscribed on the list of colonists assembled by the colonial commissioners: their change of citizenship came only at the completion of the purification, which confirmed that list in the same way that the censorial *lustrum* confirmed the validity of the citizen rolls.[27] Just as did the censors at Rome, moreover, the *IIIviri* who founded Latin colonies divided the citizenry into subunits: tribes and the census classes of *pedites* and *equites*. The commissioners probably assembled lists of those groups in advance, but the triumvir who performed the *lustrum* ritually established and confirmed the units and the status that accompanied membership in them; he made the lists real.

In the *lustrum* as in other religious rituals of the Roman state, exact performance of the proper procedures was required. Indeed, irregularities could serve to nullify an entire census. Thus, L. Iulius Caesar and P. Licinius Crassus, censors in 89, improperly took the auspices before holding the assembly for the *lustrum* and afterward the fault served as a reason for the *lustrum* to be ruled unfortunate (*parum felix*) — perhaps for that reason, new censors were chosen after a shorter than normal interval.[28] Reports apparently circulated concerning prodigies, such as the wind tearing the *vexillum* from the hands of the bearer and carrying off the victims from the altar, which called into question the validity of C. Gracchus's foundation of Carthage.[29]

Censorial, military, and colonial *lustra* took place in an analogous spatial framework. Because the colonial commissioners assembled the roster of colonists at Rome, some envision the triumvirs also performing the *lustrum* there.[30] Colonial commissioners and colonists approached the site of the colony in a body, and the use of the verb *deducere* ("to lead from") to denote the process of establishing a colony may call to mind a formal march from Rome.[31] Thus, the colonial *lustrum* and the census that preceded it can be seen as taking place in Rome and the culminating procession behind the standard as the beginning of the march itself.

But the listing of colonists can be set apart chronologically and spatially from the *lustrum* of the *coloni* and from the start of the journey.[32] Thus, colonists enrolled under the terms of the *lex Atinia* of 197 probably did not attain their new status until some time after the lists had been made, and the colonial commissioners of 219, charged with founding the colonies of Placentia and Cremona, called for the colonists to assemble close to the colonies rather than in Rome, where they probably enlisted them.[33] At Placentia and Cremona at least, the march to the site did not originate at Rome and the future colonists may never have been collected as a group there. Thus, if the *lustrum* took place at Rome, it must have been separate from the beginning of the journey to the colony. The lustral procession and the census associated with it, therefore, may be clearly separated chronologically and geographically either from the beginning of the march to the colony, or from the compilation of the list of settlers, or more probably from both. The most likely location for the *lustrum* was in the territory of the colony. Indeed, Plutarch (*CG* 11), listing a sequence of prodigies surrounding C. Gracchus's foundation of the colony at Carthage, clearly placed in Africa those affecting the procession *sub vexillo*.

The *lustrum*'s location can be further clarified by examining closely the sites where censors and generals performed their *lustra* and the places to which they led the processions that ended them. In the case of the Roman census both points were clearly fixed. The censor purified the people on the *campus Martius* outside the Roman *pomerium* and, after the completion of the various rites, led the citizens back into the city.[34] During the course of a campaign, however, generals purified their armies on a number of occasions: when they first formed their armies, when they took over an army from its previous commander, when they merged previously separate forces, when they collected scattered detachments from their winter quarters, when they divided a single army with another commander, and when they regrouped their forces to prepare for battle after a long march.[35] Naturally, they would have performed those *lustra* at many different places. Yet the setting for the rites was analogous to that in Rome. Just as the censors performed the rites outside the *pomerium* on the *campus Martius*, generals also purified their armies outside of their camps.[36] Indeed, Livy (3.22.4) held that when those conscripted had gathered as instructed outside the *porta Capena*, L. Cornelius Maluginensis (cos. 459) first established a camp and then purified the army.

Just as the censors led their processions inside the *pomerium*, generals probably led theirs back to the camp rather than beginning a march, even in the case of *lustra* performed before starting a campaign.[37] Following the purification, generals can be found paying the soldiers and giving them animals for sacrifice, addressing the army from a tribunal, and performing a sortition from a *templum*;[38] places for all of those activities were provided in the camp.[39] In fact, in one atypical case, the commanders, because of the strength of their opponents, performed the entire ceremony inside the camp.[40] The colonial commissioners, then, probably purified the colonists outside the *pomerium* of the colony and led the colonists into the city.

The chronological relationship between the formal constitution of the citizen body and the ritual demarcation of the *urbs* is obscure.[41] In an account placed after his description of the plowing of the furrow in which he called the act the first after the foundation of the city, Plutarch (*Rom.* 13) had Romulus divide the citizenry into three bodies, the legion, the people, and the senate, an operation similar to the census, although Plutarch did not explicitly link the two. Yet Cicero, if his grammar can be trusted, placed the *lustrum* before the foundation, and thus before the establishment of the colonial *pomerium*.[42]

The two different orders of events both create anomalies. Plutarch seemingly placed the creation of the sacrificial pit first, then the establishment of the *pomerium*, and finally the creation of the citizenry. The ritual at the pit would have attached the colonists to their new city, but in Plutarch's version, that would have taken place before the colonists had become citizens and before they had severed ritually their ties with their old communities. In Cicero's order of events, on the other hand, the citizen body would have been formed and the new status given before the new city existed. It is likely, then, that those ritual acts were kept as close together in time as they were in space. Indeed, one rite may have directly led into the others. Plutarch and Ovid, in their accounts of the deposition of firstfruits into the sacrificial pit made no mention of a procession, but the circumstance — a large group of men performing in sequence the same act at the same place — easily could have involved one; conceivably, the procession ending the *lustrum* may itself have ended with the colonists depositing their offerings.[43]

The formal foundation of city and citizenry took place in a complex of rituals probably spread over several days. In the ceremonies of the *sulcus primigenius*, the colonial commissioners defined the religious limits of the new city and, in the ceremonies of the *lustrum*, performed in close proximity to the new city spatially and to its formal foundation chronologically, they defined the new citizens, assembled as a group, established their proper subdivisions, and separated them formally from others who continued to reside in the territory of the new settlement. The city and its citizen body, however, required magistrates, priests, and senate or *curia*. The founders also established and filled these positions in the context of the other founding ceremonies.[44]

The *deductores* gave the essential elements of local government to the new community in a formal charter or *lex data*, and the practice of issuing a written law in some form certainly reached back at least into the third century.[45] The only substantially intact law of this type, the *lex coloniae Iuliae Genetivae*, which governed the Caesarian colony of Urso in Spain, shared the formal style of other *leges*.[46] As was the case with other laws, the founding commissioners probably publicly proclaimed the *lex data* to an assembly of the colonists who were to be governed by it. This public announcement may have taken place among the other ceremonies of the foundation. Certainly it took effect upon their completion: in the *lex Ursonensis*, no distinction in time can be made between the phrases "after this law was given" (*post hanc legem datam*) and "after the colony was deducted" (*post coloniam deductam*).[47] The first colleges of officials and priests appointed by the colonial commissioners took office at the same time. Cicero witnessed colonial magistrates of an ephemeral colony at Capua that "had just been deducted" (*colonia iam deducta*) performing some of their functions within a few days of the foundation of the settlement, while in the *lex Ursonensis* the first officials are described as holding office *post coloniam deductam*.[48]

In the same formal declaration, the founders also established the frontiers of the community itself, the outer limits of the jurisdiction of the magistrates of the new settlement. The triumvirs, in other words, created an *ager* to complement the *urbs* formed by the *pomerium*, the same arrangement found at Rome and its environs. Probably after a personal inspection of the area, the commissioners granted in a verbal formula, announced to the assembled colonists at the same time as the *lex data*, the limits of the territory their settlement was to receive.[49] Hyginus (pp. 118–19L) preserved a formula of definition, which he maintained must be included among the laws governing the colony: "the fields, places, and buildings which I shall have given and assigned within those *fines*, and within that river, and within that road, in these fields let there be *iuris dictio* and *coercitio* for that colony." Hyginus went on to note that the phrase "the fields, the places, and the buildings which . . ." was not needed if the entire territory fixed by the boundaries was assigned to the jurisdiction of the colony, and the words "let there be *iuris dictio* and *coercitio* for that colony within that *fines* and that river" would suffice. Here, as was the case with *leges templorum*, the *lex* contained a definition of the area it was to govern. The formal proclamation of these boundaries to those affected by them would have been separated in time and place from the actual establishment of markers—the two events by their very nature could not have taken place at a single time and place.

The practice of defining major political boundaries in such a manner reaches back at least to the early second century, for Q. Fabius Labeo (pr. 189), as praetor or propraetor, gave a portion of the limits of the Macedonian kingdom by specifying one of the boundaries as an ancient royal road, and some of Hyginus's phrasing reaches back at least into the second century, for the framers of the agrarian law of 111 regularly used the formula "the fields, the places, and the buildings" to describe the land covered by provisions of the law itself and by the actions of the Gracchan commissioners.[50]

An inscription may provide a detailed example of a similar announcement. In 117, the senate sent two legates to define the territory of the Langenses Veturii and fix their relationship to Genua, to which they had been attributed. The legates announced publicly their findings to both parties and again at Rome:[51]

> The boundaries of the private land of the Langenses are: from the lowest part of the stream which rises from the spring on Manicelum to the river Edus; there a *terminus* stands. From there, along the stream upward to the river Lemuris. From there along the river Lemuris uphill to the stream Comberanea. From there along the stream Comberanea uphill to the valley Caeptiema; there two boundary markers stand on either side of the *via Postumia*. From these boundary marks . . .

II. THE SPACES NECESSARY FOR PUBLIC LIFE

The order outlined by the colonial commissioners — establishing the colonial *pomerium* and the *ager*, constituting the citizen body, proclaiming the colony's constitution, and introducing into office new magistrates and priests — was expected to function in the Roman fashion, requiring the colonies to have a civic life patterned after, though not necessarily identical to, Rome's own — Aulus Gellius (16.13.9), after all, described them as resembling little images of the Roman people. In a series of rites, some of which fulfilled goals set in the formal foundation, officials created *templa*, temples, altars, sacred groves, and the necessary public meeting places.

Although the lines of development and the degree of standardization in colonial constitutions are controversial, certain elements are clear. In citizen colonies, the chief officials generally were *praetores* or, as was the case at Urso, *duoviri*; lesser magistrates were called aediles, and the members of the town council were known as *decuriones*. Urso had not just *duoviri*, but also aediles, decurions, pontiffs, and augurs, and in his speech against the proposed agrarian law of P. Servilius Rullus, Cicero (*Agr.* 2.35.96) speculated that the founders of a citizen colony at Capua might set up one hundred decurions, ten augurs, and six pontiffs. Latin colonies may have had more complicated governments. The settlers were divided into classes, and that division probably had constitutional implications. A more complete list of Roman titles certainly can be found in such colonies. At

Ariminum (268) and Beneventum (268), for example, the chief magistrates were known as *consules*, but, just as in citizen colonies, the most common title was praetor, the council sometimes was called the senate, and some colonies had tribunes and quaestors (Venusia), quaestors (Firmum), aediles (Narnia), and censors (Copia and Beneventum).[52]

Colonial priests and magistrates were expected to proceed more or less as did the analogous figures at Rome itself. The *lex coloniae Iuliae Genetivae* set forth rules to govern the arrangement of public business and gave instructions in the form appropriate to *leges*, some covering private citizens in matters of significance for the community and others providing detailed tasks for magistrates and priests: when *comitia*, *quaestiones*, and meetings of the *decuriones* were to be held, who was to supervise festivals, games, sacrifices, and *ludi scaenici*, how they were to be financed, and where and when the performances were to take place. Cicero (*Agr.* 2.34.92–93), moreover, claimed to have witnessed the magistrates of Capua performing a sacrifice in the Roman manner shortly after the colony was founded. To make such operations possible, the *lex Ursonensis* assigned to magistrates the attendants and ritual attributes typical of Roman officials. The *duoviri* and the aediles were to wear the magisterial *toga praetexta* and have wax torches (*funalia*) and candles (*cereos*). Each *duovir* was to have two lictors to carry the *fasces* (the same number the urban praetors had at Rome), an *accensus*, two *scribae*, two *viatores*, a *librarius*, a *praeco*, an *haruspex*, and a trumpet player, while each aedile was to be attended by a scribe, a *praeco*, an *haruspex*, a flute player, and four public slaves in girded aprons.[53]

Officials and priests operating in the Roman manner customarily acted in certain well-defined places, so that a range of public spaces had to be set aside. Although the layout could vary depending on the nature of the terrain and the degree to which earlier inhabitants had built on the site, Roman colonies possessed certain highly standardized elements. From the fourth century, the urban core was organized around a square or *forum* and a high place or *arx*, and clustered around those places (and elsewhere in the town) was a range of public buildings and temples, including a *Capitolium* patterned after the temple of Jupiter Best and Greatest on the Capitol at Rome.[54] At Cosa (273), for example, the highest point in the settlement was turned into an *arx* on which a *Capitolium* later was constructed — an open space in front of this temple may have been intended to serve the same function as the Roman *area Capitolina* — the largest level area was turned into a *forum*, a *comitium* and a *curia* similar to those at Rome were constructed adjacent to the *forum* (as was the case at Rome), and the *arx* and the *forum* were connected by a processional way as were the Roman versions.⁵⁵ In colonies, the size of *fora* may have been determined according to a fixed ratio based on the number of citizens.⁵⁶

Like those spaces in the urban core, certain places within the colonial *ager* and along its outer limits had important roles in the settlement's political and religious life. Hyginus Gromaticus (p. 199L) recommended that those supervising the foundation of colonies mark some crucial positions on the frontiers with inscribed stones and others with altars; the *Liber coloniarum I* (p. 241L), one of the texts of the *Corpus Agrimensorum Romanorum*, also mentioned the use of altars (*sacrificales aras*) in conjunction with other markers (*terminos Augusteos*) in similar circumstances. The placement of visible signs of the limits of large territories was a well-established practice in Rome. The legates of 117 determined where markers should be placed, while in other cases magistrates or promagistrates performed the operation. Thus, Livy (32.28.11) reported that the senate instructed two of the praetors of 197 to mark the boundaries separating the newly established provinces of Hispania Ulterior and Hispania Citerior, while the Elder Pliny (*Nat.* 5.25) held that Scipio Aemilianus made a ditch, the *fossa regia*, to distinguish previously Carthaginian territory assigned to the kings of Numidia from that forming the new province of Africa.

Some boundary markers were created in ceremony and had an enduring ritual importance. The definition of the territory of an *urbs* through the altars and other sacred spots was certainly quite old in Rome.⁵⁷ Despite the great expansion of Roman territory, the early territory of Rome itself, the *ager Romanus antiquus*, was fixed in such a fashion no later than the beginning of the republic and it remained of religious significance well into the imperial period.⁵⁸ The defining sacred places were concentrated on routes into the *ager Romanus*: the sanctuary of the god Terminus on the sixth mile of the *via Laurentina*, the statue of Mars at the fourth mile of the *via Appia*, the sanctuary of *Fortuna muliebris* on the fourth mile of the *via Latina*, and the sacred groves of Robigo at the fifth mile of the *via Claudia*, of Dea Dia at the fifth mile of the *via Campana*, and the "place called *Festoi*" between the fifth and sixth milestone of an unknown route. As apparently was the case with the boundary sanctuaries of colonies, these sacred places were at first occupied by simple shrines, altars, and groves; at Rome, monumental structures came later, perhaps in the second century.⁵⁹

The use of inscribed boundary stones apparently goes no further back than the late second century, but other forms of markers were available, which by their very nature would have left no traces.⁶⁰ Various works preserved in the *Corpus Agrimensorum Romanorum* contain references to wooden stakes or *pali sacrificiales*. Some marked the limits of private estates and may have been placed by private action.[61] Others signaled official boundaries, and the founders of colonies would have determined their placement, although these officials may not have been responsible for actually erecting the posts. Some apparently marked places in centuriated land, since they were placed on *limites* in Campania.[62] Others established the limits of the colony's territory. During either its original foundation in the second century or its refoundation with veterans in the first, the territory of Pisaurum was defined by the courses of rivers and streams, by *termini*, and by *pali sacrificiales*.[63]

Sacred places on the frontier of the *ager Romanus* were the scenes of recurring rituals: certain priests performed the sacrifice of the *Ambarvalia* at a "place called *Festoi*" and at several other places along the boundary; on some festival days Roman priests led processions from the city to the ancient frontier; on others they performed sacrifices first in the city and later at a border shrine.[64] Like the boundary sanctuaries of the *ager Romanus*, the altars and *pali sacrificiales* used to define the frontiers of a colony probably were also the sites of regular, recurring rituals through which the colonial priests and magistrates confirmed possession of their territory.[65]

The construction of the necessary places both inside the *urbs* and in the countryside—*forum, comitium, curia*, temples, altars, and other locations for rites—required more than merely noting their positions. Just as the major categories of *urbs, ager*, and citizenry took shape in the rites of the formal foundation, so also other sequences of ritual actions formed additional elements necessary to a civic order. Festus (p. 358L) claimed that Etruscan *libri rituales* contained not only instructions for the rites by which cities were founded and armies and citizen bodies formed, but also the rituals needed to sanctify walls and establish the *ius* of gates. Within the town and the surrounding *ager*, temples, altars, and shrines had to be inaugurated and dedicated, and the appropriate ritual forms and formulas, such as the framing of the words needed to define a *templum in terra* from a high place, had to be established.[66]

Just who sanctified the walls, inaugurated the *templa*, and dedicated shrines, altars, and boundary markers is unclear. The founding triumvirs themselves placed the colonial *pomerium* and they defined at least verbally major points along the boundaries of the territory. Within the town walls, moreover, they were clearly responsible for the overall layout of the settlement. The use of what was apparently a common body of rules to lay out the necessary public spaces and temples points to official action by Roman magistrates and their attendants, the ones on the scene most likely to have been familiar with the principles. When needed, moreover, the commissioners established the lines of the streets — with the same techniques they would use in defining the fields and other magistrates used in the camps — and they granted house sites to the settlers.[67]

Yet the colonial commissioners certainly did not perform all the tasks needed to turn the site into a town. The construction of public buildings and temples on their designated sites would have taken many decades — open altars and small shrines probably sufficed at first — and these operations certainly took place under the authority of local magistrates.[68] Colonial magistrates, pontiffs, and augurs, in office immediately following the formal foundation, certainly could have performed some of the necessary rites, if only at the direction of the triumvirs.[69]

In this matter, the writers preserved in the *Corpus Agrimensorum Romanorum* do not provide much help, for while some indicate that those responsible for the foundation of colonies regularly placed altars and identified sacred groves in the territory outside the *urbs*, they are vague about the position of those who performed the accompanying rites. Thus, Hyginus Gromaticus (pp. 199.5–10L) held that the founders were to place (*ponere*) altars marking territorial boundaries, while the leaders of neighboring peoples — outside the jurisdiction of the colony and of the colonial commissioners — were to consecrate (*consecrare*) altars facing them; that difference in verbs may indicate that the founders located the altars for the colonists but did not actually dedicate them or inaugurate the necessary *templa*. Elsewhere, Hyginus Gromaticus recommended that the founders note the location of sacred groves — another essential religious element of a city and the site of regularly recurring rites — but did not indicate who established the rules of cult governing them. Two surviving *leges lucorum*, governing groves in the territories of the colonies of Luceria (314) and Spoletium (241) and dating to the late third century, leave unidentified their authors.[70]

The magistrates of the colony, entering into office while the colonial commissioners were still present, probably immediately began to perform some of the functions of their office and especially the rituals that would define the civic life of their communities. Indeed, such a period when the authority of colonial commissioners and magistrates of the colony overlapped could have served as a training period. Colonial priests and officials, after all, probably would never had done such things before — they would not have occupied a suitable public position in Rome itself — and they may have needed some guidance and practice, while the colonists may have needed time to become accustomed to their new leaders.

III. TERRITORIAL SUBDIVISIONS INTENDED FOR PRIVATE USE

In addition to founding a city and its civic order, the triumvirs also turned lands to the use of individuals or they specifically removed sections from permanent private use. As part of the organization of spaces for the new city, the colonial commissioners set aside tracts of land to provide revenue for the city—local officials actually held the necessary auctions and gave the *leges dictae* according to principles similar to those that governed the same process at Rome.[71] They also reserved lands under the control of Roman officials and assemblies, for the decision to use them was made there and the magistrates handling the arrangements were dispatched from that city, and they established areas where the remaining native inhabitants of the region could continue to live and farm.[72] Like colonial commissioners, the ambassadors sent to Genua in 117 also had to identify which sections of a territory were private and public, and they announced their findings publicly by proclaiming the features that defined the boundaries and by arranging for the placement of *termini*. The triumvirs may have also defined verbally and in formal circumstances the lands set aside for certain ends and supervised the erection of the necessary markers.

The single most onerous and time-consuming of the founders' responsibilities would have been the division of substantial tracts of land into separate plots for assignment to individual colonists. By constructing the necessary network of *limites*, often over an extensive area, colonial commissioners and their attendants excluded the previous inhabitants from a portion of their old territory, eliminated all signs of their fields, and changed the lines of many or most of their roads and paths. When colonists took up their farms and prepared them for cultivation, they would have completed the final stage of domestication, for surveyors and farmers would have created a new landscape, retaining few signs of its previous use.

The founders of the colony decided which lands were to be divided based on a number of factors, most importantly the availability of cultivatable land and the location of the urban center of the community. Hyginus Gromaticus (pp. 180–81L) recommended that those in charge locate the starting point for the network not far from the town itself, and, if possible, in the *forum* of the colony, with the *decumanus maximus* and the *kardo maximus* leaving the town by each of the four gates; he called this the custom in camps, identified it as ideal, and claimed it to have the advantage of dividing the assigned land into four clear regions, each equally near the colonial *forum*. The *agrimensor* noted, however, that the land did not always allow the *limites* to be set out in an equal distance in all directions, for mountains or the sea could intervene. The ideal form certainly was not always attained, and surviving examples are relatively late. Hyginus Gromaticus's illustration was chosen from Africa, and the centuriation of Roman Carthage, either Gracchan or Caesarian, had its center in the Byrsa.[73] Hyginus Gromaticus also noted, however, that convenience often required another arrangement, with the founders placing the network where most of the land they intended to divide was located. Furthermore, he (pp. 178–79L) claimed that the "ancients," because of the fear of sudden attack, often located the city on a high place that was difficult of access and without cultivatable territory near the walls. In such cases, he (p. 194L) recommended that the founders establish their grid wherever sufficient land was available as near as possible to the habitations of the colonists. When there was insufficient land near the town, land could be assigned in several places and subsidiary settlements established in addition to the *urbs*.[74]

Founding magistrates and their assistants began the survey with ceremony, possibly in view of the colonists or their leaders, and the actions taken at that moment effectively determined the shape and location of the entire grid.[75] First, the *groma* was placed in the presence of a commissioner who had just taken the auspices. From that point, the defining roads were "sent out" according to the appropriate rules of orientation. If regular centuriation was used, the *decumanus maximus* was supposed to run from east to west and the *kardo maximus* from north to south, but in practice those conducting the survey placed the network so that it would encompass easily the necessary amount of cultivatable land while permitting the *decumanus* to be longer than the *kardo*. Just as a magistrate or priest defined the lines of a *templum* with words and gestures, so also the *conditor* may have defined the two lines that established his grid. In the act of first placing the *groma*, then, the magistrate and surveyors in accordance with the auspices effectively announced the beginning point of the network, the orientation of its axes, and, by implication at least, the approximate area to be measured and divided.

From that central point, teams using the *groma* and measuring rods began to lay out the pattern of roads that defined the grid. Systems tended to be rigidly rectangular, and if the most regular form of limitation was being used, square blocks of twenty *actus* a side were defined. Within each block, individual allotments were defined by paths (*limites*) or lines (*rigores*). Colonies with large individual allotments would have required many modules, but those units would have had few internal divisions. In those colonies in which the allotments were small, on the other hand, the overall number of modules may not have been great, but the number of internal *limites* or *rigores* would have been substantial.

All the modules were blocked out before the internal divisions were established. Hyginus Gromaticus (p. 199L), describing the practice under the Empire, held that the available land was first divided into *centuriae* in order to determine the total amount. Then, having compared the extent of this land to the number of potential recipients and to the amount each was to receive as a discharged soldier, those in charge were able to calculate the number of centuries that would have to be subdivided and the number that could be reserved until later. Finally, when they had determined how many allotments each *centuria* could hold, they marked off the boundaries within each module.

The triumvirs who founded the colony at Copia in 194 used a similar procedure, a strong indication of continuity in the basic techniques. According to Livy (35.9.7–9), the commissioners found that enough land was available to give each of the *equites* sixty *iugera* and each of the *pedites* thirty, but, because they wished to reserve some land for a possible later supplement, on the recommendation of L. Apustius Fullo, the senior triumvir, they gave only forty *iugera* each to the former and twenty to the latter. These magistrates, then, clearly knew the amount of land available— an indication that they had already determined the broad outlines of the grid—before deciding on the size of the allotments, a necessary precondition to the establishment of subdivisions within the modules. This feature may explain why *centuriae* of two hundred *iugera* were so common, for the use of a standardized module makes sense if the size of the plots later to be formed within it was unknown. As a point of contrast, note that Hyginus Gromaticus envisioned a situation in which the size of the allotments was fixed by the amount of the award due to a soldier on discharge, while the commissioners of 194 themselves determined the scale of the allotments by comparing the number of colonists with the land that had been centuriated.

In the foundation of colonies, the scale of the operation could vary considerably from case to case. In general, the founders of Latin colonies divided more land than those triumvirs who established citizen colonies, for the former were larger than the latter, and although their colonists received allotments that varied in size according to the class of the recipient, even colonists of the lowest class in Latin colonies generally received plots larger than any of those assigned to settlers in citizen colonies. At the Latin colony of Vibo (192), the colonists, 3,700 *pedites* and 300 *equites*, received, in plots of 15 *iugera* each for the *pedites* and 30 for the *equites*, a total of 64,000 *iugera* (ca. 160 square kilometers); at Copia (193), 3,000 *pedites* each received 30 *iugera*, and the 300 *equites* were given 60 each, for a total of 108,000 *iugera* (ca. 270 square kilometers); in Mutina, a citizen colony founded in 183, the 2,000 colonists divided equally 10,000 *iugera* or 25 square kilometers, while at Parma, another large citizen colony founded in the same year, the colonists divided 16,000 *iugera* (40 square kilometers).[76] The extremes can only be conjectured. If each of the colonists in a small citizen colony of 300 *coloni* received 5 *iugera*, a common allotment in such a settlement, the founders would have had to divide only 1,500 *iugera*, slightly more than 2 square kilometers; a large Latin colony of 6,000, such as Placentia and Cremona, or a colony with especially large allotments such as Aquileia would have required much more land.

Clearly, the number of modules founders would have had to establish varied considerably from project to project. Using centuries of 200 *iugera* and excluding from consideration land that might have been included in *centuriae* but which was unsuitable for cultivation, triumvirs and surveyors would have had to define a minimum of 50 *centuriae* for the 2,000 *coloni* of Mutina, of over 500 for the settlers at Copia, only two-thirds of which were subdivided and assigned, and of over 300 for the colonists at Vibo. A small colony of 300 with small allotments may have required no more than 8.

The preparation of land for division in such a fashion required the efforts of individuals occupying a range of statuses. In the late republic and under the Principate, when nonsenatorial experts in a variety of spheres can be found, a body of professional surveyors emerged to serve as intermediaries between the officials in ultimate authority and those who actually worked with the necessary instruments.[77] In the *Corpus Agrimensorum Romanorum*, the essential source on such matters, some authors set forth instructions for centuriating land and allotting plots to settlers, but left the position of those actually directing the operations obscure. Siculus Flaccus and Hyginus, for example, used the phrase "the originator of division and assignment" (*auctor divisionis et assignationis*) to describe the person who chose the lands to be surveyed and assigned, identified those to be reserved for another time, located shrines and other sacred places, and set the outer limits for the territory;[78] the experts worked under their broad directions.

Like Siculus Flaccus and Hyginus, Hyginus Gromaticus was generally vague about the status of those whose works he was describing and the position of the audience he was addressing. While providing directions for the proper orientation of the system and its spatial relationship to the town site, methods for determining the size of allotments and for assigning them to individuals, and recommendations for locating sacred sites such as altars and groves, he generally addressed his audience in the first person plural and referred to those who had established certain projects in the past, the creators of the examples that provided his general principles, in the third person plural. Above Hyginus Gromaticus's "we" and "they," however, was the figure of the *conditor*, a republican term for the founder of a colony, who assigned lands their proper legal status, initiated the centuriation itself, and authorized variations from the rules.[79] This founder certainly performed functions that were magisterial in mid-republican terms.[80] Hyginus Gromaticus, then, made a distinction between the *conditor* with ultimate authority and an intermediate group, who gave closer supervision to elements of the process.

The presence of intermediaries in the middle and late republic, however, is more problematic.[81] Nonius (pp. 11–12L) claimed that the *agrimensores* (a term that designated the later experts) earlier were known as *finitores* because they established boundaries or *fines*. Some authors of the republican period did use the term *finitor* to describe actors who performed many, if not most, of the functions of the imperial experts. Imperial *agrimensores* certainly defined a range of *fines* under a variety of circumstances: they placed the roads and paths that formed limitation networks, as well as boundaries between communities, between public land and private, and between the estates of private citizens. *Finitores* also performed at least some of these operations. Likening himself to a *finitor*, Plautus, in the preface to the *Poenulus* (49–50), announced that he would mark out *regiones, limites*, and *confinia* of the play, but he did not specify the nature of the boundaries whose construction he was parodying.[82] Cicero (*Agr.* 2.13.32, 2.13.34) used *finitor* to describe certain persons who could define the boundaries between public land and private under a proposed agrarian law in 63, although they may also have had other responsibilities. Although Plautus and Cicero, the earliest sources for the use of the term, did not explicitly link *finitores* to centuriation, such a connection is likely, given the similarity in functions between them and the later *agrimensores*.

Yet Nonius's equivalence between *finitor* and *agrimensor*, supported by their overlapping areas of activity, need not require that both titles in fact describe individuals with identical roles and positions. When performing their various functions, expert *mensores* deferred to those occupying certain traditional public roles.[83] *Conditores* made crucial decisions on centuriation, which the experts implemented. Surveyors marking the boundaries between private estates reported to a *iudex* appointed by a magistrate to hear the dispute, and that judge would rule on the matter, accepting or rejecting their report. In disputes between communities and over the location of boundaries between public and private lands, higher officials sent surveyors, who reported for confirmation their findings to the one who had sent them. Cicero's *finitores*, nonmagistrates who certainly possessed no technical skills, also made certain decisions on the scene but they also were dispatched by a magistrate and their decisions became valid only after being reported to and accepted by that official.[84] This clear subordination and lack of full independence should indicate that imperial *mensores* and late republican *finitores* extended the range of an official's activities by taking over, under his direction, certain magisterial responsibilities.

For most of the republican period matters were probably much simpler and magistrates much closer to the actual operations. In the middle republic, and to a certain extent in the late republic and early Empire, magistrates were responsible for marking boundaries between communities and between public land and private. In some cases, at least, elected officials also supervised centuriation. Livy, after all, described the triumvirs for Placentia in 218 as engaged in measuring the fields, and he characterized the triumvirs for Copia as deciding the size of the allotments after the land had been divided into modules but before those modules themselves were subdivided, an operation Hyginus Gromaticus described as being managed by an indefinite "we."[85]

Indeed, the term *finitor* may first have described a magisterial role occupied by a single individual only for a limited period of time. In form, the word merely denotes the individual who placed a boundary. This task need not have been the only public operation the person so designated performed nor need it have taken up much of his public career, as it did for the later *agrimensores*. The similar nouns *conditor* and *deductor*, for example, do not designate experts in the founding of colonies, but rather the magistrates (colonial triumvirs) given this responsibility for a few settlements to be established during their tenure in a single office. In fact, Plautus (*Poen. praef.* 49–50), whose use of the word *finitor* is the earliest attested, may have intended to describe the holder of a magistracy, not a professional surveyor, since he pictured the functionary performing a ceremony and placed that rite in the context of a range of other actions that were clearly the responsibilities of magistrates.[86] The supervision of the construction of a network of *limites* may not have required much technical skill. Those in charge operated according to a fairly rigid pattern with little room for variation, and the triumvirs themselves, landowners on some scale as were other members of their class, would have been able to identify lands suitable for cultivation.

The best guide is the analogous procedure by which camps were laid out for armies at the end of a day's march. As was the case with surveying fields, the procedures surrounding the camps also required the establishment of rectangular blocks and a regular network of roads by building out from the center according to a fixed plan, and that operation involved the use of the *groma* and the *decempeda*, instruments used to measure out straight lines and right angles and employed almost exclusively for public projects. In the imperial period, a *praefectus castrorum* of equestrian status supervised those who actually used those instruments, but in earlier times a military tribune directed the process and mid-republican tribunes were magistrates, not technicians, and some were themselves senators.[87] The twenty-four military tribunes assigned to the first four legions were elected by the *comitia tributa*—fourteen had to have served at least five campaigns and ten had to have served for ten, the minimum necessary to seek higher office—while those attached to the other legions were chosen by commanders. The official in charge of the construction of a camp, then, was an elected official in office for a short time, and thus he and the colonial commissioners occupied the same position with respect to those who assisted them.

According to Polybius (6.27–42), when the army was near the place of encampment, the commander deputed a military tribune and centurions, sending them ahead to the site.[88] After inspecting the area, they identified the camp's center, the place where the commander's tent was to be erected, choosing it to have the best view and be most suitable for issuing orders, and established the camp's orientation, assigning the legions the side most convenient for water and for foraging. At that central point, the surveyors placed the *groma*—Polybius apparently called the spot the *gramma* for that reason—and measured out first the *praetorium* and then the straight streets and rectangular blocks, all fixed in size and number, that defined the camp, marking the places where the various units would stay with flags and spears. For Polybius, the very rigidity of the plan was one of its chief advantages.

In his account, Polybius (6.41) claimed that certain specially chosen centurions assisted the tribune in the operation, but their role is obscure, for he did not claim that they possessed any technical skill or that they would be given any special training—he merely noted that they were selected to help choose the site. There is no reason to believe, therefore, that they were experts in the principles of castrametation or in the use of the *groma* and *pertica*.⁸⁹ The rank of centurion, moreover, was a temporary one, attached to a particular army and not necessarily carrying over into another army under a different general or into civilian life.⁹⁰ As a result, it would have been inappropriate for those possessing special technical expertise.

An examination of the actual foundation of the camp may clarify the matter. After noting that the tribune and centurions chose the site for the commander's tent and the orientation of the camp as a whole, Polybius then described the manner in which "they" measured out the central square, established the lines for roads, and marked the crucial locations with flags and spears. Polybius's use of the third person plural certainly should be seen as including others beyond the tribune and the centurions, for the number of the latter is likely to have been small — Polybius (6.24) noted that there were only sixty centurions in a legion and the great majority of them certainly remained with their troops. Some workers must have used the measuring rods, others probably actually placed, and carried, the flags and spears used as markers, while others again probably used the *groma*. Indeed, Polybius (6.41) claimed that the camp could be marked out quickly, and that would have required the simultaneous efforts of a substantial group, probably organized into several work parties, with each working out from the center, possibly under the supervision of a centurion.

In the case of the camps, then, the army commander had intermediaries of two ranks between himself and those who actually used the instruments and much of the operation would have taken place outside of his presence. Tribunes, however, would have been close to the entire process: the camp, after all, was not large — a singular consular army of two legions probably required a camp of approximately the same dimensions as a *centuria* of two hundred *iugera* — and all the centurions and workers must usually have been visible to the supervising tribune.⁹¹ Unlike army commanders, the triumvirs most probably lacked subordinates with the same ability as tribunes to operate at a distance. Indeed, the commissioners, although they may have chosen colonists to supervise groups in the manner of the centurions, probably oversaw the process of centuriation with a degree of attention similar to that exercised by tribunes in the camps.

Those who used the *groma*, then, were the only experts at centuriation present at the foundation of mid-republican colonies, and they probably were among the commissioners' *apparitores*, those attendants of much lower status who assisted magistrates in the performance of many of their tasks.⁹² A substantial number probably were available at most times. Each general commanding an army, after all, had experts with the *groma* accompanying him. Since the number of armies in existence in any given year varied, a reserve of surveyors would have been necessary. That, indeed, would have created a situation analogous to other magisterial *apparitores*, who served occasionally.

IV. THE ASSIGNMENT OF PLOTS

When completed, a colony contained private land in both city and countryside. After defining the town plan and centuriating a sufficient amount of land, the founders of colonies assigned house sites and fields to individual colonists through the process of sortition (*sortitio*), the casting of lots. While doing so, they dealt directly with the colonists en masse as well as with smaller groups of would-be neighbors. Sortition was an old practice in Rome, and the casting of lots in one form or another permeated Roman public life.[93] Its primary public use was to establish sequences or to assign specific benefits or tasks among equals, individuals as well as groups, and, as in other areas of concern to the larger community, magistrates supervised the procedure. Thus, consuls and praetors cast lots among themselves to determine the assignment of consular and praetorian provinces; consuls presiding over the *comitia centuriata* cast lots to determine the voting order of the centuries; tribunes presiding over the *concilium plebis* cast lots to determine the order of the tribes and also the one tribe in which the Latins present would vote; officials supervising the *dilectus* used the lot to determine which tribes would furnish soldiers and the order in which tribal contingents would be called; and the elder Ti. Gracchus, as censor in 169, picked by lot the urban tribe in which all freedmen were to be registered.[94]

Hyginus and Hyginus Gromaticus both described the sortitions that led to the assignment of fields. Hyginus Gromaticus's account (pp. 199–201L) is the more detailed. Using as an example a case in which those in charge had divided the land into modules of two hundred *iugera*, had decided to give each recipient sixty-six and two-thirds *iugera*, and accordingly had divided each *centuria* into three equal plots, he presented the first stage of sortition as aimed at dividing all the colonists into groups of three. Colonists could form such units voluntarily, but the names of those who failed to do so were entered on lots (*sortes*) which were placed in an urn. The first three names out of the vessel formed the first group, the second three the second, and so on until all the settlers had been assigned. Then the name of one member from each group was inscribed on a lot, which again was placed in the urn. Although Hyginus Gromaticus gives the impression that the groups of three received their allotments in the order in which they were formed, a sortition using the second group of *sortes* probably arranged the matter, for otherwise the second inscription of names on lots would be left without a clear purpose. Finally, the officials recorded the identifying coordinates of each century on a lot; the first one from the urn went to the first group, and so on. Hyginus Gromaticus did not specify the way in which individual plots within a century were given to each colonist in the group of three; perhaps another sortition was involved.

Hyginus Gromaticus, then, envisioned a procedure with at least three separate sortitions, one to form groups of colonists, the second to place those groups in a sequence, and the third to determine the order in which *centuriae* would be distributed. Hyginus (p. 113L) recommended a variant of that process, which he claimed to be both necessary and fair. First, all of those who were to receive allotments were to be divided into groups of ten (*decuriae*), probably by lot, and then blocks of *centuriae* sufficient to contain the plots of ten men were defined on the *forma*. When a sufficient number had been so defined, the location of each was then inscribed on a *sors* in the following form: "first lot, first, second, third, and fourth *dextra decumanum* and the same *citra cardinem*." Thus, by moving through successive sortitions, individuals would be matched with plots. Quite obviously, the accounts diverged, and in an interesting way. For Hyginus, from colony to colony groups of recipients remained constant at ten, while the size of the modules or of the collection of modules was adjusted to accommodate their plots. In Hyginus Gromaticus's scheme, the amount of land was set first (at one *centuria*) and the number of colonists was varied to match it;[95] in cases in which the plots did not fit evenly into a single century, a group of several centuries may have been formed.[96]

Both Hyginus and Hyginus Gromaticus envisaged a process where separate sortitions formed groups of colonists, determined the order of those groups, and set the sequence in which the modules would be distributed; the results of each of those stages would probably have been recorded on lists compiled by *scribae*. For small citizen colonies with only three hundred *coloni*, that task would have been easy, but in larger colonies, the procedure would have been onerous and time-consuming—perhaps for that reason, colonists were encouraged to form the primary groups voluntarily. In some colonies, at least, tribes, classes, and *vici* divided the citizenry;[97] the last clearly was a residential unit and the first may have been also, for that was the basis of the Roman tribes. Membership in tribe or *vicus*, then, would have been closely related to the location of the settlers' plots, and if these groups had been formed in advance, they may have served as intermediate elements in the process of sortition, allowing the officials to deal at any one time only with a fraction of the colonists. Like the assignment of fields, the granting of houses or of sites for houses was arranged through sortitions.[98] Since the *urbs* itself need not always have been the sole settlement site for colonists, separate sortitions may have been arranged for each location, giving each settler land near the place where he was to dwell.

Hyginus and Hyginus Gromaticus left unclear the role of the magistrates in that chain of sortitions, but they are likely to have supervised the process; certainly in colonies with only three hundred settlers intermediaries would not have been necessary. *Sortitiones* had clear religious associations—benefits distributed by lot can be seen as the results of divine favor—and they were connected to augural practice, which alone may have justified the presence of the magistrate, the chief actors in matters of the state religion.[99] In Rome and elsewhere, magistrates made their sortitions in *templa*, and, as in other acts in such places, the formalities were to be observed.[100] While on campaign against the Ligurians, Q. Petilius Spurinus and C. Valerius Laevinus, consuls in 176, having decided on two separate lines of march, cast lots to assign each consul his route;[101] Valerius was successful in his campaign, but Petilius was killed, although his army won the victory. Since there were rumors concerning Petilius's conduct, the senate ordered the augurs to investigate, and the priests, after consulting the consul's *pullarius*, the keeper of the sacred chickens essential to taking the auspices on campaign, found among other offenses that while Valerius had properly (*auspicato*) made the sortition because he had been in the camp's *templum*, Petilius had performed some crucial portion outside, creating a *vitium*.[102] Augural procedures, then, determined the proper form of sortition, and indeed, coins with augural symbols sometimes included a pitcher for casting lots along with the *lituus*.[103]

The casting of lots needed to assign fields to individuals, a public act conducted under the authority of magistrates, then, probably also took place in a *templum* constructed either in the *urbs* or outside, like the temporary enclosures in camps. Here, a space within the town is more likely—Hyginus Gromaticus (p. 204L) described the supervising officials as leading those who had received plots "into the fields" after the casting of lots—and the series of sortitions, especially for larger colonies, may have taken several days. Some elements, such as the inscription of names on lots and the voluntary construction of subgroups, would have required the presence of the colonists, and they may also have witnessed the successive drawings.

Citizens of the new colony, then, were matched to their plots in a procedure taking place in public (and probably in their presence), according to the proper rules, and possibly with considerable formality. But colonists still had to find their lands. When the sortitions had been completed, the officials led each colonist to his own portion, where they assigned him his *fines*, a transfer probably accompanied by some ceremony.[104] Such an operation, even in the smallest colonies, would have been too large to accomplish in one day, while leading the colonists out in one large mass. Instead, the officials probably took the colonists from the city in smaller groups, those units formed by the first sortition, the members of which were to be settled together in the same centuries. Here, the location of the centuries probably determined the order in which they were filled; Hyginus Gromaticus (p. 201L) held that the farthest centuries should be filled first, thus forming the outer *fines* of the centuriated land.

V. AFTER THE FOUNDATION

In the long process of foundation, the triumvirs created a new community with an urban core, a citizen body to inhabit it, priests and magistrates to lead the citizens, and an elaborate system of spaces to organize the proper functioning of civic and private life. This new city had an important role in the activities of the Roman state, for it was to provide local government loyal to the founding city, maintain good order in its territory, and raise its quota of soldiers to serve in Roman armies.[105] Colonists and their leaders had the primary responsibility for fulfilling these functions and for preserving the arrangements made by the founders, although circumstances peculiar to each settlement may have determined the degree to which the colonists were able to maintain them in or near their original form.

But there could be occasions when Roman officials again had to intervene. In some cases, colonial magistrates failed to perform their functions in a way that Roman officials found satisfactory. During the Second Punic War, ambassadors from twelve colonies reported to the consuls at Rome that they no longer could provide the soldiers required of them, and toward the end of the war, when Roman officials could devote time to less pressing matters, the consuls summoned ambassadors from these places to Rome where they informed them that from this time the settlements would have to provide even more soldiers and also pay a regular tax.[106] On other occasions, disputes between a colony and its neighbors required Roman mediation. According to Livy (45.13.10–11), when a dispute erupted in 168 between the citizen colony of Luna (177) and the allied city of Pisa, the senate sent five ambassadors to determine and establish the boundary between the two communities. Here, the people of Luna certainly claimed that the land under dispute had been given by the colonial commissioners to the community as a whole and not to individuals: the founding triumvirs, as we have seen, established individual settlers on their plots, but the colonial commissioners clearly had not placed any of the Lunenses on the contested land, for as the Lunenses themselves admitted the Pisani clearly were in possession until expelled by the colonists.

Most interventions by Roman officials reflected concerns over the number of colonists, either because the first contingent had proven inadequate or because the colonists had suffered extensive losses through war or desertion. Thus, in 206, when ambassadors from Placentia and Cremona complained that many of their colonists had scattered due to raids by the neighboring Gauls, the senate instructed a praetor to protect the towns with his army and requested the consuls to issue an edict instructing all colonists to return — the number of deserters who complied, if any, is unknown.[107] Twenty years later, the consul Sp. Postumius reported that he had found the colonies of Sipontum and Buxentum to be deserted and the senate ordered that the urban praetor T. Maenius supervise the election of triumvirs to enroll new colonists and lead them to the sites.[108]

The decision to send additional settlers to a place was taken according to the appropriate rules and in the proper places. In Livy's representations, the inhabitants of the settlement first sent ambassadors to Rome asking for reinforcements — they were probably chosen in their cities and instructed after the appropriate formalities; if the Roman senate then decided to dispatch them, it issued a decree instructing a consul or a praetor to supervise the election of triumvirs who were to arrange the matter.[109] Since an earlier plebiscite would have authorized the original foundation, it is uncertain whether a new one would now have been required. Those triumvirs did not vary noticeably in status from the commissioners that founded colonies: the college that led the supplement to Narnia in 199 contained two consulars, P. Aelius Paetus (cos. 201) and Cn. Cornelius Lentulus (cos. 201), and the triumvirate that installed new settlers at Sipontum and Buxentum (186) contained three praetorians.[110] Like other commissioners, moreover, those who led supplements probably recruited their settlers in the city and led them as a group to the colony.

There, additional land, if it had not already been centuriated by the original commissioners, would have been surveyed and marked according to the normal practices, and distributed to the colonists in the same way that the original triumvirs did. The task of such commissioners probably would have required some ritual acts involving all the colonists, old as well as new. Since no new definition of the *pomerium* would have been required, the complete ceremonies of the formal foundation of the *urbs* and its citizens would have been unnecessary, and, indeed, in the years between 200 and 167, when Livy recorded the foundation of virtually every colony, he recorded the completion of no refoundations, only the election of the commissioners. Yet some of those rituals may have been repeated: the community had new citizens, possibly organized in new tribes, and thus a new census and a new *lustrum* would have been needed.[111]

VI. CONCLUSION

The triumvirs led the colonists en masse to the site of the colony. In the months they spent on the scene, they inspected the territory of the community, identified the portions to be used for different ends, and made all necessary contacts with neighboring peoples. The process of installing a colony required the commissioners not only to divide lands and assign them to individuals but also make the necessary arrangements for the creation of a functioning civic order. Here, the rules and practices that governed the city of Rome, its environs, and its inhabitants served as a pattern for the organization of the *urbs*, the *ager*, and the citizens of the new community.

While founding a colony, the commissioners mustered under varying circumstances and for different purposes their attendants and the colonists. Some of those occasions had clear ritual identities of their own. In them, the founders led the colonists, as a mass, as individuals, or in various subgroups, through a series of elements mixing the religious and the secular in an atmosphere of ritual and formula; from those occasions, permeated by religion and ceremony, essential features of the new civic order took form and were confirmed. Thus, in the ritual of the *sulcus primigenius*, the triumvirs set the *pomerium* marking the core of the new *urbs* and, in the process, began the organization of spaces that were to shape its future civic life; in a related ceremony, the *lustrum* of the colonists, they established and defined the citizen body. By setting up boundary altars and other places for sacrifices — and by encouraging neighbors to do the same — the triumvirs delimited the territory of the settlement. Within those limits, the colonial commissioners divided the land into plots through a process that began in ceremony and in terminology resembled certain of the central rites of the Roman state. Under the supervision of those founders and again in a context with religious associations, the colonists were marshaled into groups of would-be neighbors and those neighbors were assigned to their own lands. Such occasions, then, gave order and structure to the entire process, and in them began those rituals, performed by the priests and magistrates of the new colony, which would define the public life of the place.

5

VIRITANE ASSIGNMENTS & AGRARIAN COMMISSIONS

In the foundation of a colony, senate and assembly announced the territory into which the colony was to be sent and its size, and the people chose three commissioners to recruit the colonists, lead them to the site, provide them with houses and fields, and grant them the necessary urban organization. Roman officials also distributed small plots to individuals (*viritim*), citizens as well as Latins, without creating a new city or *urbs* to act as an intermediary between the governing authorities at Rome and the settlers. Legislators framed laws authorizing viritane assignments according to the same broad principles that governed the construction of colonial legislation, although they included provisions that served to distinguish the two as separate categories. The implementation of these projects has left fewer traces in the literary sources, perhaps a result of the lowly status of the communities that resulted from them. The competent magistrates, however, probably led the settlers through ceremonialized occasions, some identical to those surrounding the founding of colonies while others differed in detail but served analogous ends. As was the case in the previous two chapters, the emphasis will be on the mid-republic.

I. THE LAWS

Like those who sought to found colonies, the framers of measures instructing that viritane assignments be made, whatever their personal motivations, used a form that was thought appropriate in only a limited range of circumstances. Judging by the places where grants were made, the designers of projects generally intended that settlers be sent into some region peripheral to the core of Roman territory at the time.[1] The resulting settlements, moreover, had only the most rudimentary governmental structure, and the settlers were not organized for self-defense — viritane assignments, therefore, generally were made near previously established colonies.[2] In the last third of the third century and the first third of the second, only three viritane assignments are recorded, while at least twenty-two colonies were founded in the same years.

Although informal discussion may have preceded public action, those advocating assignments acted according to the appropriate forms in both the construction of their proposals and in the process by which they sought approval by senate and people.[3] In an account given without context in the annalistic style, Livy (42.4.3–4) illustrates clearly certain aspects of the authorizing process and of the forms appropriate to the legislation. In 173, the senate decreed that land recently taken from the Ligurians and the Gauls be divided *viritim*, the urban praetor secured the election of a special commission of ten members to manage the project, and these *decemviri* assigned ten *iugera* each to citizens and three to Latins; Livy provided neither the name nor the rank of the official who first summoned the senate to discuss the matter. As was the case with the law or decree authorizing the foundation of a colony, the *senatus consultum* ordered that lands be given in a well-defined area and instructed a regular magistrate to secure the election of a college of special magistrates to arrange matters. Livy mentioned neither an authorizing plebiscite nor the number of settlers to be installed, but the latter omission probably is more significant than the former.

Livy's account of another project is less straightforward, since it is divided into three notices, spread over slightly more than a year, with no explicit references to any connections between them.[4] In the first, he reported that the senate had decreed at the end of 201 that the urban praetor arrange for the election of decemvirs to measure and divide public land in Apulia and Samnium, presumably taken in the recent war, among veterans who had fought "under the leadership and auspices" of Scipio Africanus in Africa and that the college was chosen. During the following year, again in an entry without context, Livy noted that the senate had decreed that veterans receive two *iugera* of land for each year of service in Spain or in Africa; *decemviri* were to arrange this. Finally, in a list of the assignments given to magistrates in 199, Livy stated that the senate extended the *imperium* of C. Sergius Plautus, urban praetor of the previous year, so that he could arrange for the distribution of land to veterans who had served for many years in Spain, Sicily, and Sardinia.

Those three notices, which overlap considerably in their provisions, probably record the initial passage of a program and two later modifications to the project.[5] The authorizing resolution instructed a regular magistrate to arrange the election of a special commission, which was to take settlers to a specific region, two adjacent territories, and assign them land. Unlike the assignment of 173, here the senate specified a narrow group from which the colonists were to be chosen. The nature of the adjustments, however, is unclear. The second decree may have included veterans from Spain for the first time, or it may have set the size of the allocations at two *iugera* for each year of service, or both. The third notice presents similar difficulties. The senate assigned to a promagistrate responsibility for managing distributions to veterans from Spain, Sicily, and Sardinia. The assignment of the responsibility to a former urban praetor — a new task for this functionary — rather than to the decemvirs may represent the final decree's innovation, for the Spanish veterans were covered by the earlier measures and the Sicilian soldiers may have been also, since Scipio mounted the invasion of Africa from there. The special commission may have had a term of only a year, since it was chosen at the end of 201, while the propraetor took over early in 199, almost exactly one year later.[6]

As tribune in 232, C. Flaminius framed the only measure explicitly stated to have been embodied in a plebiscite, but Livy's text for that period does not survive and the fragmentary evidence, scattered through works by a number of authors, is ambiguous on a number of points. The legislator regularly appears in many works in the guise of the typical demagogue and is given the attributes appropriate to such a figure. One act expected from a popular leader, especially to those writing after the reforms of the Gracchi, was the passage of an agrarian law against the will of the senate, and Flaminius reportedly carried such a measure in this fashion.[7] Despite the rhetorical and political coloration of many of the accounts, the descriptions of the actual provisions of the *lex Flaminia agraria* are consistent and reasonable. Polybius claimed that the law instructed that land taken from the Senones in the part of Gaul known as Picenum be divided among citizens, and his contemporary, Cato the Elder, described the land as the *ager*

Gallicus between the colony of Ariminum and Picenum; later authors identified the territory as either the *ager Gallicus* or both the *ager Gallicus* and Picenum.[8] The Romans had conquered those territories well before the passage of the law — Picenum fell in 286 and the *ager Gallicus* in 283 — and they sent several colonies to the region prior to 232: Sena Gallica (283), Ariminum (268), Firmum (264), and Aesis (247).

The measures of 201 and 173 each specified that ten commissioners be chosen to implement the projects. The extant accounts of the *lex Flaminia* do not identify the responsible magistrate or magistrates, but a college of agrarian commissioners, probably of the same size as the other two, was active at approximately the right time. Summarizing the funeral oration given in 221 by Q. Caecilius Metellus (cos. 206) in honor of his father, L. Caecilius Metellus, the Elder Pliny (*Nat.* 7.139) gave a list of the father's official posts: pontifex, consul twice (251 and 247), dictator (224), magister equitum (249), and *quindecemvir agris dandis*. Colleges of fifteen, later found in the priesthood of the *quindecemviri sacris faciundis*, are otherwise unattested for special commissions charged with secular tasks, including agrarian commissions. The manuscripts, however, have *XVvir*, and a simple scribal error, the duplication of the "v," would have changed *Xvir*, a common post in viritane distributions, to Pliny's *XVvir*.[9] Pliny identified neither the project on which Metellus worked nor the year in which he held the office, but the *lex Flaminia* instituted the only known viritane assignment in the years covered by the recorded offices; Metellus, then, may have served as a commissioner on the college authorized by that plebiscite.[10]

The three viritane assignments instituted between 232 and 173, then, shared a number of similarities with each other and with contemporary colonial legislation. The initiating decree or plebiscite instructed that land be divided and assigned in a specific *ager* or in adjacent *agri* and it ordered a regular magistrate to secure the election of a special commission, ten for viritane assignments and three for colonies, to arrange the matter. Unlike colonial legislation, however, the authorizing measures in viritane assignments apparently did not indicate the number of *coloni* to be settled, although they sometimes specified a narrow group from which the settlers were to be chosen and the amount of land each was to receive.

Some of those features may have been present in earlier assignments. Having defeated as consul in 290 the Samnites, Sabines, and Praetutti, M'. Curius Dentatus reportedly arranged the division of some land to Roman citizens with the amount each settler was to receive set in the authorizing measure.[11] Almost half a century earlier, other distributions were made on land taken from the people of Privernum, captured in 341, and from the Latins and Campanians defeated in 340. Each Roman citizen receiving land was given two *iugera* in Latium or three in the *ager Falernus*.[12] In the accounts of these early projects, the identity of the responsible officials is generally left unstated.[13] Regular magistrates or promagistrates, possibly the victorious generals who conquered the regions, may have arranged some of the settlements.[14] The Romans, then, may have developed specialized commissions for viritane assignments well after they had determined the form of college typical of colonization.

II. THE COMMISSIONERS

The authorizing resolutions of 201 and 173, like the laws instituting colonies, instructed a regular magistrate — in both cases the urban praetor — to hold the necessary electoral *comitia*. The presiding magistrate would have followed in those meetings the same procedures used in the assemblies that elected colonial commissioners and would have had the same ability to shape the results.[15]

Like colonial triumvirates, decemvirates included important members of the governing elite. According to Livy (31.4.3), the college elected late in 201 contained P. Servilius (he gave no *cognomen*), Q. Caecilius Metellus, C. Servilius Geminus, M. Servilius Geminus, L. Hostilius Cato, A. Hostilius Cato, P. Villius Tappulus, M. Fulvius Flaccus, P. Aelius Paetus, and T. Quinctius Flamininus. Of those, three were consulars: Q. Caecilius Metellus (cos. 206), C. Servilius Geminus (cos. 203), and his brother M. Servilius Geminus (cos. 202).[16] Three other commissioners certainly were praetorians: Aulus Hostilius Cato (pr. 207), P. Villius Tappulus (pr. 203), and P. Aelius Paetus (pr. 203). The remaining decemvirs were more junior at the time of their election to the college. The only M. Fulvius Flaccus known to have been active at the time served as tribune in 199, and T. Quinctius Flamininus, the famous consul of 198, reportedly was chosen consul after serving as quaestor.[17] P. Servilius is otherwise unknown, a clear indication that he never reached the offices of consul or praetor.[18] The only known L. Hostilius Cato served as legate in 190 on a mission with A. Hostilius Cato, also a *decemvir* on this college.[19]

That decemvirate contained three consulars, three praetorians, and four who had not yet attained either office. The next college, elected in 173, had fewer high-ranking members, but again consulars and praetorians were prominent. According to Livy (42.4.4), the commission contained M. Aemilius Lepidus, C. Cassius, T. Aebutius Parrus, C. Tremellius, P. Cornelius Cethegus, Q. Apuleius, L. Apuleius, M. Caecilius, C. Salonius, and

C. Munatius. One was a former consul and another may have been.[20] M. Aemilius Lepidus served as consul in 187 and 175 and the censor in 179. Two individuals with the name P. Cornelius Cethegus are known to have held office around the time: one had served as praetor in 185 and the other in 184 and one of the two had reached the office of consul in 181.[21] Two others were praetorians. T. Aebutius Parrus held the office in 178. The only known office-holding C. Cassius is the C. Cassius Longinus who was consul in 171, and he probably served as praetor, since he was chosen consul after the passage of the *lex Villia annalis*—two vacancies are available, both before his service on the commission.[22] Less is known of the remaining six: C. Tremellius probably reached the office of praetor, but only after he had served on the commission, L. Apuleius may have been the L. Appuleius Saturninus who served as praetor in 166, and the only C. Salonius known to have held official position in the second century served as a colonial commissioner for Tempsa in 194.[23] Q. Apuleius, M. Caecilius, and C. Munatius are otherwise unknown.[24]

The findings, then, reinforce the broad conclusions reached earlier on the membership of colonial triumvirates. On both of the decemvirates, approximately half had served as consuls or as praetors before being elected to their commission—about the same overall percentage as found in colonial commissions and indeed in the senate itself. The commission that implemented the *lex Flaminia* of 232 may have fit the pattern: its only known member had served as consul twice before his election.

III. THE INSTALLATION OF SETTLERS

Since little direct evidence survives, the process of implementation is much more obscure than was the case for colonization. Yet some conclusions can be drawn, and they are consistent with the broad pattern found in colonization—the competent magistrates mustering the *coloni* on different occasions, some permeated by religion and ceremony, and in various groups, large and small, to achieve definite ends essential to the overall project.

Some tasks facing the decemvirs were close or even identical to those performed by colonial triumvirs. Both recruited settlers (although prospective recipients might have had to meet differing requirements), surveyed lands, constructed plots for individual assignment, and matched settlers with their fields. Decemvirs and triumvirs probably performed those operations in very similar ways—they certainly would have served as well for viritane assignments as they did for colonization. In recruitment, then, the commissioners would have made a public announcement instructing those interested in receiving allotments and eligible under the terms of the law to gather at a designated time and place for selection; after that had been completed, the supervising officials proclaimed where and when the *coloni* were to assemble. In the assignments made to veterans after the Second Punic War, the officials' task may have been slightly less onerous, for the intended recipients may already have been mustered in their camps. No certain indication of the scale of projects survives, and the authorizing law may not have set a definite number. Here, the settlement of the veterans provides the only indication, for perhaps as many as thirty to forty thousand men may have been eligible, although all or most need not have actually received, or wished to receive, allotments.[25] Indeed, viritane assignments may not have been significantly larger in scale than a substantial colonization project: enlistment probably was voluntary and the pool of eligible volunteers was not bottomless; even some colonial commissioners could not recruit their full complement of settlers.[26]

Colonial commissioners departed for the site as a group together with the colonists, and the same probably was true for decemvirs charged with making viritane assignments. Certainly members of the larger colleges did not work individually or in smaller groups at widely scattered locations, since assignments were made in a single *ager* or in adjacent *agri*. Within this region, however, the larger number of commissioners may have made possible the simultaneous performance of a number of operations and enabled them to install settlers in a shorter time.[27]

On the scene, the decemvirs would have surveyed and divided land in much the same way as did the founders of colonies. Traces of the typical Roman forms of land division have been found in areas of viritane assignments. Signs of centuriation may indicate that the decemvirs of 173 assigned land along the *via Aemilia* between Ariminum, Bononia (189), and Parma (183).[28] Early in the third century, M'. Curius Dentatus may have made distributions in the vicinity of the Veline Lake near Reate, which he reportedly drained as consul, since there are traces of seemingly early limitation in this area.[29] Finally, remains of apparently early networks of *limites* have been found in the territory of Privernum and in the *ager Falernus*, reportedly the scene of viritane assignments in the late fourth century.[30] When sufficient land had been divided, the commissioners would have begun the process of assigning plots to individuals, and here they would also have used the device of sortition.[31] That process required the mustering of all the settlers who were to receive plots in a specific area, their formation into subgroups by the casting of lots, the matching of those subgroups to individual *centuriae* by the same procedure, and the leading of the *coloni* from the place where the sortitions were performed into the fields where those in charge assigned them their boundaries.

Colonial commissioners installed their *coloni* around nucleated settlements, which became new cities with well-defined civic organizations. Like those triumvirs, magistrates making viritane assignments also established new communities and gave them the proper forms of organization; the settlers required some form of government, even if only minimal, and some means of integration into the larger apparatus of the Roman state. In the hierarchy of settlements that Roman jurists and legislators began to devise in the middle of the fourth century and elaborated over the following generations, specialists in law identified a sequence of communities— *coloniae, municipia, praefecturae, fora, conciliabula, vici,* and *pagi*—and distinguished them by the number and form of their priesthoods and magistracies, the range of actions these functionaries were permitted to perform, the rights of their citizens and officials, and the nature of their relationship with the central power.

Although the creation of colonies was firmly linked to a specific magistracy, a limited range of circumstances, and a restricted group of beneficiaries, decemvirs used communal forms that were not so restricted in origin and in purpose, for they could be established by officials arranging a variety of projects and they could also be used to organize groups recently incorporated into the apparatus of the Roman state.[32] Agrarian commissioners are not known to have founded *vici* and *pagi*, villages or country districts. But in the *lex Mamilia Roscia Peducaea Alliena Fabia*, the first-century agrarian law preserved in the *Corpus Agrimensorum Romanorum* and sometimes identified as the *lex Iulia agraria*, the framers referred to colonies founded and *municipia, praefecturae, fora,* and *conciliabula* constituted under the provisions of the law.[33] Mid-republican magistrates did not create such a wide range of communities and the Romans of the time gave the status of a *municipium* only to existing communities and did not create *municipia ex nihilo* with new settlers brought to a site.[34] Although the first century saw considerable standardization and regularization in the forms of local government, the *praefectura*, the *forum*, and the *conciliabulum* clearly were viable forms in the third and second centuries and probably also in the late fourth.[35] On the evidence of that first-century law, then, *praefecturae, fora,* and *conciliabula* all are possible forms of organization resulting from earlier viritane assignments.

The defining features jurists assigned to those communities are obscure, largely due to the very limited quantity of evidence available. Specialists may not have used the term *praefectura* to designate a certain type of community with distinctive features of internal organization, for some of the places so characterized are known to have been *municipia* and at least one may have been a *forum*.[36] Festus (p. 262L) defined a *praefectura* as a place where markets were held and officials exercised jurisdiction, noting that *praefecti*—presumably the *praefecti iure dicundo* sent by the urban praetor to administer certain forms of justice away from Rome—were sent there regularly for the purpose. Communities, then, did not become *praefecturae* because they were granted peculiar forms of internal organization, but because they were used by officials of the central power as places to exercise jurisdiction when they happened to be in the area. Experts in law, on the other hand, clearly assigned the terms *forum* and *conciliabulum* to particular forms of settlements, ones that were especially pervasive and important. Livy (40.19.3), indeed, on one occasion used the phrase "in the fields and *fora* and *conciliabula* and in the city" seemingly to refer to all Roman territory distinct from those of citizen colonies and municipalities.

When decemvirs installed settlers in a region, then, they also created new communities to govern them. Two aspects of those places are important for our purposes: the scale of settlement and the nature of their civic life. Occupying a position in the hierarchy of settlements below colonies and *municipia*, *fora* and *conciliabula* can be viewed as rural centers, and as such they would have essentially been villages that served as centers for other villages in the neighborhood organized as *vici* or *pagi*. But the range of statuses from *coloniae* down through *fora* and *conciliabula* to *vici* certainly did not involve distinctions in scale. Colonies ranged from large Latin colonies containing six thousand *coloni* to citizen colonies of three hundred, and a significant portion of settlers in the former, and probably all in the latter, lived in a single center. *Fora* or *conciliabula*, or even *vici*, as settlements, certainly would not have been smaller than those settlements, and *fora* and *conciliabula*, therefore, probably covered much of the same range in size as did the urban core of colonies.

The decemvirs, then, probably established only a limited number of nucleated settlements, some of which may have been previously inhabited by noncitizens who would have been displaced; such a practice would have been both much safer for the *coloni* and much easier for the commissioners to arrange than a more dispersed settlement pattern.[37] Thus, if the commissioners chosen in 201 to distribute land to veterans did in fact settle as many as thirty thousand, they could have done so by creating the equivalent of no more than ten small Latin colonies and no more than a few subsidiary settlements. Within such an agglomeration, the decemvirs clearly could have created, defined, and assigned house sites in the inhabited areas by the same procedures colonial commissioners used.

But to create such places, the decemvirs would have had to do more than define streets and places where houses were to be built, for those communities required their own communal organizations and the temples and spaces necessary for them to operate. As an essential part of making a viritane grant, then, officials would have had to establish in the appropriate way the civic forms necessary to the type of settlement they were creating. Unfortunately, the nature of the governments of *fora* and *conciliabula* is very obscure. Here, the *conciliabulum* is slightly less problematic: Festus (p. 33L) defined it as a place where people were gathered in an assembly (*concilium*), and assemblies required magistrates to summon and direct them. Even less is known of the *forum*, but it clearly must have possessed a simple assembly and officials of its own;[38] just as *conciliabulum* signified a place where *concilia* were held, so might *forum* indicate a place for lawcourts and assemblies. Those communities, moreover, served certain roles necessary to Roman government itself. Livy, for example, recorded a number of occasions scattered throughout the late third and second centuries when Roman magistrates held levies in *fora* and *conciliabula* and personally made certain inquiries there, along with others when they ordered their edicts to be read aloud and posted through all *fora* and *conciliabula*, a clear indication that the settlements possessed someone with the authority to summon and address the inhabitants and the necessary procedures and places for them to do so.[39]

When creating a *forum* or a *conciliabulum*, then, the decemvirs also established magistracies, assemblies with definite, although limited, powers, and cults, even if only centered on simple altars and shrines.[40] In colonies, the founders created the new civic order through an intense sequence of rituals and ceremonies involving the entire populace. The founders of *fora* and *conciliabula* probably also ceremonially established their communities, although in ways that differed formally from the procedures used in colonization.

The framers of the *lex Mamilia Roscia Peducaea Alliena Fabia*, experts who were careful with their words, made a clear distinction among the settlements established by officials acting under the terms of their law, separating colonies that they identified as "deducted" from other communities, including *fora* and *conciliabula*, which were "constituted."[41] This terminological distinction preserves an important difference in practice. Founders of colonies formed their settlements by establishing the *pomerium*. Those who established other settlements, on the other hand, did not create such a

112 • VIRITANE ASSIGNMENTS

boundary, essential to defining the powers of the officials of an *urbs*. The lesser communities were not formally organized to wage war and thus did not require the complementary spheres, *domi* and *militiae*, which physically separated the exercise of military functions from other public activities.[42] Other ceremonies of foundation, however, were less specifically connected to *urbes*: the *lustrum* of the settlers, which gave them their new civic status, the granting of the *lex data*, and the appointment of the first magistrates and priests.

As a technical term, the word *constituere*, used to describe the establishment of lesser-ranking communities, can also denote the process of establishing, creating, or ordering a range of groups, places, or practices, and it often refers to arrangements made with some ceremony and requiring the granting of a governing *lex* by a magistrate: thus, earthly *templa* were constituted through the performance of the rites associated with the *liberatio* and *effatio*; *templa* serving as visual fields were constituted through the formal identification of their limits; the Roman people themselves were constituted, in the form of the *exercitus quinquennalis*, through censors' performance of the *lustrum*; and even altars and other places for sacrifice can be said to have been constituted.[43] Those who made viritane assignments, then, probably created formally the new community and its attributes in a ceremony in which they gave the law and appointed officials in front of all of those who were to have the place for their center. Within and around the town, they would have created or ordered the creation of the necessary temples, altars, and sacred groves through the appropriate series of ritual acts.

IV. CONCLUSION

Viritane assignments, like colonies, began in formal decrees of the senate and votes of the people instructing that land in a certain district or in adjacent districts be divided and requesting that a regular magistrate secure the election of a special commission to arrange the matter. Despite that similarity, laws authorizing colonies and those beginning viritane assignments clearly formed separate legal categories, for they were never combined in a single project during the middle republic, the special commissions they established came in fixed sizes that differed for both, and the communities that resulted from each differed notably in legal status and in complexity. The commissioners certainly used the same procedures as colonial commissioners to perform some of their functions, and they probably also arranged the other major aspects in the same, or in similar, ways. Thus, like their counterparts who established colonies, the decemvirs continually mustered the settlers in various groups and led them through ritualized occasions, and from certain of these ceremonies lands were divided and assigned and the lines of government emerged.

6

THE SALE & LEASE OF PUBLIC LANDS

In the founding of colonies and the making of viritane assignments, Roman magistrates specially chosen for the task, acting on orders of senate and people, created new communities with their own institutions, established boundaries defining the territories of the settlements, and divided tracts within these lands into plots, which they then assigned to individuals. But the Roman state did not limit its formal exploitation of public land to colonies and viritane assignments. Senate, magistrates, and popular assemblies also used such land to raise revenue for public purposes.

The procedures involved in selling and leasing lands and the circumstances in which those acts were performed are the focus of this chapter. Here, as in other public projects, the responsible officials dealt directly with those who were to be the subjects of their action, but the sale and lease of public land did not create a new, and permanent, civic or religious order ruling the lives of hundreds or thousands of Roman citizens and Latins and regulating their relations with the gods. For that reason, perhaps, less dramatic ceremonies characterized the process. The practices and the basic categories of land that emerged from a completed sale or lease may have been fairly old, though the best evidence concerns the late third, second, and first centuries. In this chapter, as in earlier ones, then, the emphasis will be on the middle republic.

I. PUBLIC LANDS AS A SOURCE OF REVENUE

As was the case with the founding of colonies and the making of viritane assignments, the use of land for fiscal purposes began in the public spaces of Rome with formal decrees of the senate and laws passed by the people.[1] Like those who proposed other measures regulating public lands, the framers of laws or decrees authorizing the sale or lease of public property identified the magistrate or the magistracy responsible for managing the task, instructed him to make the necessary arrangements, indicated at least generally the area affected, and ordained the place where the sale was to take place.[2] Here, as with other forms of legislation dealing with public land, mid-republican measures instructing an official to sell or lease land did not also authorize other modes of exploitation.[3]

Those who proposed and framed measures authorizing the use of a particular segment of land to raise revenue generally intended that the funds be used to meet specific and immediate needs or to support a single and limited public institution, such as a temple, a festival, or a priesthood;[4] the money was not used to increase the general revenues of the state. Thus, officials used certain lands during the Second Punic War to provide money for the war, and afterward they assigned fields to state creditors in place of payment;[5] the augurs received the fruits of the land from plots in the *ager Veiens* and the Vestal Virgins received revenue from property bounded according to rules peculiar to the cult of Vesta;[6] the censors in 174 sold certain public places to build shops around the *fora* of Calatia and Auximum, and, over a century later, the tribune P. Servilius Rullus proposed that to sell land in order to buy other tracts for his proposed distributions.[7] Certain subordinate communities governed by Roman laws and practices acted in a similar manner. In the first century, the framers of the *lex* governing the precinct of Jupiter Liber at Furfo assigned to the aediles of the *vicus* the authority to sell or lease certain lands to raise money for the temple.[8]

Because magistrates and senate sought to use public lands in these ways, exploitation for fiscal purposes was neither systematic nor thorough, and the geographic range was limited. In the late third and early second centuries, most public land was in Italy. Those tracts used to support specifically Roman institutions and programs generally were located relatively close to Rome itself, in Latium, southern Etruria, northern and central Campania, and in western Sabinum, the areas the most secure and the most convenient to Rome. Thus, the quaestors of 205 were to sell lands taken from Capua, the consuls of 200 were to compensate public creditors with lands within fifty Roman miles of Rome, the censors in 199 sold lands "under Mount Tifata," and in 172 censors were instructed to lease the *ager Campanus*.[9] Away from this inner core, the most prominent fiscal use of cultivatable public land in peninsular Italy probably was for the support of colonies and occasionally *municipia*.

Most public land not being used for colonies and viritane assignments probably escaped an officially determined use. Even land near Rome was still available in some quantity centuries after the territory became Roman. In 210, for example, the senate believed that enough land could be found in the former *agri* of Veii, Sutrium, and Nepete — regions that had come under Roman control early in the fourth century — to provide those Campanians who were to be removed from their homes with up to fifty *iugera* each; ten years later the senate and the consuls apparently expected no difficulty in obtaining land for creditors within fifty miles of Rome.[10] Livy (42.19.1–2) reported that in 172 the *ager Campanus*, the richest land taken in the Second Punic War and convenient to Rome, had not been leased for many years after the war. Areas of lesser value probably were not thoroughly exploited if the *ager Campanus* was not.

II. THE AUCTION

The process through which public land was sold or leased fell into two broad stages, which could be separated considerably in time and in space. In one, a magistrate arranged the transaction, while in the other, necessarily prior in time to the first, an official on the scene defined physically the land in question. Once bounded, however, lands probably could be transferred again after the first agreement had expired without much further expenditure of effort, although Roman officials may not always have found it easy to recover the land.[11] Those two essential elements were conceptually distinct, for different magistrates, sometimes with separate authorization, could manage each.[12]

Magistrates charged with arranging the sale or lease did so in a public auction conducted in a public space. This event set the context in which the official made contact with those interested in buying or leasing the lands. Although consuls, proconsuls, and praetors did oversee such auctions, the task most often went to censors and quaestors, who gave their names to categories of lands, *ager censorius* and *ager quaestorius*, with their own characteristics.¹³

Auctions often took place at well-defined locations, and the supervising magistrate may not often have had much freedom of choice in the matter. Sales and the placing of leases for public lands generally took place in Rome itself, and Cicero claimed that the usual place was the *rostra*, an inaugurated *templum* in the *forum* near the *curia* and the *comitium*.¹⁴ Exceptions were possible. The proconsul Q. Fulvius Flaccus leased public land in Campania at Capua in 210, presumably in auctions held in that city, and the *rogatio Servilia agraria* of 63 gave permission for its decemvirs to sell or lease public lands wherever they wished.¹⁵ When the site of the auction was far from the lands to be sold or leased, prospective bidders probably would not have been able to inspect the land on which they intended to bid.

Like gatherings of much greater formality and significance — legislative and electoral assemblies, the *lustrum* of citizens or colonists, and the dedication of temples — contacts between bidders and those supervising the auction of public property had their own proper procedures. As a first step, the presiding official would have issued an edict giving the time and the place, a necessary preliminary for any gathering, and probably also information about the transaction, which may also have been prominently posted. The procedures for announcing the sale may have had a formal aspect — at least, they could be incorporated easily as an element of a larger ceremony. As part of the *ludi Capitolini*, given to Jupiter Feretrius, an old man was led through the *forum* wearing a *toga praetexta* and a golden *bulla* — the first, the costume of certain magistrates and of boys too young to wear the *toga virilis* and the second, a sign shared by *triumphatores* and young boys — while the *praeco* announced "Sardi venales."¹⁶

The *praeco*, one of the magistrate's *apparitores*, managed the auction, although the responsible official potentially could exercise great control over the gathering, which ideally took place in his presence.¹⁷ Thus, the Elder Cato, serving as censor in 184, ordered some publicans to be driven away from the auction at which he intended to place contracts for the collection of certain revenues.¹⁸ Sulla used the power of his presence to force bidders to raise their prices.¹⁹ Augustus too intervened in an auction: he had ordered the sale of a man convicted of a crime and his goods, but when he saw that certain *publicani* were about to purchase the man, he arranged for one of his freedmen to do so instead.²⁰

Like other public occasions in which magistrates dealt with numbers of citizens, the setting of the auction emphasized the magistrate's power, and the proceedings themselves possessed their own formalities of word and deed. The presiding official appeared with the ceremonial attributes appropriate to his rank: *toga praetexta*, either curule chair or *subsellium*, and, for higher officials, lictors. Sales were marked by the placing of a spear (*hasta*), a symbol of the authority of the state, and for this reason they could be characterized as taking place *sub hasta*;[21] Plutarch (*Publ.* 19.6) reported that in his day they were proceeded by the formal announcement of the sale of the goods left behind by Porsenna when he evacuated the city in the first years of the Roman republic. The placing of leases and other public contracts possessed their own formalities: Festus (p. 108L) held that censors auctioning the contracts for the collection of public revenues first put forward the *vectigal* from the *lacus Lucrinus*, since the name was considered to be of good omen. At the end of the auction, the *praeco* proclaimed the identity of the successful bidder, whose name was entered in the public records by a *scriba*, probably along with some indication of the location of the land in question and the amount due.[22]

The presiding official set forth the terms of the sale or lease in a *lex dicta*, either a *lex venditionis* or a *lex locationis*. These laws, probably composed after consultation with experts and advisors, shared many of the features of formal writing characteristic of other classes of *leges*. The *praeco* conducting the auction would have read aloud the formulaic language of the *lex* to the assembled bidders before the auction began in the same way that other *leges* were formally pronounced to those affected by them.[23] By bidding, individuals indicated their acceptance of the terms.

Experts gave to public leases and sales their own body of law, which evolved over time according to its own rules and logic. Despite the seeming simplicity of the terminology, the nature of the distinctions between the transactions is obscure. The vocabulary forms two groups, indicating distinct categories of agreement. In one, regularly associated with the quaestors and with *ager quaestorius*, a form of *vendere* (usually translated as "to sell") signifies the action. In the other, often associated with the censors, some form of *locare* or more specifically *locare fruendum* is taken to indicate a lease. But the defining features of these sales and leases, apparently conforming to the classical consensual contracts of *emptio venditio* and *locatio conductio*, have proven difficult to separate; the jurist Gaius (3.145) noted that it was often difficult to distinguish between them.[24] Certainly, neither sale nor lease changed the ultimate ownership of the land. Public land sold at auction remained in law the property of the Roman people, and in at least one case officials used again at a later date land sold by quaestors.[25] In leases, moreover, the status of the land itself was not affected; Festus (p. 516L) defined *censoria locatio* of public land as the sale of the fruits of the place, and the Elder Cato (*Agr.* 114) regarded the leasing of private estates in the same way.

The framers of the authorizing legislation and of the governing *leges dictae* would have constructed the necessary collection of forms needed for a particular situation by choosing among various elements, perhaps with only a narrow range of options, such as the term over which the agreement was to be valid, the form of the payments, and the way those payments were to be structured. In a passage full of anachronisms, Dionysius of Halicarnassus (*Ant. Rom.* 8.73) presented a speaker as advocating that some public land be sold and that the rest be leased for five years. Gaius (3.145), on the other hand, reported that some municipal land was leased in contracts that were valid as long as the rent was paid. Some sales may also have been valid only for a fixed term. The framers of the colonial law of Urso forbade the magistrates of the settlement to sell or lease public property for more than five years, while Hyginus made a fixed term characteristic of all *agri vectigales*, which he defined as centuriated captured land not assigned to soldiers.[26]

Payments made as a result of sale or lease were most often due in monetary form, although on occasion rents in kind were imposed.[27] The way payments were arranged might form a more basic distinction between sales and leases. A magistrate selling public lands probably sought a substantial payment, or purchase price, at the beginning of the transaction, the amount to be determined by the bidding, and a rent, perhaps only token, to be paid at regular intervals afterward.[28] Those officials placing leases, on the other hand, probably intended that the state receive regular payments of some size with no substantial initial payment.

The collection of regular payments at fixed intervals need not have placed great burdens on the machinery of the state. When properly authorized, Roman officials regularly placed in a public auction contracts with *publicani* to collect such payments.[29] Disputes between publicans and those holding the land would have been resolved through private law remedies.[30] Only those who sought to gather the revenue from large tracts probably would have been of a relatively high social standing, but to be able to gather the money at all the successful bidder would have had to be more prominent or to have higher-ranking friends than the lessee or purchaser.

III. THE ESTABLISHMENT OF BOUNDARIES

The major element of the process remaining was the more difficult. As was also the case with other *leges datae* or *dictae* that sought to establish a particular use for a space, the terms of a sale or a lease ran over an area that ought to have been clearly defined. Indeed, to some degree the necessary boundary markers and *limites* gave the land its status: Siculus Flaccus (pp. 152–54L) held that they kept land sold by the quaestors from reverting in fact, if not in law, to the condition of *ager occupatorius*—land, that is, that could be used by anyone—eliminating any special privileges the purchaser may have had.[31] Boundaries, obviously, were a necessary prerequisite to a sale or lease. In some cases, an official may have established those limits some time in the past for an earlier transaction. If they had survived, no further action may have been needed to lease or sell the area again. In other instances, however, a law or senatorial decree, often different from the one authorizing the auction, gave the responsibility for the physical definition or *terminatio* of the space to a magistrate or the future holders of a specific magistracy.[32]

In the middle republic, a well-defined group of magistracies possessed the power to define the limits of segments of public land. When the land had to be separated from the private property of Roman citizens, a situation especially likely in regions closer to Rome, the power belonged to censors, consuls, and praetors;[33] Livy (4.8.2) called this the *ius publicorum privatorum locorum*. The effort expended and the range of processes involved in the preparation of a tract for sale or lease would have varied widely. Here, the size of the territory, the ways the lands in question had come to be public, the complexity of land tenure in the region, and the number, if any, of subdivisions to be constructed within the outer limits would have been essential factors.

Magistrates performing a *terminatio* did so on the scene, entering the territory with their advisors and attendants and bearing the ceremonial accoutrements appropriate to their position. At the most basic level, the official charged with determining the borders between public land and private would have had to place visible markers at crucial locations on the periphery of these public lands.[34] Thus, Dionysius of Halicarnassus (*Ant. Rom.* 8.73) had a speaker recommend that a special college of magistrates determine which lands were public and identify segments for sale or lease by placing inscribed boundary stones, while Livy (42.1.6) reported that the senate instructed one of the consuls of 173 to go to Campania and mark the boundaries between public and private land there. That act of placing individual *termini*, as we have seen, could involve ritual, and the area may have been described verbally in a public proclamation of the findings.[35]

Such an operation clearly carried with it certain judicial responsibilities. Some landholders may have wished to contest either the location of a boundary or the identification of their land as public. Others may have intended to claim that they were using the land legally.[36] Indeed, the Gracchan agrarian commission, the first special college known to have exercised those judicial powers in cases involving Roman citizens, displayed them in their title: *triumviri agris iudicandis adsignandis*.[37] To issue rulings, magistrates would have had to make the necessary determinations in hearings in which concerned individuals would have presented their claims directly to the responsible official, who would have been surrounded by his attendants and other visible signs of his power. Magistrates performing such a task would have dealt with the targets of their actions, not as a group whose members all possessed the same characteristics, but rather as individuals, for each case could be different. Contacts of this sort would have been less easily standardized than others and thus more difficult to embed in dramatic and large-scale actions characterized by a high degree of ritual formalism. Furthermore, although some questions, such as the legal status of broad sections of land, could have been resolved in the formal spaces of a town with the customary trappings and settings, the matter of boundaries could only be decided in the fields.

Roman activities in the *ager Campanus* during and after the Second Punic War provide the best indications of the possible scale of operations and of the necessary processes. There, the Romans seemingly confiscated lands on an estate-by-estate basis within the territories of Capua, Atella, Casilinum, and the community of the Sabatini after the failure of their rebellion. In theory, these states surrendered lands bounded on the west by the sea, the north by the Volturnus River, the northeast by Mount Tifata, the east by the mountains and the territories of Suessula and Acerrae, and on the southwest and southeast by the territories of Naples and Cumae, narrow strips along the coast.[38] The Roman senate and people, however, made some concessions to the defeated and to others.[39] A decree and the following plebiscite first gave instructions by families—probably only for the upper classes—declaring the property of some to be public and selling the family into slavery. They then instructed that the remainder be judged according to their census ratings, using this criterion also to determine whether their property would be confiscated. They next ordered the property of all the senators and of those who had held office at Capua, Atella, and Calatia to be sold at Capua, while those who were to be enslaved were to be moved to Rome and sold there. Other inhabitants, remaining free, were required to take up residence by a fixed date at defined places outside of Campania. Some were permitted to remain, retaining possession of their property.[40] Certain provisions of the decree and plebiscite were modified over the succeeding years, and the most sweeping elements were never completely put into effect.[41] Indeed, the entire package may have been beyond the ability of the authorities to enforce.

One result of that decree deserves special notice. Although no source specifically describes the ways the Romans made public land taken from the defeated in other instances, they probably normally defined substantial tracts within which all land was to have this status, for the regular use of such land for colonies and viritane assignments implies that broad stretches of suitable land were available.[42] In Campania, however, the situation would have been more complicated, and public officials, when acting legally and properly, may not have been able to assume that all lands in any section were in fact public.

The first attempt to exploit some of those lands came in 210, the year following the surrender, as a response to specific demands of the war. According to Livy (27.3.1–2), the proconsul Q. Fulvius Flaccus leased confiscated lands in return for a rent paid in grain, an operation that would have required the making of judgments about the status of those who had held them. Flaccus ordered troops billeted in Capua to vacate the town so that he could match fields with houses in the city; each successful bidder, then, would have received lands and a house, a sign that only lands near the city—probably the estates of the former leadership—were treated and that either new estates were created or more probably that old ones were preserved, removing the need to create new boundaries.[43]

In the following years, other Roman officials carved out restricted segments of the territory and used it for a number of purposes: the quaestors of 205 were ordered to sell lands in an area extending from the *fossa Graeca* to the sea, six years later, the censors sold lands "under Mount Tifata," while in 197 a colonial law ordered that three small citizen colonies, Volturnum, Liternum, and Puteoli, be established along the coast.[44] The colonial commissioners probably proceeded in the ways customary for such magistrates. The quaestors apparently dealt with a naturally bounded segment along the coast, for a *fossa Gracca* is most likely to have been located north of Cumae, in the marshes or slightly inland, between this *municipium* and the site of the later colony of Liternum less than ten kilometers away.[45] The lands near Mount Tifata may have been similarly restricted and already delimited.[46]

Some of the officials active in Campania in these years certainly replicated some of the operations of the proconsul Flaccus in 210. According to Livy (28.46.4–6), while the quaestors of 205 were ordered to sell certain lands in Campania, the urban praetor was to identify those Campanians who had not left in accordance with the decree of 210 and make them go to their designated areas of settlement. Between the two notices, Livy revealed that informers, who were to receive one-tenth of the price of recovered land, were encouraged to identify properties that belonged to Campanians, so that they might become public property.

Now the Roman government regularly depended on informers or *delatores* in certain circumstances. Magistrates, when their actions were aimed at only a few known individuals, summoned them into their presence with messengers, and when they wished to confront a class of individuals with certain characteristics but whose identities were unknown, they issued through their heralds edicts instructing those fitting the description to gather at a designated time and place. The latter approach, however, depended on the willingness of those addressed to come forward, and in those cases in which magistrates found it necessary to deal with unknown members of a class who proved, or were expected to prove, uncooperative, they encouraged informers, often through a reward, to give the names of individuals who could be summoned personally, probably the simplest and most effective recourse.[47]

The rewards promised *delatores* in 205, implying a future sale of the recovered lands, would seemingly have been intended to assist the quaestors in their task. If so, the informers would have helped either by identifying fields suitable for sale within the area defined by the *fossa Graeca* and the sea, thus indicating that all the territory included within these limits was not public, or by providing information concerning such places outside of this area, although Livy indicates that the quaestors were not expected to operate there. But the call for informers need not have been intended to aid the quaestors, for their use implies a type of judicial decision on the status of lands and individuals and the location of boundaries not otherwise known to have been exercised by holders of this post. The use of informers, however, accords well with the urban praetor's task of identifying those who had not departed as instructed, an operation that would also have identified lands to be made public. The urban praetor, then, would have had to determine the sections of the decree of 210 covering an individual and implicitly, at least, the sections of that decree covering the lands in his possession. Perhaps Livy's account conceals a set of closely related instructions to a number of magistrates who were to act in Campania: quaestors who were to sell a specific strip and a praetor who was to expel members of targeted groups and identify areas that could be sold later.

Attempts to determine the proper status of lands in the region continued in later years. Early in 173, according to Livy (42.1.6–12), the senate ordered one of the consuls, L. Postumius Albinus, to go to Campania and determine the limits of public land there, joining his colleague in Liguria when he had finished. No immediate need for funds provided the reason for the assignment, but rather reports that private citizens holding land bordering on public property were moving their own boundaries forward, gradually occupying the greater portion of public lands in the area. The matter, then, had become a source of controversy within the senate or, more broadly, in Roman political life. This task necessarily required the consul's presence in Campania, and his journey formed a notorious episode in the history of Rome's relations with its Italian allies. Angry with the people of Praeneste, Postumius sent a messenger ordering the magistrates of the town to come out to meet him and to provide him quarters and entertainment at public expense as well as transport for the remainder of his journey, an act the historian claimed to have been without precedent, for the Romans provided their magistrates with mules and tents to avoid placing such burdens on friendly states.

Postumius's project proved lengthy and difficult, perhaps much more so than either senate or consul had anticipated. The consul never joined his colleague in their province as originally intended. According to Livy (42.9.7), he spent virtually his entire term in the task, returning to Rome only to supervise the election of his successors. The manner in which Postumius went about his assignment in Campania is unknown, but some speculation is possible. The consul would have required those holding lands of questionable status to justify their claims, a demand they presumably could have satisfied by showing that their ownership derived from someone belonging to one of the groups allowed to retain possession. Some documents may have been of assistance here, for lists of those condemned in 210 and records of lands leased in 210 or 209 may have existed. But the apparent source of the problem was not the ownership of specific segments but rather the boundaries between them, for private citizens were accused of moving their *fines* into public land. In the absence of a detailed land register, and the first apparently was constructed for Campania over half a decade later, these limits could have been ascertained only through the testimony of witnesses, presumably neighbors, who knew or claimed to know where the boundaries of estates made public had originally been located; in other words, a resort to informers again would have been necessary.

The lands the consul defined with so much effort did not remain for long without an officially sanctioned use. According to Livy (42.19.1–2), after Postumius had recovered the greater part of the *ager Campanus*, M. Lucretius, a tribune of the plebs for 172, proposed and carried a law instructing the censors to lease the fruits of the land recovered by the consul, so that the greed of private persons would not wander in a vacuum. Those who leased the land, it should be noted, would have to defend it against the encroachments of others, saving the state the responsibility; Dionysius of Halicarnassus (*Ant. Rom.* 8.73) put forward a similar expedient in a speech he placed in the fifth century, when he had the speaker propose that lands ruled public but claimed by private citizens be sold or leased so that the purchaser or lessee, if necessary, would have to defend his position in the courts.

That seemingly simple notice, however, conceals a difficulty, providing indications that Postumius did not finish the assignment. Lucretius, as tribune for 172, would have taken up his position in December 173, but neither at this time nor in the following twelve months were censors in office. The last college, Q. Fulvius Flaccus and A. Postumius Albinus, were elected in 174 and they completed the *lustrum* and thus ended their responsibilities in the consular year of 173, probably before Lucretius took office and certainly before he carried the legislation;[48] the next censors would not be elected until 169. Since other magistrates could arrange for such transactions, the delay has no obvious explanation. Perhaps Lucretius expected or instructed a magistrate or magistrates in the intervening years to complete the *terminatio* begun by Albinus or to prepare the land in other ways for lease, a suggestion that further actions in the area may confirm. There is no evidence that the censors of 169 performed the task Lucretius seemingly gave them.

The last known act in the matter took place seven years after the passage of Lucretius's law. According to Cicero (*Agr.* 2.30.82–83), P. Cornelius Lentulus (cos. 162) was sent into Campania with public funds to buy private estates that projected into public property—in the process encountering one individual who would not sell his land at any price, an incident that Cicero used to illustrate a point he wished to make against the proposed agrarian law of P. Servilius Rullus. Granius Licinianus (pp. 8–9 Criniti) reported the same expedition, but his text has many lacunae at this point. In his version, the senate sent Lentulus, then urban praetor (ca. 165), into the *ager Campanus*, all privately held, to buy land so that it would become public, and those in possession conceded to Lentulus the right to set the price because of his moderation. Although there are strong resemblances between the two versions, a significant difference does exist: Cicero specified that the land to be purchased was private land, while Granius Licinianus identified it as public land in the possession of private citizens—thus, the persons to be compensated were *possessores*, not owners.

Cicero's version is perhaps the more likely.⁴⁹ While Lentulus may have recovered some public lands from occupiers, an important part of his assignment clearly was the consolidation of public lands, for by purchasing private estates all the land in an area would be made public, an especially valuable trait in the *ager Campanus.*

Lentulus also took steps to prepare the area for lease. According to Granius Licinianus, the praetor divided the land, constructed a *forma,* and had it deposited in the *Atrium Libertatis,* a building closely connected with the censors. Lentulus's separation of land into segments and his production of the *forma* indicates that he arranged for the centuriation of the area—the *ager Campanus* certainly was so treated at some time in the second century—and later censors are known to have leased the area in the small lots made possible by this form of land division.⁵⁰ During the middle republic, only one other instance when the authorities may have centuriated land as a preparation for sale or lease is known. Perhaps in the early years of the third century, quaestors sold land in Sabinum in lots of fifty *iugera* (according to one account in modules of ten *actus* square);⁵¹ these *agri quaestorii* were probably located in the vicinity of Cures Sabinum, where traces of limitation with the appropriate dimensions have been discovered.⁵²

In colonies and viritane assignments, triumvirs and decemvirs themselves supervised the centuriation necessary to prepare lands for distribution, and magistrates who defined lands for sale or lease probably performed the same function when needed. The framers of the agrarian law of 111 instructed the duumvirs they would create to see to the measuring and marking of the *ager Corinthus* to prepare the land for sale, the same operation Lentulus apparently performed over half a century earlier.⁵³ The official preparing the land would have directed the work of those surveyors who had accompanied him, but since there were no colonists to serve as a work force or local magistrates to supervise or continue crucial tasks, such as the erection of permanent markers, some portions of the operation may have been turned over to publicans.⁵⁴ Preparation for sale or lease of an extensive territory, then, required an effort similar in scale to the colonization of the same area.

The amount of land Albinus and Lentulus assembled and the latter centuriated remains uncertain.⁵⁵ Granius Licinianus (pp. 8–9 Criniti) may be of some help. One passage, unfortunately fragmentary, refers to fifty thousand *iugera,* but the verb indicating the action performed on this land is lacking, and as a result its status has been the subject of speculation: some suggest it to be the amount purchased by Lentulus, which seems excessive, while others view it as the total amount recovered, consolidated, or eventually leased. Cicero (*Agr.* 2.28.76–78) claimed that Rullus in 63 wished to send five thousand colonists to Capua where each would receive ten *iugera*. If Cicero's and Granius Licinianus's fifty thousand *iugera* are the same, they should be identified with either the total amount of land determined to be public or the portion available for lease.

The agrarian law of 111, passed in the aftermath of the Gracchan reform, provides an interesting parallel. The framers of the measure provided for the election of a special commission of two and set out detailed instructions for them, among which was the task of resolving certain conflicts that had arisen in the province of Africa. In portions of this province, as a result of the actions of many different officials, the system of land tenure had become confused with many claiming legal occupancy of the same lands—a situation possibly even more complex than the one Postumius and Lentulus encountered. Within two days of some date that does not survive, perhaps their arrival in Africa, the duumvirs were to issue an edict, and those holding colonial allotments and the purchasers of certain lands were to respond within twenty-five days, apparently so that the official could confirm the arrangements as legal and perhaps construct a land register.[56] Next, it instructed a duumvir to give public lands to those who had a legal right to land, such as colonists or certain purchasers, if their lands had been sold by public officials.[57] Then, within 150 days of their election, the duumvirs were to confirm the lands that certain *decemviri lege Livia* had given to *stipendiarii*, make sure that each had received the full amount promised him, giving more if required to meet that figure, and record it all on *formae*—much of the area had been centuriated at an earlier date.[58] Finally, within 250 days of their election the commissioners were to confirm and if necessary exchange the lands given to the cities of Utica, Thapsus, Leptis Minor, Acholla, Usalis, Teudalis, and perhaps Hadrumetum.[59] The land remaining after all of this, with a few named exceptions, was to be public, and the duumvirs were to enter it on *formae*. Those operations, like the activities of Postumius, took the better part of a year.

IV. CONCLUSION

The Romans evolved a clear set of procedures to exploit public land for fiscal purposes. Each effort began in formal decisions of the senate and people that resembled those involved in colonization and viritane assignments in some of the ways individual projects were formulated. Magistrates sold or leased lands in auctions in which they summoned those interested into their presence and made the arrangements in a formal atmosphere. A necessary requirement for this auction, however, was the formal bounding of the area in question, a task that involved senior regular magistrates. In areas where lands of different statuses abutted, the process could be onerous, difficult, and time-consuming, requiring the supervising magistrate to deal individually with substantial numbers of landholders. Such an operation would have involved a considerable investment in time by senior magistrates, who had other, more pressing responsibilities: the process of preparing land in the *ager Campanus* was spread over at least eight years and, within that period, required most of the term of one consul, part of the year of an urban praetor, and possibly the time of other officials in the years between 173 and 165. This episode should be kept in mind while considering the reform of Ti. Gracchus more than thirty years later. The bulk of public land not being used for colonies and viritane assignments probably escaped exploitation. Indeed, Appian (*BC* 1.7) claimed that most public land escaped any specific public use, due to lack of time. Certainly the Roman state possessed less onerous means of gaining revenue, such as the *tributum* levied on citizens — a burden suspended in 167 when the profits gained in Rome's eastern wars made its collection unnecessary — and the contributions exacted from subordinated communities outside of Italy.

LEGES DE MODO AGRORUM

In the middle republic, the various means of exploiting public land for a specific purpose—colonies, viritane assignments, sale, or lease—began with a senatorial decree or a plebiscite instructing that a segment be put to an ordained use and instructing the holders of certain posts to arrange the matter. The implementation of such projects could not be separated from the direct actions of Roman magistrates, and the necessary operations regularly required that some officials spend time on the scene defining the limits and turning the land to its intended purpose. Laws and decrees, moreover, were bound just as closely to a specific set of political, military, or fiscal circumstances as they were to a definite and limited tract of land and to the activities of a restricted number of officeholders.

But another type of agrarian law, a *lex de modo agrorum*, in theory regulated and limited exploitation of public lands by the private initiative of Roman citizens. These rules were closely linked neither to a single stretch of land nor to one set of circumstances, but rather broadly governed public lands of a certain type. The framers, moreover, did not intend them to be implemented only once, for such a law set norms that were constantly in effect. The *lex de modo agrorum* is the most obscure of all the laws regulating the use of public lands. With colonies, viritane assignments, and sale or lease, the underlying legislation served clear ends, and the number of laws authorizing the distribution of lands can be estimated with some confidence. With laws *de modo agrorum*, on the other hand, the intent of the legislator or legislators is a matter of controversy and the number of such laws is unknown. In this chapter, the provisions contained in such legislation and the means through which the competent authorities administered them will be examined, as will the place of the measures in the official regime for public lands.

I. LAWS AND THEIR IMPLEMENTATION

Those who proposed, framed, and carried a law *de modo agrorum* set rules to regulate and limit the use of lands defined by their legal characteristics. After officials had carved out segments from the public lands of the Roman people to found colonies, make viritane assignments, or raise revenue, much remained without an officially determined use; Appian (*BC* 1.7) claimed that the excess formed the largest portion. In many areas of Italy, citizens of defeated communities continued to occupy their lands. In other places, powerful Romans used such lands privately, building estates, sometimes through the expulsion of others less powerful than they. The earliest stages of the process are very obscure, as are the extent of the estates created in such a fashion, but in the years after the Second Punic War, which resulted in the confiscation of so much land from rebellious allies, the Roman elite certainly extended its possessions into regions at some distance from Rome itself.

The results of this unofficial exploitation came to be recognized, protected, and regulated in law. Jurists classified those lands as *ager occupatorius* (or if used for pasturage, *ager scripturarius* and *ager compascuus*), while calling the process of private definition and use *occupatio*.[1] Probably at a relatively early date, *occupatio* came to be associated with the concept of possession (*possessio*), which gave to those occupying public lands the privileges of a *possessor*, including the right to seek legal recourse through private law remedies against those who challenged that possession.[2] Private occupation did not change the land's ultimate status nor did it prevent officials from using it later for public ends—a clear contrast with the practice on private property. Individuals who had occupied private lands eventually came to be considered their owners through the process of *ususcapio*; the standard period one had to use lands openly as if the owner without challenge was two years. With *agri occupatorii*, on the other hand, private citizens could not establish ownership merely through use, for private action could not change the status of things pertaining to the *res publica*.[3]

Ager occupatorius served as a reserve from which portions could be separated and used at the will of senate and people.

A law *de modo agrorum* regulated the amount of land an individual could cultivate and the number of animals he could pasture on public property, as well as the sort of labor he could employ on it. Some specific numerical limits are known, not all necessarily in effect at the same time: up to five hundred *iugera* of cultivatable land and pasturage for as many as one hundred large and five hundred small animals.[4] Like laws authorizing the foundation of colonies, the making of viritane assignments, and the sale or lease of public lands, a law limiting private exploitation of public land formed part of an independent category of legislation; no law *de modo agrorum* explicitly ordained any other use for lands freed through its mechanisms.[5] Implementation of such a law, then, did not require officials to make definite arrangements for specific portions of land, as was the case with magistrates implementing other forms of agrarian legislation. Instead, officials were to identify and punish those who had transgressed the established norms; it was essentially a criminal matter.

Although the estates thus regulated could lie at some distance from the city, the crucial administrative acts took place in the public spaces of Rome. Curule and plebeian aediles prosecuted violators.[6] Operating as a pair, a college of aediles managed their prosecutions in trials before the people, as was customary before the development of the standing courts in the late second and first centuries. No known permanent *quaestio* had responsibility for violations of rules *de modo agrorum*, indicating that the laws probably did not reach the first century as an active category; the latest known reference to such a measure in a clear political context follows closely the end of the Gracchan reform.[7]

Like other significant public acts, trials took place according to procedures that emphasized the role of the magistrate and allowed extensive opportunities for formalized actions. A properly constituted assembly of the people, in which they confirmed or rejected the decision the magistrate had earlier reached, formed the culminating stage.[8] The prosecutor publicly set the date and the place, usually the *forum*. He could, if he wished, require the accused to give sureties for his appearance. The locations of the meetings followed strict rules. So did the gatherings themselves. Meetings of the centuriate assembly, necessary if the death penalty was invoked, could be held only outside the *pomerium*, but no further than one mile from it, while the tribal assembly, which validated lesser penalties, usually met within the city itself, in places such as the *forum* and the *area Capitolina*. Within the gathering, certain formalities typical of voting assemblies were observed. In Livy's representation (25.3.8–19) of a trial held in 212, after the initial statements had been made, the presiding tribunes called the people to vote by ordering an open space be cleared and instructing that the urn used to determine the tribe in which the Latins present were to vote be brought forward—the same series of actions needed to turn the final *contio* discussing proposed legislation into the more structured gathering that accepted or rejected the measure. Livy noted that the beginning of these acts ended the ability of other tribunes to intercede, as was also the case with legislative assemblies.

Some formalities distinguished legislative from electoral assemblies; others defined judicial assemblies and separated them from both. Varro (*LL* 6.90–92), following a *commentarius anquisitionis* to be dated after 242, described a quaestor calling the people and the defendant to a trial.[9] In this case, the process required the summoning of the centuries and the cooperation of a consul or a praetor:

> You shall turn your efforts to the auspices and take the auspices in a *templum*; then you shall send to the praetor or to the consul the sign which has been sought. The praetor shall call the accused to an assembly before you, and the *praeco* shall call him from the walls. It is proper to give this command. You shall send a trumpeter to the door of the accused and to the *arx*, where he shall sound the trumpet. You shall ask your colleague that from the *rostra* he proclaim an assembly, and that the bankers shut up their shops. You shall seek out the senators that they express their opinion and you shall instruct them to be present. You shall seek out the magistrates that they give their opinion, the consuls, the praetors, the tribunes of the plebs, and your colleagues, and you shall instruct them to be all present in the *templum*; and when you send the order, you shall call together the assembly.

Varro then noted the instructions given to those who had purchased the contract to provide the trumpeter who would summon the centuriate assembly:

> They shall take care that on that day on which the assembly is to take place, the trumpeter shall sound the trumpet on the *arx* and around the walls, and shall sound it before the door of this wicked T. Quintius Trogus, so that he be present in the *campus Martius* at dawn.

As was the case with legislative assemblies, the vote in a popular assembly summoned to reach a judicial decision represented only the final and decisive stage in a series of formal public events. Prosecutors, like those attempting to carry legislation, called a sequence of preliminary gatherings or *contiones* to build support and allow opponents their opportunity to argue against them.[10] On a designated day and place, the official took position with the ceremonial attributes appropriate to his rank and began the process of fact finding that led to the initial judgment. These hearings were intended to involve a mass audience, for the people would eventually render judgment. Like magistrates who summoned *contiones* to discuss proposed laws, the prosecutor kept control of the proceedings, addressing the people himself, questioning the defendant, and summoning witnesses. The defendant himself could respond and other prominent Romans probably were permitted to speak for or against him. The hearings ended with the announcement of the magistrate's verdict and, if that verdict was guilty, of the penalty he imposed. But if the defendant chose not to accept that judgment, the people gave the final decision.

Livy's representation (26.2.7–3.12) of a dramatic trial in 211 illustrates the process. At the first *contio*, a tribune prosecuting a former praetor for treason (*perduellio*) attacked the defendant with all the powers of oratory in his possession, claiming that recklessness and carelessness had led to defeat and comparing him unfavorably to other generals who had refused to survive the wreck of their armies. The defendant responded by blaming his soldiers, accusing them of demanding a battle they were unwilling to fight, and by denying or explaining specific points raised against him. On the third day, quite atypically the character of the proceedings changed. The testimony of new witnesses, clearly introduced by the tribune, asserted that the defeated commander himself was the first to flee. At that, the crowd demanded angrily that the death penalty be imposed, and the tribune complied, replacing the fine he had earlier demanded. Consulted as to the propriety of such a change, the other tribunes replied that they would wait until their colleague had issued his condemnation before deciding whether to act; they deferred action, that is, until after the verdict was reached, but presumably before the voting assembly was formally constituted. The tribune then declared the defendant guilty and asked the urban praetor to set a day for a meeting of the centuriate assembly, for that was the gathering that would have to confirm or reject such a verdict.

Aediles who prosecuted transgressors of norms established by a *lex de modo agrorum*, like that tribune, would have acted in Rome itself. Yet the lands where the violations occurred would have been located at some distance from the city. Lands held by *occupatio*, moreover, were by their very nature largely unmarked.[11] How, then, did offenses come to the attention of an aedile, an official who usually, if not always, acted in or near the city, and what demonstrations of proof did he offer in the hearings?

For proof, prosecutors relied primarily on the verbal testimony of witnesses of the appropriate legal status — they preferred male citizens — and they expected these witnesses to testify concerning matters of which they had direct knowledge.[12] Written evidence, sometimes papers seized from the accused, could be used but served a minor role. Given the essentially uncontrolled nature of *agri occupatorii*, public documents, if any, would have had little place in prosecutions. When first made public, a written definition of the boundaries of an area may well have been made and preserved. Although such a document may have reinforced claims that the land was indeed public or at least was in an area in which public land could be found, it would have provided no indication that the proper limits had been exceeded. Undoubtedly, the persuasiveness of the witnesses and of the oratory was the primary factor in determining the outcome.

Successful prosecutions, therefore, depended on the presence of suitable witnesses. Indeed, criminal trials did not necessarily begin with the actions of an official. In the standing criminal courts of the late republic, where decisions were made by juries chosen from eligible members of the upper classes, the initiative lay with private individuals. Those wishing to lodge a complaint approached the proper magistrate on his tribunal. The official, if he accepted the accusation, would appoint the necessary judges to decide the issue, but the complainant and his friends assembled the evidence, perhaps with some official assistance, and prosecuted the case. In trials before the people during the middle republic, however, officials maintained a much more active role, leading in the presentation and interrogation of witnesses, making speeches, and presiding over the final vote. But the entire process still began with a private individual leveling a charge.[13] According to Cicero (*Clu.* 134), Scipio Africanus, while holding the census of *equites*, wished to take action against a certain C. Licinius Sacerdos. In a loud voice so as to be heard by the entire gathering, Scipio said that Licinius had committed perjury and if anyone wished to bring an accusation, he would give evidence to support it. But, as no one did so, he let the matter drop.

Aediles, then, would have became aware of violations of rules *de modo agrorum* through the action of individuals or, in notorious cases, public pressure. A significant part of the administration of criminal justice in the middle republic revolved around attempts to encourage private citizens to come forward, either against certain individuals or against those who may have committed offenses of special concern at the moment. A pre-Gracchan law *de modo agrorum* required that freemen be employed on estates specifically to watch and lay accusations, and Ti. Gracchus encouraged informers to bring charges against those who violated the similar provisions of his law.[14] The entire process, then, began with private citizens coming forward or with ambitious aediles encouraging them to do so.

If the people accepted the magistrate's verdict, the penalty he set was imposed. Appian (*BC* 1.8) noted that the pre-Gracchan law limiting the private exploitation of public lands imposed a fine on violators, and a monetary penalty was customary in aedilician prosecutions. But the money did not go into the treasury. Instead, victorious aediles financed specific projects, usually highly visible ones that would increase their own prestige. Thus, the plebeian aediles L. Aelius Paetus and C. Fulvius Curvus, having convicted graziers in 295, used the fines for games and gold bowls for the temple of Ceres, while the curule aediles of the same year, having successfully prosecuted usurers for setting interest rates unlawfully high, installed bronze thresholds on the Capitol, put silver vessels on tables in the shrine of Jupiter, placed a statue of Jupiter in a four-horse chariot on the roof, erected a statue of Romulus and Remus suckling from the wolf at the fig tree Ruminalis, and paved the road from the *porta Capena* to the temple of Mars.[15] In the years following the Second Punic War, one group of successful prosecutors of *pecuarii* built a temple to Faunus, while another set up gold shields on the temple of Jupiter, built a portico outside the *porta Trigemina*, and constructed another from the *porta Fontinalis* to the altar of Mars.[16]

The complex and burdensome process involved in punishing violators of rules restricting the public land that a single individual could exploit probably limited severely the number of prosecutions. Aediles, after all, had other responsibilities, while the opportunities for trials before the people were restricted. Investigations need not have interfered too drastically with the necessary tasks of other magistrates: different officials could conduct separate *contiones* at the same time. The same rule did not apply to voting assemblies. The calendar of the Roman state limited them to days marked *comitiales*, 195 days in all, and the number was further reduced since assemblies could not meet on weekly market days, or *nundinae*.[17] Thus, large numbers of prosecutions for any crimes would have greatly restricted the ability of the prosecutors to fulfill their other responsibilities, and they would have limited the opportunities of other officials to manage their necessary business.

A single college of aediles probably prosecuted only a relatively few violators of all kinds at a time or in their terms. The fines paid by three *pecuarii* were sufficient to pay for a temple of Faunus, while the penalty levied on a single horder of grain served to fund two golden standards.[18] If the penalties were severe enough, fines placed on only a few defendants could well have funded other projects financed in this manner. Indeed, a limited number of prosecutions against a few obvious offenders makes more sense politically than prosecutions aimed more broadly. Many, if not most, violators of rules *de modo agrorum*, after all, would have belonged to the same social group as did the prosecutors. These magistrates would have had to live the rest of their public lives among the defendants and their friends and would have been to some extent dependent on other large-scale occupants of public lands for advancement in their political careers; broad prosecutions would have created too many powerful political foes. As a result, a *lex de modo agrorum* in practice would probably have led to sporadic prosecutions of a few defendants, a finding with clear implications for any attempt to determine the goals of the framers of laws *de modo agrorum* and the place of such legislation in the administration of public lands.

II. THE HISTORY OF LAWS *DE MODO AGRORUM*

Prosecutors may have acted in response to clear violations or public pressures and from a desire to improve their political position, but the framers of the laws they sought to enforce made action possible. The history of these legislators and their laws is obscure. Livy and others placed among the Licinian-Sextian rogations of 367, traditionally a major turning point in the Struggle of the Orders, a rule establishing a limit of five hundred *iugera* to the amount of public land one individual could use.[19] Appian and Plutarch reported a similar law, but they did not place it chronologically or attribute it to a named official. Appian (*BC* 1.8) claimed that an unnamed tribune at an unspecified time carried a law limiting the amount of public land used without official intervention to five hundred *iugera*, establishing a maximum of one hundred large and five hundred small animals that could be pastured on public property, and requiring those holding such lands to employ some free labor. Plutarch (*TG* 8) noted only a law setting a limit of five hundred *iugera*. Finally, in one of his orations, the Elder Cato used a law that fixed a five hundred *iugera* limit to cultivated land and an unspecified maximum number of animals to illustrate a legal principle.[20] All the evidence may refer to only a single law.

Attempts to reconstruct the history of the legislation focus on two linked matters: the date at which the first law was passed and the time when the known numerical limits were established. Yet a firm answer for either is unlikely. First, the historicity of the *lex Licinia agraria* may easily be considered doubtful. Accounts purporting to describe detailed events or proposals at such an early date do not inspire confidence.[21] Indeed, were it not for Cato's oration the existence of any pre-Gracchan regulation might well have been seriously questioned.[22] Second, the narratives of Plutarch and Appian were strongly influenced by Gracchan propaganda.[23] Conceivably each simply reflected the search for precedents for the reform of Ti. Gracchus. Furthermore, some, calculating the extent of Roman territory and estimating the number of individuals able to carve out estates at the time, have found a limit of five hundred *iugera* far too large for fourth-century conditions, and an early date for the known limits on animals is vulnerable to a similar argument.[24]

Those who deny the existence of a fourth-century law must place its appearance at some later date; Cato's speech in 167 forms a clear terminus ante quem. Some put the measure after the conclusion of the Hannibalic war, although no certain traces can be found in that well-documented period.[25] Putting the law in the second century, it is thought, would accord better with the development of large estates, accelerated as a result of the confiscations following the war. Appian (*BC* 1.8), moreover, claimed that the original law soon fell into disuse. If so, it might appear unlikely that Ti. Gracchus would have revived, or even known about, a law dormant for over two hundred years. Others, accepting these broad arguments but influenced by the failure of the sources for the second century to mention the measure, date it before the outbreak of the Second Punic War.[26] Here, Cato's reference does not provide much help. His use of such a regulation as an illustration in a public address certainly indicates that it had a place in recent political discourse, but a measure used to make a point in this manner need not have been recently passed. The private use of public lands figured in another dispute of the time. The affair of the *ager Campanus* may have bulked large in politics in 173 and 172, and the actions ordered in those years would not have been completed until 165. A discussion of a customary measure, perhaps even an inactive one, would have been appropriate at such a time.

But a *lex de modo agrorum* certainly existed before the mid-third century. Unlike laws instructing that colonies be founded, viritane assignments made, or lands sold or leased—laws that would have had to be enacted whenever action was contemplated—a *lex de modo agrorum* need have been passed only once, for it established norms and procedures that were to be in effect until the law was repealed or modified. Prosecutions, successful or not, would have long preserved the memory of the law. And such prosecutions certainly occurred—an indication, incidentally, that Appian erred in declaring that the measure quickly was ignored. Livy recorded the successful aedilician prosecution of *possessores* in 298, while Livy, Festus, Varro, and Ovid noted convictions of graziers in prosecutions beginning in the first years of the third century and extending into the first decade of the second.[27] Without Gracchan allusions and connected with specific monuments constructed from the fines, these notices confirm the existence of a fairly early law. They also indicate that such a law was enforced for some time, if only sporadically.

Other reconstructions, aimed at resolving some of the difficulties by combining parts of earlier efforts, propose a series of laws, although no ancient author clearly noted the passage of more than one law before 133. The simplest form makes a law setting a five-hundred-*iugera* limit on cultivated lands and a maximum on animals the end of the series, placing its passage in the late third or early second century.[28] Earlier measures may have set different and presumably smaller limits.

Implicit or explicit assumptions concerning the purpose of the legislation color the debate. Here, the shadow of the *lex Sempronia agraria* looms large. The reformers of 133 apparently perceived that certain broad social developments were leading to widespread ills. They wished to inhibit the former and remedy the latter, constructing their measure to achieve these ends by adding a special triumvirate to take charge of implementation.[29] The framers of the earlier law or laws, however, relied on criminal prosecutions by the aediles to achieve their ends. Yet the traditional mechanisms of prosecution simply did not allow for vigorous and regular action against large numbers of defendants, a condition of which the framers—members of the elite and familiar with the limits of Roman administration—would have been well aware. Earlier legislators, then, need not have aimed their measures at the same goal as Ti. Gracchus, nor must they have intended to achieve any broad results. If their aims were more limited, they may have set a maximum sufficiently high to lead to only a few prosecutions. While five hundred *iugera* may have seemed modest to members of the governing elite of the late second century, it may have appeared quite substantial to Romans of earlier centuries.

III. THE LAW'S PURPOSE IN THE LITERARY SOURCES

Although personal and political motives may often have had a place, those who proposed and carried laws authorizing the foundation of colonies, the making of viritane assignments, and the sale or lease of lands began projects that served clear public ends. The public goals that the framers of a law *de modo agrorum* sought to achieve are less obvious. Those ancient authors who referred to a pre-Gracchan law often presented the measure through the lens of the reform instituted by Ti. Gracchus, and when they gave any indication of the intent lying behind an earlier law, they tended to see it as the same as the reformer's. Thus, Dionysius of Halicarnassus (*Ant. Rom.* 14.12.22) and Plutarch (*Cam.* 39) used the *lex Licinia agraria* to establish C. Licinius Stolo's credentials as a seditious tribune. Livy (6.35.4–42.9) developed that theme more fully, beginning his account with Licinius and Sextius proposing laws dealing with debt, public land, and the election of consular tribunes—the first two, a *topos* for the actions of revolutionary tribunes—and filling the narrative with Gracchan allusions, or with events that can easily be viewed as such.[30] While Livy did not indicate clearly the results that he thought the legislators expected to obtain, he seemingly viewed the measure as passed in the interest of the plebs and, together with the rules on debt, intended to provide them with tangible benefits.

Only Appian and Plutarch placed the pre-Gracchan law in a specific social and economic context and gave it an explicit purpose. Appian (*BC* 1.7–9) provided the more detailed account. The Romans, as their power steadily expanded in Italy through war, regularly established cities in conquered regions to serve as garrisons, assigned some lands to settlers, and sold or leased segments. But for the remainder, by far the largest portion, they proclaimed that those who wished to use some for a time could do so on condition that they pay a tenth of the grain and a fifth of the fruit grown on it, along with another payment for the animals pastured there. All these actions, Appian held, were taken to increase the number of the Italian peoples so that they might be stronger in war. The rich, however, gained control of most of the land and, convinced that the state would never seek to recover it, expanded at the expense of their poorer neighbors, partly by purchase and partly by force, creating large estates worked by slaves. As a result, the free population declined in numbers and was reduced to poverty, while the increasing number of slaves provided a potential source of danger. Unnamed tribunes carried a law limiting the amount of public land one person could use, establishing a maximum to the number of animals that could be pastured on public land, and requiring those holding land to use some free labor. But this law was largely disregarded. After an indefinite interval, Ti. Gracchus introduced his own measure to address the same conditions.

In general, Appian's account accords well with the traditional means by which public lands were exploited. The fundamental categories are present: lands used for colonies, those used for viritane assignments, tracts sold and leased, and the remainder open to unofficial use by private citizens. The assertion, moreover, that the bulk of public lands—what would become *ager occupatorius*—remained unused because of lack of time certainly is likely given the cumbersome nature of the procedures involved in turning lands to a more specific end. But there is one problem, perhaps an insoluble one. No other author recorded any tithe on occupied lands, even though the *gromatici* and various legal writers often discussed this category.[31] Strong administrative reasons for skepticism can also be found. In Sicily, the Romans continued to collect a tithe that the kings of Syracuse had instituted, and to do so they deployed an elaborate system of procedures, known as the *lex Hieronica* from the Syracusan king who formalized it, involving regular auctions to place the contracts for collection, extensive land registers compiled by local officials, and special courts to resolve the many disputes.[32] Appian's tithe, if collected on any scale, would have required an even more complex organization, of which there is no trace, for the determination of the lands actually subject to the tithe would have been problematic: in Sicily, all arable land in a community was subject to the tax, while in Italy only a portion would have been eligible and its boundaries would have been only generally known, for individual sections were not measured and marked.[33] Appian either was mistaken or confused on this point, or he preserved knowledge of an ephemeral and unenforceable regulation.

Plutarch's version (*TG* 8) is similar in some respects. The biographer began, as did Appian, with a history of the use of captured land. Some of the territory taken in war was sold and the rest opened to the use of the poor on condition that they pay a small rent. The rich began to offer higher rents and the poor were expelled. As a result, a law was passed to prevent this accumulation of public lands in the hands of the rich by limiting the amount one person could hold, a measure that worked for a short time until the rich began to ignore it. Thus, the rich gained control of the land, the poor resisted military service, and the number of free citizens declined while that of slaves increased. C. Laelius, the friend of Scipio Aemilianus, considered proposing legislation to deal with the situation, but relented in the face of resistance. Ti. Gracchus, however, actually carried a law to deal with the situation.

Relating Plutarch's account to the known forms is more difficult. Lands apportioned to the poor on payment of a small rent were, he claimed, subjected to a rule *de modo agrorum* when the rich gained control over them by offering to pay a higher rent. This brief description, however, fits poorly *agri occupatorii*, which a *lex de modo agrorum* regulated, for such lands were occupied, not assigned. The rent that supposedly burdened those lands, moreover, cannot be seen as a version of Appian's tithe for that was fixed, so that the rich would not have been able to outbid the poor. *Agri quaestorii* and *agri censorii*, on the other hand, although given out through competitive bidding, were not covered by provisions *de modo agrorum*. The most probable explanation is that Plutarch, uninterested in such details, compressed carelessly the account he found in his source.[34]

The identity of the source or sources underlying those two accounts and the relationship, if any, between them has provoked intense interest among scholars.[35] Both Appian and Plutarch described the earlier legislation in extended discussions of the history of the use and misuse of public lands that they used to introduce their accounts of the reforms of 133, and both used their narratives, sympathetic to the efforts of the reformer, to explain the origins of an agrarian crisis—the one Ti. Gracchus claimed he would resolve—by presenting it as arising from the increasing size and number of slave-run estates and the resulting displacement of the poor. The author (or authors) underlying the two accounts probably was strongly influenced by Gracchan propaganda and may have had a role in framing it.

Despite their differences, then, a Gracchan representation of the history of laws *de modo agrorum* should lie behind both accounts, and an examination of the motives assigned to earlier laws and projects clearly reveals the ways supporters of reform used them to support a specific program. For Appian, whose account is clearer and more detailed, the Romans intended each method of formal exploitation—the foundation of colonies, the making of viritane assignments, and the raising of revenue—to increase the size of the population and the numbers of those eligible for military service. He even presented the formation of the category of *ager occupatorius* in those terms, maintaining it to be the result of a formal proclamation aimed toward achieving the same results as the other measures. The early *lex de modo agrorum* is firmly located in the same context: the framers sought to check the spread of slave-run estates and expected that the land freed through the operation of their law would be divided among the poor. Plutarch is in essential agreement with that picture, although his account is much less detailed and clear.

Both versions, then, acknowledged only one motive behind all pre-Gracchan agrarian legislation. In that way, they implicitly maintained that the apparently unprecedented law introduced by Ti. Gracchus had in fact many precedents, for it had the same goal as all earlier projects and was especially close to its chief model, the early *lex de modo agrorum*. Another feature reinforces that conclusion. Appian, and presumably the author behind his account, presented the *lex Sempronia agraria* primarily as a *lex de modo agrorum*, but such a representation could lead to an obvious question: if the framers of the earlier measure had unsuccessfully tried to resolve the problem through the same means that Ti. Gracchus later would use, why then should the Gracchan law be any more successful? Plutarch and Appian provided an answer, for both maintained that the pre-Gracchan law was quickly ignored, a claim that the successful prosecutions of the third and early second centuries subvert. This answer explains away the apparent failure of the earlier effort and also justifies one of the most unprecedented features of the law of 133: the creation of its special commission. The aediles who enforced earlier legislation did not settle citizens on the land. That was not in their power. But the *triumviri lege Sempronia* had among their tasks both the oversight of limits on large estates and the assignment of small plots to individuals. Indeed, Appian (*BC* 1.10) explicitly claimed that they were the reason that the rich could not ignore the new law in the same way they had ignored the old. The Gracchan agrarian commission, then, made it possible to achieve a goal officials and people had set for generations.

Appian and Plutarch gave to all earlier measures the same ultimate goal as the *lex Sempronia*. Yet earlier legislators may not have seen their own laws in the same light. Indeed, many, if not most, probably did not. Demographic concerns may have long been a factor in certain types of agrarian legislation, such as colonization and viritane assignments.[36] Even so, they need not have been determining: military considerations would also have played a part. And fiscal concerns would have formed the most important consideration for the framers of laws instructing that public lands be sold or leased.[37] Nor need the recognition of the legality of *occupatio* have had a demographic end. It would have been difficult for the poor to use such lands without assistance, especially if the natives were still in possession.[38]

The motive assigned to the early *lex de modo agrorum* is similarly suspect. Appian held that the legislators expected the poor to take possession of lands held in excess of the legal limit, but he did not indicate in any way the mechanism that would have led to that end, for he noted only the imposition of a fine on violators. If the framers had intended for the poor to receive land, they could have reached that goal more easily by other means: the foundation of a colony or the making of a viritane assignment.

Both were well-developed legislative categories separate from *leges de modo agrorum*.[39] Indeed, without the passage of a law ordering magistrates to arrange such things in the field, any expectation that the poor would benefit would have been illusory.

Appian's account and, to a much lesser degree, that of Plutarch, then, may provide a fairly accurate overview of the various forms through which public lands were exploited and regulated, along with some plausible details concerning the content of specific laws. But their claims concerning the goals and the contexts of the pre-Gracchan measures should inspire skepticism. They certainly contain strong propagandistic elements. In some cases, demographic concerns may have influenced the original legislators. In others, such matters formed no part of the framers' calculations. This is especially true for the early *lex de modo agrorum*, the least likely of all the laws to have been able to achieve demographic changes on a large scale.

IV. LAWS *DE MODO AGRORUM* AS A KIND OF SUMPTUARY LEGISLATION

What good, then, could the framers of earlier rules *de modo agrorum* have seen in them? Recognizing the difficulties in the surviving accounts, some have sought to find an alternative explanation for the measures. According to one influential view, over the course of their history such laws served a variety of ends.[40] Very early legislation would have permitted the plebs to occupy public lands, a right previously possessed only by patricians. In later years, legislators added numerical limits to the possession of land to preserve public order, for without some restraints competition among the upper classes for access to public lands could easily have led to violence.[41] Finally, in the years after the Second Punic War others would have set forth measures intended to restrain the numbers of slaves, increasingly seen as a menace to good order.

Such a proposition is plausible on the surface. Still, it has certain difficulties of its own. The proper use of public lands and the identity of those who were to benefit must have been an issue from a relatively early period, for disputes over land form a common feature in agricultural societies.[42] An exclusive right to public lands held only by patricians, however, must remain doubtful. Roman authors who placed the early measure in the setting of a conflict between patricians and plebeians over access to public land may simply have thought that the issues in the Struggle of the Orders were basically the same as those of the Gracchan age.[43] Competition between *possessores*, moreover, could have been restrained more effectively through the remedies of the private law, which allowed many more cases to be heard and resolved than possible in criminal trials before the people; attempts to control conflict among the elite, in other words, may have led to the formation of the concept of *possessio* and of the procedures that protected it.[44]

The framers of the first (or only) law *de modo agrorum* certainly acted in a society in which estates deemed large existed. But their efforts need not imply that they thought the size of estates, the number of Romans who possessed them, and the magnitude of the servile population to be increasing drastically. Nor does it follow that they perceived such developments as having broad effects deleterious to many Romans and dangerous to the state as a whole. Attempting to place early legislation in such a context requires the acceptance of a Gracchan view of the matter.

Another possible motive for the legislation is confirmed by the sources. Some ancient authors assigned in passing to rules limiting the private exploitation of public land not an economic or demographic goal but a moral one. Recording the successful prosecution in 298 of *possessores* who held more land than the law allowed, Livy (10.13.14) noted that such means restrained immoderate greed. Later, in a speech he attributed to the Elder Cato but may have composed himself, Livy (34.2.1–4.20) had the orator argue against a motion to repeal the *lex Oppia*, a sumptuary law prohibiting women from owning more than one-half ounce of gold, wearing multicolored clothing, or riding in a carriage in the city or in a town near the city, by condemning extravagance and the evils suffered by the state from avarice and luxury.[45] Livy's Cato praised the *lex Oppia* and the *lex Licinia agraria* as means for controlling these vices, and even claimed that excessive greed had led to the passage of the latter. This attitude was not peculiar to Livy alone. Aulus Gellius (20.1.22–23) included the *lex Licinia agraria* in a list of sumptuary laws necessary to restrain luxury among citizens.

The moralizing attitudes contained in those passages are found only in relatively late sources, but there is no reason to believe that they were not of long standing.[46] The aediles, after all, regularly prosecuted cases involving immorality, and their enforcement of regulations against horders and usurers may have been aimed in the same directions, since they resulted only in fines, not in redistribution of their grain or capital.[47] Indeed, on one occasion, Livy (35.7.1) claimed that laws against usury held greed in check. It is possible, then, that pre-Gracchan rules *de modo agrorum* shared one goal with sumptuary laws: to preserve a semblance of equality among the elite and to prevent excess and luxury, which weakened the moral fiber of the state.[48]

A *lex de modo agrorum* aimed at restraining differentiation among the elite, curbing excess, and punishing behavior that had led to public controversy makes considerable sense administratively; a scandal, after all, would help supply the informers so necessary to successful prosecutions and would inflame the crowds that would eventually have to approve the verdict. It also would give the prosecutor clear opportunities to improve his public image. Aediles had a brief time in office to position themselves to seek a higher post. The structural limitations on how many individuals could be successfully prosecuted would have forced those aediles who wished to prosecute to focus on a few obvious cases, which would have had the greatest potential to advance their careers. The framers of the law may have expected no more.

If they did indeed act in the late fourth or early third centuries and did intend to set their limits so high that only a few could reach them, the framers of a *lex de modo agrorum* would have constructed, advocated, and carried their measure at a time when few, if any, truly large estates existed. In such circumstances, a limit of five hundred *iugera* may have seemed very large. A massive expansion in both the size and in the number of large estates, moreover, could easily have put an end to prosecutions. With so much land available as a result of confiscations from faithless allies after 200, limits may well have been seen as unnecessary and archaic, estates of more than five hundred *iugera* may no longer have appeared scandalous, and, with a large number of violators, the prosecution of a few, all that was administratively feasible, may well have seemed pointless. If there was any truth to the claim that the early *lex de modo agrorum* was not enforced, it may lie here.

V. CONCLUSION

The Romans did not have the governmental resources to control all, or perhaps even most, of the land they confiscated. Specific projects were formulated and the responsibility for implementing them assigned in sequences of meetings in the major public spaces of Rome. The use of land for colonies, viritane assignments, and fiscal purposes, moreover, required that high-ranking officials or special commissions with senior senators spend time on the scene arranging matters for restricted segments of land.

Laws seeking to regulate the unofficial use of excess lands emerged from the same political and administrative system, but unlike those other arrangements, which were essentially one-time affairs, their implementation was an ongoing responsibility of certain elected officials. Like all other laws, regulations *de modo agrorum* originated in public meetings in the city, but unlike other laws covering public lands the implementation of those rules would take place entirely within the same spaces. There, prosecutions were sporadic, aimed against a small number of individuals, and had much of the morality play about them.

THE GRACCHAN REFORM

In the middle republic, Romans attempted to govern the use of public lands according to a few well-defined and long-established patterns: colonization, viritane assignments, the sale or lease of lands, and regulation of the amount of public lands that could be exploited privately. Each form, separate and independent, began in a law that dealt only with it. Each had its own ends, was implemented by magistrates peculiar to it, and had its own sequence of administrative actions. Such measures, moreover, had limited and specific goals: those positive laws ordaining a particular use of land did so only for a restricted territory and a relatively small number of individuals, while others, establishing norms governing public lands broadly, were enforceable or intended to be enforced in only a few cases.

In 133, however, Ti. Gracchus and his supporters introduced a law intended to have much broader effects. This attempt at reform marked both a turning point in Roman political history and a change in the traditional land policy, for the Sempronian law combined elements hitherto separate and attempted to achieve results on a larger scale and at more places than did earlier legislation. The legislators, however, proved less adventurous in devising new administrative methods and made only minor changes in practice.

I. THE *LEX SEMPRONIA AGRARIA*

Early in his term as tribune of the plebs, Ti. Sempronius Gracchus introduced the proposal that eventually would become the *lex Sempronia agraria*. Various motives have been attributed to the reformer and his allies. According to Plutarch (*TG* 8), C. Gracchus claimed that a journey through Etruria on the way to Numantia led his elder brother to consider reform, when he observed the scarcity of free inhabitants and the great number of slaves in the region; Plutarch also noted that others, presumably opponents of the reformer, claimed that a desire for fame and competition with some of his contemporaries were the primary factors. Following the same broad lines, modern investigators have sought the basis of Gracchus's reform in a desire to remedy certain social problems, in a concern about the declining numbers available for military service, or in an attempt to strengthen his own political position and that of his friends—goals that need not have been mutually exclusive.[1]

Whatever the motives, Ti. Gracchus certainly wished for (or at least had promised) results beyond what could be achieved in a single colonization project or land assignment. The propaganda deployed by the Gracchi and their supporters, clearly revealed by C. Gracchus's own claim, intended that the reform be seen as a justifiable response to an increase in the size and number of slave-run estates and the dislocations this process engendered among the rural citizenry. Following pro-Gracchan accounts, Appian (*BC* 1.7–9) and Plutarch (*TG* 8) maintained that Ti. Gracchus introduced the law because the rich were creating large estates by driving the poor off the land, thus leading to a decline in the number of those eligible to serve in the legions.[2] The way the law was actually framed supports the claim that large estates formed the focus of the reformer's efforts. Rather than using a traditional method to give land, Ti. Gracchus chose a more complicated alternative that potentially would result in settling *coloni* on lands taken from *possessores*, probably in the central core of Roman territory, since tracts of land suitable for colonies and viritane assignments could be found on the fringes of Roman Italy in Cisalpine Gaul and in the far south.[3]

Ti. Gracchus did not draft his measure alone. According to Cicero (*Luc.* 5.13) and Plutarch (*TG* 9), three prominent men aided him: his father-in-law, Ap. Claudius Pulcher, consul in 143, censor in 136, and *princeps senatus*; P. Mucius Scaevola, the consul for 133 (the year of Gracchus's tribunate); and P. Licinius Crassus Mucianus, a former praetor, the father-in-law of Tiberius's younger brother Gaius and the natural brother of the consul of 133. Scaevola and Crassus were among the most important jurists of their time, and Scaevola was a major figure in the development and systematization of the study of Roman law; both would serve as *pontifex maximus*.[4] With such experienced jurists, then, one could expect a high degree of sophistication in the framing of the law.

No text of the *lex Sempronia agraria* survives nor does any single work provide an extensive summary of its provisions. Only a few scattered, frequently obscure, and sometimes contradictory fragments survive, and they are often difficult to place in context or reconcile. Ti. Gracchus, moreover, modified the proposal during the course of the debate leading up to its passage, and some provisions are specifically placed in earlier versions, so that their inclusion in the final draft is uncertain. For our purposes, however, only the broad outline of the law is necessary, and that is reasonably clear.

At the core of the *lex Sempronia agraria* was a regulation *de modo agrorum*, but one with innovative features and turned to new ends. Appian (*BC* 1.9, 1.11) held that Ti. Gracchus set the amount for a single *possessor* at 500 *iugera*, the same figure found in earlier *leges de modo agrorum*, and added to it the provision that each be permitted to retain an additional 250 *iugera* for each child.[5] Livy (*Per.* 58), on the other hand, presented the upper limit, perhaps with less probability, at 1,000 *iugera*.[6] The drafters of the law also included an important concession, which changed the legal status of certain lands. According to Appian (*BC* 1.11), the law instructed that *possessores* receive secure tenure, probably *ex iure Quiritium*, of the lands they continued to occupy within the legal limits.[7] A traditional *lex de modo agrorum* punished those few *possessores* and *pecuarii* who were widely seen as using too much public land, but, upon conviction of the violators, illegally held lands were not turned to any new public use. The similar regulation in the *lex Sempronia*, however, served a different purpose: its goal was to settle propertyless citizens on land freed from *possessores*.[8] Appian (*BC* 1.10) reported that those allotments were to be inalienable, so that the rich and powerful could not regain control.

Laws regularly included provisions for their enforcement, and they often ordered the election of special commissioners to undertake some of the necessary operations. The *lex Sempronia agraria* did the same. Indeed, Appian (*BC* 1.10) held that its college upset opponents more than other features of the law, since it meant that they could not ignore the measure as they had the earlier *lex de modo agrorum*. In the foundation of colonies and the making of viritane assignments, the authorizing legislation created triumvirates for the former and decemvirates for the latter. Again, the reformers adapted and modified a traditional form to serve a new end. Primary responsibility fell on a special commission of three members, the customary size for colleges founding colonies. The law arranged for them to be selected in a fashion that varied from the usual practice: instead of being chosen by the tribes under the presidency of a consul or a praetor, probably the usual method, the *triumviri lege Sempronia* were elected in a meeting of the plebeian assembly under the presidency of Ti. Gracchus himself.[9] Those chosen, their names announced from the tribunal by the reformer, were a closely related group: Ti. Gracchus, his father-in-law Appius Claudius Pulcher, and Tiberius's younger brother, Gaius Gracchus. In rank, the membership of the triumvirate — one very senior senator, one tribune, and one who had not yet held office — was not atypical, but the close relationship among the triumvirs clearly was.[10] Like earlier laws, the *lex Sempronia agraria* probably also set the commissioners' term in office.[11]

Earlier legislation ordaining a particular use for public land specified the area in which the responsible magistrates were to operate. The Gracchan law also covered specific segments of the public lands of the Roman people, but the law of 133 defined those territories more broadly and more abstractly. The framers of the agrarian law of 111 repeatedly introduced confirmations or modifications of the legal status of certain lands, including all of those subjected to the activities of the Gracchan commissioners, with a formula of definition indicating that the tracts to be covered must be within the public lands of the Roman people in Italy as they existed in the consulship of P. Mucius Scaevola and L. Calpurnius Piso (the consuls of 133), with the exception of those lands that C. Gracchus, in a plebiscite he had carried as tribune, had excluded from division.[12] The acceptance of the actions of the Gracchan commissioners within this area and the use of the year of Ti. Gracchus's tribunate as a base should indicate that the law of 111 reproduced the geographic limits of the Sempronian law in those sections that dealt with the results of that legislation.[13] Unlike the magistrates created by earlier laws, then, the *triumviri lege Sempronia* could act over much of Italy.

But the formula in the law of 111 specifically excluded lands set forth in the plebiscite C. Gracchus later carried. The relationship, if any, between the exceptions established by C. Gracchus and the provisions of his elder brother's law is uncertain.[14] One or both may have excluded specific *agri* — the *ager Campanus* is often mentioned in this regard — or they may have set aside lands possessing certain legal characteristics.[15] The original *lex Sempronia* did exclude from division lands defined by the legal category to which they belonged. The law of 111 shows that tracts assigned to state creditors after the Hannibalic war kept their status, and Appian (*BC* 1.18) indicated that the commissioners worked around lands assigned or sold by earlier magistrates.[16] The terms of the Gracchan law, in other words, applied to *agri occupatorii*, while public lands held according to other tenures apparently were to be left undisturbed.

That broad and abstract definition of the lands covered by the law may not have been an innovation. If they had followed the pattern of other agrarian legislation of their time, those who composed pre-Gracchan measures *de modo agrorum* would also have included a formal definition of the areas covered by the terms of their laws. These rules, however, did not cover only a few specific locations, but rather ran over lands fitting the category of *ager occupatorius*—just as did the *lex Sempronia*.[17] Instead of presenting the law of 133 as akin to a colonial law or one ordering a viritane assignment, both of which certainly would have resulted in the assignment of lands to individuals, the reformers may have chosen to claim it to be primarily a *lex de modo agrorum* specifically to allow the preservation of the broad definition of lands that may have been customary in this class of law;[18] it would serve, that is, as another means of using traditional forms to construct an unprecedented measure.

Legislators necessarily had some idea of the actions needed to implement their measures and of the powers required to achieve their goals, for they had to order and define both in their laws. The Sempronian law gave to its commissioners a task of unprecedented scale and complexity. In a system of government that emphasized direct contact between magistrates and citizens, the triumvirs were to enforce over a large territory regulations originally intended to bear on just a few, and they were to follow with the assignment of land at many places to a potentially large number of settlers. Certain traces of the means by which the framers of the law of 133 sought to make that task feasible survive.

At some time between the passage of the *lex Sempronia agraria* and his death in late summer of the same year, Ti. Gracchus carried a second agrarian law. The epitomator of Livy's book 58 maintained that it assigned the commissioners the power to determine which lands actually were public: "he also put forward a second agrarian law so that he might open land more broadly for them, that the same triumvirs should judge which land was public and which private [*ut idem triumviri iudicarent, qua publicus ager, qua privatus esset*]." Macrobius (3.14.6) may support this claim, for he referred to a speech that Scipio Aemilianus gave in 129 when attacking the use of judicial powers by those triumvirs as being "against the judicial law of Ti. Gracchus."[19] The commissioners certainly possessed such powers for their official title, recorded on a number of boundary stones, was *triumviri a(gris) i(udicandis) a(dsignandis)*.[20] This function was an important element in the practices surrounding the official use of public places, and censors, consuls, and praetors normally exercised it; Ti. Gracchus's college is the first special commission known to have had the right.

The claim that a second law granted those powers has proven problematic. The tribune and his allies, members of the governing elite of the republic, would have been familiar not only with politics but also with the actual implementation of policies. One reasonably can expect, therefore, that the framers would have included in their law the powers they thought necessary. Seemingly the reform would have required that the triumvirs be empowered to determine which lands were in fact public and which were not, especially when the land was in the possession of private citizens, often powerful ones. Yet the failure of the noted jurists who framed the law to include seemingly necessary powers in the original version is peculiar.[21] Was Livy mistaken? Is there an explanation that does not require the rejection of the notice or its interpretation to mean something beyond the simple assignment of these powers?[22]

If the epitomator represented him accurately, Livy gave a simple reason for the passage of a second law: to enable the triumvirs to open up more land. Concern over the amount of land available for distribution extends into the epitomator's following sentences: "Then, when there was less land than could be divided without offense to the plebs, since he [Ti. Gracchus] had incited them to greed by hoping for a larger amount, he offered the promulgation of a law that the money that had belonged to King Attalus be divided to those who ought to have received land by the Sempronian law." Plutarch (*TG* 14) gave a different explanation for the appropriation of the bequest of the king of Pergamum: to provide assistance in stocking and equipping the plots assigned under the agrarian law. This is the only report that recipients of allotments in any program received such help. For our purposes, one motive need not be preferred over the other, and indeed the two are not entirely incompatible, for Ti. Gracchus may have intended for the money to be used for both ends. More significantly, in his description of the second law and of the bequest of Attalus, the epitomator emphasized a consistent concern over the amount of land available for distribution, making it likely that Livy actually provided the motivation for both acts.

Appian (*BC* 1.18) also reported that the amount of available land did not meet expectations, but he did not make the addition of judicial powers the result of the discovery of the shortage—only the beginning of their use. Since those in possession failed to hand in lists of their holdings, he reported, a proclamation was issued inviting informers to come forward against them. Then, noting that a large number of legal cases immediately resulted, Appian went into an extended description of the triumvirs' attempts to identify lands for distribution. In general, vagueness and obscurity, especially in matters of chronology, characterize Appian's account of the Gracchi and their reform. Appian began this section by noting that Aristonicus's revolt in Asia was under way and that Fulvius Flaccus and Papirius Carbo had joined C. Gracchus on the college as replacements for Ti. Gracchus and Ap. Claudius Pulcher. At first glance, this introduction gives the impression that the commissioners began to use their judicial powers only with the election to the triumvirate of Flaccus and Carbo in 130, a clear impossibility.[23] Appian's narrative of the start of judicial proceedings and the difficulties encountered in them must represent some of the first stages of implementation.

The first element of that narrative reveals a crucial part of the way the reformers expected their project to develop. Appian introduced the long series of difficulties attendant to the triumvirs' use of their judicial powers by simply stating that those in possession had failed to hand in lists of their holdings, so that a proclamation was issued inviting informers to come forward against them. One earlier stage, then, preceded the first attempts to define public lands through direct magisterial actions: *possessores* were given the duty to provide lists of their holdings. Then, when too few had come forward, someone, probably the commissioners, called for informers. These actions had to have been among the earliest efforts of the triumvirs. Without lands the distribution could not have gone forward, while any hope that large numbers of occupiers would voluntarily identify their holdings probably would not have survived the first attempts to implement the law. Such a dependence on voluntary compliance must represent the original expectations of the commissioners and of the framers.

Identification of land through lists provided by *possessores* would have had obvious advantages. If a sufficient number of occupiers had complied, no further magisterial activity would have been needed to locate enough suitable land. The failure of this attempt, however, forced the triumvirs to call for informers, a common response of Roman administrators when unknown members of a targeted group had failed to appear voluntarily and one of the means by which aediles had identified for prosecution violators of rules *de modo agrorum*. The proclamation of a time and a place for declarations to be made and the acceptance of those declarations actually made could easily have taken place in the public spaces of Rome. Nor need they have taken long. Both could well have been finished before the murder of Ti. Gracchus, even before the passage of the second law.

Any expectation on the part of the reformers that *possessores* would come forward on their own certainly would have been unrealistic without a strong reason for believing otherwise. If they had intended that such declarations form an important part of the implementation, therefore, the drafters of the measure should have included provisions intended to encourage compliance. Such a feature existed. According to Appian (*BC* 1.11), Ti. Gracchus attempted to persuade opponents to support his law by claiming that the grant of secure tenure over lands *possessores* would retain was adequate compensation for lost land; all holdings legally could have been taken for public use without recompense.

Such a concession could have served ends other than administrative. The framers may have intended the grant to ease passage of the law by lessening the intensity of the opposition. If that had been its sole purpose, however, Gracchus probably would have removed it after the opponents of the measure had failed to end their obstruction. Yet that did not happen.[24] Conceivably, certain ethical concerns among the framers, perhaps among the elite at large, made some form of compensation seem essential. In the second century, when elements of the Roman upper classes increasing came under the influence of Greek philosophy (a development that affected Roman legal thought), certain Stoics debated the proper relationship between law and equity. Some held that morality required only obedience to existing laws; others maintained that both submission to the laws and fairness were necessary. The roots of much of that debate lie, at least in part, in the Spartan revolution of the late third century, when land was taken from those who had used it for generations, an action that was legal, but, in the view of many, not fair.[25] This debate had obvious implications for the Gracchan reform, since the public land to be reclaimed often had been held by families for generations.[26] The framers, then, may have included a provision for compensation in their law to address concerns of equity. Yet such conclusions do not render impossible or unlikely the presence of other motives.

The reformers' expectations and strategy at the time they were constructing the original measure are clearer. They intended to settle large numbers of citizens on the land, preferably lands reasonably close to Rome itself. Rather than taking land in a block, as in earlier projects, the legislators intended to free sections for assignment through the operation of a rule *de modo agrorum*. Now special commissioners charged with founding colonies or making viritane assignments performed the bulk of their task on the scene, dividing lands, assigning them to individuals, and establishing the necessary civic organization. The aediles, however, enforced a traditional *lex de modo agrorum* entirely in the civic spaces of Rome, where triumvirs and decemvirs recruited *coloni*. The framers of the *lex Sempronia*, experts at the law, also expected the comparable portions of their law to be implemented in the city, keeping close to their model administratively as well as legally while increasing the scale of the enforcement, for they intended the *triumviri* to leave the city only to divide land and assign it to settlers.

The failure of their original plan, however, led Ti. Gracchus and his associates to turn to direct action to acquire the necessary lands, and the tribune proposed and carried a second law, giving to the commissioners the power to locate the boundaries of public and private lands, judicial powers previously held only by censors, consuls, and praetors. That change added an enormous task to the many held by the college, requiring the performance in the field of all the most essential elements of their work. The two *leges Semproniae*, then, each represent a different conception of the implementation of the basic agrarian program, one based on voluntary compliance and the other on the exercise of judicial powers by the triumvirs. The failure of the original plan may have doomed the reform from the start.

II. THE IMPLEMENTATION OF THE LAW

The death of the tribune did not end his program. Plutarch (*TG* 21) reported that the senate, wishing to conciliate the people, ended its opposition to the distribution of lands and recommended that a commissioner be chosen to replace Ti. Gracchus; P. Licinius Crassus Mucianus (pr. before 133), C. Gracchus's father-in-law and one of the authors of the law, joined Ap. Claudius Pulcher and C. Gracchus on the triumvirate, the heart of the reform. In the following years, further deaths led to additional changes. Crassus, elected consul for 131, was killed while serving as proconsul in Asia early in 130, and Ap. Claudius Pulcher probably died at about the same time.[27] M. Fulvius Flaccus and C. Papirius Carbo, both more junior than their predecessors, took their places.[28] No further changes are known.[29]

Although they faced a task of great complexity, aggravated by the failure of the original assumptions on the way the measure would be implemented, in the months and years following the death of the tribune of 133, the commissioners made a serious effort to enforce the provisions of the *lex Sempronia agraria*. The framers of the Sempronian law showed much willingness to combine elements traditionally separate into a single law and to give one college of magistrates powers and responsibilities not shared previously by a single office. While joining tasks and rights in such a manner, however, they left the traditional ways of proceeding intact. To go along with the more extensive goal of the reform, there are no signs of new administrative procedures or of extensive delegation.[30] The commission's task, then, required a long series of direct meetings with concerned individuals, confronting occupiers of public land, most of them probably hostile, directing surveyors engaged in marking and dividing the fields, leading colonists to these fields, and finally carrying through the procedures of assignment.

Away from Rome, the commissioners performed many of the customary operations. As preparation for distribution, the triumvirs arranged for land to be surveyed and marked with the necessary *termini* and *limites*; at Carthage in 123 and 122, a triumvir supervised the matter directly.[31] That probably was also the case in earlier phases, for it was the regular mid-republican practice. A number of boundary markers provide direct evidence for the operation in Italy. One, found outside Aeclanum, carries signs interpreted as *fundus veteris possessoris*.[32] If correct, this boundary would have separated sections of public land reserved for the occupant from those open for assignment. Others noted important locations in a centuriation grid and should indicate lands in part prepared for distribution: stones from Campania and Lucania carry the number of the *kardo* and the *decumanus*, while another from Apulia bears crossing lines (a *decussis*), indicating the line of the *limites*.[33] In the city, the commissioners would have been able to recruit colonists by the same procedures colonial commissioners or the decemvirs in charge of viritane assignments used. Leading the *coloni* to the sites, they assigned land to settlers, just as did other magistrates, and they matched an individual *colonus* to his plot through the use of the lot in the normal manner.[34]

But the first major task involved the identification of available lands. Such an operation required the officials to summon occupants and other witnesses, listen to claims, hear testimony and receive oaths, issue rulings, and, in the fields themselves, set the boundaries.[35] Appian (*BC* 1.18) reported that the triumvirs encountered instances when some holding lands by tenures other than possession had encroached on neighboring tracts of public lands, obscuring in the process the boundary between public and private. L. Postumius Albinus spent his year as consul in 173 doing much the same thing in only one region, Campania, and he probably did not finish.[36] The Gracchan commissioners faced the added complication of having to determine which *possessores* were holding lands above the legal limit.

All areas in which public lands could be found would not have been equally desirable as places of operation. Unable to survey all public lands in Italy, the triumvirs would have focused on a few regions. Postumius's operation in 173 was rendered more difficult because the Romans, by restoring some lands to their previous owners, had created a situation where lands held by various tenures could be found in the same tract, increasing the number of boundaries that had to be determined. Guided by personal knowledge or informers, the commissioners would have avoided similar regions (or if they had turned to such areas would not long have continued to do so). Instead, they would have preferred areas where all lands within certain broad limits had the same status. Probably they would have favored a situation in which a broad stretch of *ager occupatorius* was held by a few *possessores*.

Appian (*BC* 1.18) provides indirect evidence for an element of the commissioners' basic strategy. After noting that the triumvirs had called for informers and then proceeded to resolve a large number of disputes, Appian gave examples of certain situations in which the college exercised its powers of judgment. On some occasions, he claimed, adjoining fields had been purchased or given to allies, and then the whole area had to be measured to identify what had been sold or given. In other cases, those on the land had failed to preserve either their contracts or their allotments. Finally, Appian noted that, as a result of the original proclamation allowing the private use of undistributed lands (apparently the same edict he described in his account of the early *lex de modo agrorum*), individuals had begun to use lands adjacent to their own and the boundaries between public and private had become obscured.[37]

Two prominent features of that account are significant. Despite the intent of the legislators to settle *coloni* primarily in the inner core of Roman territory, Appian saw the triumvirs as active in areas with lands still held by allied states, perhaps another indication of the failure of Ti. Gracchus's original assumptions. These lands clearly had been subjected to official attention in the past. Appian asserted that some had been specifically given to allies and that surveys had been made. Now a grant of lands to allies could have been made at any time following the conquest and confiscation of an area. It need not have required much effort beyond a verbal description of the area in question and the erection of a few markers. Another feature of Appian's account points toward lands subjected to more intensive operations. He noted that the triumvirs, while surveying lands, affected sections sold or allotted at an earlier time. The distribution of allotments — a feature of colonization or of viritane assignments — required a magistrate's presence in the area for a substantial period, as could the sale or lease of land.[38] Indeed, Appian noted that in these areas the commissioners made new surveys and required those who had not kept their contracts or proofs of allotment to move to other places, often uncultivatable, since, he claimed, the earlier surveys had been carelessly done. A Gracchan *terminus* indicates that the commissioners operated in Campania, where land was centuriated for lease in 165, while other evidence attests to the establishment of limits or the distribution of lands in the territories of a number of colonies: Cales, Luceria, Pisaurum, Sipontum, Suessa Aurunca, Venusia, and perhaps Paestum.[39]

Thus, in some cases the triumvirs worked on the fringes of earlier assignments, around areas where lands had been sold or leased, and in sections given to the allies. This would have been a sensible strategy. Colonies, for example, often contained some lands assigned to the previous inhabitants and others destined for sale or lease. Still more was reserved for later use, such as supplements. The markers often may have survived, and colonies themselves may have preserved verbal descriptions of the segments. Thus, under ideal circumstances the commissioners would have been able to proclaim all the lands between the outer limits of a settlement and certain designated lands as *ager occupatorius* and thus under their authority. Substantial tracts given to allied states may have possessed the same characteristics.

A broad outline of the geographical regions in which the commissioners operated and of the time they were active there can be constructed. Twelve boundary markers provide the most certain evidence.[40] These *termini* were inscribed with a regular formula giving at least the *praenomen*, *nomen*, and the filiation of the commissioners along with their title. Because of the frequent replacement of members in the first years of the reform, the names allow the stone to be dated to within a few years. The *Liber coloniarum*, included among the texts in the *Corpus Agrimensorum Romanorum*, supplements the testimony of the stones. The compiler of this work, a list of places where lands had been divided and assignments made, often noted "Gracchan limits" or distributions and colonial foundations "by the Sempronian law." The core probably was assembled under Augustus and Tiberius, possibly to assist in the settlement of veterans, and over the following years more notices were added, some apparently were modified, and epitomes made.[41] As it now exists, the text covers Lucania, Bruttium, Apulia, Calabria, Etruria, and part of Picenum. Two versions survive. The most complete (sometimes called the *Liber coloniarum I*) was compiled in the fourth century A.D., and slightly later a reedited version of some sections appeared (the *Liber coloniarum II*). The verdict on its reliability is mixed.[42] Despite interpolations and certain inaccuracies, the *Liber coloniarum* is largely reliable for identifying places where divisions and assignments were made and the authority lying behind them. The legal status assigned to the settlements created by those distributions, however, cannot be trusted, for its editors cared little for the proper terminology.[43] Neither stones nor list gives any indication of the scale of the activity.

Although there are exceptions, texts and markers show that the college confined the bulk of its activity to a few areas. Of the twelve *termini*, ten fall into two chronologically and geographically distinct groups. The seven stones of the first group, the larger and the earlier, carry the names of C. Gracchus, Ap. Claudius Pulcher, and P. Licinius Crassus. Two come from Campania, one near Capua itself, and the other from the territory of Suessula.[44] The remaining five were found in the Tanager valley in Lucania, near Volcei, Atina, and Consilinum, all along a fifty kilometer segment of the recently completed *via Annia* on its course from Capua to Rhegium.[45] The activities of the triumvirs were closely connected to this road, for the boundary stones and the associated traces of centuriation show that it was one of the main axes of the grid.[46] These *cippi*, then, reveal that the Gracchan commissioners appropriated land and began the process leading to assignments in Campania and Lucania at some time between the election of Crassus as commissioner in 133 and the death of Crassus himself early in 130.[47]

The *Liber coloniarum I* noted activity in the same area, although not necessarily during the same few years. Again, the course of the *via Annia* may have been important. Grumentum (p. 209L), within twenty kilometers of the road, received Gracchan limits. Immediately before this entry, the compiler noted that Volcei, Paestum, Potentia, Atina, Consilinum, and Tegianum were centuriated with modules of the same size. Since the boundary stones show activity by the Gracchan commissioners at Volcei, Atina, and Consilinum, the other locations—Paestum, Potentia, and Tegianum—also may have received their attentions.[48] Paestum is located less than ten kilometers south of the mouth of the Silarus River, the valley that carried the *via Annia* into the interior of Lucania, and Tegianum lies within the same distance of the road. The same text (p. 209L) records two additional locations, Consentina and Clampetia, in Bruttium further to the south, the former on the *via Annia* and the latter about twenty kilometers from the road. Although all the sites in Campania and Lucania may not have been treated in the same journey, the commissioners probably moved down a major road, with occasional detours to promising areas. Earlier in the century, colonial and agrarian commissioners may have used the *via Aemilia* in Cispadane Gaul in the same way.

An isolated *terminus* with the same names may indicate that the triumvirs followed the same procedure in another area.[49] This marker, a first-century copy, was found at Fanum Fortunae in Picenum, the point where the *via Flaminia* from Rome reaches the Adriatic coast and not far from the citizen colonies of Pisaurum and Sena Gallica. The *Liber coloniarum I* (p. 227L), incomplete for Picenum, reported assignments "by Gracchan limits" at Ancona about fifty kilometers south of Fanum on the coast.

The second group also presents a clear picture, with no overlap in time or place with the first. Two *termini* carry the names of C. Gracchus, M. Fulvius Flaccus, and C. Papirius Carbo; a third, heavily damaged, may be associated with them.[50] These markers, erected no earlier than 130, were found in Samnium and form a compact group between Aeclanum and Compsa. The exact course of the *via Appia* from Beneventum to Tarentum and then Brundisium is not always certain, but those markers certainly lie reasonably close to it.[51] The *Liber coloniarum I* mentioned Gracchan activity at Abellinum, twenty-five kilometers from Beneventum, and at Compsa and Venusia farther to the east on the same route.[52]

The second of the isolated markers carries only the names of Flaccus and Gracchus, and it must have been erected early in 130, after the death of Crassus and of Claudius but before Carbo joined the college.[53] The stone was found to the northwest of Luceria and may be associated with centuriation on the Daunian plain in Apulia.[54] The *Liber coloniarum I* (p. 210L) noted other Gracchan activity on the plain and along its fringes at Herdoniae, Ausculum, Arpi, Sipontum, and Salapia, all lying within a rectangle approximately sixty kilometers by forty. Bari, on the coast about seventy-five kilometers from Salapia, was another probable settlement area.[55]

In addition to those regions, the *Liber coloniarum* noted other areas that had received the attention of the triumvirs, although the lack of inscribed *cippi* make it difficult to determine when they worked there. Some of the places could have been reached on journeys to Campania, Lucania, Samnium, and Apulia. Cales (p. 232L) and Verula (p. 239L) lie on or near the *via Latina* on its course from Rome to Capua, while Vellitrae (p. 238L) and Suessa Aurunca (p. 237L) are located not far off this road between it and the *via Appia*. In another direction, the commissioners divided lands at Corfinium (pp. 228L, 255L) and Afile (p. 230L), the former on the *via Valeria* and the latter not far from it. One route, it should be noted, led from

Corfinium by way of Aesernia to the Daunian plain.[56] A few other places are more distant from these core areas of activity. Three sites (pp. 219L, 215–16L) are in Etruria: Arretium and Ferentum lie along the *via Cassia*, and Tarquinii is located on the *via Aurelia*. Finally, settlements were made at Tarentum (p. 211L), where they probably were connected with the later colony of C. Gracchus, and at Lupiae on the Sallentine peninsula south of Brundisium.[57]

In their years in office, then, the Gracchan commissioners implemented the program by traveling down major routes across the peninsula. In these forays, the triumvirs covered a substantial amount of territory. They probably worked very quickly.[58] Expeditions down the *via Flaminia* and the *via Annia* probably took place in 132 and 131. In the next year, the commissioners were establishing markers in Apulia, and they began to survey in Samnium no earlier than 130.

Most of the activity of the college may have been concentrated in the first three years, a period no longer than the term given to colonial commissioners, for after 129 the ability of the triumvirs to use their judicial powers fully apparently was curtailed. According to Appian (*BC* 1.19), some allied states continuing to occupy confiscated lands complained about the way the commissioners exercised these powers and secured Scipio Aemilianus as their advocate. Refraining from attacking the agrarian law itself, Aemilianus persuaded the senate that such cases should not be decided by the triumvirs, whom the allies distrusted, and early in 129, the senate assigned C. Sempronius Tuditanus, consul in that year, to judge such matters. Tuditanus was not long engaged in the task. Realizing the difficulties involved, he departed for his province of Illyria to avoid resolving the cases he had taken. As a result of these events, Appian noted that the triumvirs remained idle.

What the senate actually did is uncertain. Appian did not make clear whether Tuditanus was given jurisdiction over all cases concerning public land or only those involving allies. Nor did he specify whether the college actually lost its judicial powers and, if so, whether that loss was permanent.[59] The commissioners certainly remained in office: Appian (*BC* 1.21) reported that those in possession resorted to various pretexts to delay the division of land after the death of Aemilianus in the same year, while Livy (*Per.* 59) and Cassius Dio (fr. 84.2) presented the commissioners more actively, the former accusing them of stirring up *seditiones* and the latter claiming that they ravaged all of Italy. None explicitly mentioned the commission's judicial powers.

Attempts to reconstruct the senate's action have proven problematic, since a decree of the senate alone normally would not have invalidated a plebiscite. Some scholars have held that a law must have been carried as a result of the decision, while others have sought to find legal justification for the senate's action in various principles of Roman law.[60] But formal removal or modification of the college's judicial power may not have been necessary. In the past, the senate itself had authorized senior magistrates to determine the boundaries between Roman territory and that of other states and between public and private property; only a change in the status of public property may have required authorization by the people. The original *lex Sempronia agraria* had authorized the triumvirs to act over public land in Italy and the second law probably assigned to them judicial powers in the same territory. But these commissioners did not possess the exclusive right to determine the status of lands and their limits, for other officials, also authorized by a law or the senate, exercised certain powers over public lands in Italy in the same years. If he was the person honored by the inscription at Polla, T. Annius Rufus (pr. by 131, cos. 128) may have installed cultivators on public lands in Lucania after the passage of the Sempronian law but before its commissioners operated in the area.[61] In 124, moreover, a colony was established at Fabrateria Nova, probably by its own triumvirs, while two years later M. Livius Drusus carried a law instructing that other magistrates found colonies in Italy.[62]

The *lex Sempronia agraria*, then, probably did not bar the senate from assigning some magistrate of the appropriate rank the task of separating public lands from private in Italy. Now high-ranking officials, such as consuls, could claim jurisdiction in specific cases already being heard by officials of lesser rank, and magistrates could prohibit others of equal or lesser rank from granting judgments in individual instances.[63] Thus, Tuditanus, having been given by the senate the responsibility for establishing the limits of public land, may have preempted the *IIIviri* by taking some cases under his own jurisdiction. When he left Italy for his province, the triumvirs may have recovered their ability to act.

Although the college probably maintained its full powers after 129, the intervention of Aemilianus may have impaired permanently the triumvirs' activities. Members of the commission themselves wished to conciliate the allies after 129. Appian (*BC* 1.21) stated that some Romans proposed to give Roman citizenship to the Italians in order to lessen their resistance to the reform, and Flaccus himself introduced a citizenship law in 125 in a vain attempt to bring this about. When C. Gracchus renewed his brother's agrarian law in 123, he left out the judicial powers: the *triumviri agris iudicandis adsignandis* became *triumviri agris dandis adsignandis*.[64] These powers, never a part of the original plan, probably had proven too difficult to use. But the commission still could act in other ways. Scipio's action in 129 could have left lands already demarcated but not yet assigned. Perhaps more important, the commissioners may have been reluctant or unable to exercise their powers to determine the legal limits to *agri occupatorii*, but that does not mean they could not act on lands where that was clear, a condition that could be found in colonial territories and perhaps in other locations.

III. THE AGRARIAN LEGISLATION OF C. GRACCHUS

The laws of 133 did not end Gracchan agrarian legislation. Ten years after the tribunate of Ti. Gracchus, his younger brother Gaius, tribune in 123 and 122, carried laws on such matters as the supply of grain to the poor, appeal of magisterial decisions, the lawcourts, road building, the assignment of consular provinces, and the province of Asia.[65] Among those measures, some dealt with public lands, and this legislation reflects changes in the ways the reformers thought land reform should proceed.

Probably soon after he entered office, C. Gracchus introduced and carried a law that to a considerable extent renewed his brother's.[66] Indeed, Appian knew only of the law of Ti. Gracchus, while the framers of the law of 111, which attempted to bring order to the management of public lands after years of turmoil, mentioned only the younger Gracchus's measure and his triumvirate; both probably saw the law of 123, then, as a continuation of the first (with perhaps some additions and modifications).

The first of Ti. Gracchus's laws had not given to the commissioners the power to determine which lands were public and which private—that came only through a second plebiscite. The law of 111 and two other measures from the late 120s, however, refer to the commissioners as *III viri a(gris) d(andis) a(dsignandis)*, a title clearly distinct from that recorded on a number of *cippi*: *triumviri a(gris) i(udicandis) a(dsignandis)*.[67] C. Gracchus, then, did not grant the judicial powers contained in his brother's second measure, but that is easily explicable. The authority to determine the boundaries between public and private was not part of the original plan, and its later inclusion was a result of the failure of this plan. In the years following 133, moreover, the use of these powers had proven contentious. They had stirred up trouble with the allies, whom C. Gracchus wished to conciliate, and afforded his opponents with opportunities for attack. The triumvirs, moreover, had probably never been able to use those powers effectively. In sum, judicial powers had proven too costly and too ineffective.

C. Gracchus, then, reenacted his brother's law in its original and least controversial form. He also proposed and carried other laws dealing with public lands, reflecting a change in strategy. The emphasis turned to the foundation of colonies, a more concentrated form of settlement than the first phases of the reform allowed and one that would threaten fewer large-scale *possessores* and allied communities. Measures separate from the main agrarian law authorized these colonies. The Livian epitomator (*Per.* 60) noted that in 123 Gaius carried agrarian laws, clearly separate from the main agrarian legislation, that would bring about the foundation of colonies in Italy and one at Carthage.[68] Plutarch (*CG* 8) had Gracchus propose, in a law or laws seemingly separate from his first, that colonies be sent to Tarentum and Capua. Velleius Paterculus (1.15) reported that colonies were sent to Scolacium Minervium, Tarentum Neptunia, and Carthage in 123, but he did not specify the authority under which they were sent.[69]

The law ordaining the foundation of the colony of Iunonia at Carthage furnishes the clearest example, although an atypical one. Another tribune, Rubrius, probably an ally of C. Gracchus, carried the measure in 123, perhaps in the second half of the year.[70] The Rubrian law possessed many of the basic characteristics of a traditional colonial law. It authorized a colony (probably only one) on a specific territory, and it set for that settlement a definite size.[71] The measure, moreover, provided for the election of a special commission, a triumvirate (the customary size for such a body in those circumstances).[72] C. Gracchus and M. Fulvius Flaccus served as members of that college, but the remaining member is unknown. If the *triumviri lege Sempronia* and the *triumviri lege Rubria* had identical membership — if, that is, the distinction between the commissions existed only in law, not in practice — Carbo may have been the third.

The *lex Rubria* followed an old form, but the nature of the legislation underlying colonies in Italy is less certain. Plutarch (*CG* 8) thought that Tarentum and Capua both were authorized by a single measure; Livy's epitomator (*Per.* 60) spoke of laws (in the plural), but one was the *lex Rubria*. Conceivably, a single law ordered the foundation of all Italian colonies, but it would have been less traditional in form than the Rubrian law. A single triumvirate would have been responsible for founding the places, but this college was not a specialized colonial commission but rather the triumvirs already in existence under the terms of the main Sempronian law; at least, the law of 111 acknowledged no other triumvirate as active in Italy. The law authorizing colonies in Italy, then, assigned responsibility to an existing commission, but one that was also empowered to make other forms of settlement. The *lex Rubria* may have established a college that was separate from the other legally, if not in fact, simply because Carthage was outside the geographical limits given to the original commission, for the agrarian laws of Tiberius and Gaius Gracchus probably covered only Italy, empowering the triumvirs to act legally only there.[73]

The law carried by M. Livius Drusus complements that picture of Gracchan colonial legislation. According to Plutarch (*CG* 9–10), Drusus, tribune of the plebs in 122 and C. Gracchus's chief opponent in that year, in a successful attempt to outbid him for popular support proposed and carried a law ordering the establishment of twelve colonies (instead of Gaius's two or three), each of three thousand. Appian (*BC* 1.23) confirms the outlines of this account. Neither Plutarch nor Appian revealed whether the colonies were to be placed at specific locations or in more broadly defined areas, but at the very least broad limits probably were set.[74] Drusus's law, moreover, provided for the election of a special commission; Plutarch praised him for not serving on it, a compliment that also shows that magistrates actually were chosen.[75] Drusus's law probably was not implemented, or at least not implemented fully.[76]

Colonial commissioners traditionally founded colonies in ways that differed in certain crucial respects from the process by which decemvirs made viritane assignments, and the shift of emphasis in the reform would have required that the Gracchan commissioners perform new actions. Cicero (*Agr.* 2.12.31) held that a *lex Sempronia*, certainly one passed by the younger Gracchus, gave to the triumvirs the *pullarius* needed to take the auspices for the founding of colonies.[77] At least one of those colonies, Iunonia at Carthage, was founded by a triumvirate following the traditional stages, recruiting settlers, centuriating the land, and leading the settlers through the appropriate ceremonies of the formal foundation.

Appian and Plutarch provide the bulk of the evidence for the foundation of Iunonia, but they do so in accounts that focus to a considerable extent on signs of divine anger, possibly fabricated by C. Gracchus's opponents, that could be (and were) used to undermine the validity of the foundation and the underlying legislation. According to Appian (*BC* 1.24–25), the triumvirs supervised directly the location of the city, the centuriation of the land, and the recruitment of colonists, while reports of portents reflecting on these matters served as the basis for nullifying the entire project. Plutarch (*CG* 11) recorded the performance of the formal ceremonies of foundation, the *lustrum* and perhaps the preparations for the plowing of the *sulcus primigenius*, and also noted the appearance of signs around them.

The actions of the opponents of the reform confirm the continuing importance of the customary defining ceremonies. Divine signs and ritual flaws could nullify an official action, but only after the appropriate sequence of stages. First, someone had to report the signs to the proper authority, then the appropriate body of priests had to determine their significance, and finally the senate had to accept these corporate findings and issue its opinion.[78] Appian (*BC* 1.24–25) noted that certain priests, probably the augurs, considered the signs reported from Carthage to be bad omens, and the senate, accepting their report, decreed that an assembly should be called to repeal the authorizing law;[79] Gracchus and Flaccus were killed while preparing to contest that resolution.

The significance of the decisive signs is not clear at first glance. The agrarian law of 111 reveals that the *lex Rubria* was repealed and the colony at Carthage no longer legally existed as an *urbs*, but the assignments to individuals retained their validity.[80] According to Appian (*BC* 1.24–25), wolves destroyed the markers defining areas set aside for assignment, and Obsequens (33) confirmed this, noting that they had scattered the *limites* that C. Gracchus had placed for the division of the fields. Appian's and Obsequens's signs bore only on the land division and, by extension, on the assignments that resulted from them, yet these distributions remained valid after the *lex Rubria* was repealed and the colony had lost its legal status.

Plutarch (*CG* 11) noted a number of other portents that would more clearly have affected the legal status of the colony. While C. Gracchus was engaged in establishing the settlement, the wind reportedly broke the leading standard despite the efforts of its bearer, a storm scattered the sacrificial victims from the altar, blowing them beyond the markers establishing some outline, and wolves tore up the boundary markers themselves. Whether or not they actually occurred, these signs ostensibly took place during the ceremonies making up the formal foundation of the city, for the procession was an essential part of the colonial *lustrum* and sacrifices were a necessary accompaniment to the same rite. Plutarch did not clearly identify the outline beyond the markers of which the sacrifices were blown, but it must have lain near the place of sacrifice and the site of the future city. In the circumstances, the line of the *pomerium*, either already plowed or marked and ready to be plowed, would be the most likely candidate.[81] In Plutarch's version, it is unclear whether the markers scattered by the wolves defined the *pomerium* or the fields. Unlike signs that affected only the fields and the assignments, the bulk of these portents bore on the corporate existence of Iunonia itself, for they called into question the ceremony that formed the settlers into a new civic body and probably also those rites that located the new *urbs*. The opponents, then, presented indications of divine opposition to the division and assignment of lands and to the creation of a new *urbs*. The senate, and possibly also the augurs, accepted only the latter, determining that the Rubrian law ordered the foundation of a colony at a place forbidden by the gods;[82] the repeal of the *lex Rubria* would have been a clear remedy.

The reformers, then, shifted toward colonization programs implemented in the appropriate fashion. This change to a more concentrated form of settlement probably was a response to the difficulties involved in implementing the first Sempronian law and an attempt to avoid the problems that effort had revealed. Like the laws of C. Gracchus and the elder Drusus, other measures put forward to divide lands in the first decades after the death of the reformers in 121 also focused on traditional means of exploitation, although again the scale was to be larger than traditional projects and the competent magistracies differently defined.[83]

IV. THE TRIUMVIRS *LEGE SEMPRONIA*

In the middle republic, colonial commissions departed for the site in a group together with the colonists. At least on occasion, members of a colonial triumvirate would wait in Rome until the entire college could make the journey.[84] Such a practice certainly was not possible for the Gracchan commission. Until the triumvirs had determined the amount of land available in a region, they would not have known how many settlers to recruit and lead there. Perhaps more importantly, all three commissioners rarely were available at the same time. In one form or another, the triumvirate first established by the *lex Sempronia* of 133 lasted for at least twelve years, and during that period commissioners frequently occupied other posts.[85] C. Gracchus may have returned to Rome from Spain only late in 132, and he served as quaestor and proquaestor in Sardinia in 126, 125, and part of 124—he returned to Rome early enough to stand for election as tribune this year. Crassus was consul in 131 and proconsul until his death in 130. Flaccus, elected consul for 125, was proconsul in 124 and probably early 123; he must have served as praetor no later than 128. Carbo, consul in 120, probably was tribune when chosen triumvir; his term as praetor could have come no later than 123. Both Carbo and Flaccus conceivably could also have held the office of aedile while commissioners. The full college, then, probably could only have assembled for an extended time in late 132 and for a year or two in the early 120s. The *IIIviri lege Sempronia* had to arrange among themselves a more complex division of responsibilities than would have been necessary earlier.

Two sets of evidence may bear directly on the way the commissioners distributed the work among themselves. In a single short phrase of notable obscurity, Appian (*BC* 1.9) seems to have characterized the commissioners as "three elected men, exchanging annually" (τρεῖς αἱρετοὺς ἄνδρας, ἐναλλασσομένους κατ'ἔτος). These few words generally are interpreted in one of two ways. Some take the crucial phrase "exchanging yearly" to refer to the term for which members of the college were chosen.[86] The framers of the Sempronian law, then, would have provided for their triumvirs to be elected for one year, and each year those triumvirs would stand for reelection, gaining authorization to proceed for another year. On general principles, that is unlikely. Since the reformers pushed their measure against strong opposition, they probably would not have wished to make their commissioners fight every year for the continuation of the reform; little time would be left for other activities. Instead, the framers of the law probably would have set a term either as long as they thought necessary or as long as they could propose without arousing additional opposition.[87]

Others, translating the passage as "three elected men, alternating among themselves yearly," take the crucial phrase to refer to the manner in which the Gracchan triumvirs distributed administrative responsibilities among themselves, rather than to their term in office;[88] if so, members of that college would have assigned duties for managing all or part of the task to a different member each year. Some, moreover, view that rotation as taking place in a very regular fashion, mapped out well in advance, so that commissioners would have sole responsibility in their year and would know the years for which they could seek other offices;[89] they suggest that colonial triumvirates customarily had functioned in the same way.[90] But members of the governing elite probably would never have committed themselves to a scheme so rigid that it would interfere with the ability of the senate to extend the command of a successful governor or with the desire of an influential Roman to seek higher office when circumstances seemed right.

What did Appian mean? The crucial phrase can be made to refer to annual elections only with difficulty, and the length of their term, then, is a matter for speculation.[91] Since the membership of the commission did not change each year, Appian must have intended to describe some other change or exchange, and his use of the passive or the middle voice indicates that the commissioners were the subjects of their own actions or those of others. If the personnel of the college did not change yearly, the most likely explanation is that their internal arrangements did, for the commissioners were not all available at all times. Yet if the triumvirs exchanged tasks among themselves, they need not have done so in a fixed rotation. More likely, they would have made arrangements so as to adjust to the success of the commissioners in any particular election. Depending on those results, each year those available for service would have decided among themselves how to proceed.[92]

The college that founded Iunonia provides a clear example of the way the reformers shared responsibilities when some were holding other posts. Although it shared members with the main Gracchan commission, that triumvirate, elected as a result of the *lex Rubria* of 123, was legally separate from it.[93] Only two of the three commissioners are known. C. Gracchus was chosen while tribune for 123; he would found Carthage as triumvir in the next year, while serving again as tribune. M. Fulvius Flaccus was elected colonial commissioner not long after his return from his province and his subsequent triumph; he also would serve as tribune in 122. In this college, at least two of the three members were in another office in the year the colony was founded. At least one was so serving in the year the law was passed.

Appian and Plutarch provide the bulk of the evidence for the way the foundation proceeded. According to Plutarch (*CG* 11), having been chosen by lot, Gracchus sailed to Africa, where various portents associated with the foundation of the city took place. Gracchus completed his task in seventy days and returned to help Flaccus against Drusus. Appian's version (*BC* 1.24–25) differs substantially. Both having been chosen tribune for 122, Gracchus and Flaccus sailed to Carthage where they marked out the city on the place Scipio Aemilianus had devoted to the gods and defined lands for six thousand colonists, more than the number fixed in the law. Then they returned to Rome and invited colonists to enlist from all of Italy. Shortly afterward, Gracchus and Flaccus were killed.

The accounts imply at least two separate trips to Carthage, for the performance of the rites of foundation required that the enlistment of the settlers had already been completed, and that, according to Appian, took place only after the land had been surveyed and marked, revealing the amount available for distribution and thus the number of settlers needed to fill it. Such a process clearly must be distinguished from mid-republican practice, in which the number of colonists was fixed by the law (as the *lex Rubria*, traditional in form, did), but the size of the allotments was determined on the scene, after measuring the land. The method adopted by the commissioners at Carthage, it should be noted, probably reflects the sequence of events adopted by the *triumviri lege Sempronia* to implement that law: determining the status of the land and measuring it, recruiting the settlers needed to fill it, and leading them there to receive their allotments.

One significant difference between the two versions allows the way the triumvirs fit those journeys around their other responsibilities to be determined. Plutarch and Appian seemingly disagreed on the number of commissioners who went to Africa. For the former, Gracchus alone made the journey (he was chosen by lot to do so), while Flaccus remained in Rome to counter their enemy, M. Livius Drusus, a tribune of 122. Appian, on the other hand, had them make the trip together while both were serving as tribunes. Appian's version would have left Drusus essentially unopposed for an extended period of time; for that reason alone, Plutarch's account is more probable. But if C. Gracchus traveled alone to Carthage in 122, that does not prevent Flaccus from having made a separate voyage earlier; Appian may have represented Flaccus and Gracchus as going together because he or his source knew that both had gone to the site.

Appian and Plutarch, however, noted the completion of different elements in the colonizing process, corresponding to the two trips made to the site. Plutarch's report consists largely of a series of portents connected closely with the ceremonial foundation of a colony, rites requiring the presence of the colonists.[94] Plutarch described no event that clearly formed part of the centuriation of the land, and the time Gracchus spent in the area, seventy days, would have been too short for extensive activities of that sort. The rituals of foundation, then, must have been followed quickly by the assignment of plots to the settlers and the appointment of the colonial magistrates. Livy (*Per.* 60), or his epitomator, supports Plutarch's account, for he claimed that the younger Gracchus led out the colony.

Appian's version focused on the division of land. Going to Africa, the two commissioners first set aside the place for the city, and then they surveyed and marked fields sufficient for six thousand colonists. Returning to Rome, the two triumvirs began to recruit colonists, but reports arrived from those surveying the fields of unfavorable omens. Finally, the two met their deaths. Appian mentioned neither the transportation of settlers to Africa, nor the ceremonies of the foundation, nor the assignment of lands — indeed, the account leads directly from the beginning of enlistment to the struggle that resulted in the final act of violence. Yet the agrarian law of 111 reveals that lands actually were assigned, so that the triumvirs did recruit and transport colonists, and they probably did perform the ceremonies of foundation.[95]

Thus, the narratives of Plutarch and Appian largely are complementary. The former wrote of the foundation rites of the city, and the latter mentioned only an initial inspection of the territory and its division into individual plots. At some time not long after the passage of the *lex Rubria*, then, the commissioners (or at least two of the three) divided by lot the overall task among themselves in Rome. Flaccus was the first commissioner required to act. Probably relatively late in 123, he went to Africa with the necessary surveyors, attendants, and advisors, inspected the territory, chose the spot for the city, and located the fields in relation to it. Then, he started the process of centuriation, taking the auspices and performing the proper initial acts. In earlier colonies, the authorizing legislation fixed the number of settlers, and the commissioners determined the size of the allotments by comparing that number with the amount of land available.[96] At Carthage, however, the triumvirs ignored the limit set by law and determined the number of settlers to be recruited only after ascertaining the number of lots of a certain size that could be established. After the completion of enlistment, probably in Rome according to the traditional procedures, C. Gracchus then led the settlers to Africa in 122.[97] There, he would have purified the colonists in a *lustrum*, plowed the *sulcus primigenius*, and given the community its governing law and its first magistrates and priests. In the same seventy-day period, Gracchus probably also assigned portions by lot, through a long series of meetings with the colonists, en masse and in smaller groups, in the civic spaces of Iunonia. The whereabouts of the third commissioner during all of this are unknown.

At the colony of Iunonia, therefore, the triumvirs arranged the survey and the actual installation of settlers from the beginning as essentially autonomous elements involving separate journeys to the site by a single commissioner accompanied by different individuals. Such an arrangement clearly contrasts with the procedures followed by earlier triumvirates: those commissioners set out in a body with the necessary attendants and surveyors and with the settlers themselves.[98]

According to custom, colleagues shared certain defined powers, obligations, and privileges.[99] Thus, all those serving as consul, praetor, curule aedile, plebeian aedile, tribune of the plebs, or quaestor could perform the same range of functions proper to their office, and each had the right to the costumes and attendants appropriate to their ranks. Yet in practice, and without affecting the potential of the post, those holding a single office often performed different tasks at separate locations. Thus, the senate established the consular or praetorian provinces for a year, while the casting of lots determined which consul or praetor would hold each (and the quaestor who would accompany them).

In other cases, colleagues shared responsibility for the performance of one task. The two censors supervised the census, which took place under their leadership in Rome itself. Among special commissions, moreover, a single colonial commission could found one colony, while one duumvirate could place the contract for construction or dedicate a temple. Yet the Romans intended essential elements of any project to be led by a single individual.[100] Although their colleagues may have been present, only one magistrate took the auspices before a public act, only one colonial commissioner plowed the primeval furrow, only one tribune presided over a meeting of the *concilium plebis*, and only one censor or quaestor presided over a public auction. The presidency over a single, restricted element in a larger task could be assigned in various ways. Consuls who had combined their armies rotated daily in command as long as their armies remained together. In other cases, the official who would lead for one restricted task could be determined by mutual agreement (*comparatio*) or by lot (*sortitio*); Varro (*LL* 6.86–87) noted that the two censors cast lots on the morning of the *lustrum* to see which would preside over the day's ceremony. It is easy to envisage mid-republican colonial commissioners doing the same for the ceremonies of the *deductio* or those beginning centuriation.

Yet the commission that founded Carthage followed a procedure that conforms fully to neither model. Unlike the governors of provinces, the triumvirs established by the Rubrian law shared in the performance of one task, the establishment of a single colony. Unlike other colleges that had only one project, all of those commissioners were not present (or nearby) through all or most of the crucial stages of the effort. Instead, they broke a single task into distinct elements and treated each as if it were separate. Thus, when Gracchus received by lot the performance of the ceremonies of foundation, he gained along with it the responsibility for leading the colonists to Carthage and probably also the duty of distributing plots to each. The same sortition, on the other hand, would have assigned to Flaccus the performances associated with the beginning of centuriation, which would carry with it supervision of the entire survey. This arrangement, probably set by mutual agreement rather than by law, would allow the triumvirs to perform easily other tasks, some not closely connected with their duties as commissioners.

Although the arrangements at Carthage conceivably could have been developed just for the occasion, it is more likely that the commissioners used at that colony practices evolved for the main commission. In the countryside, the implementation of the reform would have fallen into two stages: commissioners had to determine the status of lands, survey them, and begin the process of preparing sections to receive settlers. Since the commissioners could not have predicted the amount of land available in a given area until the survey had begun, it is likely the settlers were not recruited until this procedure was well advanced. Several commissioners may have been simultaneously engaged in surveying, but in different areas, or one or more commissioners may have surveyed, while another triumvir settled *coloni* on land prepared at an earlier time.[101] Whatever the division of labor the Gracchan commissioners actually used, the necessary arrangements could not have been formed far in advance. The task established by the *lex Sempronia* was too complex for its course to be predicted. During the work, moreover, the ambitions and the opportunities of the triumvirs would be subject to change. At the same time, because of the replacements made necessary by death, new commissioners at different stages of their careers would have to be accommodated. It is possible, moreover, that different portions of the task — surveying and settlement — would have fluctuated in importance at various times. Because of the length of time and the complexity of the project, adjustments in the division of labor would have to be made from time to time, perhaps yearly; the meaning of Appian's cryptic phrase may lie here.

That process of dividing a single project into a number of semiautonomous sections would be widely followed in the following century, but with a significant difference.[102] In the implementation of the Gracchan laws, an elected official of the Roman state managed each segment, but increasingly over the course of the first century nonmagisterial and even nonsenatorial actors would be given managerial roles. It is possible, although unlikely, that C. Gracchus and his allies did the same. Appian (*BC* 1.24) reported that "those still marking lines through the city in Africa" sent word to Rome of the prodigy of the wolves, after Flaccus (and, for Appian, Gracchus also) had returned to Rome. Who, then, were those marking land in Africa and who was in charge? Conceivably, the unknown third commissioner had accompanied Flaccus to the area and had remained while his colleague returned to Rome. On the other hand, could Flaccus have performed the necessary beginning ceremonies and then left after leaving instructions to delegates?

That possibility of delegation depends on the accuracy of Appian's account, and here the signs are not favorable. Appian's brief statement forms an element in the process by which the omens at Carthage were used to undermine the validity of the foundation, for it explains the source of the reports to the senate and the augurs. Appian portrayed the receipt of the message as leading immediately to the senate's decision to negate the colonization, followed shortly by the death of Gracchus and Flaccus. Yet Appian left out the foundation of the settlement and the distribution of lands (which would have required the completion of centuriation). Given the way he constructed his narrative, for him there were no colonists on the scene to send the report, and there was no action that the portents could call into question but the survey; his claim that those measuring the land had sent the report may have been no more than speculation.[103]

V. CONCLUSION

The Gracchan reform altered the traditional system by which public lands were exploited. To achieve results on a larger scale than previously had been attempted, Ti. Gracchus and his allies framed an unusually complex law that combined categories of legislation hitherto separate and created a special commission to administer them. But while the reformers and their successors assigned officials larger tasks and new configurations of powers, these powers were customary and were exercised in the traditional ways. In other words, there were only minor administrative innovations, made de facto not de jure; the legislators attempted to make no structural changes in government.

TOWARD THE PRINCIPATE

The formulation, proposal, and passage of legislation covering public lands did not end with the Gracchan reform, for agrarian laws were a common feature of the political struggles of the last century of the republic. The originators of some later projects constructed measures considerably more complex than earlier laws, even those associated with the Gracchan reform. Although specific provisions and their place in the whole are often obscure, those who drafted authorizing legislation combined previously distinct elements even more freely than did Ti. Gracchus, apparently set forth many exceptions and qualifications and provided more detailed instructions than earlier laws, and may have attempted to achieve a higher degree of standardization in the internal arrangements of the communities that were to result from their actions than previously was the case. For our purposes, a continuous history of the legislation, detailed reconstructions of each law or program, in-depth explications of the political contexts, and thorough explorations of the attempts at implementation are unnecessary. Instead, the aim is to provide a broad overview of the forms encompassed within the laws along with a closer examination of some aspects of administration that clarify continuities and show new developments.

I. THE PROJECTS OF THE FIRST CENTURY

After the death of C. Gracchus, the political, social, and economic context of agrarian legislation grew more complex. In the following century, reforming tribunes, like the Gracchi, proposed and sometimes carried laws intended to resolve what they saw as some of the major problems of their day. In the same period, however, a series of great commanders increasingly came to dominate Roman political life. Sometimes they acted in a manner that seemingly did not differ greatly from a typical republican leader, forming alliances with fellow senators, speaking in the senate and in popular assemblies, campaigning for office, and performing the duties of the posts they had gained. On other occasions, however, they used agents, sometimes themselves senators, or led or threatened to lead their armies or veterans of their armies against their opponents in the city. The interests of these generals permeated much of the agrarian legislation of the time.

The Gracchan laws ended the rigid separation of categories found in mid-republican legislation. Like the Gracchi, late republican legislators felt free to combine elements earlier kept distinct, but again like the Gracchi they followed in very broad outline the patterns found in earlier legislation: laws instructed magistrates to perform certain operations, they created special posts to which they assigned various powers and functions, they named, often rather generally, the areas to be used, and they identified the intended beneficiaries more or less precisely. Much of the complexity of the legislation is due to the ways in which the framers sought to achieve these ends, while balancing them with other concerns.

In the middle republic, the most common form of law ordered the distribution of land to settlers either in colonies or viritane assignments and specified closely the lands it covered, identifying named tracts in Italy. (Rules *de modo agrorum* covered all lands in Italy of a certain legal type.) The framers of late republican laws followed the same broad pattern, although they tended to define their areas broadly, as did the Gracchi, and often intended that the veterans of the major commanders be the main (or only) beneficiaries. Laws carried by L. Appuleius Saturninus during his terms as tribune in 103 and 100 gave plots in Africa to Marius's veterans and ordered the division of land taken by Marius in Gaul, along with more in Sicily, Achaea, and Macedonia — some settlers, at least, were to be installed in colonies.[1] Almost a decade later, M. Livius Drusus, tribune of the plebs in 91 and the son of the tribune of 122, proposed to lead several colonies to sites in Italy and Sicily.[2]

Pompey sought for many years to secure the passage of laws providing lands for his veterans.³ In 70, one tribune, a Plotius or Plautius, proposed a law giving land to soldiers of Pompey and Metellus Pius returning from the war against Sertorius in Spain, and in 60, another, L. Flavius, attempted unsuccessfully to carry a measure providing for the veterans of Pompey's eastern wars, although he modified it to permit assignments to be made to citizens in general in order to increase the chances of passage.⁴ Pompey's efforts were successful in 59, as a result of his combination with Caesar and M. Licinius Crassus in the so-called First Triumvirate. Caesar secured the passage of a consular law (not the more common plebiscite) instructing that public land in Italy, with the exception of a specific region, the *ager Campanus*, be divided among the citizens, not just veterans (to reduce opportunities for censure).⁵ Later in the same year, Caesar carried a supplementary law that opened the *ager Campanus* and the neighboring *campus Stellas* to distribution to citizens with three or more children, probably as part of a colonial foundation.⁶

Ti. Gracchus attempted to find land for his distributions by recovering public lands that were being used unofficially by private citizens, but the difficulties involved in that project led his brother to propose that some *coloni* receive plots outside of Italy. Like the younger Gracchus, later legislators occasionally turned to tracts outside the peninsula.⁷ But some wished to grant land closer to Rome, perhaps because they intended to rely on the beneficiaries for direct political and military assistance. To provide lands in Italy, they used another expedient: the purchase of private lands with public funds. Such an operation had precedents. In 166 or 165, P. Cornelius Lentulus purchased lands in Campania to create a large block to be leased (not distributed);⁸ because of his reputation for rectitude, the landowners conceded to him the right to set the price. To purchase lands, legislators had to identify the source of the money, and they occasionally set forth the means for determining the price. The second of Saturninus's laws ordered that funds collected from Q. Servilius Caepio as a result of the affair of the gold of Tolosa be used for the purpose.⁹ The first *lex Iulia agraria* of 59 instructed that additional lands be made available through purchase from those willing to sell; the value the owners had declared for the property on the census lists would determine the price and the money would come from the booty taken by Pompey and from the tribute he had imposed on the defeated.¹⁰

These measures were proposed and sometimes carried in times of domestic peace at Rome, but others were put forward during periods of open civil war, when the contestants often were in great need of money and land for their veterans. Again these efforts had their roots in legislation, but under the force of circumstances, their actions display a mixture of the customary with various ad hoc remedies designed to resolve difficulties of the moment.[11] To reward their followers while punishing and weakening potential or actual sources of opposition, Sulla, Mark Antony, Octavian, and Lepidus resorted to confiscations on a large scale, sometimes from individuals and at other times from entire communities, taking care to claim that the lands had become public because of criminal conduct by its previous owners, according to the rules of Roman law. Despite these irregular methods, they used many of the customary forms — colonies, viritane assignments, sale, and lease — to turn property to their ends.[12]

One ultimately unsuccessful measure illustrates the complexity possible in a late republican land law. P. Servilius Rullus put forward an unusual and complicated law while tribune of the plebs in 63 — the only measure of this decade not clearly associated with Pompey's agenda.[13] The details of the *rogatio Servilia agraria* are known only through Cicero's attacks against the measure, a very uncertain source. In the course of three orations delivered while serving as consul, Cicero made many assertions about the contents of the law and quoted, or claimed to quote, directly from the text. Yet the details of the law have proven difficult to reconstruct. Cicero's characterization of the proposal is clearly tendentious, and at least some of the purported provisions are certainly misrepresentations. At times, too, Cicero blurred the distinction between provisions actually in the law and those that he claimed Rullus would put in later. Still the broad outlines of the measure are reasonably clear.[14]

Rullus assigned to the officials he wished to create an extensive and complex task, more so even than the *triumviri lege Sempronia* of 133 received, for they were to sell lands and place contracts to collect revenues, purchase tracts for distribution, found colonies, and make viritane assignments. In the law, Rullus set forth extensive instructions, sometimes identifying areas and potential sources of funds precisely and at other times in a more general manner. To raise money, for example, he ordained the sale of all things not yet sold among those whose sale the senate had authorized during the consulship of M. Tullius and Cn. Cornelius (81); of those lands, places, and buildings outside of Italy that had become public during the consulship of L. Sulla and Q. Pompeius (88); of the property to be confiscated by Pompey, campaigning in the East at the time; and of certain public revenues identified by name.[15]

The ultimate goal of Rullus's project was to place settlers on the land. His officials apparently were expected to use the funds they had raised to purchase lands in Italy for distribution at whatever price the owners set.[16]

Cicero (*Agr.* 1.6.17), claiming to quote the exact wording of the law, asserted that it instructed officials to settle *coloni* in whatever colonies and *municipia* they wished and to assign them lands wherever they wanted (in his own voice Cicero indicated that this was to take place in Italy); more specifically, Cicero also held that the measure ordered five thousand colonists to be installed at Capua and in the *campus Stellas*.[17]

II. ADMINISTRATIVE PROCEDURES

Those who framed laws and designed projects, then, included the traditional forms of exploitation and the necessary elements and definitions, although they combined freely and defined broadly. In attempting to achieve their goals, moreover, they did not eliminate the older administrative system nor did they seek to transform it on a large scale. Instead, they made adjustments to increase its efficacy or to adapt it to political conditions.

Special commissions customarily managed the assignment of lands to individuals. Unlike the mid-republican practice, where colleges came in a restricted range of sizes determined by the task—triumvirs founded colonies and decemvirs made viritane assignments—the commissions created by later legislation varied greatly in size and in powers. One of Saturninus's laws created a special commission of ten with judicial powers (*decemvir agris dandis adtribuendis iudicandis*).[18] The younger Drusus provided for another decemvirate, but one without judicial powers (*Xvir agris dandis adsignandis*), and he served as *Vvir agris dandis adsignandis* under the terms of an otherwise unknown *lex Saufeia*.[19] *Quinqueviri* may also have managed some of Sulla's distributions.[20] Rullus's project centered on a commission of ten which was to possess judicial powers and praetorian *imperium* for five years.[21] The first *lex Iulia* of 59 assigned responsibility for purchasing lands for distribution and settling *coloni* to a commission of twenty, and some members also belonged to a special commission of five (*Vvir a(gris) d(andis) a(dsignandis) i(udicandis)*) with judicial powers;[22] the relationship between these two colleges is obscure, but the framers probably created the college of five as a legally defined subcommittee or as an adjunct to the commission of twenty to identify and perhaps purchase lands for distribution.[23] In 44, the consuls Mark Antony and Dolabella carried a law creating a commission of seven to divide land among veterans and needy citizens.[24]

Legislators and administrators expected that operations would proceed through the necessary sequences of formal actions. In those cases where attempts to implement the measures actually were made, the responsible officials seemingly did so. According to Cicero (*Agr.* 2.12.31), Rullus provided his commissioners with the auspices needed for the founding of colonies and with the *pullarius* who kept the chickens necessary to auspication. Mark Antony personally directed the *lustrum* and plowed the furrow for the colony at Casilinum in 44.[25] The *XXviri* of 59 were collectively responsible for the formal foundation of the colony at Capua, although all need not have been present, and some supervised the division and assignment of lands on the scene.[26] By law, they omitted one formal element: the vigintivirs were permitted to distribute plots in the *ager Campanus* and the *campus Stellas* without the casting of lots (*extra sortem*), perhaps to allow many veterans to be settled in one place or to permit them to receive allotments before other citizens.[27] L. Decidius Saxa, probably a *septemvir* serving under the *lex Antonia agraria* of 44, participated in the measuring and marking of land for distribution.[28] Auctions also followed the proper forms, although there could be considerable freedom of choice over the place and time. According to Plutarch (*Sull.* 33), Sulla presided over sales from his tribunal, while Dio (47.14.5) held that the Triumvirs sold property of the proscribed in the same way. Cicero (*Agr.* 2.20.55) reported that Rullus's proposal permitted its decemvirs to sell land and public revenues—which Cicero pictured as taking place in auctions *sub hasta*—wherever they wished, rather than at Rome or some other specific location.

Even when legislators intended to depart from custom, they adapted traditional gatherings to accomplish the task. Rullus wished to elect his *decemviri agris dandis adsignandis iudicandis* in an unusual way. Consuls or praetors regularly supervised the elections of the members of earlier colleges. Like Ti. Gracchus, Rullus intended that an assembly under his own presidency choose the decemvirs. But this gathering was not to be a normal meeting of the *concilium plebis*; only seventeen of the thirty-five tribes would actually vote, using the same procedures found in the election of the *pontifex maximus*.[29] As a result of a change that took place sometime in the third century, a *minors pars populi*, seventeen tribes chosen by lot just before the vote, elected the chief pontiff; as a result of the *lex Domitia* of 104 this procedure was extended to cover the elections for other positions in the major priestly colleges, the members of which had previously recruited replacements through co-optation.[30]

In some projects, movement away from magistrates and toward delegation of responsibilities took place. Some late republican *leges rogatae* and *datae* are vague about the official status of those who would perform or had performed essential operations. Thus, the *lex Mamilia, Roscia, Peducaea, Alliena, Fabia*, sometimes called the *lex Iulia agraria*, identified those who were to establish settlements under its authority as "he who shall found [*deduxerit*] colonies and constitute [*constituerit*] *municipia, praefecturae, fora, conciliabula*"—on other occasions it used the equally general *curator*—and proceeded to give them instructions concerning the marking of fields and other matters.³¹ The agrarian law of 111, on the other hand, identified clearly by office those who had performed or were expected to perform certain operations: censors, praetors, *IIIviri lege Sempronia*, the otherwise unknown *Xviri lege Livia*, and the *IIviri* the law itself created.³² The first-century legislator may have intended the vagueness of his terms, when contrasted with the precision found in earlier measures, to cover nonmagistrates delegated certain functions. Such delegation certainly did occur. The framers of the *lex data* governing the Caesarian colony of Urso (44) clearly distinguished between Caesar, who made or could make the decisions appropriate to a *deductor* and may have retained the title, and the individual who actually founded the colony.³³

The construction of chains of command through a process of delegation was a feature of late republican political life. In the last century of the republic, the great commanders increasingly turned to the use of agents, generally legates of senatorial rank, to maintain control over far-flung military operations and large-scale projects of other kinds, such as the grain supply of Rome and extensive distributions of land.³⁴ When seeking to provide for their veterans, these military leaders and their allies often used the established structure of their armies to provide the necessary delegates. While he may have used special commissions on occasion, Sulla probably also had his legates lead soldiers to the towns he had designated, for his veterans were settled in their military units.³⁵ Like Sulla, Caesar, Brutus, Octavian, and Mark Antony also attempted to make large-scale distributions in colonies and viritane assignments possible by resorting to legates and prefects.³⁶

The use of agents in that way allowed the absent leader to maintain a personal link to the settlement and ensure that the project remained in the hands of those loyal to him or under his influence. Antony's supporters held that those who founded colonies for his legions should be his friends, not those of Octavian, while the law of Urso instructed that Caesar and the actual founder—"he who had the right of giving and assigning lands to colonists under the *lex Iulia* and he who would establish the colony"— were the colony's only permissible patrons.³⁷ Indeed, the use of delegates allowed the individual under whose auspices they operated to put himself in the role of *deductor*. Augustus (*Res Gestae* 3, 28) claimed to have led out to colonies or assigned fields elsewhere to 300,000 veterans, founding twenty-eight colonies in Italy and throughout the Mediterranean world. A *denarius* minted after the Perusine War by the moneyer and quaestor designate Ti. Sempronius Gracchus carried the portrait of Octavian on the obverse along with a standard (*vexillum*), a military standard (*aquila*), the plow to mark the furrow, and a *decempeda* to measure the land, all references to the settlement program, while another *denarius* of Octavian, minted in the years 29–27, shows him in the appropriate dress plowing the *sulcus primigenius*.[38] Augustus's successors also took the title of *conditor coloniae* for those settlements founded under their auspices.[39]

The consistent use of delegates allowed those in ultimate authority to control the outlines of a project and maintain that they were the true founders and thus the settlers' proper patrons. At the beginning of such a shift, there could have been much ambiguity over the identity of the benefactor. Perhaps for that reason, Caesar apparently chose in advance of the actual foundation (and perhaps proclaimed publicly) those who would be the first magistrates, priests, and decurions of his colonies, allowing the actual founder only to make the formal installation.[40] Like Caesar, Octavian occasionally wished to maintain a closer personal connection to the process of assignment. While reporting the maneuvers immediately before and during the Perusine War, Appian (*BC* 5.19, 5.16) noted that Octavian personally dispatched colonists to their sites and that on one occasion he summoned soldiers into his presence in the *campus Martius* for the division of land.[41] There, he allowed those who thought themselves especially deserving to ask him directly for special rewards, which on some occasions he granted, while he gave the undeserving less than they expected; the *Liber coloniarum I* (p. 232L) confirms that Octavian did allot lands to veterans according to achievement under arms (*pro merito*). Dio (51.4.5) reported that Octavian also allocated land at Brundisium, to which veterans were summoned in the winter of 31/30. In the first, and probably at the second, Octavian determined for each veteran the amount of land he would obtain at the colony to which he would be sent, but the assignment of specific plots probably was made by others at the site.[42]

It is not clear how much this direct personal connection between Octavian and the granting of lands to his soldiers was his customary practice. Appian's and Dio's assemblies both took place at crucial moments when Octavian may have been eager to emphasize to his soldiers that he was indeed their benefactor. Appian placed his descriptions against the background of the impending Perusine War and he noted that the assembly on the *campus Martius* took place in an atmosphere of open violence—Suetonius (*Aug.* 14) reported that Octavian almost lost his life in it—and Dio's gathering occurred just after the battle of Actium. In such moments, Octavian may have adapted a traditional form for his meetings with the soldiers. The procedure by which he granted lands on the basis of merit may have resembled other formal public occasions following military action, in which commanders publicly praised and rewarded or castigated and punished soldiers for their behavior.[43]

Such a use of agents to make possible wider action than a single magistrate or college of magistrates could achieve was not limited to projects framed in time of civil war. The *rogatio Servilia agraria* also experimented with delegation. In that measure, Rullus established for his decemvirs a range of tasks apparently without precedent in earlier legislation and permitted them to act over an extensive area; indeed, Cicero sometimes characterized certain provisions as applying wherever the commissioners saw fit, or as covering all lands outside Italy that had become public by a certain date.[44] To make the management of such a large and complex project practicable and plausible, Rullus proposed letting the decemvirs delegate certain functions. According to Cicero (*Agr.* 2.13.34), the law empowered the commissioners to yield certain tasks or powers to the quaestors; Cicero did not specify what operations could be transferred from one magistrate to another but, in the context of the law and of Cicero's passage, the sale of properties or revenues or the actual collection or storage of funds is most likely.[45] Rullus's magistrates, then, could have used other regularly elected officials as assistants.

The delegation of other functions, however, was of greater significance for future developments. In the field, each decemvir was permitted and perhaps expected to work independently. The same approach that the *IIIviri lege Sempronia* took extralegally here was authorized by law.[46] In addition, among the necessary *apparitores*— *scribae, librarii, praecones*, and *architecti*— the law gave to the college two hundred surveyors or *finitores*, assigning twenty to each commissioner.[47] Under certain conditions, these *finitores* could operate without the presence of an elected official. According to Cicero, the law permitted a single decemvir to dispatch a single surveyor to perform some task, and after completing it, to report formally to the decemvir who had sent him, who presumably would confirm the action.[48] In these operations, then, the law allowed the ten commissioners to work in ten separate areas. It permitted each to send their twenty surveyors to twenty different places in the vicinity. Under the *rogatio Servilia agraria*, the ten primary actors would be supplemented by two hundred in the field.

Changes in the legal position of the officiant in ceremonies would have carried with them shifts in form. The foundation of colonies, for example, was closely connected with the auspices and with augural practice: major parts began with the taking of the auspices, and the creation of an inaugurated zone, the *pomerium*, was a defining element in the foundation. Cicero (*Agr.* 2.12.31) reported that a special form of the auspices was required for magistrates who wished to found colonies, and while the formal *deductores* may have had the right to use them, their agents, operating only under the auspices of their leader, would not have been able to take them (or any others) at the site. Romulus founded Rome as *rex* and *augur*, and colonial triumvirs in some fashion replicated this mixture of roles; the fictions and reinterpretations that enabled legates to create inaugurated zones such as the *pomerium* when they did not possess the auspices are unknown. The changes, however, would not have meant an end to rituals of divination, only a shift in their form. The use of delegates so common in certain aspects of late republican political life resulted in some movement away from the auspices.[49] Instead, assisted by *haruspices*, the commanders of detached military forces, and perhaps also those who actually installed colonists, would have ascertained the will of the gods through the inspection of the entrails of sacrificed animals, a method not tied to tenure in a magistracy.[50] Despite their apparent conservatism, Roman religious practices did allow for adjustments.

III. THE "RATIONALIZATION" OF THE PROCESS

On closer examination, the process of delegation proves quite complex. In the implementation of agrarian legislation, innovation in administration was not limited to a simple substitution of one or more agents to act on the scene for a distant magistrate. Instead, those directing operations showed a marked tendency to divide the overall administrative process into a number of semiautonomous elements, each of which could be managed by different individuals or groups. Here, the Gracchan triumvirs had made the first step. In the middle republic, commissioners together first recruited settlers, then led them to the site in a body, prepared lands, installed *coloni*, and gave them their land. One of the Gracchan triumvirs, however, first prepared the site, having traveled there with his attendants. Then, one or more commissioners recruited settlers. Finally, a single triumvir led the intended recipients to the site, gave them their lands, and created their government. Some late republican projects were arranged in the same way, allowing a more efficient use of time and permitting a greater scale of activity.

One case provides an interesting illustration of the way a single element, or indeed a single performance, could be divorced from other parts of the process. In late April 44, while serving as consul, Mark Antony personally performed the colonial *lustrum* and established the *pomerium* at Casilinum shortly after Caesar's death, yet his participation was limited, for he spent around two weeks at the place before leaving.[51] Clearly Antony did not supervise in any direct way the centuriation of the land and the actual installation of settlers. Instead, Mark Antony, who visited Casilinum and participated in its foundation while attempting to secure support in the army after Caesar's murder, probably merely performed one of the most prominent rituals of the foundation, divorced from participation in other aspects of the settlement.[52]

At the same time, and associated with this process of definition and separation, other actors markedly lower in status came to have an important role in administrative processes. The Gracchan commissioners continued to have a magistrate, one of the members of the college, manage each stage, while later supervisors resorted to delegates. Mid-republican triumvirates and decemvirates included many senior senators—half of all known commissioners had held the office of consul or praetor—some who had only held lesser posts, and probably others who had not yet gained any office.[53] At least some of the late republican commissions probably followed the same general pattern. The *XXviri* and *Vviri* established by the Julian agrarian law of 59, for example, certainly overlapped in their membership:[54] C. Cosconius (pr. 63) served on both boards, and M. Valerius Messala (cos. 61) may have also. Two members of the First Triumvirate, Cn. Pompeius Magnus and M. Licinius Crassus were *vigintiviri* along with M. Attius Balbus (pr. by 59), and M. Terentius Varro and Cn. Tremellius Scrofa (both praetors at an unknown date);[55] some may also have been *quinqueviri*. L. Decidius Saxa, probably a *septemvir* under a law carried by Antony and Dolabella in 44, served as tribune of the plebs in the same year.[56]

Many of those used as agents occupied a similar social position or one rather close to it.[57] Ti. Claudius Nero (the father of the future emperor), who had distinguished himself as quaestor, founded colonies for Caesar at Narbo and Arelate in Gaul, Q. Hortensius (pr. 45?) founded some for Brutus, and L. Memmius, who probably had served as tribune of the plebs settled two legions at Luca in 42.[58] In 45 and 44, Q. Valerius Orca (pr. 57), *legatus pro praetore*, operated in the territory of Volaterra, while L. Plotius Plancus (who would become praetor in 43) assigned lands in the territory of Buthrotum in Epirus with C. Ateius Capito and C. Cupiennus, whose status is uncertain.[59] A few years later, C. Asinius Pollio (pr. 45), P. Alfenus

Varus (possibly a praetorian), and C. Cornelius Gallus (who may not have been a senator) as legates distributed lands beyond the Po, in the process confiscating the estates of Vergil's family.[60]

Those agents, prominent members of their leaders' circles, supervised the confiscation of lands and their centuriation, the foundation of colonies, and the installation of veterans. In the middle republic, settlers enlisted at Rome gathered at a designated place and time, and the founding magistrates led them to the site as a group. Soldiers who were to receive lands in the 40s and 30s were led to the site in formal groups, but magistrates or legates who installed the settlers did not necessarily assemble them or lead them there.[61] Veterans either remained or gathered in military units and their commanders may have provided the necessary leadership: some of Caesar's veterans were encamped in temples and sacred precincts in Rome at the time of his death, waiting to be led to their colony "under one standard" by a single individual assigned the task.[62] Perhaps on occasion the commanders of units or military tribunes serving under them conducted the soldiers to the site.

Leaders in the civil wars, then, regularly resorted to agents, some of senatorial rank and others who probably had risen to prominence through their military service — a qualification they had in common with many late and mid-republican senators. For certain tasks, on the other hand, commanders of armies and at least one legislator in more peaceful times turned to individuals who specifically were not to be senators, nor need they have possessed any aptitude for military leadership. In the middle republic, public roles formed the sphere of the senatorial order and its members generally possessed the ability to act in all appropriate areas. But in the course of the last republican century, some public functions increasingly were taken up by citizens of lesser rank. From the time of Gracchus, for example, members of the equestrian order occupied a prominent place on the juries that issued judgments in the standing courts, while some *equites* became experts in the law, a field previously the province of prominent members of the senatorial nobility.[63] In the administration of agrarian legislation, new actors increasingly appear, but not in roles that required them to gather colonists, lead them to the site, or install them on the land.

The two hundred surveyors to be created by the *rogatio Servilia* provide the clearest example. Cicero (*Agr.* 2.13.32) unfortunately did not make clear the nature of the tasks assigned to these *finitores*, but the very name of those functionaries indicates that their role involved the establishment of *fines*, either those marking the boundaries between public lands and private or the *limites* forming the networks needed as preparation for distribution, or both. In the passage just cited, Cicero primarily attacked the exercise of judicial powers—the right to determine which lands were public—by the decemvirs, which should indicate that the *finitores* also were permitted to do the same. But the surveyors may also have been able to supervise centuriation; Cicero was not defining the office of *finitor*, but was instead attacking what he wished to be seen as an opportunity for the arbitrary use of power, and here an emphasis on judicial activities would have been more appropriate.[64]

Rullus intended those surveyors to be neither of low social status nor in possession of a special technical skill. According to Cicero (*Agr.* 2.13.32), the two hundred *finitores* were to be chosen *ex equestri loco*. The exact meaning of that phrase is unclear, but those surveyors certainly were to be recruited from the *ordo* immediately below the senatorial, and eligibility may have been further restricted to a narrow group defined by a hereditary status—the sons or grandsons of those who possessed the public horse and were enrolled in the equestrian centuries.[65] Certainly Cicero presented the *finitores* in a way that implied that they had not achieved their status on their own and did not possess any special skill—on several occasions he stressed that they would be young, which would seemingly have precluded both;[66] their social position was more important than proven ability or experience. If they supervised centuriation, then, they would have directed, if only loosely, those who used the *groma* and the *decempeda*, following a well-defined pattern in the same way that mid-republican colonial commissioners did in the fields and military tribunes did in the camps.[67]

In at least one moment in their struggles, the Triumvirs used public contractors, rather than magistrates, legates, or prefects, to provide for centuriation. Early in his work, the compiler of *Liber coloniarum I* (pp. 211–13L) quoted at length what he identified as a law governing the limiting and measuring of lands in Etruria, Campania, and Apulia; among other things, provisions set forth the width of *kardines* and *decumani* and instructed that inscribed boundary stones be erected at certain points. Given in the proper forms of a *lex*, the text represents at least part of a *lex locationis*—it identifies the one who would implement the instructions as "he who will have the contract"—and its concluding lines give an approximate date, for they proclaim that Octavian, Mark Antony, and Lepidus ordered the work.[68]

Those *conductores* need not have been experts at the task they were managing. Supervision of the placement of the *limites* defining fields or the roads forming a camp—a task long managed by magistrates and not by professionals—need not have required great expertise, for those in charge worked according to a rigid and well-defined pattern; those who actually used the instruments, in other words, may have been the only ones who required any special skill. That *lex locationis*, moreover, is the only clear evidence that private contractors ever managed the installation of centuriation grids, and the passage in the *Liber coloniarum* only shows that it was used in Etruria, Campania, and Apulia;[69] the practice, then, need only have been used in these areas and perhaps only for a short time.

In later years, the supervision of centuriation or the marking of any boundaries for public land was not a matter for *publicani*. Writers on matters of surveying under the Empire found the origins of their art in those last years of the republic. The author of the late *Demonstratio artis geometricae* (p. 395L) held that a letter of Julius Caesar related to the origins of the skill. In the early years of the Principate surveying was rapidly organized as a formal profession with its own rules and hierarchies.[70] The title of surveyor covered a range of statuses from the simple user of the *groma* and *decempeda* to professionals of equestrian status, learned in geometry and the law and skilled in setting out boundaries and in measuring the area of enclosed spaces.

In their relations with those above them, these specialists followed knowingly or unknowingly the pattern Rullus had proposed for his surveyors in 63. Decemvirs dispatched Rullus's *finitores* and *conditores* and judges sent the later *agrimensores*, and both groups of agents reported their activities to the official who had sent them for confirmation. *Finitores* and *agrimensores* both received pay at regular rates from the state and were dispatched by the order of the emperor or some other competent authority — they were public functionaries rather than private contractors.[71] In fact, claiming it to have been the opinion for a long time, the jurist Ulpian (*Dig.* 11.6.1) held that there could be no contract of *locatio-conductio* with a *mensor*; although Ulpian's opinion was explicitly concerned only with surveyors working for private individuals, the same probably held true for those engaged in public business.

IV. CONCLUSION

In the late republic, there was a considerable amount of variation in the definition of projects dealing with public lands and in the combination of processes they required. From the time of the Gracchi, framers of legislation combined goals that earlier were separate and gave officials new arrays of powers. But they expected their administrators to perform the necessary functions through the customary operations, including the ceremonies that structured and symbolized them. Indeed, when they wished to perform some new task or an old one in a new way, the legislators and administrators adapted to that end a traditional form.

From an administrative perspective, the most important change, one that would be expanded in the imperial period, involved the introduction of new categories of actors to perform necessary operations. In the middle republic, magistrates—either those holding regular offices or those specially elected for the task—managed essential processes and led the proper rites, while in the late republic major administrative roles were occupied by nonmagistrates and even some who were not senators. This insertion of new actors involved the end of the unity of the settlement process, for parts could be assigned to a number of different agents, not all of the same social and political status. Some segments, including ones that involved dealing with the intended beneficiaries, were often managed by legates and prefects of senatorial rank. Others could be delegated to persons of lesser status, and here one clear result of the separation of the settlement process into distinct elements was the opening of space for the development of specialists. If the word "rationalization," when applied to matters of government, is taken to denote an organization of processes to permit greater efficiency, the delegation of authority resulting in chains of command, and the beginnings, at least, of some professionalization and specialization, then no matter how imperfectly each was achieved, late republican administration could be said to have begun to be rationalized.[72]

CONCLUSION

Roman government was largely a matter of rites and forms. Around offices clustered repertories of formal acts, of ritual occasions, some exclusive to one office, others shared by several or many. Certain rites were necessary, more were optional. Magistrates performed some at fixed times each year, while they arranged for others whenever the proper occasion arose. These ceremonial occasions were essential to the proper functioning of government. In some, divine approval was sought and the wrath of the gods averted. In others, magistrates mustered citizens into groups essential to larger operations, gave them necessary instructions, and led them through various operations. These collections of formal acts, moreover, not only set the proper form for official action, but they also helped form perceptions of processes, of social groups, and of spaces — all central to the passage and implementation of agrarian legislation.

That emphasis on proper form shaped both the laws that sought to regulate the use of public lands and the processes by which those measures were implemented. In the late third and early second centuries, the Romans possessed a system for exploiting public lands that was highly compartmentalized in conception and very formal in practice. Its roots may well lie at least a century earlier, at a time not long after the beginnings of the large-scale territorial expansion of the Roman state. Members of the elite who proposed projects or regulations were expected to accommodate them to one of a limited range of types and to include the necessary elements peculiar to the class, for each had its own ends, its own magistracies, and its own specific sequences of ceremonial acts. In most cases, those who initiated a project sought to turn a specific tract or adjacent tracts of land to a single use: the establishment of a colony, the making of viritane assignments, and the sale or lease of land. The framers of laws followed a basic pattern. At the most general level, they set the desired goal, identified the area the measure covered, indicated the officials who were to implement it, and ordained that they perform specific operations. Only the authors of laws *de modo agrorum* constructed rules that supposedly covered broad tracts of land, but they also identified the lands regulated by the *lex* (by legal category) and gave specific and limited tasks to the holders of a post.

In addition to those general features, each category of legislation had its own particular rules. Choosing from a limited range of options, the authors of colonial legislation set the number of settlements, their size, and legal status, and they also ordered a regular magistrate to secure the election of *tresviri coloniae deducendae*. The framers of laws aimed at making viritane assignments again identified the region and sometimes those eligible to receive land and also instructed that a special commission—*decemviri agris dandis adsignandis*—be chosen. Each category had not only its own magistracy, but also its own communal form, for while the new communities that resulted from the activities of the decemvirs may not have differed greatly in size from those founded by colonial commissioners, they varied markedly in their legal status and in the complexity of their constitutions.

The ways magistrates put forward, carried, and implemented laws was shaped by ritual, formula, and the rules and concepts (some explicitly religious in nature) that set forth the necessary operations and identified where, when, and how they must be performed. These officials were expected to operate in direct contact with those concerned, and many of those contacts, including the most important, were embedded in ceremonies. Thus, the officeholder who first brought forward a proposal, the occupant of a post possessing the right to call the senate into session, summoned senators to meet in one of the proper places as determined by augural rules, and the meeting of the senate, conducted according to the necessary procedures, resulted in a formal decree couched as a recommendation in the appropriate language. Then, the official designated by that decree, usually a tribune of the plebs, secured the necessary popular approval by summoning the people to meet in one of the major public spaces of Rome itself and there leading them through the proper rituals of the legislative assembly. The texts of the laws themselves were characterized by verbal patterns identical to those found in certain practices of the state religion, a reflection of the important role of priests as experts in public and private law.

The passage of the authorizing legislation was not the only part of the process conducted with ceremony in Rome itself. *Leges de modo agrorum* were implemented entirely through rites held there. The aediles who enforced the measure usually operated in the city and they summoned those accused to defend themselves, held the necessary preliminary meetings with the people, and conducted the resulting criminal trials before a popular assembly in the public spaces of Rome. Magistrates charged with recruiting settlers for colonies and viritane assignments operated in the same places and in the same fashion by summoning to them those interested in going. When land was to be sold or leased, the official in charge made the necessary contact with prospective purchasers or lessees again in a ceremonial public meeting held in a prominent public place, often in Rome itself.

In agrarian legislation, crucial elements of the administrative process took place at the site of the future colony or viritane assignment or on lands to be sold or leased. Officials charged with installing settlers or preparing lands for auction organized their activity through fixed chains of formal actions, and each method of exploitation possessed its own sequences of necessary rites. Ritual and formula were especially prominent in colonization and viritane assignments, which involved the formation of new communities, with their own governments, cults, and public spaces. In ceremonies in which they participated along with the settlers, colonial commissioners organized the system of religious and political spaces of the new city, formed the colonists into a citizenry, and assigned them their own magistrates, priests, laws, and territory. The definition of the colonial territory itself was accomplished formally, and the subdivision of a portion of that territory into numerous plots began in the same fashion. In ceremonies in the new city, moreover, officials formed groups of neighbors and matched them to specific tracts. Some of these features, such as the *urbs* and its complementary *ager* were not only established in rites but formed essential elements in a body of ritual knowledge. Viritane assignments probably proceeded through many similar stages.

Roman administration, then, involved the construction by various magistrates of sequences of ritualized actions, and Roman administrative science consisted in large part of a body of ceremonies to be deployed in the proper circumstances at the appropriate place and with the necessary people. Some rites, such as those involved in taking the auspices, were used in the same form as part of a very wide range of activities. Others were used in a limited number of projects. The formal auction could be used to place a range of government contracts and sell a variety of public property, while the *lustrum* could be used to purify and form the Roman citizen body, an army, or a group of colonists. Yet other ceremonies filled only one function: the plowing of the primeval furrow served to create the defining *pomerium* of an *urbs*.

In the system of government of the mid-republic, the number of individual actors who could arrange projects at any one time was limited, and the emphasis on direct and ceremonial action kept magistrates close to the projects they were managing and limited greatly the scale of activity. Those aediles who wished to prosecute violators of rules *de modo agrorum* were required to devote many popular meetings to the task, and as a result the number of violators who could be punished necessarily was limited. Officials who operated away from the city had even longer and more onerous tasks to perform, and the number of settlers they could install or the amount of land they could sell or lease again was limited. Regular magistrates with the *ius publicorum privatorum locorum*—consuls, praetors, and censors—were few in number, and as the chief officials of the state they had many more important duties. Even special commissions of three and ten included many senior senators with other responsibilities and goals.

Ti. Gracchus and his allies disrupted that collection of traditional practices and procedures. Unlike their predecessors, the reformers of 133 wished to make broad changes in the ways large segments of public land were used. To achieve results on a grand scale, they did not invent new forms or procedures but rather combined old ones in new ways. In practice, their program proved too difficult to administer, especially since those in possession of public lands did not cooperate as expected. Ti. Gracchus's younger brother Gaius, when tribune himself in 123, returned to a more conventional form of activity, emphasizing the foundation of a relatively few colonies.

Like the reforming tribune of 133, some later legislators also wished to achieve broader results than earlier practices had allowed. In their laws, they again combined previously distinct forms of exploitation and also defined special commissions in unprecedented sizes. In certain cases, however, the framers of laws or those for whom they were acting were more willing than the Gracchi to experiment with administration. They did not abandon the traditional operations, nor did they create new ones that were not also encompassed in ceremony. Instead, they introduced new, nonmagisterial actors to enable projects to be arranged at many locations simultaneously. In the process, they divided the long sequence of necessary formal acts into segments that could be assigned to different individuals and groups. Some remained the province of members of the senatorial order. Others were turned over to nonsenators, opening ground for later professionalization.

Although evidence is lacking, it is probable that the emphasis on the exact performance of those religious rites that formed essential parts of the administrative process declined. Ritual flaws in sacrifices, sortitions, and rites of divination served in the past to call into question the validity of those acts, as did those signs the gods sent in the course of governmental actions. In effect a check on magistrates who acted improperly, the same practice would have achieved a broader result in the changed conditions of the late republic. Rather than limiting or nullifying the deeds of one actor among many, a focus on formal flaws would have possessed the potential to disrupt the policies of the great dynasts of the age by requiring not only that they themselves perform ceremonies properly but that all their agents do so also. One would expect that reports of such faults would have been discouraged in the more controlled atmosphere created by the victors in civil wars to protect the image of the dynast and to prevent the failure of lesser officials from negating the programs of the greater.

Ceremonial appearances by magistrates, moreover, not only set the proper form for official action, but they also would have helped to form perceptions of government and of officials. Here, there were perhaps the beginnings of a more significant shift in the late republic, involving a potential change in the ways all concerned viewed the rites and the positions of those involved in them. Mid-republican ceremonial provided the necessary context for the contacts between public officials and those who were to be the subjects of their actions, the rites themselves formed part of broader administrative processes, and the performances focused on magistrates and elevated them above the other participants; the officiants, moreover, were the highest single human authority in their area of activity—beyond them were only collective groups, such as the senate and people, and the gods.

But in later settlements, a greater leader, one far away, dominated the proceedings, which were taking place at his orders and which often announced or confirmed decisions he had made. The official on the scene, ostensibly the focus of the rites, was only acting for another, and this circumstance may even have been openly acknowledged in some way during the ceremonies. With the benefactor separated from the actual grant of the benefaction, moreover, the tight link between the leaders in certain ceremonies and the actual administrators would have begun to loosen. Thus, Antony purified the colonists at Casilinum in 44 and established the colonial *pomerium*, certainly the most prominent of all the rituals involved in establishing a colony, but did little else to install the settlers, while Octavian inserted new forms, not strictly necessary for settlement, into the process to maintain personal contact with his veterans.

In the projects of the first century, then, the individual in ultimate authority grew farther away from the actual rites that had defined public office earlier, breaking the connection between political power, responsibility for forming policy, and leadership in ritual and separating specific ceremonies from the broader administrative process in which they had been embedded, creating a potential division between rites that elevated those in authority and those that were "pragmatic." It would be another project to investigate the ways Roman ceremonial shifted to accommodate the roles of the emperor and his subordinates.

NOTES

In the following notes, Latin and Greek authors will be cited according to the abbreviations of the *Oxford Latin Dictionary* (Oxford, 1968), and Liddell and Scott's *A Greek-English Lexicon* (Oxford, 1940). Modern works will be cited by the author's last name and a short form of the title. Complete citations of books and articles will follow in the bibliography, where the title of the journals in which articles appear will be abbreviated according to the system used in *L'Année philologique*. Certain modern works, however, will be regularly cited in the following abbreviations.

AE	*L'Année épigraphique* (cited by year and number of the inscription).
ANRW	H. Temporini and others, eds. *Aufstieg und Niedergang der römischen Welt. Geschichte und Kultur Roms im Spiegel der neueren Forschung*. Berlin and New York, 1972–.
Broughton, *MRR*	T. R. S. Broughton. *The Magistrates of the Roman Republic*. 3 vols. New York and Atlanta, 1951–85.
CIL	T. Mommsen and others, eds. *Corpus Inscriptionum Latinarum*. Berlin, 1863–.
De Martino, *Costituzione*	F. De Martino. *Storia della costituzione romana*. 6 vols. 2nd ed. Naples, 1972–75.
Diz. Epig.	E. De Ruggiero and others. *Dizionario epigrafico di antichità romane*. Rome, 1886–.
FIRA	S. Riccobono and others, eds. *Fontes Iuris Romani Anteiustiniani*. 3 vols. 2nd ed. Florence, 1943–68.
HRR	H. Peter, ed. *Historicorum Romanorum Reliquiae*. 2nd ed. Leipzig, 1914.
IG	*Inscriptiones Graecae*. Berlin, 1873–.
ILLRP	A. Degrassi, ed. *Inscriptiones Latinae Liberae Rei Publicae*. Florence, 1957–63.
ILS	H. Dessau, ed. *Inscriptiones Latinae Selectae*. Berlin, 1892–1916. Reprint, Chicago, 1979.
Mommsen, *Ges. Schr.*	T. Mommsen. *Gesammelte Schriften*. Vols. 1–8. Berlin, 1905–13.
Mommsen, *Str.*	T. Mommsen. *Römisches Staatsrecht*. Vols. 1–2. 3rd ed. Leipzig, 1887. Vol 3. Leipzig, 1887.
Mommsen, *Straf.*	T. Mommsen. *Römisches Strafrecht*. Leipzig, 1899. Reprint, Darmstadt, 1955.
ORF	E. Malcovati, ed. *Oratorum Romanorum Fragmenta Liberae Rei Publicae*. 4th ed. Turin, 1976.
RE	G. Wissowa and others, eds. *Real-Encylopädie der classischen Altertumswissenschaft*. Stuttgart, 1894–.

INTRODUCTION

1. All dates are B.C. unless otherwise noted.

2. The modern literature is too vast to be examined here. Instead, the positions of modern scholars will be discussed at the appropriate points in the text and notes.

3. For the definition, see Weber, "Essay on Bureaucracy," pp. 196–244.

4. See, for example, Hirschfeld, *Verwaltungsbeamten*. For subsenatorial elements of that government, see Pflaum, *Les procurateurs équestres*, and *Les carrières procuratoriennes*; Boulvert, *Esclaves et affranchis*; Weaver, *Familia Caesaris*.

5. See Hopkins, *Conquerors and Slaves*, pp. 74–96.

6. See, for example, Millar, *Emperor in the Roman World*, and Saller, *Personal Patronage*.

7. Thus, Turner, *Forest of Symbols*, p. 19, defined ritual as "formal behavior for occasions not given over to technological routine, having reference to beliefs in mystical kings or powers." Gluckman, *Politics, Law and Ritual*, p. 251, distinguished between "ritual," which "people believe . . . help[s] by mystical means outside of sensory observation and control" and "ceremonial, highly conventionalized performances in which this 'mystical' element is not present," and Goody, "Religion and Ritual," pp. 143–64, once defined ritual as "a category of standardized behaviour (custom) in which the relationship between the means and the end is not 'intrinsic' i.e. is either irrational or non-rational." Geertz, *Negara*, who takes ritual as an activity much more seriously, also presents the rituals of the traditional Balinese state as distinct from the activities that directly produced clear social and economic results.

8. See the comments of Goody, "Against Ritual," pp. 28–29.

9. For works framed in such terms, see Warde Fowler, *Religious Experience*, and Latte, *Römische Religionsgeschichte*.

10. In their interpretations of Roman religion, such scholars share, often quite explicitly, many of the evolutionary assumptions of nineteenth-century anthropology; see Kuper, *Invention of Primitive Society*.

11. For a recent anthropological study along these lines, see Geertz, *Negara*. Price, *Rituals and Power*, uses a similar approach to study the ways local elites in the Roman Empire represented to themselves and their fellow citizens a distant imperial power.

12. North, "Religion in Republican Rome," p. 609. Elsewhere, North ("Conservatism and Change," p. 3) notes: "public life in particular was full of minor religious duties, of vows and prayers and sacrifices and the taking of auspices; every act had its ritual accompaniment, token perhaps, but to be ignored at one's peril."

13. For arguments against making belief central to interpretations of ritual and its cultural role, see Price, *Rituals and Power*, pp. 7–11. Liebeschuetz, *Continuity and Change*, p. 29, points out that some rites maintained their importance despite exploitation for political advantage.

14. For the legal forms of communal organization, see Chapter 1, section II. Roman surveying will be examined in Chapter 2, sections V and VI, while the early history of ceremonies will be discussed when the rites are examined.

15. For the early history of Roman historiography, see Badian, "Early Historians," pp. 1–38; Frier, *Libri Annales*. The fragments of the earlier historians are collected in HRR.

16. See Chapter 4, section I.

17. For the development of Roman antiquarianism, see Rawson, *Intellectual Life*, pp. 233–49.

18. This feature was not a late addition to Roman historiography. Fabius Pictor (fr. 19 P), the first Roman historian, described the processions associated with the *Ludi*

Magni, which he attributed to their first performance in 490, but the account owes much to the practices of his own time; see Frier, *Libri Annales*, pp. 242–43. Dionysius of Halicarnassus (*Ant. Rom.* 7.71–73), who preserved the account, claimed to have witnessed a similar procession in his own day.

19. For areas known to have been surveyed, see Dilke, "Archaeological and Epigraphic Evidence," pp. 564–68.

20. K. Lachmann (L) edited these texts, which he published in the first volume of F. Blume, K. Lachmann, and A. Rudorff, *Die Schriften der römischen Feldmesser* (Berlin, 1848). C. Thulin (*Corpus Agrimensorum Romanorum* [Leipzig, 1913]), reedited the texts of five of the authors, Siculus Flaccus, Frontinus, Hyginus, Hyginus Gromaticus, and Agennius Urbicus.

21. See Dilke, *Roman Land Surveyors*, pp. 126–32; Panerai, "Gli agrimensori romani," pp. 112–14; and Chouquer and Favory, *Les Arpenteurs*, pp. 7–13.

CHAPTER 1

1. See Astin, *Lex Annalis*.
2. On the *publicani*, see Badian, *Publicans and Sinners*, and Cimma, *Ricerche sulle società di publicani*.
3. For the senate, see Willems, *Le sénat*; Talbert, *Senate of Imperial Rome*; and Bonnefond-Coudry, *Le sénat*.
4. For the assemblies, see Botsford, *Roman Assemblies*; Taylor, *Roman Voting Assemblies*.
5. See Hopkins, *Death and Renewal*, pp. 31–119.
6. See Szemler, *Priests*, and "Priesthoods and Priestly Careers," pp. 2314–31; Scheid, "Le prêtre et le magistrat," pp. 243–81; and Beard, "Priesthood," pp. 19–48.
7. For the pontiffs, see Wissowa, *Religion und Kultus*, pp. 501–23, and Bouché Leclerc, *Les pontifes*. The augurs will be examined at greater length in Chapter 2, section I.
8. Kunkel, *Herkunft und soziale Stellung*, pp. 6–133, and Wieacker, "Die römischen Juristen," pp. 183–214, both note that nonsenatorial experts in the law are not found until the first century.
9. From the late republic (and probably much earlier), some authors grouped the various areas of activity into larger spheres that were firmly distinguished in rule and action—according to one scheme public, sacred, and private—but the strongest division was between the first two, on the one hand, and private matters on the other; see Crawford, "*Aut sacrom aut poublicom*," pp. 93–98; Scheid, "Le prêtre et le magistrat," pp. 243–44; and Catalano, "La divisione del potere," pp. 667–91. Thus, the jurist Ulpian (*Dig.* 1.1.1.2) divided public law into laws concerned with rites, with priests, and with magistrates and assemblies. Cicero maintained the same division, defining (*Rep.* 1.25.39, 1.27.43, 1.32.48) the term *res publica* itself as all the property of the people and everything of concern to them and treating (*Leg.* 2.27.69) laws governing magistrates after those concerned with priests and *sacra*. Two centuries later, Gaius (2.2–11) set forth a different system, dividing matters into divine and human, with the former subdivided into *res sacrae* and *res religiosae* and the latter into *res publicae* and *res privatae*. Following Gaius, Watson, *State, Law and Religion*, pp. 117–18 n. 11, maintains that the crucial divide was between the human world and the divine, arguing that Crawford's demonstration that magistrates and senate controlled the boundary between public and sacred is irrelevant to his conclusion that the two spheres were especially closely related, since public officials also controlled the boundary between public and private. But, having determined the boundaries between public and private and those between public and

sacred, the state did not act in the private sphere beyond providing judges to rule on disputes between private citizens; the same was not true of religious matters.

10. The demands of various roles could conflict; see Bleicken, "Kollisionen," pp. 446–80.

11. See North, "Religion in Republican Rome," pp. 589–90.

12. For *commentarii*, see A. von Premerstein, *RE* 4, pt. 1 (1900), cols. 726–59, s.v. *commentarii*. For the priestly literature, see Linderski, "Libri Reconditi," pp. 207–34.

13. The entering consuls, for example, supervised the Latin festival and ended it with a sacrifice to Jupiter Latiaris on the Alban Mount (Livy 21.63.6–15, 41.16.1–5), the urban praetor presided over the apparently archaic procession of the *Argei* and also over the *Ludi Apollinares* (Dion. Hal. *Ant. Rom.* 1.38; Livy 25.12.3–15, 26.23.3, 27.11.6, 27.23.5; see also Scullard, *Festivals*, pp. 120–21, 159–60), while the curule aediles were responsible for the *Ludi Romani* and the plebeian aediles managed the *Ludi Plebii* (Scullard, pp. 183–86, 196–97).

14. See Cic. *ND* 2.4.11; *Div.* 1.17.33; Varro *LL* 6.90–92.

15. For conscription, see Chapter 3, section III; for the *lustrum*, see Chapter 4, section I.

16. See, for example, Livy 36.36.5–6, 40.34.4–6.

17. See Chapter 2, section I.

18. For an overview of Roman practices, see Nicolet, *Rome et la conquête*, 1:270–97; Salmon, *Making of Roman Italy*, pp. 40–72. More detailed investigations on the nature and development of those practices can be found in Rudolph, *Stadt und Staat*; Sherwin-White, *Roman Citizenship*; Galsterer, *Herrschaft und Verwaltung*; and Humbert, *Municipium*.

19. For colonization, see Chapters 3 and 4. For viritane assignments, see Chapter 5.

20. See Mommsen, *Str.*, 1:332–93; Purcell, "Apparitores," pp. 125–73; and Cohen, "Some Neglected *Ordines*," pp. 23–60. *Apparitores* should not be confused with members of a modern bureaucracy; according to Kunkel, *Roman Legal and Constitutional History*, pp. 18–19, "The practical influence of these magistrate's servants (generically called *apparitores*, from *apperare*, 'to be at someone's orders') was also in general inconsiderable, since the magistrates exercised their office personally and by word of mouth whenever possible. Not until the Principate did the beginnings of a bureaucracy emerge."

21. See Johnson, "Roman Tribunal"; Ulrich, *Roman Orator*.

22. Executions: see Hinard, "Spectacle des exécutions," pp. 111–25; sale: see Chapter 6, section I; trial: Livy 6.15.1–2; payment of soldiers: Livy 2.12.6–16. The tribunal may have been the typical setting for a magistrate and his *apparitores* from an early period. Colonna, "Scriba cum rege sedens," pp. 187–95, interprets a scene on an Etruscan relief of the fifth century as representing officials on a tribunal, apparently presiding over games, and accompanied by a lictor and a *scriba*.

23. For Roman ritual dress, see Bonfante Warren, "Roman Costumes," pp. 584–614.

24. In the formula, the consul is called a *iudex* (see also Cic. *Leg.* 3.3.8). Magdelain, "L'inauguration de l'*urbs*," p. 29, suggests that the use of this term maintains a distinction between *imperium domi* and *imperium militiae*; for the meaning of these terms, see Chapter 2, section I. For the *accensus*, see Fraccaro, "Accensi," pp. 133–46.

25. Varro *LL* 6.86–93. For a further discussion of those operations, see Chapter 4, section I, and Chapter 7, section I.

26. See Johnson, "Roman Tribunal," pp. 37–64.

27. See Buckland, *Textbook of Roman Law*, pp. 610–16; Jolowicz and Nicholas, *Historical Introduction*, pp. 176–87.

28. For the prohibition of the words and the expiation, see Varro *LL* 6.30; for the prin-

ciples, see also Macr. 1.16.14; Festus p. 348L; and Gaius 4.29. On *nefas* in the calendar, see Michels, *Calendar*, pp. 61–68.

29. Mentioned in the Twelve Tables, the *legis actiones* gradually began to be replaced by the more flexible formulary system, where the praetor to guide the *iudex* constructed a formula, composed of highly formalized sections, each with its own appropriate language, to deal directly with the special circumstances of the case as explained by the parties. Gaius (4.29–30) characterized the change as the introduction of litigation by *concepta verba*, phrases adapted to the case, in place of the *certa verba* of the earlier system; see Jolowicz and Nicholas, *Historical Introduction*, pp. 199–208. According to Gaius (4.30), the shift began with a *lex Aebutia* and ended with *leges Iuliae* of Augustus; it was never fully completed. The date of the *lex Aebutia* is uncertain, but it probably is to be placed in the second century and most probably in the latter half of that century; see Jolowicz and Nicholas, pp. 218–25.

30. For the process and the evidence, see Pietilä-Castrén, *Magnificentia publica*, pp. 15–144; Ziolkowski, *Temples of Mid-Republican Rome*, pp. 193–234.

31. See Chapter 3, section I.

32. See Chapter 6, section I. Ziolkowski, *Temples of Mid-Republican Rome*, pp. 203–14, mistakenly identifies the *locatio* with the inauguration of the temple enclosure.

33. See Chapter 2, sections I and IV.

34. For electoral assemblies, see Chapter 3, section II.

35. For inauguration, see Chapter 2, section I. For *ludi*, see Pietilä-Castrén, *Magnificentia publica*, p. 159.

36. Livy 40.44.8–10, 42.3.1–11.

37. A similar pattern can be found in colonization, where Livy regularly noted the passage of the law authorizing the colony, the election of the special commission to arrange it, and the performance of the rituals of the foundation that signified the completion of the process. On one occasion, however, Livy described other activities by colonial commissioners when they were caught up in the Gallic uprising that preceded Hannibal's entry into Italy. See Chapter 3, section I.

38. For the tribunes, see Livy 25.3.12–19. For the importance of the *fasces*, see Marshall, "Symbols and Showmanship," p. 138.

39. See, for example, Cic. *ND* 2.4.11; *Div.* 1.17.33; *Har.* 11.23.

40. Gracchus: Cic. *ND* 2.4.11; *Div.* 1.17.33; census: see Wiseman, "Census in the First Century," pp. 62–65.

41. Petilius: Livy 41.14.7–18.16; Flaminius: Livy 21.63.6–15.

CHAPTER 2

1. See Sherwin-White, *Roman Citizenship*, pp. 34–35.

2. For an examination of augural responsibilities and practices, see Linderski, "Augural Law," pp. 2146–2312.

3. For the terms, see Catalano, "Aspetti spaziali," pp. 440–553; Sherwin-White, *Roman Citizenship*, pp. 19–26. Catalano (p. 496) points out that the augural distinction between *ager peregrinus* and *ager hosticus* must have developed after the change in meaning of *hostes* from "foreigner" to "enemy." De Martino, *Costituzione*, 2:17–18, put this change of meaning in the fourth century.

4. Catalano, "Aspetti spaziali," pp. 493–94; Mommsen, *Str.*, 3:824–25; and A. Schulten, "Finis," *Diz. Epig.* 3:92–95. For the rituals, see Chapter 4, section II.

5. The exact nature of *ager Gabinus* is unclear. Mommsen, *Str.*, 3:598 n. 4, thought it must include the territory of all Latin states, but Catalano, "Aspetti spaziali,"

pp. 494–95, holds that it included only the territory of Gabii, while Latin territory was considered *ager peregrinus*.

6. See Magdelain, *Recherches sur l'"imperium,"* pp. 40–48, 57–67.

7. Linderski, "Augural Law," pp. 2156–58.

8. Although the *pomerium* was inaugurated, the city itself was not a *templum*; see Valeton, "De templis Romanis," 23:55–64, and Catalano,"Aspetti spaziali," pp. 482–85.

9. In this work, the word *templum* (in Latin) will denote a *locus inauguratus* or the visual field used in divination (see section VI), while temple (in English) will denote a shrine.

10. Varro *LL* 5.33, 5.143; Gell. 13.14.1.

11. Cic. *ND* 2.4.11; *Div.* 1.17.33. Mommsen, *Str.*, 1:97, thought that the auspices Gracchus neglected were the *auspicia peremnia*, taken when magistrates crossed the *amnis Petronia*, a small stream that magistrates leaving the city and going to the *campus Martius* had to pass over (see Festus p. 296L), but Magdelain, *Recherches sur l'"imperium,"* pp. 47–48, shows that the auspices were those needed to cross the *pomerium*.

12. Marius Victorinus *Ars grammatica* 1.4.42 (= *Grammatici Latini* VI, p. 14 Keil). Linderski, "Augural Law," p. 2157, notes that this implies that the *fines* were clearly marked so that the place to auspicate would be known.

13. On the political implications of the *pomerium*, see Magdelain, *Recherches sur l'"imperium,"* pp. 40–48, 57–67. The addition of that strip outside the *pomerium* allowed holders of *imperium* to preside over meetings of the centuriate assembly on the *campus Martius*, to meet with the senate, and to attend meetings of the plebeian assembly in the *circus Flaminius* without crossing the *pomerium*; see Taylor, *Roman Voting Assemblies*, p. 20.

14. See Mommsen, *Str.*, 3:926; Catalano, "Aspetti spaziali," p. 474.

15. See Varro *LL* 6.86–87, 6.91.

16. See Fraccaro, "Polibio e l'accampamento romano," pp. 154–61, and Walbank, *Commentary on Polybius*, 1:709–23.

17. Hyginus *De munitionibus castrorum* 11. The text unfortunately is corrupt at this point—the version cited is that of A. von Domaszewski (*Hygini Gromatici liber de munitionibus castrorum* [Leipzig, 1887])—and other editions provide different readings, although all agree on the presence of the altar, on the relative positions of the tribunal and the *auguratorium*, and on the purpose of the latter; see *Hygini Gromatici liber de munitionibus castrorum*, ed. G. Gemoll (Leipzig, 1879); Hyginus, *De metatione castrorum*, ed. Grillone (Leipzig, 1977); and Pseudo-Hygin, *Des fortifications du camp*, ed. M. Lenoir (Paris, 1979).

18. For the dedication, see Livy 2.8.6–8, 9.46.6–7; Cic. *Dom.* 52.133; Plut. *Publ.* 14; Sen. *Cons. ad Marc.* 13.1. All the stages are outlined by Serv. *A.* 1.446. See also Wissowa, *Religion und Kultus*, pp. 394–95 n. 7.

19. For Livy's use of formulas in the construction of narratives, see Ogilvie, *Commentary on Livy*, p. 92, and Kunkel, "Zum römischen Königtum," pp. 11–12.

20. *CIL* III.1933.

21. See *ILS* 112; *CIL* I.2.756, X.3513.

22. See Pliny *Ep.* 10.50; Festus p. 165L; Serv. *A.* 7.26.1. Festus (204L) finds it worthy of comment that the temple of Ops had no surviving law.

23. *CIL* IX.3513.

24. See, for example, *CIL* III.1933; *ILS* 112, 4907–8. On the use of the law as a pattern, see Palmer, *Roman Religion and Roman Empire*, pp. 57–78.

25. *CIL* I.2.401.

26. *CIL* I.2.366.

27. *ILS* 8208; for the date of Sentius's praetorship, see Broughton, *MRR*, 2:465. For burial sites on the Esquiline, see Dion. Hal. *Ant. Rom.* 20.16, and *CIL* I.2.591.

28. See Horace *S.* 1.8.6–16 for the *cippus*, and Gaius 2.2–9 for the legal status of tombs.

29. See Macr. 3.9.1–16. Macrobius identified his source as a certain Furius, probably Aemilianus's friend, L. Furius Philus (cos. 136); see Le Gall, "Evocatio," p. 521, and Palmer, *Roman Religion and Roman Empire*, p. 142. For the rite of *evocatio* in general, see also Basanoff, *Evocatio*.

30. See Chapter 4, section I.

31. The exact nature of the distinction between *leges datae* and *leges dictae* is obscure. Bleicken, *Lex publica*, pp. 58–71, takes *lex data* to refer to *leges colonicae, leges templorum, leges ararum*, and *leges lucorum*, while Magdelain, *La loi à Rome*, pp. 28–31, uses *lex data* only for colonial laws and *lex dicta* for the others.

32. *ILS* 4914: *Haec area intra hanc definitionem cipporum* . . . ; *ILLRP* I.485: . . . *Nequis intra terminos proprius urbem ustrinam fecisse velit neive stercus, cadaver iniecisse*; see also *CIL* III.1933. The regulations for the dedication of a shrine in 58 to Jupiter Liber at the *vicus* of Furfo also indicate that the area was defined by stones, although the details are unclear; see *CIL* I.2.756 (= *ILS* 4906). For *templa*, see Varro *LL* 7.13. For Romulus, see Livy 1.44.4–5.

33. See Daube, "*Finium demonstratio*," pp. 39–52.

34. Thus, Siculus Flaccus pp. 152–53L, 154L.

35. Festus p. 505L; Dion. Hal. *Ant. Rom.* 2.74; Plut. *Num.* 16, *Quaest. Rom.* 15. For the *crimen termini moti*, see R. Taubenschlag, *RE* ser. 2, 5 (1934), cols. 784–85, s.v. *terminus motus*.

36. See, for example, Livy 5.50.2; *ILS* 26, 5922c, 5923d. Rules may have assisted restoration: Dolabella (pp. 302–3L), a late writer preserved in the *Corpus Agrimensorum Romanorum*, held that the *fines* for deserted shrines where no traces of the original limits survived were to be set at fifteen Roman feet from the entrance.

37. See Chapter 7, section I.

38. See, Plut. *Num.* 16; Pliny *Nat.* 18.8; Festus p. 505L.

39. On the date of the prophecy, see S. Weinstock, *RE* ser. 2, 8, pt. 1 (1953), cols. 577–81; Zancan, "Il frammento di Vegoia," pp. 217–19; Heurgon, "Date of Vegoia's Prophecy," pp. 41–45; Harris, *Rome in Etruria and Umbria*, pp. 31–40; and Pfiffig, "Eine etruskische Prophezeiung," pp. 55–64. Turcan, "Encore la prophétie de Végoia," pp. 1009–19, however, puts the prophecy in the third century. Hinrichs, *Gromatischen Institutionen*, p. 80, places the prophecy early in the imperial period without argument and without citing any of the modern studies on the question.

40. On the Terminalia, see Scullard, *Festivals*, pp. 79–80. Wissowa, *Religion und Kultus*, pp. 136–38, denied that Terminus was a separate deity, since he shared a temple with Jupiter. For a detailed study of the deity, see Piccaluga, *Terminus*.

41. Ovid *Fast.* 2.639–84; Plut. *Quaest. Rom.* 15, *Num.* 16. See also Varro *LL* 6.13. For the rites defining the early *ager Romanus*, see Chapter 4, section II.

42. Cato fr. 24 P; see also Livy 1.55.4–7, 5.54.7; Dion. Hal. *Ant. Rom.* 3.69.5–6; Ovid *Fast.* 2.667–70; Serv. *A.* 9.446; Aug. *CD* 4.23, 4.29, 5.21.

43. For later practices, see Chapters 8 and 9.

44. See Chapter 3, section I, and Chapter 5, section I.

45. See Chapter 6, section III.

46. Livy 42.1.6, 42.19.1–2.

47. See Mommsen, *Str.*, 1:243, 2:618–24.

48. Livy 9.46.6; Cic. *Dom.* 49.127–50.128. For the date and the contents of the *lex Papiria*, see Tatum, "*Lex Papiria*," pp. 319–28.

49. Livy 45.13.10–11 (Broughton, *MRR*, 1:431–32, counts the five as magistrates, in the category of special commissions, apparently because Livy referred to them as *quinque viri*, but the historian clearly stated that the senate sent [*misit*] them so that they probably should be regarded as legates); *CIL* I.2.636, I.2.584. For more examples, see Scuderi, "Decreti del senato," pp. 371–415.

50. See, for example, *IG* VII.413.

51. *ILS* 24. For other examples, see Chapter 8, section II.

52. See, for example, *ILS* 9376: *C. Caninius C. f. pr. urb. de sen. sent. poplic. ioudic*; See also *ILS* 5922a–c. Under the Empire, practice shifted. At the beginning of the reign of the emperor Claudius, markers identified the authority of the officials who erected them with phrases such as *ex auctoritate Ti. Claudi Caesaris*, rather than the earlier *ex s. c.*, whereas those placed in the mid-second century A.D. gave the emperor's name in the nominative and that of the individual who actually performed the operation in the ablative; see Eck, "Senatorial Self-Representation," pp. 136–37.

53. For an analysis of the passage, see Linderski, "Augural Law," pp. 2256–96.

54. See also Cic. *Div.* 1.17.31; Varro. *LL* 7.9. The words *regiones determinavit* occur frequently in augural practice. *Regiones* can be used to refer both to the lines separating and dividing a place or to the parts themselves created by such a process of separation. The basic meaning, however, is that of the lines of separation (see, for example, Gell. 13.14.1). The sources are collected in Valeton, "De templis Romanis," 20:370–73.

55. Some ritual formulas, characterized as *certa verba*, were fixed and unchangeable, but Varro's use of *concepta verba* indicates that those words could be rephrased according to circumstance; for a discussion of the meaning of this passage, see Linderski, "Augural Law," pp. 2266–67. The distinction between *certa verba* and *concepta verba* was also important in private law where the change from the former to the latter marked the change from the rigid *legis actio* to the more flexible formulary system; see Jolowicz and Nicholas, *Historical Introduction*, pp. 199–200.

56. Norden, *Aus altrömischen Priesterbüchern*, pp. 3–106, 281–86, provides the most important attempt to reconstruct the formula; for others, see Latte, "Augur und Templum," pp. 143–59, and Peruzzi, "La formula augurale," pp. 449–56.

57. Torelli, "Un templum augurale," pp. 293–315.

58. The purpose of such precincts is uncertain: Valeton, "De templis Romanis," 20:374, thought that the *minus templum* served to mark a place after the performance of the *liberatio* and the *effatio*, but before a permanent enclosure or the walls of an *aedes* could be built. Linderski, "Augural Law," pp. 2274–79, suggests that one use for those *templa* was for the taking of the auspices in military encampments; Serv. *A.* 4.200 reported that the same or a similar enclosure was marked by *hastae*, seemingly appropriate for such a location.

59. *ILS* 112: . . . *his legibus hisque regionibus dabo dedicaboque, quas his hodie palam dixero.* . . . See also *CIL* III.1933: . . . *ollis legib(us) ollisque regionibus dabo dedicaboque, quas hic hodie palam dixero* . . . ; *CIL* IX.3513 (58 B.C.): . . . *olleis legibus illeis regionibus.* . . .

60. Piso fr. 13 P (= Pliny *Nat.* 28.4.14–16). See also Dion. Hal. *Ant. Rom.* 4.59.2–61.4.

61. On the legal importance of the demonstration of boundaries, see Daube, "Finium Demonstratio," pp. 39–52.

62. Daube, "*Finium Demonstratio*," pp. 40–41; see also Rudorff, "Gromatischen Institutionen," pp. 234–36.

63. See Chapter 4, section I.

64. Dion. Hal. *Ant. Rom.* 4.13.1–3; Gell. 13.14.3–4; Tac. *Ann.* 12.23; Sen. *Dial.* 10.13.8. The instances when the *pomerium* supposedly was enlarged are either of the regal period or of Sullan times or later; the ritual of the plowing, then, may have been first

turned to the *pomerium* of Rome itself long after it began to be used to establish the *pomeria* of colonies.

65. *CIL* I.2.584, esp. lines 1–5.

66. See Chapter 4, section I.

67. For the trees and *cippi*, see Varro *LL* 7.8–9; Torelli, "Un templum augurale," pp. 293–315.

68. Festus p. 146L; Serv. A. 4.200. For the purpose of such places, see n. 58.

69. Hyginus Gromaticus p. 199L.

70. *Liber coloniarum I* pp. 218.8L, 222–23L; *Liber coloniarum II* p. 257L; Latinus and Mysrontius p. 347L. See Chapter 4, section II.

71. It must be emphasized that *terminatio* and *limitatio* describe different processes with differing goals. The outer limits of a territory could be defined without any subdivision within the boundaries.

72. For the development of Roman surveying practices, see Hinrichs, *Gromatischen Institutionen*, pp. 23–57; Chouquer and Favory, *Les paysages de l'antiquité*, pp. 69–138; Gabba, "Per un'interpretazione storica della centuriazione," pp. 265–84. For specific projects, see Dilke, "Archaeological and Epigraphic Evidence," pp. 580–83. For Roman surveying in its broader historical context, see Kain and Baigent, *Cadastral Map*.

73. Castagnoli, "I più antichi esempi," pp. 3–9; "La centuriazione di Cosa," pp. 147–65; *Le ricerche sui resti della centuriazione*; Vallat, "Ager publicus, colonies et territoire agraire," pp. 187–98; Hinrichs, *Gromatischen Institutionen*, pp. 23–57; and Muzzioli, "Note sull'ager quaestorius," pp. 223–30.

74. For the process, see Dilke, *Roman Land Surveyors*, pp. 82–97, and Chouquer and Favory, *Les paysages de l'antiquité*, pp. 139–52.

75. Hinrichs, *Gromatischen Institutionen*, p. 56. Hinrichs, however, identified the surviving physical traces, based on modules of 210 *iugera* measuring 20 *actus* by 21, with the foundation of the colony in 218. Two of the *gromatici*, Frontinus (p. 30L) and Hyginus Gromaticus (p. 170L), mention *centuriae* of these dimensions at this colony and assign them to the Second Triumvirate after 43. Close study of the remains, however, has revealed signs of an earlier division based on squares of 200 *iugera*, and those modules probably belong to the earliest assignment in 218; see Tozzi, *Storia padana antica*, p. 23.

76. Hinrichs, *Gromatischen Institutionen*, pp. 56–57. *ILS* 24 allows the *kardo maximus* and the *decumanus maximus* to be identified in the *ager Campanus*. The road from Capua to Atella formed the chief *decumanus* and the east-west route to Calatia the *kardo maximus*; the two intersected just south of Capua. The traces of centuriation around Carthage may be attributed either to the Gracchan or to the Caesarian colony; there the intersection of *kardo maximus* and *decumanus maximus* took place in the *forum* of Carthage itself; see Wightman, "Plan of Roman Carthage," pp. 29–46.

77. See Hyginus pp. 111–28L for the principles.

78. *ILS* 24.

79. Granius Licinianus p. 9 Criniti. Fragments of such a *forma* survive for the Roman colony at Orange; see Piganiol, *Les documents cadastraux d'Orange*.

80. See della Corte, "Groma," pp. 5–100.

81. Castagnoli, *Orthogonal Town Planning*, pp. 96–97, 104, 120–21; Brown, "Cosa, I," p. 24. See also Ward-Perkins, "Early Roman Towns," pp. 127–54; *Cities of Ancient Greece and Italy*, pp. 22–32; and MacKendrick, "Roman Town Planning," pp. 126–33.

82. Castagnoli, *Orthogonal Town Planning*, pp. 100–103.

83. For the use of the *groma*, see Hyginus *De mun. castr.* 12; and for *scamna* and *strigae* in the camps, see Hyginus *De mun. castr.* 1, 14, 15, 19, 20, 36–37, 40, 43, 48. Polybius (6.27–42) provides a detailed description of the plan of a camp, used, he claimed, in all

times and in all places; see Fraccaro, "Polibio e l'accampamento romano," pp. 154–61, who placed the document that served as Polybius's source in the period of the Pyrrhic War, and Rawson, "Literary Sources," pp. 13–31, who placed it at the end of the Second Punic War. Note that the *via praetoria*, running at right angles to the *via principalis* and the *via quintana*, was less marked and did not run completely through the camp; see Walbank, *Commentary on Polybius*, 1:709–19.

84. The use of the term *kardo* for the north-south axis of a centuriation grid may reinforce the link, for it signifies a hinge, pivot, or axis and has the special meaning of the axis around which the universe circled the earth; see Dilke, *Roman Land Surveyors*, p. 231. The *haruspices* and *augures* are not known to have used the term, but their name for the celestial axis has not been preserved. In light of the meaning of *kardo*, would the north-south *limites* have been known as *kardines* before one was singled out as the *kardo maximus*?

85. For the word *groma*, see Dilke, *Roman Land Surveyors*, pp. 66–67; for the *asteriskos*, see Dilke, "Archaeological and Epigraphic Evidence," pp. 569–73.

86. For Greek colonial practices, see Chouquer and Favory, *Les paysages des l'antiquité*, pp. 79–89.

87. Hinrichs, *Gromatischen Institutionen*, pp. 23–48.

88. Thus, Hinrichs, *Gromatischen Institutionen*, pp. 80–81. But Gabba, "Per un'interpretazione storica della centuriazione," pp. 267–68, notes that claims of Etruscan derivation clearly cannot be accepted if taken as referring to the archaic period, while they can be accepted if taken only as indicating that the Romans took account of Etruscan practices when developing centuriation.

89. Thus, Hinrichs, *Gromatischen Institutionen*, pp. 78–84, rejects any link between certain religious practices and centuriation and claims that he will seek a "pragmatic" source for the techniques—which he finds in the Roman camp, the laying out of which certainly involved the same instruments and techniques. But Hinrichs's solution then brings up the question—which he does not ask—of the origins of the layout of the camps. Weinstock, "Cosmic System of the Etruscans," p. 129, separates "theological speculation" from "gromatical practice." Castagnoli, *Orthogonal Town Planning*, pp. 78–81, holds that the technical writers artificially superimposed cosmic theories on standard surveying practice, placing the imposition without argument in the late republic.

90. See Thulin, *Die etruskische Disciplin*, 1:15–22. Dumézil, *Archaic Roman Religion*, pp. 637–49, argues that the Etruscan *libri fulgurales* and lightning lore in general had by the late republic largely been merged with Roman ideas.

91. Valeton, "De modis auspicandi," 17:282–85, held that only one type of *templum* was involved in auspication and it served equally for signs *ex caelo* and *ex avibus*. But Linderski, "Augural Law," p. 2270, pointing out that the observer of signs such as lightning looked up while the auspiciant watching the flight of birds from the *arx* looked down over the city and the fields, noted that one type of *templum* must have been defined against the sky and the other against the surrounding landscape. Other evidence confirms this: Magdelain ("L'auguraculum de l'arx," pp. 253–69) has shown that the inscriptions on the *cippi* set up in the *auguraculum* at Bantia to assist the auspiciant in the construction of a *templum* make it clear that the *cippi* were used only for the observation of birds. See also Regell, "Die Schautempla der Augurn," pp. 597–637. For the definition of *auguraculum*, see Festus p. 17L.

92. See Linderski, "Augural Law," pp. 2261–67.

93. Linderski, "Augural Law," pp. 2269–72, holds that the term *templum in terra* refers only to the defined field of vision, while Catalano, "Aspetti spaziali," pp. 467–68, main-

tains that the term refers both to the field of vision and to the earthly *templum* in which the person taking the auspices stood.

94. Linderski, "Augural Law," pp. 2279, 2287 n. 561, observes that Livy's augur seems to have made the *pomerium* the eastern limit of his space, but he notes that by doing so the auspiciant also used the *pomerium* to divide his field of vision into the two opposite augural spheres of *urbs* and *ager*. Valeton, "De modis auspicandi," 18:246–48, held that the *pomerium* divided the field of vision into two registers, an upper for the observation of high-flying birds, *aves praepetes*, and a lower for low-flying birds or *aves inferae*.

95. Magdelain, "L'auguraculum de l'arx," pp. 253–65, and Torelli, "Un templum augurale," pp. 293–315.

96. Dilke, "Varro and the Origins of Centuriation," pp. 353–58, and "Religious Mystique and the Training of Agrimensores," pp. 158–62, lists some similarities with augural practice, but he does not address the significance.

97. In those *templa* that were fields of vision, the entire space clearly would lie in front of the observer, but the matter is less clear with regard to earthly *templa*. Müller and Deecke (*Die Etrusker*, 2:137) and Regell ("Die Schautempla der Augurn," p. 601 n. 3), followed by many scholars, assumed that the auspiciant himself sat at the *decussis*, where the dividing axes crossed in the middle of the *templum*, and constructed his field of vision. In such a case, like the centuriation grid, half of that *templum* would lie behind him. But it is more likely that the auspiciant sat on the periphery with the entire *templum* before him: Torelli, "Un templum augurale," p. 41, points out that the inscriptions giving the divisions and the significance of the fields of vision placed in the *auguraculum* at Bantia can only be read by an observer to the west of the *templum*; see also Linderski, "Augural Law," pp. 2257–60.

98. This passage immediately follows Hyginus Gromaticus's relation of Varro's views on the origins of centuriation. The situation Hyginus Gromaticus described—the *conditor* present and taking the auspices—would not have been the customary practice after the late first century (see Chapter 9, section II), which may reinforce the possibility that Varro was the source.

99. Plautus did not explicitly link his *finitor* to centuriation, for he did not identify the nature of the *regiones*, *limites*, and *confinia* that the surveyor would mark out, and these terms can refer to boundaries in a range of forms and circumstances. For the status of mid-republican *finitores* and the range of their responsibilities, see Chapter 4, section III.

100. See Slater, "Plautine Negotiations," pp. 131–46. Plautus, according to Slater, began the parody by asserting authority over the audience (ordering the *praeco* to silence the crowd before asking the herald himself to be silent) and by likening himself to an *imperator histricus* using the proper verbal forms. For *ne* with the subjunctive as a feature of edicts, see Daube, *Forms*, pp. 37–49.

101. Compare Plautus's declaration as a surveyor with *ILS* 112, *CIL* III.1933, and *CIL* IX.3513.

102. For Rome, see Richardson, "*Honos et Virtus*," pp. 240–46, and Coarelli, *Il Foro Romano I*, pp. 100–103. For Cosa, see Brown, Richardson, and Richardson, "Cosa II," p. 13; Magdelain, "Le pomerium archaïque," pp. 83–84. Ziolkowski, "Between Geese and the Auguraculum," pp. 213–17, holds that Livy's augur must have looked exactly to the east from the *arx*, since Livy did not describe him as looking to any topographical point. But Livy turned a formula into a narrative (see n. 19), so that whatever direction was named as east for the purpose of the rite would have become true east in his account. Ziolkowski also maintains that the presumed *auguraculum* at Cosa may be seen as oriented almost exactly east-west as easily as north-south and (while questioning the

proper identification of the place) assumes a similar orientation for the augural field of vision. But he did not note that the proper definition of a *templum in terra* required the auspiciant to construct a field of vision crossed by the *pomerium* and looking out over *urbs* and *ager*—from any position on the *arx* at Cosa, those requirements could be met only with a more or less northward orientation.

103. See n. 76.

104. The rules of orientation probably were more complex than our sources reveal. Varro (*LL* 7.6–7), for example, had his *templum in caelo* oriented toward the south, Cicero (*Div.* 1.17.31) had Attus Navius also face south for the *augurium stativum*, and Livy (1.18.6–10) had Numa Pompilius face to the south while the officiating augur faced toward the east. Frontinus (pp. 27–28L) and Hyginus Gromaticus (pp. 166–67L), however, claimed that Varro had the centuriation grid oriented toward the west, and the former noted that certain architects also recommended that temples face in that direction; Vitruvius (4.5) certainly did so.

105. The resemblance between surveying and augury has proven treacherous for those who assume that similar processes must have similar ends. Thus, some think *centuriae* must have been *templa*; see, for example, Müller and Deecke, *Die Etrusker*, 2:128–30; Rudorff, "Gromatischen Institutionen," pp. 335–45; Nissen, *Das Templum*. But Valeton, "De templis Romanis," demonstrated that *centuriae* had nothing to do with *templa*. Others have maintained the contrary position: since the two processes did not lead to the same result, they must have had nothing in common; see Catalano, "Aspetti spaziali," pp. 468–70, and Hinrichs, *Gromatischen Institutionen*, pp. 78–84.

106. Gell. 14.7.7 explicitly stated that the temple of Vesta was not also a *templum*. Frothingham, "Circular Templum," pp. 302–20, mistakenly thought that a *templum* could be circular.

107. For example, Hinrichs, *Gromatischen Institutionen*, p. 78, holds that the connection between surveying and orientation originated in the late republican antiquarian speculation.

108. Thus, Castagnoli, "La centuriazione di Cosa," p. 160.

109. Gabba, "Per un'interpretazione storica della centuriazione," pp. 274–76, suggests that the large tracts of relatively flat land available in Cispadane Gaul, where the Romans began to place colonies and viritane assignments in the middle and late third century, provided the opportunity to make the system much more regular.

CHAPTER 3

1. On colonization in general, see E. de Ruggiero, *Diz. Epig.* 2:415–58, s.v. *colonia*; E. Kornemann, *RE* 4 (1900), cols. 511–87, s.v. *colonia*; Rudolph, *Stadt und Staat*, pp. 129–56; Salmon, *Roman Colonization*; Galsterer, *Herrschaft und Verwaltung*, pp. 41–64; and Keppie, *Colonisation and Veteran Settlement*.

2. Beginning: 40.43.1 (Luca); end: 34.45.3–5 (Sipontum, Tempsa, and Croton), 39.44.10 (Potentia and Pisaurum), 39.55.6–8 (Parma and Mutina), 39.55.9 (Saturnia), 40.29.1–2 (Graviscae), 41.13.4–5 (Luna); beginning and end: 32.29.3–4, 34.45.1–2 (Volturnum, Liternum, Puteoli, Salernum, and Buxentum), 34.53.1–2, 35.9.7–8, 35.40.5–6 (Vibo Valentia and Copia), 37.46.9–47.2, 37.57.7–8 (Bononia), 39.55.5–6, 40.34.2–3 (Aquileia). Both the authorization and the formal foundation of Placentia and Cremona lie before Livy's text resumes with book 21 (for the foundation, see *Per.* 20), but the commissioners and colonists were caught up in Hannibal's invasion of Italy in ways that reveal much about other details of the process; see section III in this chapter and

Chapter 4, section I. The same general features, it should be noted, are found in Livy's accounts of temple dedications; see Chapter 1, section II.

3. Thus Mommsen, *Str.*, 2:624–27, and De Martino, *Costituzione*, 2:102. For examples, see Livy 32.29.3–4, 34.53.1–2, 37.46.9–47.2, 39.23.3–4, 39.55.5–6 (see also 10.21.7–10).

4. In Livy's differing treatment of separate instances, some have seen signs of procedural distinctions between colonies of differing status or an indication that the process evolved over time. Thus, Willems, *Le sénat*, 2:678–83, maintained that a law was required only for citizen colonies, while Latin colonies could be founded with only a decree of the senate (but note that Livy [34.53.1–2] attributed the sequence of senatorial decree and plebiscite to two Latin colonies). More recently, Hinrichs, *Gromatischen Institutionen*, pp. 10–12, made a distinction between military colonies and civilian ones, with only the latter requiring a plebiscite, but that division, unlike the separation into citizen and Latin, has no parallel in Roman law and is without textual support. Botsford, *Roman Assemblies*, pp. 350–51, and Rudorff, "Gromatische Institutionen," p. 331, held that plebiscites were necessary only after the Gracchi. The variation in Livy's notices is best ascribed to stylistic considerations.

5. For the senate in general, see Willems, *Le sénat*; Talbert, *Senate of Imperial Rome*; Bonnefond-Coudry, *Le sénat*.

6. Bonnefond-Coudry, *Le sénat*, pp. 394–413, notes that some sessions of the senate were poorly attended and that magistrates might plan to take advantage of that to achieve their goals; no quorum was required except in a few matters, especially those concerning religion and elections.

7. See Bonnefond-Coudry, *Le sénat*, pp. 31–160.

8. See Gell. 14.7.1–13.

9. For the procedure in legislative assemblies, see Botsford, *Roman Assemblies*, pp. 48–65, 119–38; Taylor, *Roman Voting Assemblies*, pp. 34–83; Fraccaro, "La procedura del voto," pp. 235–54; Hall, "Voting Procedure," pp. 267–306.

10. See Livy 34.53.1–2 (see also Livy 10.21.7–10).

11. Botsford, *Roman Assemblies*, pp. 139–51; Taylor, *Roman Voting Assemblies*, pp. 15–33, 56–58.

12. For the use of such a *carmen*, see Livy 39.15.1.

13. Note that a number of magistrates could hold *contiones* at the same time; see Gell. 13.16.1–2.

14. See Taylor, *Roman Voting Assemblies*, pp. 2–3.

15. For the linguistic peculiarities of *leges*, see Magdelain, *La loi à Rome*, pp. 23–54. For the identification of a *lex* in its various forms—*lex rogata*, *lex data*, and *lex dicta*—as a ritual text, see Magdelain, *La loi à Rome*, pp. 12–22, and Kaser, *Privatrecht*, 1:30.

16. Daube, *Forms*, pp. 50–56, 109.

17. Schulz, *History of Roman Legal Science*, pp. 87, 96–98.

18. See Magdelain, *La loi à Rome*, p. 23. The term *lex* and the features associated with it were not restricted to laws passed by popular assemblies. The same phrasing and use of third-person imperatives in that form were also characteristic of *leges datae* and *leges dictae*, in which specific sets of instructions were given to named individuals or classes of individuals by the word of a magistrate authorized to do so. Such laws were issued for a number of purposes: to regulate the public life of a colony and its colonists; to set forth the conditions of a public sale or contract (*lex locationis* or *venditionis*); and to regulate the use of a temple, altar, or sacred grove (*lex templi*, *arae*, or *luci*); see Magdelain, pp. 23–54. Contracts of sale and for various works among private citizens also followed the same pattern; see Lübtow, "Catos leges venditioni et locationi dictae," pp. 227–441.

19. Daube, *Forms*, p. 87; Magdelain, *La loi à Rome*, pp. 26–27.

20. See, for example, Livy 22.10.1–10; Festus 160L; Macr. 1.16.19, 3.10.7; see also Magdelain, *La loi à Rome*, pp. 24–25; Watson, *State, Law and Religion*, pp. 39–43.

21. See Chapter 8, section I, and Chapter 9, sections I and II.

22. For the nature of Latin rights and their development, see Sherwin-White, *Roman Citizenship*, pp. 108–16.

23. Three hundred: Tarracina (328), Volturnum, Liternum, Puteoli, Salernum, and Buxentum (all founded in 194); see Livy 8.21.11, 34.45.1–2. Archaeological studies at the *castra* of the citizen colonies of Minturnae (296) and Pyrgi (before 218) indicate that these were no larger; see Salmon, "*Coloniae Maritimae*," pp. 18, 23–24; *Roman Colonization*, 71–72. Two thousand: Mutina and Parma (183) and Luna (177); see Livy 39.55.6–8, 41.13.4–5.

24. The twelve cases where the number of original colonists is known range from a low of 2,500 men at Cales (334) and Luceria (314) to a high of 6,000 at Alba Fucens (303), Placentia (219), and Cremona (219). Bononia (189) and Aquileia (181) held 3,000 *pedites* and an unknown number of *equites*. Interamna Sucasina (312), Sora (303), Carseoli (302 or 298), and Vibo (194) had 4,000; see Livy 8.16.14, 9.26.5, 9.28.8, 10.1.1–2, 10.3.2, 35.9.7–8, 35.40.5–6, 37.57.7–8, 40.34.2; Asc. *Pis.* p. 3 Clark; Polyb. 3.40.4. Dion. Hal. *Ant. Rom.* 17/18, fr. 10, gave the number of settlers at Venusia as 20,000, but that figure is unlikely to be correct. The Latin colony of Copia had 3,300 settlers, but the number who actually enrolled may have fallen short of expectations: see Livy 35.9.7–8.

25. See the following section.

26. Colonial Triumvirates: Livy 3.1.6, 4.11.5, 5.24.4, 6.21.4, 8.16.14, 9.28.7–8, 9.46.3 (= Licinius Macer fr. 18 P), 10.21.7–10, 21.25.1–7, 31.49.6, 32.2.6–7, 32.29.3–4, 34.45.1–5, 34.53.1–2, 35.9.7–8, 35.40.5–6, 37.46.9–11, 37.57.7–8, 39.23.3–4, 39.44.10, 39.55.5–9, 40.29.1–2, 40.43.1, 41.13.4–5, 43.17.1; Asc. *Pis.* p. 3 Clark; Dion. Hal. *Ant. Rom.* 9.56.1–6; Festus 458L; Polyb. 3.40.3–10. Terms: Livy 32.29.3–4, 34.53.1–2. Colleges of larger size in the middle republic were responsible for viritane assignments; see Chapter 5, sections I and II. The last known colonial triumvirate founded the Gracchan colony at Carthage; see Chapter 8, sections III and IV.

27. The triumvirate established in 190 to lead supplements to the Latin colonies of Cremona and Placentia illustrates the lack of a distinction between commissions that founded new settlements and those that reinforced old ones, for later in the year, when the senate decided to establish new Latin colonies in the same region, the same triumvirate was assigned the task (Livy 37.46.9–47.2).

28. See Livy 32.29.3–4, 34.53.1–2, 37.47.2, 39.55.5–6, 40.43.1.

29. For the *lex Aelia*, see Livy 34.53.1–2, 35.9.7–8, 35.40.5–6.

30. Livy 21.25.1–7 (see also Polyb. 3.40.3–10), 34.45.3–5, 39.44.10, 39.55.6–9, 40.29.1–2, 41.13.4–5.

31. One colony: Croton (194), Sipontum (194), Tempsa (194), Copia (193), Vibo (192), Saturnia (183), Aquileia (181), Graviscae (181), Luca (elected in 180), Luna (177); two colonies: Placentia and Cremona (219), Bononia and an unidentified colony (189), Potentia and Pisaurum (184), Mutina and Parma (183); five colonies: Volturnum, Liternum, Puteoli, Salernum, and Buxentum (197). For the sources, see n. 42.

32. One exception is certain and one possible. The first is the commission chosen in 190 to lead a supplement to the two Latin colonies of Placentia and Cremona, which was later given the task of founding two additional Latin colonies (Livy 37.46.9–47.2, 37.57.7–8). The second is the commission authorized under the *lex Atinia* of 197; if Livy's wording (32.29.3–4) can be trusted, the fifth of the small citizen colonies may have been added later. But note that the majority of commissions only founded a single colony and thus clearly derived their powers from one law or decree of the senate.

33. See Polybius 3.40.3–10 and Livy 39.55.6–8. The only apparent exception was the *lex Aelia*, which authorized Copia (where 3,300 settlers actually were installed) and Vibo Valentia (where 4,000 received lands), but the number of settlers at Copia may have been fewer than expected; see Livy 34.53.1–2, 35.9.7–8, 35.40.5–6. The land law of M. Livius Drusus (tr. pl. 122) instructed that its commissioners establish twelve colonies, each of 3,000 *coloni*; see Plut. *CG* 9.2.

34. Note also that the commission instituted by the *lex Atinia* of 197 established five small citizen colonies along the coast of the Tyrrhenian Sea, and the distance between the northernmost colony, Volturnum, and the southernmost, Buxentum, is approximately 200 kilometers. If Livy's phrasing can be trusted, however, Buxentum, separated from the others by the greatest distance, was added later and thus the original four, Volturnum, Liternum, Puteoli, and Salernum, would have formed a more compact group, separated by less than 100 kilometers; see Livy 32.29.3–4.

35. Livy 37.46.9–47.2.

36. Note that the *rogatio Servilia agraria* of 63 defined certain attributes of its decemvirs by references to the *lex Sempronia agraria* of 133 and the manner of their election by analogy with that of the *pontifex maximus*; Cic. *Agr.* 2.7.18, 2.12.31. In the *lex data* that governed the Caesarian colony at Urso, some powers of colonial magistrates and priests were defined by reference to their equivalents at Rome; see *FIRA* I, no. 21, cap. 66 and 103.

37. Conceivably the citizen colonies of Tempsa, Croton, and Sipontum, established in 194 by three triumvirates on scattered locations, could have been authorized by the same law; see Livy 34.45.3–5.

38. See Livy 10.21.7–10, 34.53.2, 37.46.9–11, 39.23.3–4. Willems, *Le Sénat*, 2:681, held that election was required only for the founders of citizen colonies and that the commissioners for Latin colonies were appointed; there is no evidence to support such a distinction.

39. Taylor ("Gracchus' Last Assembly," pp. 65–66; *Roman Voting Assemblies*, pp. 46, 133 n. 40) denied that Livy's notice referred to electoral *comitia*, since she thought the Capitol too small for all tribes to vote simultaneously, and she maintained instead that the *comitia* mentioned must be the *comitia curiata*. Fraccaro ("La procedura del voto," pp. 235–54), followed by Hall ("Voting Procedure," pp. 267–306), showed that in meetings of the tribal assembly for judicial and legislative purposes the tribes voted in succession, while in electoral assemblies they voted simultaneously, but Fraccaro (and Hall) suggested that before the appearance of the written ballot in 139 the tribes also voted in succession in elections. There is no reason to believe that these electoral *comitia*, which must have largely lacked controversy, were well attended. For the size of assemblies, see MacMullen, "How Many Romans Voted?," pp. 454–57.

40. For procedures in elections before the tribal assembly, see Taylor, *Roman Voting Assemblies*, pp. 59–83.

41. See Earl, "*Professio*," pp. 325–32. Asconius (*Tog.* p. 89 Clark) reported that the consul of 66 rejected the candidacy of Catiline, after consulting his advisory *consilium*. Livy (39.39.10–15) noted that over a century earlier the consul who was to preside over the election of a suffect praetor conducted, on the advice of the senate, a number of *contiones* seeking to force a candidate deemed unsuitable by the tribunes to withdraw; when the candidate refused, the senate decided that a sufficient number of praetors had already been chosen and the position remained unfilled.

42. Foundation of Placentia and Cremona (219–218); Polyb. 3.40.3–10, Livy 21.25.1–7, Asc. *Pis.* p. 3 Clark; supplement to Venusia (election of commissioners in 200): Livy 31.49.6; supplement to Narnia (election in 199): Livy 32.2.6–7; foundations of Volturnum, Liternum, Puteoli, Salernum, and Buxentum (election in 197, foundation in 194):

Livy 32.29.3–4, 34.45.1–2; foundation of Sipontum (foundation in 194): Livy 34.45.3–5; foundation of Croton (founded in 194): Livy 34.45.3–5; foundation of Tempsa (founded in 194): Livy 34.45.3–5; foundation of Vibo Valentia (election in 194, foundation in 192): Livy 34.53.1–2, 35.40.5–6; foundation of Copia (election in 194, foundation in 193): Livy 34.53.1–2, 35.9.7–8; supplement to Placentia and Cremona (elected in 190, Bononia founded in 189): Livy 37.46.9–47.2; 57.7–8; refoundation of Sipontum and Buxentum (elected in 186): Livy 39.23.3–4; foundation of Potentia and Pisaurum (founded in 184): Livy 39.44.10; foundation of Parma and Mutina (founded in 183): Livy 39.55.6–8; foundation of Saturnia (founded in 183): Livy 39.55.9; foundation of Aquileia (elected in 183, founded in 181): 39.55.5–6, 40.34.2–3; foundation of Graviscae (founded in 181): Livy 40.29.1–2; foundation of an unnamed Latin colony, probably Luca (elected in 180): Livy 40.43.1; foundation of Luna (founded in 177): Livy 41.13.4–5; supplement to Aquileia (elected in 169): Livy 43.17.1. More than one commission may have been active at Placentia in 219–218; see Gargola, "Colonial Commissioners of 218," pp. 465–73.

43. In the following discussion, Broughton's identifications in *MRR, sub anno*, will be accepted unless there is a reason for doubt (in which case the matter will be discussed at the appropriate point). Note that between seven and nine vacancies can be found in the praetorian *fasti*, most after the passage of the *lex Villia annalis* in 180. Since this law required individuals to hold the office of praetor before that of consul, those commissioners known to have held the office of consul after 180, but having no known term as praetor, can be assumed to have held this office in one of the free years; see Astin, *Lex Annalis*, pp. 19–30.

44. Sage and Wegner, "Administrative Commissions," p. 29, suggest that those commissioners not known to have ever held a regular office were not part of "the office-holding class." Those triumvirs easily could have held any or all of the magistracies up to and including aedile without leaving any traces.

45. Former consuls: C. Terentius Varro (cos. 216) who was chosen to lead a supplement to Venusia in 200; P. Aelius Paetus (cos. 201) and Cn. Cornelius Lentulus (cos. 201), who were to install additional settlers at Narnia in 199; M. Servilius Geminus (cos. 202), elected in 197 to found Volturnum, Liternum, Puteoli, Salernum, and Buxentum; L. Valerius Flaccus (cos. 195), chosen in 190 to lead a supplement to Placentia and Cremona; and P. Cornelius Scipio Nasica (cos. 191) and C. Flaminius (cos. 187), elected in 183 to found Aquileia. Former praetors: M. Minucius Rufus (pr. 193) for Vibo in 194, L. Apustius Fullo (pr. 196) for Copia in the same year, L. Valerius Tappo (pr. 192) for the supplements to Placentia and Cremona, L. Scribonius Libo (pr. 192), M. Tuccius (190), and Cn. Baebius Tamphilus (pr. 199) for the resettlement of Sipontum and Buxentum in 186, L. Manlius Acidinus (pr. 188) for Aquileia, and Q. Fabius Buteo (pr. 181) in 180 for an unnamed colony, probably Luca (for the identity of the colony, see n. 95). The sources for the commissions are given in n. 42.

46. Consulars: Q. Lutatius Catulus (cos. 220) for Placentia and Cremona in 219 and 218, M. Aemilius Lepidus (cos. 187) for Parma and Mutina in 183, P. Claudius Pulcher (cos. 184) for Graviscae in 181, M. Aemilius Lepidus (cos. 187) for Luna in 177; serving consul: Q. Fabius Labeo (pr. 189, cos. 183) for Saturnia in 183; praetorians: two unnamed praetorians founded Placentia and Cremona in 219 and 218, M. Helvius (pr. 197) for Sipontum in 194, L. Cornelius Merula (pr. 198) for Tempsa in 194, Cn. Octavius (pr. 205) and C. Laetorius (pr. 210) for Croton in the same year, Q. Fabius Labeo (pr. 189) for Potentia and Pisaurum in 184, L. Quinctius Crispinus (pr. 186) for Parma and Mutina in 183, C. Afranius Stellio (pr. 185) for Saturnia in 183, C. Calpurnius Piso (pr. 186) for Graviscae in 181, Cn. Sicinius (pr. 183) for Luna in 177, possibly along with P. Aelius Tubero, then serving as praetor. The manuscripts have a *lacuna* in the passage reporting the last commission (Livy 41.13.4–5), so that only the *praenomen* and *nomen*

of a P. Aelius are preserved. Broughton, *MRR*, 1:399, identified him as P. Aelius Tubero, praetor in that year, but another candidate, P. Aelius Ligus (cos. 172) is available. For the sources, see n. 42.

47. See section IV in this chapter.

48. Q. Fabius Labeo (pr. 189), serving as consul when he founded Saturnia would then rank only as a former praetor, while P. Aelius Tubero, if he was indeed a commissioner for Luna, would not yet have achieved that rank; see n. 46.

49. C. Afranius Stellio (pr. 185), who settled Saturnia in 183.

50. For the distribution of ranks in the senate, see Willems, *Le sénat*, 1:305–80.

51. Placentia and Cremona (219–218): a consular and two former praetors; Placentia, Cremona, and Bononia (190–189): L. Valerius Flaccus (cos. 195) and L. Valerius Tappo (pr. 192); Narnia (chosen in 199): P. Aelius Paetus and Cn. Cornelius Lentulus, both consuls in 201; Croton (194): Cn. Octavius (pr. 205) and C. Laetorius (pr. 210); Sipontum and Buxentum (chosen in 186): L. Scribonius Libo (pr. 192), M. Tuccius (pr. 190), and Cn. Baebius Tamphilus (pr. 199); Mutina and Parma (183): M. Aemilius Lepidus (cos. 187) and L. Quinctius Crispinus (pr. 186); Saturnia (183): C. Afranius Stellio (pr. 185) and Q. Fabius Labeo (pr. 189), who was serving as consul at the time (Liguria was his province), but probably was only a praetorian when elected; Aquileia (183–181): P. Cornelius Scipio Nasica (cos. 191), C. Flaminius (cos. 187), and L. Manlius Acidinus (pr. 188); Graviscae (181): P. Claudius Pulcher (cos. 184), C. Calpurnius Piso (pr. 186), and C. Terentius Istra (pr. 182) (If the election had been held in the previous year, Terentius would have been serving as praetor, but his province was Sardinia and he probably would not have been elected triumvir *in absentia*; his election to the commission, then, probably was earlier than his election as praetor. It is just conceivable that Claudius's election as consul followed by a short interval his election to the college.); Luna (177): Cn. Sicinius (pr. 183) and probably also M. Aemilius Lepidus (cos. 187) (The manuscripts have a *lacuna* between the *nomen* of the first triumvir, P. Aelius, and the *cognomen* of the second; the gap probably contained Aelius's *cognomen*, along with the *praenomen* and *nomen* of the second member. The *cognomen* of the second triumvir is corrupt, for the *legibus* of the manuscripts makes no sense in the context; it is usually emended to Lepidus, an easy change, and the M. Aemilius follows easily. The P. Aelius is usually identified as P. Aelius Tubero, who was praetor in 177, the year in which the colony was founded; see Broughton, *MRR*, 1:399. Aelius probably would not have held the office when elected triumvir.). For the sources, see n. 42.

52. Venusia (chosen in 200): C. Terentius Varro (cos. 216); Volturnum, Liternum, Puteoli, Salernum, and Buxentum (197–194): M. Servilius Geminus (cos. 202) (the other two members were elected praetors shortly after they were placed on the commission); Sipontum (194): M. Helvius (pr. 197); Vibo Valentia (194–192): M. Minucius Rufus (pr. 197); Copia (194–193): L. Apustius Fullo (pr. 196); Potentia and Pisaurum (184): Q. Fabius Labeo (pr. 189); Luca (chosen in 180): Q. Fabius Buteo (pr. 181); Aquileia (chosen in 169): no consular or praetorian members. For the sources, see n. 42.

53. Two consulars and a praetorian: Aquileia in 183; consular and two praetorians: Placentia and Cremona in 219–218; three praetorians: resettlement of Sipontum and Buxentum in 186. Note that the membership for the triumvirate that founded Tempsa is incomplete, and the college, therefore, is not part of this discussion. For the sources, see n. 42.

54. Consular and a praetorian: supplement to Cremona and Placentia (190), Parma and Mutina (183), Graviscae (181), and Luna (177) (in the last three, only the foundation is reported and the ranks given are those of one year before that date); two consulars: supplement to Narnia in 199; two praetorians: Croton (194) and Saturnia (183). For the sources, see n. 42.

55. One consular: supplement to Venusia (200) and Volturnum, Liternum, Puteoli, Salernum, and Buxentum (197); one praetor: Sipontum (194), Vibo Valentia (194), Copia (194), Potentia and Pisaurum (184), and Luca (180). For the sources, see n. 42.

56. Nine colleges founded or led supplements to citizen colonies and nine established or supplemented Latin ones. Among the former, one held three praetorians (resettlement of Sipontum and Buxentum), two had two praetorians each (Croton and Saturnia), three each had a consular and a praetorian (the pair of Mutina and Parma, Graviscae, and Luna), one had one consular (Volturnum, Liternum, Puteoli, Salernum, and Buxentum), and two had one praetorian each (Sipontum and the pair Potentia and Pisaurum). Among the latter, one had two consulars and a praetorian (Aquileia), another a former consul and two former praetors (Placentia and Cremona), a third had one consular and one praetorian (supplement to Placentia and Cremona and foundation of Bononia), a fourth included two consulars (supplement to Narnia), a fifth had one consular (supplement to Venusia), three more had one praetorian each (Vibo, Copia, and Luca), and the last, no consulars or praetorians (supplement to Aquileia). For the sources, see n. 42.

57. For the sources, see Broughton, *MRR*, 1:343, 348, 352, 357.

58. For the sources, see Broughton, *MRR*, 1:347, 351, 367–68.

59. For the sources for his praetorship, see Broughton, *MRR*, 1:365, 369. For the embassy, see Livy 39.54.11–55.4.

60. For the presence of a praetorian army, see Eckstein, *Senate and General*, pp. 26–27.

61. Zonar. 8.20. Eckstein, *Senate and General*, p. 329 n. 12, claims Catulus campaigned in Istria against Demetrius of Pharos.

62. For the sources, see n. 42.

63. Pisa was the anchor of the Roman frontier against the Ligurians in the west, and Roman armies used it as a base (Livy 39.32.1–4). In 180, the Pisatans offered land for a colony to Rome, and the senate accepted the offer. The colony, then, was established at Pisa's request, and it need not have formed an important element in Rome's strategy in the area, which apparently focused more on Luna at this time. Although the front around Pisa was active for a few more years, Luca (unlike Luna) was never mentioned in accounts of the fighting after 180. This silence may indicate that military activity by both sides in that area was not on a large scale. Indeed, early in 180 Roman armies attacked the Apuani, the tribe that most threatened the area of Luca, and the commanders deported a large number of Ligurians, while later that year the consul Q. Fulvius Flaccus, attacking from Pisa, captured and deported another seven thousand men (Livy 40.41.3–4). As a result of these actions, the territory of Luca might not have been considered dangerous.

64. The only exception is the college that led a supplement to Aquileia in 169, for it included no members of consular or praetorian rank. At this time, however, the large number of senior senators on public business as a result of the Third Macedonian War may have made it difficult to find a former consul or praetor free to work on a colonial supplement. Indeed, in 170, the urban praetor, M. Raecius, recalled to Rome all senators not engaged in public business and ordered them to remain near the city (Livy 43.11.4–5), a sign that they were urgently needed in Rome.

65. Livy 8.16.14; Festus p. 458L; see Broughton, *MRR*, 1:141, 159.

66. For the use of some form of *scribere* in this connection, see Livy 5.24.4, 8.16.14, 31.49.6, 37.47.1, 39.23.4.

67. Livy 37.47.1–2. Livy gave no indication why the colonial commissioners did not perform the task in this case.

68. Note that Rullus in 63 gave the decemvirs to be created by his proposed land law *scribae* and *praecones*; see Cic. *Agr.* 2.13.32.

69. For the use of *nomen dare* to describe an action by prospective colonists, see Livy 1.11.4, 10.21.10, 34.42.6; Cic. *Dom.* 78; Festus p. 13L; Sen. *Ad Helviam* 7.7.

70. The words *nomen dare* may indicate that prospective colonists freely volunteered, but this need not always have been the case, for the same phrase was also used to describe military conscription: see Brunt, *Italian Manpower*, p. 630. Salmon, *Roman Colonization*, p. 24, holds that Roman citizens could legally be compelled to join citizen colonies, but he cites no evidence. With respect to Latin colonies, the situation is clearer, for Roman citizens could not be forced to give up their citizenship; according to Cicero (*Caec.* 33.98), citizens joined Latin colonies of their own will or to escape a legal penalty; Salmon, p. 168 n. 26, saw in the latter a reference to citizens' *ius exilii*.

71. For the term, see Festus p. 13L; Livy 34.42.6. Smith, "Citizenship in Roman Colonies," p. 19 n. 15, points out that in its strictest sense *adscriptio* means inclusion on a list, but that the word, when used more loosely, can denote the act of becoming a member of a colony.

72. For the legal meaning of that requirement, see Daube, "Patterns of Manumission," pp. 68–72.

73. Brunt, *Italian Manpower*, pp. 28–31, and Salmon, *Making of Roman Italy*, p. 65.

74. On the *iura* of the Latins, see Sherwin-White, *Roman Citizenship*, pp. 108–16.

75. A report preserved by Livy (34.42.5–6) provides the only direct evidence: in 195, Latins enrolled in citizen colonies were claiming Roman citizenship, and the senate rejected the claim (which Livy called a *novum ius*). Mommsen (*Str.*, 2:636, 3:622) and Kornemann (*RE* 4 [1900], cols. 571–72, s.v. *coloniae*) saw the incident as proof that Latins could not legally serve in citizen colonies, but Smith, "Citizenship in Roman Colonies," pp. 18–20, suggests that the Latins' citizenship would not have been made real until the actual foundation—the *novum ius* would have been the claim that entry on a list sufficed to give the status. Smith's interpretation has been widely followed; see Salmon, *Roman Colonization*, pp. 184–85 n. 165; Briscoe, *Commentary on Livy Books XXXIV–XXXVII*, pp. 115–16; Badian, "Roman Politics and the Italians," pp. 385–86. Piper, "Latins and the Roman Citizenship," p. 39, writing against Smith's thesis, admits that Smith's interpretation "does seem to express what Livy actually wrote." The rights of Latins in this regard probably contracted through the second century. At the end of that century, the *lex Appuleia* gave Marius the right to grant Roman citizenship to three individuals in each of the colonies authorized by the law, a privilege he used to give citizenship to a Latin (see Cic. *Balb.* 21.48). Marius probably would not have expended one of those positions if a Latin could have gained Roman citizenship as an ordinary colonist. Some scholars, holding that Latins could serve in citizen colonies, have sought to avoid the difficulty posed by this case by holding that Marius's colonies were Latin and that the *lex Appuleia* gave him the right to make three individuals in each Latin colony Roman citizens; see Smith, "Citizenship in Roman Colonies," pp. 18–20, and Sherwin-White, *Roman Citizenship*, p. 112. Against Marius's colonies being considered Latin, see Badian, *Foreign Clientelae*, p. 206, and Piper, "Latins and the Roman Citizenship," pp. 39–43. Certain rights of Latins, such as the ability to come to Rome and take up some of the privileges of citizenship there, seem generally to have been eroded during the second century; see Sherwin-White, *Roman Citizenship*, pp. 110–11. Among the lost privileges may have been the right to join citizen colonies.

76. Note that the act of submitting one's name as a colonist and the similar action of those who came forward, voluntarily or not, for military service both were described with the words *nomen dare*, while those chosen had their names recorded on a list and

were instructed, after having sworn an oath, to assemble again later at a designated time and place. For the military uses of the phrase, see Brunt, *Italian Manpower*, p. 630, and Deniaux, "Le passage des citoyennetés locales," p. 268 n. 10; for the list of those chosen to serve in the army, see Brunt, *Italian Manpower*, pp. 637–38; and for soldiers and colonists instructed to reassemble later, see Polyb. 3.40.3–10, 6.21.6–7.

77. Livy 5.19.4; Polyb. 6.19.5–6.

78. Livy 2.28.5, 3.41.7, 43.14.2; Varro *apud* Non. p. 28L; V. Max. 6.3.4.

79. Polybius presented the *dilectus* as taking place entirely at Rome. Some scholars, such as Brunt, *Italian Manpower*, pp. 625–34, have felt with some justification that the collection of all citizens of military age at Rome was impossible, or at least unlikely, in the late third and second centuries, given the large number of citizens and the extent of Roman territory; indeed, some instances of conscription away from Rome are known. But Polybius's version of the *dilectus* need not represent archaic practices or antiquarian reconstructions of such practices, referring to a time when the citizen body and the territory were small enough for the draft to be managed in such a manner. Even if many soldiers were conscripted in gatherings away from Rome, some certainly were enlisted in the city, as various notices concerning the *dilectus* in the second century clearly show; see Rawson, "Literary Sources," p. 15. For our purposes, the extent to which part of the *dilectus* took place away from Rome is irrelevant; the choice of colonists would not involve the same problems of scale and thus could easily be accomplished at Rome, perhaps for small colonies even on a single day.

80. Rawson, "Literary Sources," pp. 13–31. Note that Polybius mentioned neither the auspices that probably preceded the *dilectus* nor the ritual and formula that may have accompanied it. The absence of both can be explained either by Polybius's apparent lack of interest in such matters or by the focus on the tribunes rather than on the consuls, who would have taken the auspices and performed some, at least, of the ceremony. The date of Polybius's source is unknown, but the historian noted a few of the details that were different in his own day, and Rawson holds this to imply that the overall procedure had remained essentially unchanged. For the election of military tribunes, see Suolahti, *Junior Officers*, pp. 51–57.

81. Livy 37.4.1–2, 36.3.13–14.

82. Livy 34.42.5–6. Note that the consul of 190 (Livy 37.4.1) gave the time and place of assembly for his army at a *contio* held some time after the completion of conscription. If colonial commissioners followed a similar procedure when they had not given instructions at enlistment, the colonists may have had to wait at Rome for a public announcement.

83. For the presence of a praetorian army, see Eckstein, *Senate and General*, pp. 26–27.

84. Livy 21.63.9, 27.40.7, 31.14.1, 41.10.5–13, 42.49.1, 44.22.17, 45.39.11; Varro *LL* 7.37; Cic. *Fam*. 13.6a.1; Ulpian *Dig*. 1.16.1. Augustus instructed those about to depart to make vows at his new temple of Mars Ultor on the Capitol; see Dio 55.10. For the departure, see Mommsen, *Str.*, 1:63–64, 375, 430; and Magdelain, "L'inauguration de l'*urbs*," p. 11, who notes that those practices formed a necessary transition between the spheres *domi* and *militiae*.

85. See Livy 32.29.3–4, 34.42.5–6, 34.45.1–2. See also Broughton, *MRR*, 1:336, 339 n. 3.

86. Livy placed the passage of the law in 197, but C. Atinius, who carried the plebiscite, was tribune for 196, so that the law probably was passed between late December 197 and the end of February 196. Carcopino, *Autour des Gracques*, pp. 161–62, used this college to illustrate his theory that all triumvirates, including the Gracchan agrarian commission, used a form of regular rotation over a college's term with only one commissioner working in any given year: Geminus, then, would have been the sole commissioner in 196, Thermus in 195, and Longus in 194. The Romans, however, probably would not

have committed themselves to a scheme so rigid, and there are difficulties with the rotation — Thermus certainly returned from Spain well into his supposed year as manager, while Longus actively served as consul during his; arrangements probably were made on an ad hoc basis. Seibert, "IIIviri lege Sempronia," pp. 63–64, and Briscoe, *Commentary on Livy Books XXXI–XXXIII*, pp. 225–26, suggest that the tribune C. Atinius who passed the law was not the C. Atinius who served as tribune in 196 and propose instead an otherwise unattested tribunate for another C. Atinius in 197; Seibert advanced that suggestion specifically to spread the work of the college over four consular years rather than three in order to undercut Carcopino's suggestion about rotation. Briscoe and Seibert base their arguments on two points: (1) the position of the notice within the narrative of the events of the year indicates that the plebiscite was passed earlier in 197; and (2) two Gaii Atinii were active at the time, one, probably to be identified with the tribune of 196, was praetor in 190 and the other was praetor in 195. They suggest that the tribunate of the praetor of 195 should be placed in 197. The notice of the plebiscite's passage, however, is annalistic in style and is without context in the narrative; its place in the accounts of that year, then, need not indicate its actual chronological position. Furthermore, although it is reasonable to assume that the praetor of 195 had held the office of tribune, no evidence places it in 197 and a tribunate in this year would leave a very short interval between the two offices. Carcopino's thesis, intended to explain the mode of operation of the Gracchan agrarian commission, will be examined in greater detail in Chapter 8, section IV.

87. Livy 33.43.5–8, 34.10.1–7.

88. Livy 33.43.9, 34.43.3–9.

89. The matter will be examined in greater depth in Chapter 8, section IV, and in Chapter 9, section IV.

90. Livy (21.25.1–7) and Polybius (3.40.3–10) both held that the same triumvirate founded both colonies, but Livy, who provides most of the information on the identity of the commissioners, is confused here, giving eight names for three places. As a result, some scholars have held that each settlement was founded by a separate college; see Broughton, *MRR*, 1:241–42 n. 12; Walbank, *Commentary on Polybius*, 1:375; and Bandelli, "La fondazione di Piacenza e di Cremona," p. 41. But a close examination of the sources reveals that only one triumvirate was involved and that Livy's confusion resulted from the election of a new triumvirate to complete the foundation of Placentia after the capture of the original commissioners; see Gargola, "Colonial Commissioners of 218," pp. 465–73.

91. The officials who founded Copia and Vibo Valentia, both authorized by the *lex Aelia*, clearly could not work individually at separate sites, for while the law authorized two colonies on nonadjacent sites separated by difficult terrain, it authorized separate triumvirates for each settlement.

92. For this college, see Chapter 8, section IV.

93. Bononia (one year): the decision making began in December 190 or in January 189 (Livy [37.47.1–2] reported that C. Laelius [cos. 190] persuaded the senate to send the colony while supervising the election of his successors) and the foundation day was December 30, 189 (Livy 37.57.7–8); Copia (one year or less): Livy (34.53.1–2) noted the authorizing law was passed late in the consular year of 194 and he (35.9.7–8) reported the foundation in the consular year of 193; Vibo Valentia (between one and two years): it was authorized by the same law as Copia, and Livy (35.40.5–6) reported the foundation in the consular year of 192; Aquileia (at least two years): the decision to found was made no earlier that the early summer of 183, for Livy (39.55.4–6) noted that the senate issued its decree after M. Claudius Marcellus, one of the consuls of that year, had defeated the Gauls in his province and was seeking to begin a war with the Istrians, while the foun-

dation took place in 181 (Livy 40.34.2), probably no earlier than the late spring, for Livy (40.26.1–3) reported that the Istrians were hindering the foundation of the colony, and that Q. Fabius Buteo, one of the praetors of the year but apparently already in his province, had begun a war against them for that reason; Luca (at least two years): see nn. 95 and 96.

94. For the term, see Livy 32.29.3–4, 34.53.1–2.

95. As praetor in 181, Buteo held Gaul as his province and campaigned actively against the Istrians, and his command was prorogued, probably for the entire year; see Livy 40.36.13. In other cases that year, Livy noted those magistrates whose term was extended only until their successors arrived (see 40.36.7), and his failure to do the same with Fabius, when coupled with the fact that Gaul was not assigned as a province to any of the magistrates of 180, makes it likely that Fabius served there for at least one more year. When reporting the election of the college, Livy (40.43.1) only identified the settlement as being near Pisa. Some have identified Livy's colony with the citizen colony founded at Luna by a different triumvirate in 177, assuming that the senate had changed its mind about the legal status of the settlement and its triumvirate; see Marquardt, *Römische Staatsverwaltung*, 1:39; and Salmon, "Last Latin Colony," pp. 30–35; *Roman Colonization*, p. 109. Others, noting Velleius Paterculus's report of the foundation of Luca (see following note), accept the foundation of two colonies, a Latin one at Luca, and a citizen colony at Luna, and this is the most likely position; see Salmon, *Making of Roman Italy*, pp. 95, 199 n. 331, who changed his position and accepted both Luna and Luca based on archaeological evidence that shows a Roman settlement at Luca at the right time. Luca certainly was a Latin colony, for after 90 it became a *municipium* (Cic. *Fam.* 13.13.1), as a Latin colony would have, rather than remaining a colony as would have been the case for a *colonia civium Romanorum*.

96. Livy did not report its foundation (perhaps it lies in one of the many lacunae in books 40 through 42), but Vell. Pat. (1.15.2) placed the foundation of Luca in the fourth year after the foundation of Graviscae, an event Livy placed in 181, so that counting inclusively, the formal establishment of Luca probably can be placed in 178. But Velleius's chronology is often confused; Livy and Velleius agree on the date for the foundation of Bononia in 189, but Velleius's dates for Pisaurum and Potentia and Aquileia and Graviscae are one year earlier than Livy's. Yet both placed Aquileia and Graviscae in the same year and both gave the same interval between the foundation of those two places and the establishment of Potentia and Pisaurum. The difference can be explained by a single, simple error: the miscalculation by Velleius or his source of the interval between the foundations of Bononia and Potentia and Pisaurum or the corruption of the number in the manuscripts.

97. For the history of both colleges, see Livy 34.53.1–2, 35.9.7–9, 35.40.5–6.

98. Livy 34.62.16–17. Elsewhere, Livy (34.62.16–18) implied that the dispute came to the senate's attention shortly after the consuls of 193 left for their provinces, and thus after the colonial commission was chosen, for their election would have followed closely the plebiscite in late 194.

99. See Livy 40.26.2.

100. The absence of one or more triumvirs on other tasks may also be inferred in other triumvirates where the year in which the law was passed and the college chosen is unknown: at Graviscae, one of the members of its college, C. Terentius Istra, was praetor in the year preceding its foundation in 181, and at Saturnia, Q. Fabius Labeo was consul in the year of its foundation, 183; see Livy 39.45.1–3, 39.51.5, 39.55.9, 40.29.1–2. The latter instance need not show that the presence of a consular or praetorian was not required: another member of the commission, C. Afranius Stellio, had served as praetor in 185; see Livy 39.23.2.

CHAPTER 4

1. For earlier use, see Livy 23.35.3, 24.7.10, 24.13.7, 25.20.1.
2. Livy 34.53.1–2, 35.9.7–8, 35.40.5–6.
3. Livy 34.53.1–2, 35.9.7. Note that Livy (32.2.6) recorded that the colonists of Narnia complained in 199 that others in their community were acting as if they were colonists.
4. Forms of two verbs usually denoted the act of establishing a colony. The more frequently encountered expression, preferred by writers affecting the annalistic style, was some form of the words, *coloniam deducere*, while another, less frequently used phrase was *coloniam condere*. For *deducere*, see Livy 9.28.7, 10.21.7, 34.45.1–5; Cic. *Phil.* 2.40.102; *Div.* 1.45.102; for *condere*, Ovid *Fast.* 4.827–28; Cato 18P; Festus p. 271L; Varro *LL* 5.143. For the late third and early second centuries, Livy customarily recorded the foundation of colonies with some form of *deducere* (for the sources, see Chapter 3, n. 42). Livy 37.57.7–8 shows that the founding was considered to have been achieved on a single day.
5. Saticula: Festus p. 458L; Brundisium: Cic. *Sest.* 131; Placentia: Asconius *Pis.* p. 3 Clark; and Bononia: Livy 37.57.7. The manuscripts of Asconius place the foundation of Placentia on December 31, 218. Madvig, *Disputationis de Q. Asconii Pediani et aliorum in Ciceronis orationes commentariis appendix critica*, pp. 20–21, emended the date to May 31 to fit his perception of the events of that year; in this he has been followed by subsequent editors. For a defense of December 31, see Gargola, "Colonial Commissioners of 218," pp. 465–73.
6. For Placentia, see Livy *Per.* 20, 21.25.1–7; Polyb. 3.40.3–10.
7. Scholars have identified different events with the foundation day and have placed it at different points in the process of colonization. Mommsen, *Str.*, 2:637–39, followed by E. Kornemann, *RE* 4 (1900), cols. 577–78, s.v. *coloniae*, held it to be the day on which the *lustrum* ending the census of the colonists was performed, an act, he maintained, that came at the end of the entire process; Mommsen, however, argued neither position in detail. Salmon, *Roman Colonization*, p. 26, again placed the foundation day at the end; for him it was the day on which the commissioners signaled the completion of their task by having the bronze tablets containing the *forma* and the *lex colonica* erected and the *groma* removed. That act, however, was mentioned only by a late source, M. Junius Nipsius (p. 295L), who did not specifically connect it with the formal foundation or even with the end of the founders' responsibilities. Eckstein, "Foundation Day," pp. 85–97, clearly demonstrates that our sources identified the formal foundation of a city, including Rome itself, with the plowing of the *sulcus primigenius* around the site of the town. For Rome, see Ovid *Fast.* 4.825–32; Plut. *Rom.* 11; Dion. Hal. *Ant. Rom.* 1.88; and Tac. *Ann.* 12.24. See also Cato fr. 18 P (= Serv. *A.* 5.755); Varro *LL* 5.143; Festus pp. 270–71L, 392L. Eckstein correctly placed that act relatively early in the process, when the colonists arrived at the colonial site. Salmon, *Roman Colonization*, p. 24, holds without argument that the *sulcus primigenius* was established only for colonies placed at previously uninhabited sites, but the example of the citizen colony at Capua (see next note) shows him to be mistaken.
8. The Caesarian citizen colonies of Capua and Urso both had *pomeria* marked by the plow (see *CIL* X.3825; *FIRA* I, no. 21, cap. 73. Varro (*LL* 5.143) claimed the ritual was used to found *oppida* in Latium, probably a reference to Latin colonies, while Cato (18P) used the general *civitates*.
9. Valeton, "De templis Romanis," 23:17, 67, held that the augurs of the new colony themselves inaugurated the colonial *pomerium* from a place near, but not at, the future city, using as evidence Ennius's description (*Ann.* 77–96 V = Cic. *Div.* 1.48.107–8) of Romulus taking the auspices from the Aventine for a city he would found on the Palatine. Catalano, "Aspetti spaziali," p. 486 and n. 178, points out that the augury was part of the

contest between Romulus and Remus over who would be founder and thus it concerned the identity of the founder and not the location of the colony or the day of its foundation. Like Romulus, the colonial commissioner clearly placed the *pomerium* by plowing the furrow; the role, if any, of the colony's augurs is unknown.

10. Varro *LL* 5.143. Cicero (*Div.* 1.17.30) had Romulus divide the heavens by *regiones* to take the auspices *ex avibus* on the day of foundation.

11. Plut. *Rom.* 11; Ovid *Fast.* 4.827–28.

12. Cato fr. 18 P (= Serv. *A.* 5.755); see also Don. Ter. *Ad.* 1.583.

13. Dion. Hal. *Ant. Rom.* 1.88; Plut. *Rom.* 11.

14. For the use of the furrow in the colonies of the dynasts of the last years of the republic, see *CIL* X.3825; *FIRA* I, no. 21, cap. 73; Cic. *Phil.* 2.40.102. For the coinage, see Levick, *Roman Colonies*, pp. 35–37.

15. See Brown, *Cosa*, pp. 16–17, 51; Brown, Richardson, and Richardson, "Cosa II," pp. 9–14.

16. See Mommsen, *Str.*, 2:332–33; Wiseman, "Census in the First Century," pp. 59–75. On the census itself, see Piéri, *L'histoire du cens*; Nicolet, *World of the Citizen*, pp. 49–88.

17. For Latin colonies, see Livy 35.9.7, 35.40.5–6, 37.57.8; Asc. *Pis.* p. 3 Clark. Note that Augustus's citizen colonies in southern Asia Minor had tribes of their own; see Levick, *Roman Colonies*, pp. 76–78.

18. For the *lustrum*, see Mommsen, *Str.*, 2:412–13; Ogilvie, "Lustrum Condere," pp. 31–39; Berve, *RE* 13 (1927), cols. 2040–58, s.v. *lustrum*; Hülsen, *RE* 13 (1927), cols. 2029–39, s.v. *lustratio*; Piéri, *L'histoire du cens*, pp. 77–98.

19. Livy 1.44.1–2; Varro *LL* 6.86, 6.93; see also Dion. Hal. *Ant. Rom.* 4.22.1–2.

20. For the sacrifice itself, see Festus 372–74L. Serv. *A.* 1.283, called the procession an *ambilustrum*.

21. Cic. *De Orat.* 2.268; Suet. *Aug.* 97; V. Max. 4.1.10.

22. Varro *LL* 6.93: *quod censor exercitum centuriato constituit quinquennalem, cum lustrare et in urbem ad vexillum ducere debet*.

23. Cic. *Phil.* 2.40.102; see also *Agr.* 2.32.86; Plut. *CG* 11.

24. See Mommsen, *Str.*, 2:332; Piéri, *L'histoire du cens*, pp. 77–97. Varro (*LL* 6.93), indeed, claimed that the purification rite established the citizenry in the form of the *exercitus quinquennalis*.

25. Berve, *RE* 13 (1927), cols. 2056–57, s.v. *lustrum*; Latte, *Römische Religionsgeschichte*, p. 119.

26. The terminology may indicate that the connection between censorial and colonial *lustra* was closer than the tie between either of the two and military lustrations. The *lustrum* of the censors at Rome was "founded" (*conditum*), as was also the case with cities and colonies; see Mommsen, *Str.*, 2:332, and Ogilvie, "Lustrum Condere," pp. 31–39. Perhaps because the colonial *lustrum* was a typical and prominent ritual of colonization, founders could be known either as *deductores* or as *conditores*; see, for example, Don. Ter. *Ad.* 1.583.

27. See Daube, "Patterns of Manumission," pp. 68–72; Smith, "Roman Citizenship in Roman Colonies," pp. 18–20. *Contra* Piper, "Latins and Roman Citizenship," pp. 38–50.

28. Festus p. 366L; see Wiseman, "Census in the First Century," pp. 59–75.

29. Plut. *CG* 11. See also App. *BC* 1.24. For a discussion of those passages, see Chapter 8, section IV.

30. Eckstein, "Foundation Day," pp. 91–93, closely associates in time the drawing up of the list of prospective colonists with the *lustrum*. Following A. S. Pease, *M. Tulli Ciceronis de Divinatione Liber Primus* (Urbana, Ill., 1920), p. 283, Eckstein essentially sees *lustra* as preparations for departures, viewing in that way military *lustra* and even the censors' *lustrum*, which ended in a march back into the city, and for that reason, he

places the colonial *lustrum* at Rome as a preparation for the departure to the colony. While the *lustrum* certainly was performed before beginning campaigns, the ceremony essentially formed a body of men, citizens or soldiers, into a unit with the necessary subgroups: the censors' *lustrum*, after all, began no project and the procession that ended it was in essence a ceremonial entry of the newly reconstituted citizens into their city. Salmon, *Roman Colonization*, is confused on this point: at p. 24, he makes no reference to the *lustrum* and takes the procession *sub vexillo* to refer only to a formal march from Rome to the colonial site, while at p. 168 n. 27, while discussing the *sulcus primigenius*, he says that the ceremonies were identical to the censors' *lustrum* without mentioning any of the ceremonies associated with it.

31. For the vocabulary, see n. 4.

32. Colonial commissioners, if they followed the same general procedures as generals did with their armies, may have purified the colonists on a number of occasions, especially when they had first collected the settlers and were preparing to depart for the colony, but one *lustrum* probably was definitive with regard to the colonists' civic status.

33. For the *lex Atinia*, see Chapter 3, section III. For Placentia and Cremona, see Polyb. 3.40.3–10.

34. Varro *LL* 6.93.

35. See, for example, App. *BC* 4.88–89, *Iber.* 19; Dio 47.38.4; Hirtius *BG* 8.52.1; Livy 3.22.3–4, 23.35.5, 38.12.2–10, 38.37.8, 41.18.6–10; Plut. *Brut.* 39; *Caes.* 43; Tac. *Ann.* 15.26.

36. Dio 47.38.4 and Plut. *Brut.* 39 both claim that a location outside the camp was customary.

37. Livy (38.12.2–10) claimed that the march of Cn. Manlius Vulso's army began a few days after he had purified his army.

38. App. *BC* 4.88–89, *Iber.* 19; Livy 38.12.2–10, 41.18.6–10; Plut. *Brut.* 39, *Caes.* 43; Tac. *Ann.* 15.26.

39. See Chapter 2, section I.

40. Dio 47.38.4; Plut. *Brut.* 39.

41. Mommsen, *Str.*, 2:636–38 (followed by Kornemann, *RE* 4 [1900], cols. 577–78), who held that the *lustrum*, rather than the plowing of the *sulcus*, marked the foundation day of the colony, thought that the colonial *lustrum* should come at the end of the entire process of colonization and he placed it at the colonial site after lands had been assigned; the *lustrum*, however, ended the census and no evidence requires that the census be one of the last official acts of the founders.

42. Cicero's phrase (*Div.* 1.102) — *in lustranda colonia ab eo qui deduceret* — may indicate that the *lustrum* preceded the *deductio*, if the use of the imperfect subjunctive of *deducere* indicates that, with respect to the time of the *lustrum*, that act was still to come.

43. Note that in some military lustrations, the soldiers themselves sacrificed in camp after the ceremony: see Plut. *Brut.* 39.

44. For the commissioners giving a charter and filling the offices, see Mommsen, *Str.*, 2:637–38. Salmon, *Roman Colonization*, pp. 85–86, held without discussion that Latin colonies were free to chose their own constitutions, but how could they have decided on such a matter without magistrates and assemblies?

45. According to Livy (27.38.3–5), in 207 ambassadors from a number of *coloniae maritimae* read to the senate documents supporting their claim for exemption from military service. Note that Salmon, *Roman Colonization*, pp. 26, 167 n. 14, makes no clear distinction between the *lex rogata* that authorized a colony and the *lex data* that governed it.

46. For the style, see Chapter 3, section I.

47. Thus, Hardy, *Three Spanish Charters*, p. 9.

48. Cic. *Agr.* 2.34.92; *FIRA* I, no. 21, cap. 69, 93.

49. Siculus Flaccus (p. 135L) noted that "we proclaim, however, the *regiones* within the *fines* of which there is the free power of *ius dicendi* and *ius coercendi* for the magistrates of individual colonies." He considered that definition part of the *lex data* of the colony, and thus it would have been proclaimed along with it to the settlers at the ceremonies surrounding the *deductio*; see pp. 163–64L. Here, it should be noted that the *lex data* governing the Caesarian colony of Urso specified that *fines* had been given to the colony, but not the stage at which that occurred: *FIRA* I, no. 21, cap. 77, 78, 104.

50. See Livy 39.27.10; *FIRA* I, no. 8, passim (the law of 111 will be cited according to Riccobono's text, since it is more widely available, and Lintott's new edition, published in his *Judicial Reform*, will be cited only when it varies in a way that is significant for our investigation). For the definition of large territories, see also Chapter 2, section IV.

51. *CIL* I.2.584. Dilke, *Roman Land Surveyors*, p. 36, assumes that surveyors must have been employed in the boundary dispute, but this is unlikely. Instead, the magistrates probably examined the territory, the witnesses, and perhaps the documents.

52. *Praetores:* Cora: *CIL* X.6527; Signia: *CIL* X.5969; Setia: *CIL* X.6466; Cales: *CIL* X.4651; Interamna Lirenas: *CIL* X.5203; Beneventum: *CIL* X.480; Aesernia: *CIL* IX.2664; Spoletium: *CIL* XI.4822; *quaestores*: *CIL* IX.438–40, 5351; tribunes: *CIL* IX.438–40; *aediles*: *CIL* XI.4125; *censores*: *CIL* IX.1635, X.123; see Beloch, *Römische Geschichte*, pp. 489–92; Sherwin-White, *Roman Citizenship*, pp. 117–19. Local senates are attested in the Latin colonies of Brundisium, Venusia (*CIL* I².402); Paestum (*CIL* I².1682); Firmum (*CIL* I².1921); and Aquileia (*CIL* I².2197); see Laffi, "I senati locali," pp. 59–74.

53. *FIRA* I, no. 21, cap. 62. The *lex Plaetoria* provided that the urban praetor at Rome was to have two lictors when he exercised jurisdiction; see Censorinus *De die natali* 24.3.

54. See MacKendrick, "Roman Town Planning," pp. 126–33; Ulrich, *Roman Orator*. For later elaborations, see Ward-Perkins, "From Republic to Empire," pp. 1–19.

55. Brown, *Cosa*, pp. 9–11, 23–24, 53–54. Brown notes that similar *comitia* and *curiae* were built at the Latin colonies of Alba Fucens and Paestum.

56. For the suggestion, see Brown, *Cosa*, pp. 15–16.

57. They were also important from an early date in the Greek world; see Polignac, *La naissance de la cité grecque*.

58. For the early *ager Romanus*, see Catalano, "Aspetti spaziali," pp. 492–94. For the points that defined it, see Momigliano, "Interim Report," pp. 100–101; Alföldi, "Ager Romanus Antiquus," pp. 187–88; *Early Rome*, pp. 296–304; Quilici Gigli, "Confini del territorio di Roma primitiva," pp. 567–75.

59. See Scheid, "Les sanctuaries de confins," pp. 583–95.

60. For the use of inscribed markers, see Chapter 2, section III.

61. See, for example, Frontinus p. 43L.

62. *Liber coloniarum I* pp. 221–22L.

63. *Liber coloniarum II* p. 257L. For markers defining an unknown, but apparently official, boundary at Sutrium (the Augustan colony?), see *Liber coloniarum I* pp. 217–18L.

64. For the rites, see Strabo 5.3.2. Scheid, "Les sanctuaries de confins," pp. 585–86, identifies the priests in question as the pontiffs and derives Strabo's notice from Polybius and perhaps Fabius Pictor. On the festival of the Robigalia, performed on April 25, the *flamen Quirinalis* led a procession to the site at the fifth milestone on the *via Claudia*; see Ovid *Fast.* 4.905–42; Festus p. 325L; and Scullard, *Festivals*, pp. 108–10.

65. Some *pali*, located between Rome and Portus, were replaced by order of the emperor Trajan, but before that they were annually renewed, presumably by local officials, and if ritual was involved in their placement (as their name indicates), so probably was it a part of their renewal; see *Liber coloniarum I* pp. 222–23L.

66. An *auguraculum* was an essential part of a Roman city: when Bantia became a *mu-*

nicipium at the end of the Social War, an *auguraculum* was established according to Roman rules on the local *arx*; see Torelli, "Un templum augurale," pp. 293–315. Such a place would require its own formula to define the necessary *templa* to observe the flight of birds; see Chapter 2, section VI. Frederiksen, *Campania*, pp. 270, 279 n. 65, noted that the colony of Puteoli absorbed preexisting local cults, such as the temple of Apollo at the high point of the city.

67. For the techniques of surveying in the towns and the fields, see Chapter 2, section V. For the assignment of house sites (and fields), see section IV in this chapter.

68. Brown, *Cosa*, pp. 31–62. But the triumvirs were present when the walls of Placentia were being built; see Livy 21.15.1–7.

69. For the dedication of temples by colonial officials, see *CIL* III.1933; *ILS* 112.

70. *CIL* I.2.366, 401.

71. See, for example, *FIRA* I, no. 21, cap. 82. For the procedures involved in selling or leasing public lands, see Chapter 6.

72. Thus, Livy (35.9.7–9) held that the colonial commissioners who founded the Latin colony in the *ager Thurinus* in the years 194–193 surveyed more land than they wished to assign and withheld from the colonists one-third of that land so that a supplement could be sent later if the Roman senate and people so desired. Indeed, the practice of withholding land may have been common, for the sending of supplements was not unusual; see Livy 31.49.6, 32.2.6–7, 37.46.9–11, 39.23.3–4, 43.17.1.

73. Wightman, "Plan of Roman Carthage," pp. 29–46.

74. At Cosa (273), there was insufficient space inside the walls of the colony for all the colonists to have received house sites. Some, then, clearly lived elsewhere, and a secondary fortified center was created at about the same time some distance away; see Brown, *Cosa*, pp. 15–28.

75. See Hyginus Gromaticus p. 170L. For the orientation of the system, see Chapter 2, sections V and VI. Note that Hyginus Gromaticus's representation of the placing of the *groma* after the *conditor* had taken the auspices would apply primarily to the period before the mid-first century, for after that date practice shifted; see Chapter 9, section II.

76. For the number of settlers and the size of their plots, see Livy 35.9.7–8, 35.40.6, 39.55.6–8.

77. See Chapter 9, section III.

78. Siculus Flaccus pp. 157L, 160L, 164L, 165L; Hyginus pp. 120L, 125L.

79. See, for example, Hyginus Gromaticus pp. 169L, 201L, 203L. Note, however, that the late author Agennius Urbicus (pp. 21–22L), in his commentary on Frontinus, explicitly (but probably mistakenly) identified the *conditor* with the *mensor*.

80. Hyginus Gromaticus p. 170: *posita auspicaliter groma, ipso forte conditore praesente*. . . .

81. The *rogatio Servilia agraria* of 63 provided for the appointment of *finitores* of equestrian status to work under its decemvirs. Hinrichs, *Gromatischen Institutionen*, p. 84, thinks this to have been customary earlier. The law of 63, however, probably represented an innovation in this regard; see Chapter 9, section III.

82. For a discussion, see Chapter 2, section VI.

83. See Hinrichs, *Gromatischen Institutionen*, pp. 85–89; Nicolet, *Space, Geography, and Politics*, p. 150.

84. For the relative positions of magistrates and *finitores*, see Chapter 9, section III.

85. Livy 21.25.5, 35.9.7–9; Hyginus Gromaticus p. 199L. Note that Hyginus Gromaticus described an operation in which the size of the plots given to individual settlers was determined by an existing formula—years of service—so that there was no need to decide that on the scene, as colonial commissioners must have done.

86. See Chapter 2, section VI.

87. For the role of republican tribunes in forming camps, see Suolahti, *Junior Officers*, p. 47; for their position and the process of selection, see Suolahti, pp. 51–57.

88. For an examination of Polybius's account, see Walbank, *Commentary on Polybius*, 1:709–23. Rawson, "Literary Sources," pp. 13–23, thinks that the account derives from a military tribune's *commentarii*, since their role is emphasized and the commander's largely ignored. Polybius did not note any religious acts involved in setting up a camp, perhaps because of lack of interest or perhaps as a result of his emphasis on the role of the tribunes. The central square, however, contained a *templum* or *auguratorium* (see Chapter 2, section I), and that enclosure would have to have been ritually defined, probably by the commander after he had led the army into the place where the camp was to be constructed. For the use of the *groma*, see Hyg. *De mun. castr.* 14.

89. Rawson, "Literary Sources," p. 23, holds that Polybius (6.41) reveals that "the tribunes are accompanied by (and doubtless take less real part than) specially trained centurions," and Hinrichs, *Gromatischen Institutionen*, pp. 82–84, claims that Polybius's centurions actually used the *groma*, but those positions do not reflect Polybius's wording. As part of his insistence that civilian and military operations formed entirely separate spheres, Hinrichs holds that all military surveyors (used in establishing camps and, he thinks, also in founding Latin colonies) were centurions, while the surveyors who marked lands for citizen colonies, viritane assignments, and sale or lease were of equestrian status.

90. According to Polybius (6.24.8–9), military tribunes chose centurions for their steadiness. Livy (42.33.6) gave to the consuls the right to appoint all officers, and Mommsen, *Str.*, 1:120 n. 4, suggests that the consul delegated the power to the tribunes for the sake of convenience.

91. On the size of the camp, see Walbank, *Commentary on Polybius*, 1:709–15.

92. Note that Cicero (*Agr.* 2.13.32) included *finitores* provided by the *rogatio Servilia* among the *apparitores*.

93. There is no extensive study of Roman sortition, but G. Sundwall is currently writing a dissertation on the subject at the University of North Carolina: "*Sortes Romanae*: Religion, Politics, and Random Chance." The Roman sections of V. Ehrenberg's survey in *RE* 25 (1926), cols. 1451–1504, s.v. *Losung*, are inadequate; on occasion, such as at cols. 1493–94, he holds, against evidence he has just cited, that its use was restricted to unimportant matters.

94. Provinces: see, for example, Livy 35.41.6, 36.1.6–2.7; order of voting: Livy 24.7.12, 27.6.3; Cic. *Phil.* 2.33.82; *dilectus*: Livy 4.46.1; Polyb. 6.20.1–2; Gracchus: Livy 45.15.5–6.

95. This situation could easily fit many, but not all, of the assignments in colonies of the second century, when *centuriae* of two hundred *iugera* were common: at Copia, for example, *equites* and *pedites* each received either forty or twenty *iugera*; at Mutina and Parma, founded by the same college, the colonists each were granted five *iugera* at the former and eight at the latter; while at Saturnia, each plot contained ten *iugera* and at Graviscae five. See Livy 35.9.7–9, 39.55.6–9, 40.29.1–2.

96. After describing the process of sortition, Hyginus Gromaticus (p. 204L) gave a procedure for giving an allotment when parts of it were located in several *centuriae*. First, he said, we centuriate, and then we terminate (*terminavimus*) the individual plots, inscribing them on a bronze *forma*. Then, a *sors* is inscribed. Thus, with a plot of sixty-six and two-thirds *iugera* over three centuries the lots should read "six and two-thirds *iugera* in D(extra) D(ecumanum) I K(itra) K(ardinem) I, fifteen *iugera* in D(extra) D(ecumanum) I K(itra) K(ardinem) II, forty-five *iugera* in D(extra) D(ecumanum) II K(itra) K(ardinem) II. Note that this instance seemingly concerns a single plot given to a single person apparently without a mediating group, but the recipients could be arranged in groups if the amount of excess was regular and predictable, that is, if the

same fraction resulted from each century. Some second-century colonial distributions certainly gave plots that would not fit evenly into a single century of 200 *iugera*; see, for example, Livy 35.40.5–6, 37.57.7–8, 39.44.10, 41.13.4–5. Salmon, *Roman Colonization*, p. 178 n. 111, holds that the land of a Latin colony was not technically *centuriatus ager* and that its allotments, therefore, did not need to have been made in suitable fractions of a *centuria*. The evidence he cites for that conclusion (Festus p. 47L), however, indicates nothing of the sort.

97. For tribes and classes, see n. 17. In Cales (334) and Ariminum (268), the *vici* were named after those of Rome; see Sherwin-White, *Roman Citizenship*, p. 99. For the *vici* of later colonies in Asia Minor, see Levick, *Roman Colonies*, pp. 76–78.

98. Verg. A. 5.755–56: *interea Aeneas urbem designat aratro sortiturque domos*.

99. Ehrenberg, *RE* 25 (1926), col. 1465, s.v. *Losung*, insists on the separation of the religious and the political meanings of the lot, but in this he is certainly mistaken. Plautus, in *Cas.* 346–49, 382–83, 389–90, 402, 410, 417–18, linked it to divine favor, while Cicero (*Div.* 1.45.103, 2.40.83) described the determination of the *praerogativa* in meetings of the *comitia centuriata* as an *omen comitiorum*; see Taylor, *Roman Voting Assemblies*, pp. 73–74, 143 n. 30. Linderski, "Augural Law," p. 2175, suggests that the drawing of lots could have been taken as a kind of augury through which Jupiter expressed his will.

100. Catalano, "Aspetti spaziali," p. 474. Note that Catalano specifies that sortitions were performed *in templo* within the first milestone of Rome, but Livy 41.18.7–16 shows that sortitions in camps were also performed in a *templum*.

101. Livy 41.18.7–16.

102. Livy 41.18.7–8. Unfortunately the clause recording Petilius's fault is corrupt and the exact nature of the *vitium* is obscure; see Linderski, "Augural Law," pp. 2173–75.

103. See Taylor, "Symbols of the Augurate," pp. 352–56; *Roman Voting Assemblies*, p. 144 n. 32.

104. Hyginus Gromaticus p. 204L: *sortitos in agrum deducemus et fines assignavimus*. For the use of ceremony in such circumstances, see Chapter 2, section IV.

105. For discussions of the ways these quotas were set, see Brunt, *Italian Manpower*, pp. 545–48, and Baronowski, "Formula Togatorum," pp. 248–52.

106. Livy 27.9.1–14, 29.15.1–15.

107. See Livy 28.11.10–11.

108. Livy 39.23.3–4. Note that Livy described only the report and the election of the commissioners and did not report any foundation. This should indicate that, despite being abandoned, Sipontum and Buxentum still were considered to be legally in existence.

109. See, for example, Livy 31.49.6, 32.2.6–7, 37.46.9–11, 39.23.3–4, 43.17.1. For the election of colonial commissioners and their ranks, see Chapter 3, section III.

110. Livy 32.2.6–7, 39.23.3–4.

111. In the *forum* at Cosa, the excavators found a number of sockets arranged in rows, which they interpreted as the places for posts that were to mark lanes for voting. If so, Cosa originally had three tribes, and the excavators suggest that two were eventually added, for a total of five, an event they link to the arrival of new colonists; see Brown, *Cosa*, p. 41.

CHAPTER 5

1. In the late third and early second centuries, C. Flaminius sent *coloni* to the *ager Gallicus* and Picenum, special commissioners installed Scipio's veterans in Samnium and Apulia, and the decemvirs of 173 assigned lands in the *ager Gallicus* and Liguria. Early

assignments followed the same pattern. M'. Curius Dentatus installed settlers on the western limits of Sabinum, which he had just conquered. Almost half a century earlier, others were sent to the *ager Falernus*, also recently seized. All of those projects are discussed in greater detail in the following pages of this section.

2. Taylor, *Voting Districts*, p. 49.

3. Again, as was the case with the colonial law, the sources sometimes specify a decree of the senate and on other occasions a law, but the normal practice probably was for both; see Chapter 3, section I. Hinrichs, *Gromatischen Institutionen*, pp. 10–12, suggests that a plebiscite may not always have been required for mid-republican colonies.

4. Livy 31.4.1–3, 31.49.5, 32.1.6.

5. Colonization laws also were occasionally modified after the initial measure had been passed. The commission chosen in 190 to lead supplementary settlers to Placentia and Cremona was later assigned the task of founding two new settlements (Livy 37.46.9–47.2), and the college chosen in 197 to found five citizen colonies may have had the fifth added later (Livy 32.29.3–4).

6. Briscoe, *Commentary on Livy Books XXXI–XXXIII*, p. 167, explains the change by postulating that either a magistrate with *imperium* was required for some reason or that the commissioners were involved in some other task. Toynbee, *Hannibal's Legacy*, 2:202, holds that either the task had proven to be too large for the commissioners (in which case it is difficult to see how a single promagistrate could have accomplished it) or that the decemvirs had been negligent. The senate's modifications, however, may have extended the decemvirs' task so that they could not complete it within the designated period. For one year as a possible term for commissioners in viritane assignments, note that Livy's report of the assignment of 173 combines in a single annalistic entry the senatorial decree, the resulting creation of the commission, and the completion of the task of that college—the use of the perfect tense, *diviserunt*, to describe the operation they performed on the land should indicate that the task had been completed—unlike the practice in annalistic descriptions of colonization for the same period, where beginning and end were in separate notices in different years, reflecting the time it took to establish the settlement.

7. Cic. *Inv.* 2.17.52; *Luc.* 5.13; *Sen.* 4.11; *Brut.* 14.57; V. Max. 5.4.5; Polyb. 2.21.7–9. Some scholars, building on the accounts of senatorial opposition, hold that the land covered by the law was in the possession of rich senators or had been rented out by the state and that this was the source of senatorial opposition; see Càssola, *I gruppi politici*, pp. 93–94; Frank, *Economic Survey*, 1:60. Beloch, *Römische Geschichte*, p. 344, and Valvo, "Il modus agrorum," pp. 179–224, held that the law contained a provision *de modo agrorum* limiting the amount of land rich Romans could occupy on their own initiative. Both positions are unlikely, since rich Romans of the time probably did not possess much land in a region so far from Rome and subject to Gallic attacks; see Gabba, "Caio Flaminio e la sua legge," pp. 159–63.

8. Polyb. 2.21.7–9; Cato *Orig.* fr. 43 P (= Varro *R.* 1.2.7); Cic. *Sen.* 4.11; *Brut.* 14.57; V. Max. 5.4.5.

9. For other decemvirates implementing agrarian legislation, besides the two examples given above (201 and 173), see *ILS* 48 (= *CIL* I^2.1, p. 198) (Saturninus); *ILS* 49 (the younger Drusus); Cic. *Agr.* 2.7.16–18 (Rullus).

10. Thus, Corbett, "L. Metellus," pp. 7–8. Note that Pliny's text contains either Metellus's most recent—the earliest certain one is his first consulship—or his most important offices: there is no mention of any term as praetor, aedile, tribune of the plebs, or quaestor, and he certainly would have held some of those. Metellus probably held the listed offices in the later part of his career.

11. Livy *Per.* 11; Fron. *Str.* 1.8.4, 4.3.12; Flor. 1.10.1–3; Plut. *Apophthegmata M'. Curii*, 1;

Pliny *Nat.* 18.4.18; Columella 1, *praef.* 14; 1.3.10; Auctor *Vir. Ill.* 33.5–6. Note that Frontinus said that the senate authorized Dentatus to receive a larger allotment of land than others, but the author of *Vir. Ill.* attributed the decision to the people. Some scholars maintain that Dentatus carried through his distributions against the will of the senate; see, for example, Forni, "Manio Curio Dentato," p. 200; Càssola, *I gruppi politici*, p. 92; Triebel, "Ackergesetze und politischen Reformen," pp. 10–11. Reportedly, there was hostility between Dentatus and the senate, but the sources did not link it to land, and in 290, the year of the law, the senate gave him two triumphs; see Harris, *War and Imperialism*, p. 180. Columella 1, *praef.* 14, held that another distribution took place under C. Fabricius (cos. 282, 278).

12. Livy 8.1.3, 8.11.13–14.

13. Livy (6.21.4–6) claimed that in 383 the senate ordered the *ager Pomptinus* to be divided among Roman citizens and had *quinqueviri* created to manage it. Colleges of five are not otherwise known to have distributed land until the *quinqueviri agris dandis adsignandis lege Saufeia* of the early first century; see *ILS* 49.

14. Thus, Mommsen, *Str.*, 2:629.

15. For the procedures, see Chapter 3, section II.

16. See Broughton, *MRR*, 1:322. Each of the three consulars are the only individuals of those names known to have been active at the time. See Briscoe, *Commentary on Livy Books XXXI–XXXIII*, pp. 63–64; Badian, "House of the Servilii Gemini," pp. 50–51; Scullard, *Roman Politics*, p. 83. The three praetorians to be discussed in the following sentence are also the only ones of those names known to have been active in these years.

17. Flaccus's tribunate: Livy 32.7.8–11; Plut. *Flam.* 2.1–2. Flamininus: Livy 32.7.8–9, 32.7.12. Badian, "House of the Servilii Gemini," p. 51, acting on the assumption that Livy or his source gave the names in order of their rank, held that Flaccus should have been a praetor since the next name on the list was a praetorian, and thus he suggested that Flaccus be emended to either Nobilior or Centumalus. The words *ex quaestura* used to describe Flamininus's status on election to his consulship indicates only that the highest post he had reached was that of quaestor—it need not mean that he was actually holding the office of quaestor at the time of election; see Broughton, *MRR*, 1:329 n. 2.

18. Badian, "House of the Servilii Gemini," p. 51, and Sumner, in his review of Briscoe's *A Commentary on Livy Books XXXI–XXXIII*, p. 321, reject this name on the assumption that the list is in order of rank, which would require that the first name be that of the most senior consular.

19. Livy 38.55.5. Briscoe, *Commentary on Livy Books XXXI–XXXIII*, pp. 63–64. Sumner, in his review of Briscoe, again working on the assumption that the list was in order of rank, identified the L. Cato who served on the college with the C. Hostilius Cato who was praetor in 207 along with A. Hostilius Cato, who also served on the commission, and suggested that the text be emended accordingly. Broughton, *MRR*, 1:322, identified L. Cato as the praetor of 207, but he corrected the error at *MRR*, 3:103.

20. See Broughton, *MRR*, 1:409–10.

21. F. Münzer, *RE* 4 (1900), col. 1280, s.v. "Cornelius (95)," and Broughton, *MRR*, 1:410 n. 6, both identify the commissioner with the consul of 181 (and praetor in 185?) on the grounds that the consul who moved Ligurians to Samnium where he assigned them land would have been a likely choice to assign land among the Ligurians to Romans.

22. Consulship: Livy 42.28.5. For his praetorship (the available years are 175 and 174), see Broughton, *MRR*, 1:406 n. 1; Münzer, *Römische Adelsparteien*, pp. 218–19.

23. For Tremellius: Varro (*R.* ? 4.2), referring to a Tremellius who was his contemporary, said that the family had produced seven praetorians in a row. One of these may have been the decemvir, but if so his term as praetor is otherwise unattested, and thus must have been one of the vacant positions in 175, 174, and 170. Of those years, 170 is the

most likely, since there are stronger candidates for the others; see Broughton, *MRR*, 1:420. For Appuleius: Livy 45.44.2. For Salonius: Livy 34.45.3–5.

24. M. Caecilius Denter was sent on an embassy to the east in 173 and a M. Caecilius was sent to purchase grain in southern Italy in 172; see Livy 42.6.4–5, 42.27.8. Broughton, *MRR*, 1:410 n. 7, held that the decemvir should not be identified with the legate of 173, but gives no reason.

25. Gabba, *Esercito e società*, pp. 100–104. Brunt, *Italian Manpower*, p. 69, says "40,000 veterans could well have been given allotments" on the apparent assumption that all who were legally eligible would have been settled. Toynbee, *Hannibal's Legacy*, 2:659–60, table V n. 2, suggests that Scipio's veterans were settled around Telesia, Cubulteria, Caudium, and Abellinum in Samnium and Herdoniae, Aecae, and Arpi in Apulia.

26. See, for example, Livy 10.21.7–10.

27. Note that decemvirs may have had a term of only one year; see n. 6.

28. See Ewins, "Colonization of Cisalpine Gaul," pp. 54–71; Dilke, *Roman Land Surveyors*, pp. 146–47; Regoli, "Centuriazione e strade," pp. 106–7.

29. Draining of the Veline lake: Cic. *Att.* 4.15.5; Serv. *A.* 7.712. Forni, "Manio Curio Dentato," p. 224, identifies the consulate mentioned by Varro as Dentatus' first (290). Connection between limitation and Dentatus's distributions: Hinrichs, *Gromatischen Institutionen*, pp. 41–42; Brunt, "Enfranchisement of the Sabines," pp. 123–24.

30. Vallat, "*Ager publicus*, colonies et territoire agraire," pp. 192–98.

31. The agrarian law of 111 does indicate the sortition was used to assign plots in contexts other than colonial foundations; see *FIRA* I, no. 8, lines 3, 15, 16. Note, however, that Mommsen, *Ges. Schr.*, 1:97ff., followed by Kaser, "Die Typen des römischen Bodenrechts," pp. 11–12, thought that the references must refer to land given in colonies, since he held that sortition was not used in viritane assignments. Such a distinction between colonies and viritane assignments, without clear justification in the sources, is unlikely; see Johannsen, "Die Lex Agraria des Jahres 111," pp. 212–17, and Lintott, *Judicial Reform*, p. 206.

32. The circumstances in which the formation of *fora* and *conciliabula* was deemed appropriate are controversial. Many hold that the rank of *forum* was given to places intended to serve as rural trading centers; see Brunt, *Italian Manpower*, pp. 570–76, and Galsterer, *Herrschaft und Verwaltung*, p. 27. Others suggest that *fora* were to be road stations servicing *viae*; see A. Schulten, *RE* 7 (1910), col. 62, s.v. *forum*; Rudolph, *Stadt und Staat*, p. 164; G. Radke, *RE* suppl. 13 (1973), cols. 1428, 1497–98, s.v. *viae publicae Romanae*; Salmon, *Making of Roman Italy*, p. 183 n. 14; Sherwin-White, *Roman Citizenship*, pp. 74–75. Still others suggest that *fora* differed from *conciliabula* only because one form was thought suitable for communities that had grown naturally, while the other served for a settlement created entirely by official action; see Mommsen, *Str.*, 3:775, 798 (who suggested that *fora* were founded by consuls and censors, while *conciliabula* grew naturally), and Ruoff-Väänänen, *Studies on the Italian Fora* (who suggested that all *fora* were preexisting communities given a new status). On their own, each definition is unsatisfactory. Although *fora* did serve as the site for certain commercial activities, the right to hold a market (the *ius nundinarum*) was not strictly limited to this class, for markets also were held in *vici*; see Ruoff-Väänänen, *Studies on the Italian Fora*, pp. 8–9. In some cases, moreover, both *fora* and *conciliabula* were established to provide for new settlers. The *lex Mamilia Roscia Peducaea Alliena Fabia* reveals that those who founded the communities (including *fora* and *conciliabula*) authorized by the law centuriated their territories; see *FIRA* I, no. 12, cap. 5. The *forum* and the *conciliabulum*, then, probably did not serve only a single purpose, and among the ends they could serve would be to organize new settlers.

33. *FIRA* I, no. 12. For a new examination of the text and the features of the law, see Crawford, "Lex Iulia Agraria," pp. 179–90.

34. Sherwin-White, *Roman Citizenship*, p. 170.

35. Thus, Rudolph, *Stadt und Staat*, pp. 159–67; Galsterer, *Herrschaft und Verwaltung*, p. 26; Ruoff-Väänänen, *Studies on the Italian Fora*, pp. 24–29, 48–52.

36. See Sherwin-White, *Roman Citizenship*, pp. 74–75. Abbott and Johnson, *Municipal Administration*, p. 10, state that "*praefectura*, in fact, may be thought of as a generic term applicable to any community which lacked the full right of self-government."

37. Arthur, *Romans in Northern Campania*, pp. 35–37, suggests that the *coloni* settled in the *ager Falernus* in 340 were established en bloc in the two *fora*, *forum Claudii* and *forum Popilii*, attested for the area, although he admits that evidence for the date at which they were settled and the period when they became *fora* is uncertain. Viritane assignments, it should be noted, were generally made near previously founded colonies, which probably provided the necessary protection (see Taylor, *Voting Districts*, p. 49), but this does not mean that the settlements resulting from such an assignment were small, merely that they were not organized for war.

38. The evidence and the modern literature is surveyed in Ruoff-Väänänen, *Studies on the Italian Fora*, pp. 38–47, who suggests that the magistrates of *fora* only possessed aedilician powers. Sherwin-White, *Roman Citizenship*, p. 75, suggests that *fora* possessed a local assembly, some magistrates, and perhaps a local council.

39. Livy 25.5.6, 39.14.7–8, 43.14.10; see Sherwin-White, *Roman Citizenship*, p. 74.

40. No source specifically places temples or other signs of cult in a *forum* or a *conciliabulum*, but since higher-ranking communities, such as colonies and municipalities, possessed them, as did lower-ranking ones, such as the *vicus* and the *pagus*, it is likely that *fora* and *conciliabula* also had at least a simple religious organization. For cult in a *vicus*, see *CIL* I.2.756.

41. *FIRA* I, no. 12: *Quae colonia hac lege deducta quodue municipium praefectura forum conciliabulum constitutem erit* . . . ; KL V: *qui hac lege coloniam deduxerit, municipium praefecturam forum conciliabulum constituerit.* . . . Note that Festus (74L) also described *fora* as constituted.

42. Note that officials of *fora* and *conciliabula*, unlike their counterparts in *municipia* and *coloniae*, could not conscript soldiers, and thus either Roman officials went to those places to arrange the matter or they issued edicts through *fora* and *conciliabula* ordering young men to report to Rome for conscription; see, for example, Livy 25.5.5–6, 43.14.7–10.

43. For the use of *constituere* to describe the formation of earthy *templa*, see Linderski, "Augural Law," pp. 2277–78; for *templa* as fields of vision, see Varro *LL* 7.9; for the *lustrum*, see Varro *LL* 6.93; for altars and places of sacrifice, see Verg. A. 11.185; Festus p. 57L. Ruoff-Väänänen, *Studies on the Italian Fora*, p. 19, suggests that the distinction between "deducted" and "constituted" found in the *lex Mamilia Roscia Peducaea Alliena Fabia* indicates that the verb *constituere* must denote only the process of giving rights to an already existing community experiencing a change in its legal status. But the words *deducere* and *constituere* clearly refer to a process appropriate to the formal establishment of a community of a certain legal status, and not to any previous condition of this community.

CHAPTER 6

1. See Livy 27.11.8, 28.46.4, 41.27.10–2, 42.19.1–2; Cic. *Agr.* 2.14.35–37; *FIRA* I, no. 8, line 97; Hyginus p. 115L; Siculus Flaccus p. 136L. See also Marquardt, *Römische Staats-*

verwaltung, 2:155–56; Willems, *Le sénat*, 2:346–47; Burdese, *Studi sull'ager publicus*, p. 43; De Martino, *Costituzione*, 2:207–9.

2. See, for example, Livy 27.11.7–8, 28.46.4, 42.19.1–2; Cic. *Agr.* 2.14.35–37; *FIRA* I, no. 8, line 97.

3. In the first century, the founders of Caesar's colony at Urso set aside land to be sold or leased by colonial officials; see *FIRA* I, no. 21, cap. 82. These founders, however, did not lease or sell the land themselves nor did they seek to use the revenue for projects originating in Rome itself or to support institutions located in this city; see Chapter 4, section III. If mid-republican colonial commissioners did the same, and that seems likely, they also probably determined neither the time nor the occasion for their use. Magistrates occasionally failed to follow the instructions they had been given; see Cic. *Agr.* 2.14.37.

4. Marquardt, *Römische Staatsverwaltung*, 2:155–56; Burdese, *Studi sull'ager publicus*, p. 44.

5. Livy 28.46.4, 31.13.1–9.

6. Festus p. 204L; Hyginus p. 117L.

7. Livy 41.27.10; Cic. *Agr.* 1.2.5, 2.19.51. Other forms of public property were exploited in the same fashion during times of need; see, for example, Orosius 5.18.

8. *CIL* I.2.756.

9. Livy 28.46.4–6, 31.13.1–9, 32.7.3, 42.19.1–2.

10. Livy 26.34.6–12, 31.13.1–9. For the availability of land near Rome, see Liverani, "L'ager veientanus," pp. 39–43. Göhler, *Rom und Italien*, p. 72, suggests that land for the creditors in 200 was confiscated during the Hannibalic war, but no ally that close to Rome is known to have revolted. The *Liber coloniarum I* (pp. 216L, 219L, 232L, 237L, 239L) records that the Gracchan agrarian commissioners found public land in Latium and southern Etruria in the years after 133.

11. Livy (45.18.3–4) noted that the senate decided not to lease captured land in Macedonia in 167 because the publicans would effectively end public rights over the land.

12. See, for example, Livy 42.1.6, 42.19.1–2; *FIRA* I, no. 20, cap. 82.

13. Leasing by consuls and praetors: Cic. *Agr.* 2.14.37; Granius Licinianus pp. 8–9 Criniti; *FIRA* I, no. 8, line 74.

14. Cic. *Ver.* 2.3.40; *Agr.* 2.21.55–56. Note that the framers of the agrarian law of 111 (*FIRA* no. 8, lines 74–76) established provisions to sell lands in Africa at Rome, while the authors of the first-century *Tabula Heracleensis* (*FIRA* I, no. 13, lines 33–37) instructed that the *quaestor urbanus* place certain public contracts openly in the *forum*.

15. Livy 27.3.1. Cic. *Agr.* 2.21.55–56. Livy did not specify the authority, if any, that allowed Flaccus to hold the auctions in Campania.

16. Plut. *Rom.* 25.5; Festus. p. 430L. See also Wissowa, *Religion und Kultus*, p. 117; Scullard, *Festivals*, pp. 194–95. Note that the *Ludi Capitolini* were not staged by magistrates or public priests, but by a special association, known in later times at least as the *collegium Capitolinorum*.

17. For the *praeco*, see K. Schneider, *RE* 20, pt. 1 (1922), cols. 1193–99, s.v. *praeco*; Rauh, "Auctioneers," pp. 451–71.

18. Livy 39.44.8–10; see also Plut. *Cat. Mai.* 19.

19. Plut. *Sull.* 33.

20. Suet. *Aug.* 24.

21. Cic. *Phil.* 2.26.64; Livy 24.18.10–11. For the symbolism of the *hasta*, see Alföldi, "Hasta," pp. 1–27.

22. *FIRA* I, no. 8, line 46, apparently in the context of public sales of land, referred to entries *in tableis [publiceis]*.

23. For the form, see Magdelain, *La loi à Rome*, pp. 32–46.

24. To some extent, the two forms were associated with different magistracies. The actions of the quaestors in this area are regularly described by some form of the verb *vendere*—indeed Siculus Flaccus defined *ager quaestorius* as land the Roman people sold (*vendiderunt*) by quaestors—while the actions of the censors are often described with the verb *locare*. But that connection was not exclusive. The noun *locatio* and the verb *locare* commonly were used to describe actions by the censors, but they can also describe arrangements made by other officials, and *vendere*, in its various forms, was used to describe quaestorian sales, but it can also refer to those arranged by the censors (see Livy 27.3.1, 41.27.10). Mommsen, "Die Anfänge von Kauf und Miethe," pp. 262–65, suggested that sale and lease became differentiated over time because they were associated with different magistracies.

25. Marquardt, *Römische Staatsverwaltung*, 2:155–56; Zancan, *Ager publicus*, p. 33; Burdese, *Studi sull'ager publicus*, pp. 42–48. The framers of the *lex Ursonensis*, FIRA I, no. 8, cap. 82, explicitly instructed that land sold by local officials was to remain the public property of the colony. For later reuse, see *Liber coloniarum II* p. 253L.

26. *FIRA* I, no. 20, cap. 82; Hyginus p. 116L.

27. In classical Roman law, payments under a contract of *locatio conductio* were for a fixed sum of money to be paid at fixed times, and that probably was the regular procedure when public lands were involved; see Nicholas, *Introduction to Roman Law*, p. 184. But Cato held that rents on private estates should be calculated as a fixed portion of the crops, and Livy (27.3.1) noted that a proconsul in 210 had leased land for grain. Cicero (*Agr.* 2.29.81), however, reported that the rent due from the *ager Campanus*, leased by the censors, never varied and was immune to the weather and other calamities—clearly a fixed payment, probably in money. The procedure in 210 may have been a response to difficulties in procuring grain as a result of the war.

28. Thus, Burdese, *Studi sull'ager publicus*, pp. 45–46; Kaser, "Die Typen des römischen Bodenrechts," pp. 43–45; Marquardt, *Römische Staatsverwaltung*, 2:155–56; Rudorff, "Gromatische Institutionen," pp. 287–88.

29. *FIRA* I, no. 8, line 85, refers to officials, probably the censors, contracting with *publicani* for the collection of the *vectigal* on the fruits of public land.

30. For such remedies later in the second century, see Lintott, "Le procès devant les *recuperatores*," pp. 1–11.

31. In those case in which the location of the limits had been recorded in a *forma*, that document could enable the boundaries to be restored if lost, and perhaps for that reason Sulla tampered with the *forma* made for the *ager Campanus* by the urban praetor in 165, apparently as a prelude to an attempt to change the status of the land; see CIL VI.919; Granius Licinianus p. 9 Criniti.

32. See, for example, Livy 42.1.6, 42.19.1–2; *FIRA* I, no. 8, line 97.

33. Mommsen, *Str.*, 2:435. For an early first century example, see CIL I.2.2516, a *cippus* recording the separation on the senate's advice of public land from private near the Tiber by the urban praetor C. Caninius; for the date of Caninius's praetorship, see Broughton, *MRR*, 2:463.

34. See Livy 42.1.6, 42.9.7, 42.22.5–6, 44.16.7; CIL I.2.2516; ILS 26. This practice was still followed under the Empire: see CIL V.1265.

35. See Chapter 2, section IV.

36. Note that in 167 Prusias, king of Bithynia, asked that land taken from Antiochus and occupied by the Galatians be assigned to him. The senate ordered that an investigation be made to determine if the land was public land and also if it had already been assigned to another; see Livy 45.44.10–11. The agrarian law of 111 established procedures for cases in which individuals had purchased land in Africa at Rome and later found it to be legally held by another; *FIRA* I, no. 8, line 66.

37. For the Gracchan commission, see Chapter 8, section I.

38. For the limits, see Levi, "Sui confini dell'agro Campano," pp. 604–16; Frederiksen, *Campania*, pp. 31–46.

39. Livy, our chief source in the matter, presented two different accounts of that settlement and placed them in different years. In the first, placed in 211, he (26.14.1–16.13) noted that the Romans executed about seventy of the leading senators, imprisoned about three hundred members of the upper classes, confiscated all the land and buildings, and sold the citizens into slavery, while preserving the city of Capua itself as a dwelling place for artisans, merchants, and the cultivators of the soil, but without the civic institutions of assembly, senate, and magistrates — Cicero (*Agr.* 2.32.88–33.90) also noted that the Romans had deprived Capua of its civic institutions, leaving it only as a home for laborers. Livy's second account (26.30.1–34.12), placed early in 210, is more detailed and presents a slightly different result. The first notice ostensibly represents the action of the general receiving the surrender, while the latter records a senatorial decree and the plebiscite that confirmed it. For the relationship between the two, see Ungern-Sternberg, *Capua*, pp. 81–82.

40. Some speculation on the identities of those who kept their property is possible. Livy (23.31.10) reported that the Romans gave three hundred Campanian *equites* who had refused to join the revolt citizenship in a neighboring *municipium* and that they exempted daughters from families that were to be sold into slavery from that penalty, if they had married into other families before the surrender. Frederiksen, *Campania*, p. 270, suggested that the *equites* may have retained their lands after the settlement of 210, and it is possible that those daughters kept their dowries. Members of the Roman upper classes, moreover, had intermarried with their Campanian counterparts for several generations, with the likely result that some of the land within the *ager Campanus* had probably come into Roman hands.

41. Many, if not most, of the Campani remained in place, and without specific governmental actions to prepare places for them — of which there are no signs — they would probably not have moved without force; thus, Frederiksen, *Campania*, pp. 248–49. Indeed, Livy (28.46.6) noted that the senate instructed an urban praetor in 205 to assure that Campanians were living only in designated places and to deal severely with those who were not, a good indication that the relevant portions of the original decree were not being widely followed. The Campanians eventually had their citizenship restored; see Livy 38.28.4, 38.36.5–6.

42. Indeed, the legates sent by the senate in 117 to resolve a boundary dispute between the people of Genoa and the Langenses Veturii, who were dependent on them, included in the proclamation of their findings a verbal description of those public lands of Genoa in the possession of the Veturii in which the boundaries were given by rivers, streams, mountains, hills, ridges, and the occasional boundary marker, and within this seemingly extensive tract the ambassadors included no exceptions; see *CIL* I.2.584.

43. Levi, "Una pagina di storia agraria romana," pp. 54–55, suggests that the Romans placed a tithe on the entire *ager Campanus*, as they did in Sicily. Vallat, "Statut juridique et statut réel des terres," pp. 87–96, suggests that the magistrates active in Campania in 210 and 209 granted the bulk of the land to members of their own *gentes* — Fulvii, Cornelii, Sempronii, and Claudii — who in turn distributed portions for a rent to dependents, finding evidence in the fact that members of those *gentes* were regularly associated with agrarian legislation concerning the *ager Campanus* in the following decades. But members of these prominent families were regularly associated with all sorts of public activity. The leasing of lands, perhaps in the same fashion, continued in the following year, for Livy (27.11.8) noted that a senatorial decree and a plebiscite instructed the censors chosen in 209 to do so. The extent of the lands the proconsul and censors

transferred is unknown, but given their other responsibilities and the circumstances of the war the amounts may not have been great.

44. See Livy 28.46.4–6, 32.7.3, 32.29.3–4, 34.45.1–2.

45. For the location, see Frederiksen, *Campania*, pp. 272, 279 n. 71. Vallat, "Statut juridique et statut réel des terres," p. 89, describes the area as "globalement la partie occidentale," but that certainly overstates the case.

46. Levi, "Una pagina di storia agraria romana," p. 53 n. 2, suggests that the lands in question formed part of the estate of the temple of Diana on Mount Tifata. Note that the temple certainly possessed estates in the area, for Sulla gave or confirmed the limits of its lands, while Augustus and Vespasian later restored those bounds; see *CIL* X.3828 (= *ILS* 251).

47. For the importance of informers in judicial proceedings of the late republic—and for rewards for informing—see Alexander, "*Praemia*," pp. 20–32.

48. Livy 41.27.1, 42.10.1–4. Note that Livy reported the passage of Lucretius's measure in the consular year of 172, so that he did not carry the law early in his term. Laws could carry instructions addressed to future holders of magistracies; see *FIRA* I, no. 8, line 28.

49. Scardigli, *Grani Liciniani Reliquiae*, p. 40, suggests that abusive *possessores* had reoccupied the land in the years following the *terminatio* of Albinus, but also (p. 41) notes that Cicero's account seems to imply that those paid were the true owners; Lentulus may have recovered some land from *possessores* and purchased other land from owners. For a discussion of the question, see Cardinali, *Studi graccani*, pp. 118–21. For a definition of *possessio*, see the following chapter.

50. For leasing in small lots, see Cic. *Agr.* 2.30.82–31.84. Numerous traces of centuriation on the *ager Campanus* survive, indicating that the plain was divided into a grid formed of regular centuries of twenty *actus* a side. A Gracchan boundary marker (*ILS* 24) allows the two major axes to be identified: the *decumanus maximus* was the main road from Capua to Atella, and the *cardo maximus*, which intersected it just south of Capua, was the east-west road to Calatia; see Bencivegna, "Un nuovo contributo," pp. 79–89; Frederiksen, *Campania*, pp. 273–74. Frederiksen ascribes the centuriation to Postumius, but the consul was instructed to perform a *terminatio*, while the leasing of the land, a process that could be helped by centuriation, was not ordered until the following year. Note that centuriation allowed the area of plots, useful for calculating the rent, to be determined. Both *ager quaestorius* and *ager censorius* clearly can be associated with that method of surveying and marking the land; see Gabba, "Per un'interpretazione storica della centuriazione," pp. 265–84; Levi, "Ricerche sulla genesi della *centuriatio*," pp. 409–15. In some cases, officials may have transferred land to intermediaries. Hyginus (p. 116L) noted that certain individuals had purchased the right to a *vectigal* on some land and that they sold or leased those lands *per centurias* to neighboring *possessores*. Note, however, that Hyginus's description cannot refer to the leasing of the *ager Campanus* in the years 172–165, for there the neighboring landholders were the source of the problem and the land was leased to keep them within their proper bounds.

51. Siculus Flaccus p. 136L; *Liber coloniarum II* p. 253L; *Libri Magonis et Vegoiae* p. 349L. None provides a date for the arrangements, but the author of the *Liber coloniarum* noted that Caesar or Augustus ordered another centuriation of the area some time after the earlier division. The original sale of that land, necessarily earlier than the mid-first century, may well date to the period of the conquest of the region in 290 and the viritane assignments that followed: Gabba, "Per un'interpretazione storica della centuriazione," pp. 268–69; Muzzioli, "Note sull'ager quaestorius," pp. 223–30; Taylor, *Voting Districts*, p. 62. Some scholars have placed the original survey in the time of Sulla—see Bozza, *La possessio*, p. 175 n. 2, and Burdese, *Studi sull'ager publicus*, p. 44—

but no evidence links the the land with Sulla, and the arrangements may have been made considerably earlier, as the division into smaller modules rather than *centuriae* of two hundred *iugera* may indicate.

52. The author of the *Liber coloniarum II* specifically placed the land in question there. Siculus Flaccus and the author of the *Libri Magonis et Vegoiae* used the more general term Sabinum to indicate the location of the lands in question, but Latin authors frequently used Sabinum to refer specifically to land around Cures; see Taylor, *Voting Districts*, pp. 60–64, esp. 62 n. 58; Gabba, "Per un'interpretazione storica della centuriazione," pp. 268–69; Muzzioli, "Note sull'ager quaestorius," pp. 223–30. Muzzioli discovered traces of centuriation based on limits of ten *actus*, as described in the sources, in the vicinity of Cures and identifies them with these *agri quaestorii*.

53. *FIRA* I, no. 8, line 97.

54. The framers of the agrarian law of 111 (*FIRA* I, no. 8, lines 97–98), after instructing the *duumviri* to prepare the *ager Corinthus* for sale by having it measured and *termini* placed, seemingly set forth instructions for contracting out the work. Hinrichs, *Gromatischen Institutionen*, p. 90, interpreted the passage as indicating that the entire process of centuriation in cases where land was being prepared for sale or lease was performed by publicans of equestrian rank, who had successfully bid for the contract, a conclusion that accords well with his position that those who centuriated camps and the land in Latin colonies differed from those who surveyed land in citizen colonies and that used for fiscal purposes; his distinction between military and civilian spheres, each with different experts performing the same task, is unattested in the sources. Mommsen, *Ges. Schr.*, 1:145, noting that *Dig.* 11.6.1 *pr.* held that a contract of *locatio/conductio* did not exist with a *mensor*, argued that the *mensor* who seemingly would have centuriated the *ager Corinthus* was permitted to form the contract because it was with a community and not a private individual. But the assumption that the contract of line 98 covered the survey ordered in line 97 is unnecessary and, as the *Digest* indicates, probably false, for the text is fragmentary and the phrases connecting the two segments are lost. Indeed, Lintott, *Judicial Reform*, p. 280, suggests that some other public work was involved. Centuriation, it should be noted, involved matters beyond the measuring out and marking of the appropriate intervals with *groma*, *decempeda*, and stakes. Occasionally boundary ditches had to be dug and inscribed markers erected. In colonies, the colonists would have been available as a work force, and colonial magistrates would have been available to supervise them. The same would not have been the case for land prepared for sale or lease. Hyginus Gromaticus (p. 172L) recorded that Augustus placed a contract for marking fields that had already been surveyed.

55. On the basis of the detectable traces of centuriation, some hold that all of the *ager Campanus* with the exception of the meadows along the Volturnus to the north and the marshes by the river Clanius to the west was included in a grid made up of 550 *centuriae* or 110,000 *iugera*; see Frederiksen, *Campania*, pp. 273–74. Other magistrates, however, are known to have operated in the area much later, and since such grids could easily be extended, the eventual size of the network provides no evidence for the extent of the original division.

56. Lintott, *Judicial Reform*, pp. 249–54, suggests that their first task in Africa (outlined in lines 52–61 of the law) was to create a register of previous allotments and of unfulfilled claims to land, probably by receiving declarations by those holding land or wishing to do so and ruling on their validity.

57. See Lintott, *Judicial Reform*, pp. 256–60.

58. Lintott, *Judicial Reform*, pp. 265–66, suggests that the *stipendiarii* paid a fixed rate calculated on area, since according to Cicero (*Ver.* 3.12) all Punic peoples paid a *certum stipendium*. Appian (*Pun.* 135.641) mentions a tax on land and on persons, and Lintott

suggests the latter was an alternative to the land tax for nomads and craftsmen. For centuriation in the area, see Chapter 8, section IV.

59. On those cities, see Lintott, *Judicial Reform*, p. 266.

CHAPTER 7

1. For *occupatio* and *ager occupatorius*, see Burdese, *Studi sull'ager publicus*, pp. 13–36; Bozza, *La possessio*, pp. 9–70. Scholars disagree over the period at which jurists first formed these concepts and also over the date at which the practices conceptualized in such a fashion first appeared. For our purposes, however, it is sufficient to note that the basic features that concern us — the legal recognition of private occupation of public lands and the determination that use of such lands in that way did not give full ownership — appeared relatively early. Indeed, *leges de modo agrorum* themselves, a category that may reach back into the fourth century, implicitly acknowledged both the legitimacy of *occupatio* — as long as it was accomplished in the approved manner and within the established limits — and the state's continuing authority over the land; thus, Burdese, p. 51.

2. For the connection of *occupatio* with *possessio*, see Jolowicz and Nicholas, *Historical Introduction*, pp. 259–61, and Nicholas, *Introduction to Roman Law*, p. 130. The date at which the various praetorian interdicts protecting possession first appeared is unclear, but two, *uti possidetis* and *unde vi*, were certainly in force in the second century: Terence (*Eu.* 319) alluded to a basic formula of the former (known from *Dig.* 43.17.1), while the second is first attested in the agrarian law of 111 (*FIRA* I, no. 8, line 18); see Jolowicz and Nicholas, pp. 261–63; Watson, *Law Making*, p. 41.

3. Zancan, "Sul possesso," pp. 71–96, proposed that such *possessiones* at first became fully private through *usus* and placed the supposedly later prohibition of *ususcapio* in the second century, associating it with the activities of L. Postumius Albinus in the *ager Campanus* in 173. Against this, see Bozza, *La possessio*, pp. 43–69; and Tibiletti, "Il possesso dell'*ager publicus*," 26:176–79. Rather than representing an innovation, the case of the *ager Campanus* would have had clear precedents, except in scale; see Chapter 6, section III. The position that *usus* did not confer ownership of certain lands was old in Rome, for the framers of the Twelve Tables knew of land (and land that was not intended for a religious use) whose ownership could not be gained in that manner; see Cic. *Leg.* 1.21.55.

4. For the pre-Gracchan regulations, see section II in this chapter.

5. Thus, Tibiletti, "Il possesso dell'*ager publicus*," 26:198.

6. See Livy 10.13.14, 10.23.11–13, 10.47.4, 33.42.8–11, 34.53.4, 35.10.11–12; Festus p. 276L; Varro *LL* 5.158; Ovid *Fast.* 5.283–94.

7. See Cic. *De Orat.* 2.284.

8. See Mommsen, *Straf.*, pp. 151–74.

9. Mommsen, *Str.*, 2:543 n. 2, and Schulz, *History of Roman Legal Science*, pp. 36–37, place the account after 242, since it assumes the existence of more than one praetor and thus must be placed after the year in which the second praetor was added. Latte, "Origins of the Quaestorship," 24–33, puts the document in the first half of the second century on linguistic grounds.

10. For *contiones* in prosecutions, see Livy 4.40.5, 26.2.7, 38.51.6; Cic. *Vat.* 47.40.

11. *Agri occupatorii* need not be included in any *forma* that resulted from a survey; see Siculus Flaccus p. 138L.

12. Mommsen, *Straf.*, pp. 400–420.

13. See Plautus *Aul.* 415–20; Livy 25.3.8–19, 39.14.3–17.3.

14. App. BC 1.8, 1.18. Tibiletti, "Il possesso dell'*ager publicus*," 26:200–201, holds that the informers mentioned in the earlier law were intended to watch slaves and report on their conduct and were not to watch the *possessor* and report on his conduct, although Appian's language would appear to support the opposite position. To support this interpretation, he notes that Appian held that the law was intended to restrict the development of large estates and limit the danger to the state posed by large numbers of slaves; the numerical limits of the *lex de modo agrorum* addressed the former, but unless those free informers were intended to watch slaves, the latter would have remained unresolved. Such a view, however, requires the acceptance of an essentially Gracchan representation of the context and the intent of pre-Gracchan law (see section III in this chapter). Tibiletti found further support in Suetonius's report (*Caes.* 42) that Caesar instructed graziers to employ free herders as one-third of the work force, but Suetonius did not claim that they were to watch the slaves; instead, he held the Caesar was concerned about the size of the free population.

15. Livy 10.23.11–13.

16. Livy 33.42.8–11 (see also 34.53.4), 35.10.11–12. For other examples, see Livy 38.35.5–6; Festus p. 276L; Ovid *Fast.* 5.283–94.

17. See Taylor, *Roman Voting Assemblies*, pp. 17–18, 118 n. 4.

18. Livy 33.42.10, 38.35.6.

19. Livy 6.35.4–42.9; Vell. Pat. 2.6.2–3; Dion. Hal. *Ant. Rom.* 14.12.22; Plut. *Cam.* 39; Varro R. 1.2.9; Gell. 20.1.23; Pliny *Nat.* 18.14.17; V. Max. 8.6.3; Auctor *Vir. Ill.* 20.2–4; Columella 1.3.11 (Columella gave the maximum as fifty *iugera* and clearly is in error; see Tibiletti, "Il possesso dell'*ager publicus*," 26:219 n. 3).

20. Cato fr. 167 *ORF* = Gell. 6.3.37.

21. Tibiletti, "Il possesso dell'*ager publicus*," 26:209–17, saw Livy's account of the *lex Licinia agraria* as a means of filling out the role of turbulent tribunes traditionally assigned to Licinius and Sextius, but he also thought some fourth-century law of the type, perhaps with different terms, should be accepted as historical.

22. But Maschke, *Römischen Agrargesetze*, pp. 57–59, considers Cato's speech to be a later fabrication, although he has no strong arguments to support his position. Cardinali, *Studi graccani*, p. 151 n. 1; Tibiletti, "Il possesso dell'*ager publicus*," 26:191–92; Burdese, *Studi sull'ager publicus*, p. 58, all accept the authenticity of the passage.

23. See the following section.

24. Niese, "Das sogennannte licinisch-sextische Ackergesetz," pp. 410–23, began the discussion concerning the five hundred *iugera* limit, using three hundred senators and eighteen hundred *equites* (the size of those orders at a later date) as the number of potential *possessores*. Tibiletti, "Il possesso dell'*ager publicus*," 27:9–12, furnished the calculations concerning pasturage. Others find neither limit implausible for that time. See, for example, Allen, "Niese on the Licinian-Sextian Law," pp. 5–6; Brunt, *Italian Manpower*, pp. 28–29 n. 5; Burdese, *Studi sull'ager publicus*, pp. 55–57; De Martino, "Riforme del IV secolo," p. 39; *Storia economica*, 1:27–29.

25. Niese, "Das sogennannte licinisch-sextische Ackergesetz," pp. 410–23, argued that the notice may have appeared in one of the lacunae found in surviving books of Livy or that it was never mentioned, since Livy may have considered it unimportant. To support such an argument, Tibiletti, "Ricerche di storia agraria romana," pp. 185–87, attempted to show that Livy had no interest in agrarian affairs in these years, an argument that is implausible for a historian writing after the Gracchi.

26. Some identify the law with the *lex Flaminia* of 232; see Beloch, *Römische Geschichte*, pp. 343–44; Nap, *Die römische Republik*, p. 107; Valvo, "Il *modus agrorum*," pp. 179–224. Against that view, see the strong arguments of Gabba, "Caio Flaminio e la

sua legge," pp. 159–63, who points out the implausibility of assertions that wealthy Romans possessed *latifundia* in these distant regions, open to attack by Gauls.

27. Livy 10.13.14, 10.23.13, 10.47.4, 33.42.8–11, 35.10.11–12; Festus p. 276L; Varro *LL* 5.158; Ovid *Fast.* 5.283–94. The prosecuting aediles mentioned by Festus, Ovid, and Varro—L. and M. Publicius Malleolus—held office either in 241 or 238; see Broughton, *MRR*, 1:220 n. 3. Tibiletti, "Il possesso dell'*ager publicus*," 26:228–29, holds that Livy's report (10.21.14) concerning the prosecution of *possessores* in 298 represents an authentic early case of a violation of a law *de modo agrorum*, but he suggests that the early cases involving *pecuarii* did not involve violations of such a law (he placed limits on herds later, when he thought they would better fit conditions), and instead involved some unknown fault on the part of those *publicani* who farmed the collection of the *scriptura*—Cicero (*Ver.* 3.17) used *pecuarius* to describe them. Ovid, however, clearly thought that the convicted *pecuarii* actually owned the cattle and used the land.

28. Soltau, "Aechtheit des licinische Ackergesetze," pp. 624–29; Botsford, *Roman Assemblies*, pp. 334 n. 1, 363 n. 1; J. Vancura, *RE* 23 (1924), cols. 1164–71, s.v. *leges agrariae*; Göhler, *Rom und Italien*, pp. 90–93; Tibiletti, "Il possesso dell'*ager publicus*," 26:173–236, 27:3–41; Nicolet, *Les Gracques*, pp. 119–31; Sterckx, "Les premiers règlements *de modo agrorum*," pp. 309–35.

29. See the following section and Chapter 8, section I.

30. Both the *lex Licinia agraria* and the *lex Sempronia agraria* established a five hundred *iugera* limit; the patricians who opposed the first law persuaded some unnamed tribunes to interpose their veto, a clear parallel to the confrontation in 133 between Ti. Gracchus and M. Octavius; in response, Sextius and Licinius used their powers of intercession to block the election of most officials for five years, a move reminiscent of the less dramatic suspension of public business instituted by Ti. Gracchus as part of his dispute with Octavius; over an extensive period, moreover, Licinius and Sextius were elected tribunes of the plebs, and the next reported attempt to hold consecutive terms as tribune was Ti. Gracchus's.

31. On legal grounds, Zancan, *Ager publicus*, pp. 10–11, and Burdese, *Studi sull'ager publicus*, pp. 63–68, deny the existence of a *vectigal* on *agri occupatorii*. Cardinali, *Studi graccani*, pp. 104–6, Fraccaro, *Studi sull'età dei Gracchi*, pp. 67–68, and Tibiletti, "Il possesso dell'*ager publicus*," 26:183–89, accept Appian's claim.

32. For the *lex Hieronica*, see Carcopino, *La loi de Hiéron*, and V. Scramuzza, "Roman Sicily," in Frank, *An Economic Survey of Ancient Rome*, 3:237–40.

33. For the uncontrolled nature of such lands, see Siculus Flaccus p. 138L. But Toynbee, *Hannibal's Legacy*, 2:242–43, De Martino, *Costituzione*, 2:403, and Stockton, *The Gracchi*, pp. 214–15, suggest without evidence that it was possible for the tithe to have been collected, but that it probably was only collected sporadically. Occasional collections also would have required some form of land register.

34. Fraccaro, *Studi sull'età dei Gracchi*, pp. 74–75, and Cardinali, *Studi graccani*, pp. 99–100, suggest that Plutarch has confused a rent on *ager censorius* with Appian's tithe on *ager occupatorius*. Attempting to defend the accuracy of Plutarch's account, Tibiletti, "Il possesso dell'*ager publicus*," 26:207, suggests that Plutarch focused on only one method by which *latifundia* were formed (rather than giving a broad account such as the one he saw Appian as providing). Ignoring the formation of estates through *occupatio*, Plutarch would have mentioned only a process by which the very rich acquired land in public auctions by offering higher rents than the less rich (but still not poor) could afford. One would think that the amounts offered in an auction would bear a closer relationship to the supposed productivity of the land than to the ability of the lessee to pay. In any case, a law *de modo agrorum* would not have regulated such lands.

35. Some hold that Plutarch and Appian were both following a common source, possibly one of the Gracchi; see Cardinali, *Studi graccani*, pp. 45–70; Fraccaro, *Studi sull'età dei Gracchi*, pp. 11–29; Burdese, *Studi sull'ager publicus*, p. 59; and Tibiletti, "Il possesso dell'*ager publicus*," 26:192–209. Gabba, *Appiano e la storia delle guerre civili*, p. 37 n. 1, denies the possibility of a common source.

36. Livy (27.9.11), for example, noted that Latin colonies were founded to increase the number of Latins.

37. Thus, Gabba, *Appiano e la storia della guerre civili*, p. 40.

38. Thus, Tibiletti, "Il possesso dell'*ager publicus*," 26:194, who thinks that land open to *occupatio* was uncultivated, which seems unlikely as a general rule.

39. See Tibiletti, "Il possesso dell'*ager publicus*," 26:198–200.

40. Thus, Tibiletti, "Il possesso dell'*ager publicus*," 27:20–41.

41. Tibiletti, "Il possesso dell'*ager publicus*," 26:218–25, thought that certain scattered passages (Siculus Flaccus pp. 136L, 137L, 138L; Agennius Urbicus p. 2L; Columella 1.3.13) indicated earlier stages without specific numerical limits. They seemed to limit *possessio* to only those lands actually cultivated or to lands reserved with the expectation that they would be cultivated (*in spem colendi*). Siculus Flaccus attributed the rule to the age of the Gracchi, but Tibiletti held him to be in error, for he thought the use of the word *mos* must represent a stage prior to the development of formal law. In his view, the earliest practice *de modo agrorum* limited possession only to those lands which were actually cultivated, and specific numerical limits would have formed a later stage. Such a customary limit is unlikely. A regulation *de modo agrorum* should restrict the amount of public land one person could exploit, but the phrases extracted from the works of Siculus Flaccus, Agennius Urbicus, and Columella established no such limits, for the wealthy, who would have been most able to actually use large segments of land, would have faced the least restraint. Instead of setting boundaries, those phrases amount to a definition of *occupatio*, not to a limit placed on it—one could not claim rights deriving from the use of certain lands unless one was actually cultivating them or had taken steps to prepare them for cultivation. The existence of such a definition is compatible with the existence of a law establishing firm limits—one could possess, for example, only that land actually being used up to a maximum of five hundred *iugera*—and they should be considered as complementary features.

42. For a possible context of disputes over land and debt in fourth-century Rome, see Cornell, "Recovery of Rome," pp. 323–34.

43. See, for example, Livy 6.35.4–38.13.

44. Labruna, *Vim fieri veto*, pp. 143–286, suggests that the early *lex de modo agrorum* was intended to protect the poor and that the early *lex* and the praetorian interdict *uti possidetis* were related measures designed to achieve that end. There is no evidence for this position beyond the text of Appian, tainted, as we have seen, with Gracchan propaganda, and the combination of public law and private law remedies to achieve the same goal would be unusual. The praetor's interdict protected *possessores* from forcible expulsion, but at no time could the poor reasonably be expected to use it against the rich and powerful.

45. The speech is Livy's composition, not Cato's; see Briscoe, *Commentary on Livy Books XXXIV–XXXVII*, pp. 39–43. That point is clearly illustrated by a speech of Cato's alleged opponent, L. Valerius, who attempts to use Cato's *Origines* against him (Livy 34.5.8), but according to Nepos (*Cato* 3), Cato only began that work in his old age; see Briscoe, p. 56, and Tibiletti, "Il possesso dell'*ager publicus*," 26:226. Cardinali, *Studi graccani*, p. 137, thought the speech to be substantially authentic.

46. Tibiletti, "Il possesso dell'*ager publicus*," 26:226–27, thinks the passages too vague

to be of use. For another link between morality and the amount of public land in one's hands, see also Pliny *Nat.* 18.4.17–18 (on the modesty of M'. Curius Dentatus).

47. For the aediles' responsibilities, see Mommsen, *Str.*, 2:492–93; Lintott, *Violence in Republican Rome*, pp. 96–97; Bauman, "Criminal Prosecutions," pp. 245–64.

48. Maschke, *Römischen Agrargesetze*, pp. 56–58, also linked laws *de modo agrorum* and sumptuary legislation. For sumptuary legislation, see Bonamente, "Legge suntuarie," pp. 67–92; Baltrusch, *Regimen morum*.

CHAPTER 8

1. The literature on the tribunate of Ti. Gracchus is vast. For an overview, see Badian, "From the Gracchi to Sulla," pp. 197–245; "Tiberius Gracchus," pp. 668–731. For later works, see Bernstein, *Tiberius Sempronius Gracchus*, and Stockton, *Gracchi*. Earl, *Tiberius Gracchus*, Rich, "Supposed Manpower Shortage," pp. 287–331, and Shochat, *Recruitment*, deny the reality either of an agrarian crisis or a military one.

2. See Chapter 7, section III.

3. Tibiletti, "Il possesso dell'*ager publicus*," 26:181, holds it unlikely that Roman *possessores* had extended their *possessiones* into all parts of Italy at the time of the Gracchan reform. Later legislators certainly chose the option of colonies within Italy; see section III in this chapter, and Chapter 9, section I.

4. For their careers, see Bauman, *Lawyers in Roman Republican Politics*, pp. 230–312.

5. Earl, *Tiberius Gracchus*, pp. 17–18, held that both sons and daughters were to benefit from the additional portion. For other *praemia patrum*, see Astin, *Scipio Aemilianus*, pp. 322–24.

6. See also Auctor *Vir. Ill.* 65. Some scholars hold that this 1,000 *iugera* represents the basic 500 *iugera* plus 250 more for each child up to a maximum of two; see Molthagen, "Die Durchführung der gracchischen Agrarreform," p. 423 n. 5, and Hermon, "La loi agraire de Tiberius Gracchus," p. 182. Against this view, see Badian, "From the Gracchi to Sulla," p. 210 n. 52; "Tiberius Gracchus," p. 702; and Stockton, *Gracchi*, p. 41 n. 3. Earlier laws *de modo agrorum* also regulated the size of the herds that could be pastured on public land and the number of slaves that could be employed on it, but no such provisions are recorded for the *lex Sempronia agraria*, which need not have contained them. The goal of the Gracchan law, after all, was not to completely regulate all aspects of the use of *ager occupatorius* or to ordain the ways *possessores* used the public land they were permitted to retain, but rather to free cultivatable land for distribution; much of the land used exclusively for pasturage must have been uncultivatable.

7. See Burdese, *Studi sull'ager publicus*, p. 84. Plut. *TG* 9 mentioned compensation given to *possessores*, but its nature and its relationship to other benefits—additional land for children and secure title on lots held within the legal limits—are unclear. Some concessions may have been removed in a second version of the law. Plutarch (*TG* 10) reported that Ti. Gracchus made his proposal harsher following resistance to his proposal and simply ordered the large landholders to vacate excess land without compensation.

8. App. *BC* 1.9; Plut. *TG* 8.1. Appian (*BC* 1.7, 1.9) claimed that Tiberius wished to help Italians, not just Romans, although no other source indicates that noncitizens were to be aided by the measure. Some scholars accept Appian's account; see, for example, Shochat, "Lex Agraria of 133," pp. 25–45. Others, with greater probability, regard Appian as mistaken; see Carcopino, *Autour des Gracques*, p. 83; Zancan, *Ager publicus*, p. 86; Cardinali, *Studi graccani*, pp. 169–72; Boren, *Gracchi*, p. 49; Badian, "Tiberius

Gracchus," pp. 701–2; Earl, *Tiberius Gracchus*, pp. 20–23; Molthagen, "Die Durchführung der gracchischen Agrarreform," p. 430; Bernstein, *Tiberius Sempronius Gracchus*, pp. 137–44.

9. Cic. *Agr.* 2.12.31; Livy *Per.* 58; Vell. Pat. 2.2.3.

10. For the membership of colonial commissions, see Chapter 3, section III.

11. Most modern commentators suggest that the commission either served for a year and was reelected annually or that it had an indefinite term, but both are dependent on an obscure passage and probably are incorrect; see section IV in this chapter. Some speculation about the term is possible. Terms for four special colleges are known. Three colonial commissions each held office for three years; see Livy 32.29.4, 34.53.2. The decemvirs to be established by the law of P. Servilius Rullus (tr. pl. 63) and the *triumviri rei publicae constituendae* of 43 both had a five-year term; Cic. *Agr.* 2.13.32; Dio 47.2.1–2. Rullus occasionally claimed to be following Gracchan precedents (see, e.g., Cic. *Agr.* 2.12.31). The Gracchan college was elected originally early in 133, so that a five-year term would have expired early in 128 and an extension of similar length would have ended early in 123. If the Gracchan commission had been given a fixed term, a new law probably would have been necessary to extend it. The *triumviri* of 43 formed the only known commission whose term in office certainly was extended, and they at first simply declared their term to be extended for an additional five years—an option not open to members of colleges with less wide-ranging powers—although they later felt a law to be necessary; see Dio 47.2.1–2, 48.54.6; App. *BC* 5.95. Obsequens (28a), in a passage that unfortunately is mutilated, connected M. Fulvius Flaccus, in his position as triumvir, with dissension caused by the passage of laws in 129. In 124, C. Gracchus ran for the post of tribune for 123, and one of his actions in office was to secure the passage of an agrarian law, which presumably renewed his brother's. In order to stand for election in 124, Gaius, then a proquaestor, left the army of the proconsul L. Aurelius Orestes in Sardinia before his commander departed, an action for which he was strongly criticized and for which he took some risk of censure by the censors; see Plut. *CG* 2.4. Perhaps there was some reason to hurry.

12. *FIRA* I, no. 8, lines 1, 2, 4, 6, 10, 15, 20, 27.

13. Johannsen, "Die Lex Agraria des Jahres 111," p. 186.

14. For differing views on the matter, see Mommsen, *Ges. Schr.*, 1:98, 108; Cardinali, *Studi graccani*, pp. 159, 192; Johannsen, "Die Lex Agraria des Jahres 111," pp. 198–201; Lintott, *Judicial Reform*, pp. 202–4.

15. Note that the broadly framed laws of the first century often excluded areas by name; see Chapter 9, section I.

16. *FIRA* I, no. 8, lines 31–32. For a discussion of Appian's passage, see the following section.

17. For the lands covered by earlier *leges de modo agrorum*, see Chapter 7, section III.

18. Note that Appian (*BC* 1.9), Plutarch (*TG* 9–10), and Livy (*Per.* 58) emphasized the rules *de modo agrorum* of the *lex Sempronia*.

19. For the context of that speech, see Astin, *Scipio Aemilianus*, p. 193 n. 2; Gabba, *Appiani bellorum civilium liber primus*, p. 60.

20. For the markers, see the following section.

21. For that reason, Cardinali, *Studi graccani*, p. 159 n. 1, and Earl, *Tiberius Gracchus*, p. 91 n. 1, reject the notice.

22. Bauman, "Gracchan Agrarian Commission," pp. 391–401, seeks to explain the notice in a way that allows those powers to be present in the original law, but his positions depart greatly from the ostensible meaning of the text. He suggests that the second law allowed the triumvirs to initiate criminal prosecutions of violators *apud populum*—something no sources say they did—or that it gave them the right to delegate their ju-

dicial powers, although he admits (p. 399) that such powers could not normally be delegated. The epitomator clearly stated that the second law gave to the triumvirs the right to determine which lands were public.

23. On the implementation, see the following section.

24. Plutarch (*TG* 9) held that his compensation, whatever it was, was removed for just that reason. The provision for secure tenure, however, was preserved: a Gracchan boundary marker found near Aeclanum has marks which have been interpreted as signifying *f(undus) p(ossessoris) vet(eris)* (see Mommsen, in *CIL* I.2.645), while the agrarian law of 111 mentions the land of the *vetus possessor*; see *FIRA* I, no. 8, lines 21–23.

25. See Erskine, *Hellenistic Stoa*, pp. 152–61; Nicolet, "L'inspiration de Tiberius Gracchus," pp. 142–58.

26. See Behrends, "Tiberius Gracchus und die Juristen," pp. 25–121, and Bauman, *Lawyers in Roman Republican Politics*, pp. 249–55. Later writers, perhaps reflecting the propaganda of the Gracchan period, did use arguments based on fairness against the law; see Flor. *Epit.* 2.1; App. *BC* 1.10.

27. On Crassus's death, see Fron. *Str.* 4.5.16; V. Max. 3.2.12; Obsequens 28; Vell. Pat. 2.4.1; Justin 36.4.8. Obsequens puts Crassus's death in 130 and Velleius calls him proconsul at the time. Justin put his death *extremo annis tempore*, but this probably refers to the end of his command, which would cease when his successor arrived; see Magie, *Roman Rule in Asia Minor*, 1:151, 2:1039–40. The year of Claudius's death is less certain, but 129 provides a secure terminus ante quem, for Livy (*Per.* 59) recorded a different name in his place on the college in this year. The deaths certainly were close in time, for the inscriptions on the Gracchan *termini* are all either before the deaths of Crassus and Claudius or after the deaths of both; for the stones, see n. 40.

28. Livy *Per.* 59. The inscription on a *terminus* (*AE* [1955], no. 222) from Apulia bears only the names of Gracchus and Flaccus, showing that the latter joined the college before Carbo. Vell. Pat. (2.6.4) states that Gaius filled his brother's place with Flaccus, ignoring Crassus; this may mean that Flaccus filled the spot held by Crassus, who then would have died before Claudius (Carcopino, *Autour des Gracques*, p. 137). Auct. *Vir. Ill.* (65.4) seems to place C. Gracchus, Flaccus, and Crassus on the commission at the same time, thus making Flaccus succeed Claudius whose death would be before that of Crassus. For a discussion, see Russi and Valvo, "Note storiche sul nuovo termine graccana," pp. 238–49. Flaccus's rank in the senate at the time of his election is unknown—his only recorded office beside triumvir was consul in 125, but his praetorship must have been no later than 128; see Sumner, *Orators*, p. 63. Carbo probably served as tribune of the plebs in 130 and may have held that office when elected *IIIvir*: Carbo's tribunate usually is dated either to 131 or 130, but the later is the more probable; see Sumner, pp. 58–59.

29. No source reports the presence of Flaccus after 125, but he probably was still a member in 121 when he was killed along with C. Gracchus. Carbo is not attested as a triumvir after 129, but he may have continued in that office until the end. Cichorius, *Römische Studien*, pp. 113–17, attempts to determine the membership of the commission after the deaths of C. Gracchus and Flaccus from a heavily restored inscription found at Carthage (*ILS* 28). This stone, an imperial replacement of an original that does not survive, provides no certain evidence for the Gracchan college, and may record the actions of different magistrates assigned some other task in Africa; see Broughton, *MRR*, 1:522–23 n. 5, and Molthagen, "Die Durchführung der gracchischen Agrarreform," pp. 437–38.

30. Note that the agrarian law of 111 clearly linked changes of status under the terms of the Gracchan law with the actions of the *IIIviri*; see *FIRA* I, no. 8, lines 2–7, 11–12, 16–17, 22–23. Bauman, "Gracchan Agrarian Commission," pp. 398–99, suggests that

the triumvirs could delegate their power to determine which lands were public, but the evidence does not support that conclusion; see n. 22. Tibiletti, "Les *treviri lege Sempronia*," pp. 277–81, suggests that the commissioners used *praefecti*, for otherwise the law could not have been generally enforced. There is no evidence for any such subordinates nor any indication that the law was enforced generally.

31. The operations of the commissioners who founded Carthage will be examined in section IV in this chapter.

32. See Mommsen, *CIL* I.2.645.

33. *CIL* I.2.640 (= *ILS* 24), 639 (= *ILLRP* 471); *ILLRP* 469. Hinrichs, *Gromatischen Institutionen*, pp. 58–61, suggests that markers and centuriation do not necessarily indicate that an area was prepared for distribution, maintaining instead that they show areas in which the commissioners exercised their judicial powers; *contra* De Martino, "Gromatici e questioni graccane," pp. 3141–42. In Hinrichs's view, the commissioners started by constructing a centuriation network so that a *forma* could be compiled covering a very large stretch of land. Then, within that area, they plotted all the estates, so that they could identify and recover the surplus. More probably, the commissioners began by identifying a region held by a few large *possessores* and then centuriated that region, restricting the original occupants to only a few centuries; the rest would have been distributed.

34. The agrarian law of 111 confirms that the Gracchan commissioners gave and assigned (*dedit adsignavit*) plots and that they did so by lot; see *FIRA* I, no. 8, lines 3, 15, 16.

35. The commissioners may have permitted *veteres possessores* to choose the lands they would retain; see *FIRA* I, no. 8, line 2: . . . *vetus possessor sibei] agrum locum sumpsit reliquitve. quod non modus maior siet, quam quantum unum hominem ex lege plebeive sc(ito) sibei sumer[e* . . . The exact nature of the actions by *veteres possessores* is difficult to determine. *Sumere* is usually taken to be the equivalent of *occupare*; see Burdese, *Studi sull'ager publicus*, pp. 74–79; Johannsen, "Die lex agraria des Jahres 111," p. 203. But *relinquere* is more difficult. Hardy (*Roman Laws and Charters*, p. 56) translated *relinquere* as "to retain," but that it not a normal use of the word. Burdese (74–79) took it to indicate lands a *vetus possessor* had transferred to another through a mechanism such as inheritance. Lintott, *Judicial Reform*, pp. 204–5, translated *relinquere* as "to maintain in a former state." The fragmentary nature of the passage does not make it clear whether official action also was necessary. Mommsen (*Ges. Schr.*, 1:96) and Zancan (*Ager publicus*, p. 74 n. 1) wished to interpret the word as it was used in lines 7, 11, and 81 of the law, where it referred to the triumvirs themselves maintaining lands in their original condition, for the *possessor* himself should not have possessed the right to do so. Johannsen (p. 203) rejects that interpretation on linguistic grounds, but she accepts that further triumviral action was needed, for in lines 16 and 17, the framer of the law referred to lands held by *veteres possessores* as having been "given, assigned, and restored" (*dedit adsignavit reddidit* or *datus adsignatusve*) by the commissioners.

36. See Chapter 6, section III.

37. For an examination of Appian's account of the early *lex de modo agrorum*, see Chapter 7, section III.

38. Thus, Gabba, *Appiani bellorum civilium liber primus*, p. 58. The bulk of Appian's chapter must refer to land held by Roman citizens, since they were most likely to have held public land through the formal actions of Roman officials.

39. *Liber coloniarum I* pp. 210, 219, 232, 237L. For Paestum, see n. 48. Pani, "Il nuovo cippo graccano dauno," pp. 389–400, holds that the single marker from the Daunian plain (*AE* [1955], no. 222) was placed in the *ager Lucerinus*, but Russi and Valvo, "Note storiche sul nuovo termine graccana," pp. 225–49, propose the *ager Taurasinus*.

40. *CIL* I.2.639, 640, 641, 642, 643, 644, 645, 719 (on the second to the last of these the names of the commissioners do not survive); *ILLRP* 469 (= *AE* [1945], no. 25); *ILLRP* 472; *AE* (1955), no. 190; *AE* (1955), no. 222. One stone is a first-century copy, but the others in general follow the description of Gracchan markers provided in the *Corpus Agrimensorum Romanorum* (p. 242L): a round column one or one and a half feet in diameter and three or four feet high.

41. See Thomsen, *Italic Regions*, pp. 265–74.

42. Mommsen, "Libri Coloniarum," pp. 145–226, attacked the reliability of this source. Its basic accuracy was defended by Pais, "Il Liber Coloniarum," pp. 55–93, 377–411; Thomsen, *Italic Regions*, pp. 261–310; De Martino, "Gromatici e questioni graccane," pp. 3125–50.

43. Keppie, *Colonisation and Veteran Settlement*, pp. 8–12, points out that all places in the segment of the first *Liber coloniarum* covering the *provincia Lucania* are identified as *praefecturae*, while in the following portions, covering the *provincia Brittiorum* and the *provincia Apulia*, each place is characterized as an *ager* followed by an adjective giving the identity of the community. In the *provincia Tuscia*, moreover, all places were called *coloniae*, even though some are known not to have held that rank.

44. *CIL* I.2.640 — found at Sant'Angelo in Formis not far from Capua; *CIL* I.2.641.

45. *CIL* I.2.639, 642; *ILLRP* I.472; *AE* (1945), no. 25; *AE* (1955), no. 190. For the identification of the road as the *via Annia*, see n. 61.

46. Bracco, "Un nuovo documento della centuriazione graccana," pp. 29–37.

47. Carcopino, *Autour des Gracques*, makes a more precise dating of the stones; see section IV in this chapter.

48. Thus, Pais, "Il Liber Coloniarum," pp. 56–57.

49. *CIL* I.2.719.

50. *CIL* I.2.643, 644, 645. On the last, the names of the commissioners do not survive.

51. For the overall course of the *via Appia*, see Chevallier, *Roman Roads*, pp. 132–33.

52. *Liber coloniarum I* pp. 210L, 229L. Note that other sources call the settlement at Abellinum Livian; see n. 76.

53. *AE* (1955), no. 222.

54. See Pani, "Il nuovo cippo graccano dauno," pp. 389–400.

55. *Liber coloniarum I* p. 211L. The texts have Varinum, which Thomsen, *Italic Regions*, pp. 52–53, identifies as Bari.

56. The later *via Valeria* probably was first constructed in the first half of the second century, and although they are poorly known, a number of roads — one beginning at Corfinium — led across central Italy to Luceria and Herdoniae; see Salmon, *Samnium*, pp. 19–21, and Nagle, "Allied View of the Social War," p. 373. Those routes, however, were not the only ones that led to Apulia; the imperial *via Traiana* ran east from Beneventum through Ausculum and Herdoniae to Brundisium by way of Bari — the surveys at Bari and Lupiae may result from this route — and in some form the road was in use in republican times, probably at least as early as the late third century; see Wiseman, *Roman Studies*, p. 135.

57. For the identification of the *territorium Lyppiense* as Lupiae, northeast of the modern Lecce, see Thomsen, *Italic Regions*, pp. 52–53. The same passage that mentioned Tarentum and Lypia also gave the *territorium Austranum*; its location is unknown, but it probably was in the same area.

58. When describing the commissioners resurveying certain lands, Appian (*BC* 1.18) noted that the original surveys were inaccurate, since they were done in haste. One can doubt whether the triumvirs were more careful in this matter than their predecessors.

59. Carcopino, *Autour des Gracques*, p. 84, and Gabba, *Appiani bellorum civilium liber primus*, p. 60, believe they recovered full powers after Scipio Aemilianus's death.

60. See Bauman, "Gracchan Agrarian Commission," pp. 403–6, and Pani, "Potere di *iudicatio*," pp. 131–46.

61. The identity of the man honored in *ILS* 23 is uncertain, but T. Annius Rufus (pr. by 131, cos. 128) is the most likely; see Wiseman, "*Viae Anniae*," pp. 21–37; "*Viae Anniae* Again," pp. 82–91. For P. Popillius Laenas (pr. by 135, cos. 132), see Degrassi, "Un nuovo miliario," pp. 259–65; Hinrichs, "Der römische Strassenbau," pp. 162–76, "Nochmals zur Inschrift von Polla," pp. 251–55. Less probably, Bracco, "L'elogium di Polla," pp. 5–38, has proposed T. Annius Luscus, the consul of 153, and Verbrugghe, "*Elogium* from Polla," pp. 25–35, identifies the subject as Ap. Claudius Pulcher (cos. 143) on the mistaken assumption that only agrarian commissioners could distribute land. The Gracchan *termini* found in the area bear the names of Gracchus, Claudius, and Crassus and thus are to be dated before 130.

62. For Fabrateria Nova, see Vell. Pat. 1.14.4; Drusus's law will be discussed in the following section.

63. For examples, see V. Max. 7.7.6; Cic. *Ver.* 2.1.119.

64. For the law of C. Gracchus, see the following section.

65. For the legislation of C. Gracchus, see Stockton, *Gracchi*, pp. 114–61.

66. Livy (*Per.* 60) reported that C. Gracchus "carried the agrarian law that his brother had carried"; Vell. Pat. (2.6.2), who knew of the law of Ti. Gracchus, held that Gaius "divided fields, forbidding any citizen from having more than five hundred *iugera*, which was ordered once by the *lex Licinia*"; and the author of *De viris illustribus* (65) said that "he carried an agrarian law and constituted himself, Fulvius Flaccus and C. Crassus [*sic*] as triumvirs for the division of lands." Plut. (*CG* 5) merely stated that one of the laws he proposed was agrarian.

67. Law of 111: *FIRA* I, no. 8, line 15; Latin Law of Bantia: *FIRA* I, no. 6, lines 14–15 (= *CIL* I.2.582); Judiciary Law: *FIRA* I, no. 7, lines 2, 13, 16, 22 (= *CIL* I.2.583). The agrarian law of 111 certainly used the phrase *III a.d.a.* to refer to the Gracchan commissioners and the same probably is true for the *lex de rebus repetundis*, usually identified as the *lex Acilia*, which was probably passed shortly after C. Gracchus's agrarian law; see Lintott, *Judicial Reform*, pp. 166–69. The date of the *lex Latina Bantiae* is controversial, with some placing it in the Gracchan age while others put it later in the century; see Hall, "II-Iviri a.d.a.," pp. 199–206. In any case, the agrarian law and the judicial law clearly show that the titulature of C. Gracchus's commission excluded judicial powers. Note, however, that Carcopino, *Autour des Gracques*, pp. 247–48, held that the law of 123 continued those powers, since he thought that some of the *cippi*, all of which mention judicial powers, are to be dated to 123 and later; there is no evidence to support the assertion, clearly contradicted by the legal texts.

68. Livy probably placed the colonial legislation in 123. The epitomator (*Per.* 60) separated the colonial legislation from the earlier agrarian law by a phrase indicating that the tribune had been continued in office for another year. Stockton, *Gracchi*, pp. 229–30, notes that Livy covered events of 122 in book 61 and thus the epitomator (and Livy) must have placed all the laws in 123 (since they are reported in book 60); the phrase "continued in office" would refer only to the election not to actually taking office the second time.

69. Appian (*BC* 1.23) reported that the younger Gracchus proposed to found many colonies. The *Liber coloniarum I* (pp. 216L, 219L, 229L, 233L, 237L, 238L) noted colonies at Ferentinum, Tarquinii, Abellinum, Cadatia, Suessa Aurunca, and Vellitrae that were founded *lege Sempronia* or *lege Graccana*, but the legal status assigned to communities by that document are unreliable; see Keppie, *Colonisation and Veteran Settlement*, pp. 8–12.

70. Livy (*Per.* 60) saw C. Gracchus as responsible, but Plut. (*CG* 10) reported that

Rubrius actually carried it, a claim the law of 111 confirms; see *FIRA* I, no. 8, line 59. The year of Rubrius's tribunate is uncertain, but much of the difficulty derives from a failure to distinguish between various stages of colonization, for the passage of the law and the foundation of the colony frequently took place in different years. Indeed, for the years following the Second Punic War, Livy regularly distinguished between the decision to found a colony (and the choice of commissioners) and the ceremonial foundation; see Chapter 3, section I. Vell. Pat. (1.15.4) placed the colony's foundation (*colonia condita est*) in 123. Appian (*BC* 1.24) and Plutarch (*CG* 11) had the colonial commissioners in Africa in 122. In *CG* 10, Plutarch reported the law itself after recounting the passage of Drusus's colonial law in 122, but he did not date the former closely, for he used the notice to lead into C. Gracchus's trip to Africa. Writers in the Livian tradition probably placed the legislation in 123, leaving the foundation for a later year. For the epitomator, see n. 68. Eutropius (4.21) stated that Carthage was founded by the order of the senate, clearly an error, and he dated the colony to 123, but it is uncertain whether he was describing the authorization or the actual foundation. Orosius (5.12.1) is clearer: in 123, Carthage was ordered restored (... *Carthago in Africa restitui iussa* ...) — this declaration should represent the passage of the *lex Rubria* itself.

71. Appian (*BC* 1.24; *Pun.* 136) reported that C. Gracchus settled six thousand *coloni* at Carthage — more, he noted, than the law allowed.

72. Livy *Per.* 60; Appian (*BC* 1.24) spoke of the founders as being especially chosen for the task. Yet Carcopino, *Autour des Gracques*, pp. 278–92, held that Flaccus and Gracchus were not members of a special commission established to found Iunonia but, instead, supervised the colonization as members of the agrarian commission instituted in 133 by Tiberius Gracchus. This scheme is part of Carcopino's overall thesis on the nature of the Gracchan agrarian commission and suffers from the same weaknesses; see section IV in this chapter.

73. See nn. 12 and 13.

74. The law of the younger Drusus, tribune of the plebs in 91 and the son of the tribune of 122, may provide some indications of the range. According to Appian (*BC* 1.35), Drusus proposed to lead to sites in Italy and Sicily several colonies that had been authorized some time before but not established; the earlier measure may have been his father's.

75. According to his elogium, the younger Drusus served as *Xvir agris dandis adsignandis lege sua*; see *ILS* 49. If he did copy certain provisions of his father's law, he may also have used a commission of the same size.

76. The *Liber coloniarum I* p. 229L claimed a colony was installed at Abellinum *lege Sempronia*, but the title of the colony was Veneria Livia (see *CIL* X.1117), leading Beloch, *Der italische Bund*, p. 63, and Boren, "Livius Drusus," pp. 31–32, to identify it as one of Drusus's colonies.

77. Note that Ti. Gracchus's law provided for viritane assignments, and thus its commissioners would not have needed the auspices for colonial foundations. It is unclear, however, whether C. Gracchus gave that right in a colonial law, which would have added to the powers of the commission reestablished by his land law earlier in the year, or if it was the main agrarian law itself, in which case the switch to colonization already had been planned at the time this measure was framed. In either case, this commission was the first to be empowered both to found colonies and to make viritane assignment.

78. For the process with respect to the augurs, see Linderski, "Augural Law," pp. 2151–90.

79. Appian used the word μάντεων to describe the priests, a term that can refer either to augurs or to haruspices. Rawson, "Religion and Politics," p. 197, identifies the priests as augurs, while Thulin, *Die etruskische Disciplin*, 3:102, and MacBain, *Prodigy and Ex-*

piation, p. 75, hold them to be Etruscan *haruspices*—for MacBain on the grounds that augurs only dealt with signs during comitial proceedings or from birds. But the augurs also dealt with signs in situations away from the city and studied signs that included actions by four-footed animals, lightning, thunder, and storms; see Linderski, "Augural Law," pp. 2162–68. Here an important distinction in religious law is crucial. Portents, the concern of *haruspices* and of the *decemviri sacris faciundis*, reflected upon the health of the state in general. The signs that formed the specialty of the augurs, however, only determined the acceptability of actions actually being performed at the time; see Linderski, "Cicero and Roman Divination," pp. 30–31. The signs and principles of augural law, then, are more appropriate to the situation at Carthage.

80. For the continuing legality of the assignments, see Lintott, *Judicial Reform*, pp. 253–55.

81. Plutarch used ὑπογραφῆς to describe an outline defined by markers, and that word seems more appropriate to the outline of the city than to the grid of lines defining divisions within the fields. Note that Livy (1.44.4–5) pictured Romulus as marking the Roman *pomerium* with fixed *termini*.

82. Opponents could easily have found a clear reason for divine disapproval. After having urged the gods of Carthage to abandon the place in the rite of *evocatio*, Scipio Aemilianus next vowed a portion of the city, its fields, and certain places to the Roman gods in the complementary rite of *devotio*; see Macr. 3.9.1–16; Le Gall, "Evocatio," p. 521; and Palmer, *Roman Religion and Roman Empire*, p. 142. Gracchus and his supporters, on the other hand, may have claimed that the vow was invalid. Reporting the same dedication, Cicero (*Agr.* 1.5) suggested that Scipio had consecrated the place either to mark the victory, proclaim the destruction of Carthage, or for some religious reason. Perhaps these options indicate that the legal basis for Aemilianus's action was contested. Line 81 of the agrarian law of 111 may contain a reference to these dedicated lands; see Johannsen, "Die lex agraria des Jahres 111," p. 377, and Lintott, *Judicial Reform*, p. 268. The oblique nature of the passage may indicate that the framers were trying to avoid taking a stand on the legal status of the lands.

83. See Chapter 9, section I.

84. See Chapter 3, section IV.

85. See Seibert, "IIIviri lege Sempronia," pp. 53–86.

86. Thus, Mommsen, *Str.*, 2:632–33, Cardinali, *Studi graccani*, p. 158, Fraccaro, *Studi sull'età dei Gracchi*, 1:84, De Martino, *Costituzione*, 2:103, and Johannsen, "Die Lex Agraria des Jahres 111," p. 86 n. 68. For a strong argument against this position, see Carcopino, *Autour des Gracques*, pp. 132–33.

87. For possible terms, see n. 11.

88. See Carcopino, *Autour des Gracques*, pp. 129–303. Carcopino also thought the college's term significant. Starting from the fact that the terms of special commissions are known in only a few cases, he (141–44) argued that those boards were atypical and that the normal practice would have been for colleges to have no fixed terms, but instead to serve until the task was completed. The examples he cited, however, are questionable. No source described the basis of those commissions' long tenure in office—the same situation we face with the Gracchan college; for the weakness of the evidence, see Seibert, "IIIviri lege Sempronia," pp. 57–58. Indeed, a practice permitting officials to hold office indefinitely on their own authority is unlikely; even the *triumviri rei publicae constituendae* of 43 had a fixed term (five years); see Dio 47.2.1–2. The Triumvirs, it should be noted, at first simply declared their term extended for an additional five years, but later they felt that procedure to be inadequate and secured the passage of an authorizing law; see Dio 48.54.6; App. *BC* 5.95.

89. Here, the supposed practices of the *decemviri legibus scribundis* of 451 served Car-

copino as a model. Zonaras (7.18) described each decemvir sitting alone in judgment on a regular daily rotation (he used the adverb ἐναλλάξ to describe this exchange); Livy (3.33.8) gave the same college a similar rotation. Ogilvie, *Commentary on Livy*, p. 457, thought this rotation improbable and was in fact based on accounts of the rotating presidency of the Athenian βουλή. Using the known offices of the triumvirs, Carcopino, *Autour des Gracques*, pp. 175–209, constructed an outline of that alternation: Ap. Claudius would have been the sole active triumvir in 133, Ti. Gracchus would have served in 132, C. Gracchus in 131. In 130, the sequence would have begun again with Claudius's replacement. Carcopino found support in the boundary markers left by members of the college, for the order of the names on the stones varies (on different occasions Crassus, Gracchus, and Flaccus each are named first), and that variation, he maintained, must indicate that the commissioner named first actually was in charge when the land in question was surveyed. Seibert, "IIIviri lege Sempronia," p. 63, notes that Ti. Gracchus's attempt to secure reelection as tribune for 132 (see Plut. *TG* 16; App. *BC* 1.14) would conflict with Carcopino's account of his position on the college and the way it operated, that Plut. *TG* 13 implies that Ti. Gracchus intended to work in 133, and that C. Gracchus was reelected tribune for 122, his year of duty according to Carcopino.

90. Carcopino, *Autour des Gracques*, pp. 161–62, thought he had found another example of regular rotation. The *lex Atinia* of 197 created a triumvirate to found several colonies, but two members of its triumvirate were elected praetors shortly afterward and received provinces, and both commands were extended for at least part of the following year; one of those two, moreover, was elected consul for the third year of the college's existence. Carcopino held that one triumvir served as sole active commissioner in 196, another held primary responsibility in the second year, while the third managed in the final year. This rotation, moreover, was known in advance, so that the members would know the years in which they could seek other offices. The evidence, however, does not allow this conclusion, for the second commissioner would have returned from his province well into his alleged year as manager, while the third would have been actively serving as consul during his. In this college, arrangements for the division of responsibility could not have been made in advance, for no one could have predicted that two would be successful as candidates for praetor, nor could anyone have foreseen that their terms would be prorogued, and certainly no one could have predicted that one later would be elected consul. This college is discussed at greater length in Chapter 3, section IV.

91. Indeed, taking both the words αἱρετούς and ἐναλλασσομένους to refer to annual elections is redundant, for then the entire phrase would read "three elected men, elected yearly." For the range of meanings of ἐναλλάσσω and related words, see Seibert, "IIIviri lege Sempronia," pp. 81–82. For some speculation about the term, see n. 11.

92. Seibert, "IIIviri lege Sempronia," pp. 82–85, suggests that each commissioner may have received responsibility for a single geographic area and would have worked on it whenever he had the time; each triumvir, then, would have been in sole authority in his province, just as praetors, while members of a college, each had their own *provinciae*.

93. For the date of the law, see previous section.

94. See section III in this chapter.

95. See, for example, *FIRA* I, no. 8, lines 60–61.

96. See Chapter 4, section III.

97. For the process of enlistment, see Chapter 3, section III. Appian (*BC* 1.24) held that the colonists were recruited from all of Italy, but that does not mean that he thought the formal enlistment necessarily took place at many locations, only that he thought individuals from all of Italy were eligible to present themselves at the announced time and place.

98. See Chapter 3, section IV.

99. For the principles of collegiality, see Mommsen, *Str.*, 1:30–31.

100. See Mommsen, *Str.*, 1:37–46.

101. There is some slight evidence that the Gracchan commissioners customarily worked alone. Because members of the duumvirate established by the agrarian law of 111 were always mentioned in the singular, Mommsen, *Ges. Schr.*, 1:141, suggested that they had a divided area of competence, one working in Africa and the other in Greece. Johannsen, "Die lex agraria des Jahres 111," 304–5, rejects that position, pointing out that the law also refers to members of the Gracchan triumvirate in the singular, yet each possessed the same area of competence. But in line 81 of the law of 111, the drafter noted that the *decemviri lege Livia* assigned land to Utica, an action he described with a plural subject and plural verbs. Thus, the Gracchan commissioners, while they possessed the same powers and shared in the same task, may have worked individually, and the framers of the law of 111 may have expected their duumvirs to operate in much the same way. Note also that the decemvirs to be established by the proposal of Rullus in 63 were to work in that fashion; see Chapter 9, section II.

102. See Chapter 9, sections II and III.

103. Note that Plutarch's omens (*CG* 11–12), which bore on more of the major elements of foundation, supposedly took place while C. Gracchus was on the scene, but since Plutarch did not link repeal of the law with the portents, he would have had no reason to explain how the signs came to the attention of the senate. Conceivably, someone who had accompanied Gracchus to the site, or a member of the entourage of the governor of the province of Africa, or an inhabitant of a neighboring city served as the ostensible source, but in any case after the foundation no reporter would have been engaged in dividing lands.

CHAPTER 9

1. First law: Auct. *Vir. Ill.* 73.1; second law: Livy *Per.* 69; Plut. *Mar.* 29; Auct. *Vir. Ill.* 73.5. Niccolini, *I fasti dei tribuni della plebe*, pp. 199–202, suggests that the earlier provided for viritane assignments while the later established colonies. Some *coloni* may actually have been settled in Africa. The *elogium* of Julius Caesar's father (*Inscr. Ital.* 13.3.7) records that he led colonists to the island of Cercina. There is, however, little evidence for extensive Marian settlements in Africa; see Brunt, *Italian Manpower*, pp. 577–80.

2. The law of the younger Drusus ordered the foundation of colonies in Italy and Sicily, which Appian (*BC* 1.35) noted that had been authorized earlier but not founded—perhaps these colonies formed part of his father's program. For the program of the elder Drusus, see Plut. *CG* 9–10; App. *BC* 1.23.

3. For the political context of the legislation, see Gruen, *Last Generation*, pp. 387–404.

4. Cic. *Att.* 1.18.6 provides the only explicit reference to the *lex Plotia agraria*, but Cicero did not give a date or specify its provisions, beyond noting that it resembled the later *rogatio Flavia agraria*. Dio (38.5.1), in a speech supposedly given in support of the *lex Iulia agraria* of 59, has Pompey refer to an earlier law, approved by the senate, which provided land for his soldiers and those of Metellus, probably a reference to the Plotian law. The Plotius in question is usually identified with the Plotius who sponsored other bills in 70; see Gabba, "Lex Plotia Agraria," pp. 66–67; Smith, "Lex Plotia Agraria," p. 82. Marshall, "*Lex Plotia Agraria*," pp. 43–52, accepts the identification, but holds that the measure was never actually passed. Plutarch (*Luc.* 34) made Clodius in a speech refer to Pompey's veterans settled on fields and in towns and that may refer to colonies,

although it could also refer to soldiers settled *viritim* in the territories of established places. For the *rogatio Flavia agraria*, see Cic. *Att.* 1.18.1, 1.19.4; 2.1.16; Plut. *Cat. Mi.* 31; *Luc.* 42; Dio 37.49.2–37.50.6. Cic. *Att.* 1.18.1 noted that the two measures were similar.

5. Dio 38.1.1–7 provides the most detailed account of the law. Taylor, "Caesar's First Consulship," pp. 254–58, and Gruen, *Last Generation*, p. 397, place the measure late in January, but see Linderski, "Constitutional Aspects," pp. 434–40.

6. Dio 38.7.3; App. *BC* 2.10; Suet. *Iul.* 20; Vell. Pat. 2.44.4 noted that the measure resulted in the *ius urbis* being restored to Capua.

7. See, for example, Suet. *Iul.* 42; Aug. *Res Gestae* 3, 28.

8. For Lentulus's activities, see Chapter 6, section III.

9. For the law, see Livy *Per.* 69; Plut. *Mar.* 29; Auct. *Vir. Ill.* 73.5.

10. See Dio 38.1.3–4; Plut. *Caes.* 14.1–2; Cic. *Dom.* 23.

11. Cic. *Agr.* 2.78 shows that some of Sulla's colonies were authorized by a law, while the law of Urso, founded as a result of Caesar's victory in the civil wars, refers to lands given and assigned by a *lex Iulia*, a *lex Antonia*, decrees of the senate, and plebiscites; *FIRA* I, no. 21, cap. 97, 104.

12. Those projects are discussed in greater detail later in the chapter.

13. For suggestions on the political context of the measure, see Sumner, "Cicero, Pompeius, and Rullus," pp. 569–82, and Gruen, *Last Generation*, pp. 392–94.

14. For some attempts to reconstruct details of the law, see Afzelius, "Das Ackerverteilungsgesetz des P. Servilius Rullus," pp. 214–35; Jonkers, *Social and Economic Commentary*. For the identification of quotations from the law in Cicero's text, see Ferrary, "Rogatio Servilia Agraria," pp. 141–64.

15. Cic. *Agr.* 2.14.35–37, 2.15.38–46, 2.18.47–49, 2.19.51–20.55. For the location of places to be sold and the type of revenues to be placed, see Jonkers, *Social and Economic Commentary*, pp. 57–137.

16. Cic. *Agr.* 2.23.62–27.72.

17. Cic. *Agr.* 1.6.20–21, 2.28.76.

18. According to his *elogium*, C. Iulius Caesar Strabo held the post of *decemvir agris dandis adtribuendis iudicandis*; *ILS* 48. On the basis of the known offices, his service must have been before 90, but the presence of judicial powers shows that this college and the decemvirs established by Drusus's law of 91 were not identical. One of the laws of Saturninus probably created the college; thus, Broughton, "*Elogia* of Caesar's Father," pp. 323–30; Frank, "New Elogium of Caesar's Father," pp. 90–93. Gabba (*Appiani bellorum civilium liber primus*, pp. 102–3; "Ricerche su alcuni punti di storia mariana," pp. 12–24) suggests that Caesar was elected under the terms of the law of 103, since the legislation of 100 was abrogated and the colonies were not actually established, but Cicero (*Balb.* 48) reveals that the list of colonists was assembled—a sign that commissioners had been chosen.

19. See *ILS* 49.

20. According to the *Liber coloniarum* I (p. 236L), *quinqueviri* founded a colony at Praeneste. Mommsen (*Str.*, 2:628) suggested that they operated under the *lex Iulia* of 59, but neither of the laws of this year are known to have authorized a colony at Praeneste, while a Sullan *lex Cornelia* certainly did; see, Harvey, "Sullan Colony," pp. 38–39 n. 17.

21. See Cic. *Agr.* 2.12.32.

22. Dio 38.1.5–7; Cic. *Att.* 2.6, 2.7.

23. Thus, Mommsen, *Str.*, 2:628 n. 4. Rudolph, *Stadt und Staat*, p. 188 n. 2, suggested that the quinquevirs were established by the first law and the vigintivirs by the second, but this is unlikely.

24. Cic. *Att.* 15.19.2; *Phil.* 5.7, 5.21, 8.26, 12.23; Dio 45.9.

25. Cic. *Phil.* 2.100–104; *Att.* 14.20, 14.21.

26. The *Liber coloniarum I* (p. 231L) speaks of Capua as being "deducted" by the vigintivirs. For the division of land, see *Liber coloniarum I* p. 231L; Varro *R.* 1.2.9–10; Pliny *Nat.* 7.176.

27. Suet. *Iul.* 20. Suetonius claimed that Caesar assigned the lots in this manner, but that may only mean that he included such a provision in his law, for Dio 38.1.6–7 noted that Caesar specifically excluded himself from membership in the college. Caesar *Civ.* 1.14 implied that some veterans were settled in Campania.

28. Cic. *Phil.* 14.10. No source actually places Saxa on the college of VII, but see Syme, "Who Was Decidius Saxa?," pp. 133–36. Since Cicero elsewhere (*Phil.* 11.12) described Saxa as *castrorum metator*, A. Schulten, *RE* 7, pt. 1 (1912), cols. 1889, 1891, s.v. *Gromatici*, identified him as the first known *praefectus castrorum*, an official under the Empire who specialized among other things in the laying out of camps. Syme argued against regarding Saxa as a *praefectus castrorum*—an office certainly attested only with Augustus—and maintains: "In the Roman army in the time of Caesar there is no trace of a separate corps of engineers, surveyors, or the like."

29. Cic. *Agr.* 2.7.16.

30. See Botsford, *Roman Assemblies*, pp. 391–92; Taylor, *Roman Voting Assemblies*, p. 82. Cicero (*Agr.* 2.8.21) suggested that the lot would be used to determine the voting of the tribes for Rullus's commission.

31. 263–66L. The identification of the law and of the five individuals who gave it its name has proven to be extremely contentious. A link with Caesar's agrarian legislation is probable, either one of the laws of 59 or some later measure during the civil wars or less probably in the mid to late 50s; for a brief discussion and a list of the relevant modern literature, see Crawford, "Lex Iulia Agraria," pp. 179–90. For our purposes, no closer identification is necessary. Note that Cicero (*Agr.* 2.7.17) used *curatores* to encompass the holders of magistracies—specifically the triumvirs, quinquevirs, and decemvirs customarily elected according to the provisions of agrarian laws—but Festus (p. 42L) only defined a *curator* as one placed in charge of the grain supply or the dividing of lands.

32. See *FIRA* I, no. 8.

33. *FIRA* I, no. 21, cap. 66. See also *CIL* X.3825.

34. See Schleussner, *Legaten*, and Thomasson, *Legatus*, pp. 14–25.

35. For his distributions, see Livy *Per.* 89; App. *BC* 1.95–96, 1.100, 1.104; see also Hinrichs, *Gromatischen Institutionen*, pp. 66–75. For Sullan *quinqueviri*, see n. 20.

36. For the use of legates and prefects, see Cic. *Fam.* 13.7 (for the title *praef(ectus)*, see Crawford, *Roman Republican Coinage*, 1:486, no. 476; Grant, *From Imperium to Auctoritas*, pp. 7–11); Dio 47.14.4; App. *BC* 5.14; Suet. *Tib.* 4; *CIL* XIV.2264; Q. Hortensius, whose coins call him *praef(ectus) colon(iae) dedu(cendae)*, served under Brutus (Grant, p. 10). For their projects, see Vittinghof, *Römische Kolonisation*, and Keppie, *Colonisation and Veteran Settlement*.

37. App. *BC* 5.14; *FIRA* I, no. 21, cap. 97.

38. For the coin of Gracchus, see Crawford, *Roman Republican Coinage*, 1:529–30, no. 525; for the coin of 29–27, see Grueber, *Coins of the Roman Republic*, 2:17, no. 4363.

39. See *CIL* III.374, 1443, 3279; VIII.17841, 17842.

40. Thus, Hardy, *Three Spanish Charters*, p. 8, following chapters in the *lex Ursonensis* (*FIRA* I, no. 21, cap. 66, 125).

41. Keppie, *Colonisation and Veteran Settlement*, p. 96, holds that Appian's report that Octavian dispatched colonists shows that Octavian himself served personally as *deduc-*

tor, but Appian clearly stated that Octavian "sent out" the settlers, rather than "led them out."

42. Hinrichs, "Das legale Landversprechen," pp. 539–41, holds that Octavian assigned the plots, using a *forma* constructed as a result of the surveying and marking of the lands in question. But the subdivisions within centuriation modules could not have been created until the size of allotments was known, and it is most probable that the same individuals would have handled both the construction of the grid and of the plots within modules. Some assignments were made on the scene. In his description of the use of sortition to match settlers and plots, Hyginus Gromaticus (pp. 199–201L) used as an illustration veterans of the legion *V Alaudae*, and that example might have been derived from the actual settlement of members of this legion at Emerita in 25; thus, Keppie, *Colonisation and Veteran Settlement*, p. 94.

43. See, for example, Cic. *De Orat.* 2.272; Livy 5.47.7–1, 24.18.3–10, 27.11.14–15; V. Max. 2.9.7.

44. Cic. *Agr.* 1.3.7, 2.21.56–57.

45. Nicolet, "Les *finitores*," p. 99, suggests without argument that the words *quaestori permittant* should be emended to *quaesitori permittant*. It is unclear what such a person would have investigated and determined, since the same passage indicates that the measure instructed *finitores* to issue decisions, presumably about boundaries and the status of the land; given the tasks in the sphere of competence of the quaestors, no emendation is necessary.

46. Cic. *Agr.* 2.13.34. For the Gracchan commission, see Chapter 8, section IV.

47. Cic. *Agr.* 2.13.32: *finitores ex equestri loco ducentos, vicenos singulorum stipatores corporis constituit, eosdem ministros et satellites potestatis*. Instead of *finitorēs*, the manuscripts give either *ianitores* or *iam lictores*, but in the context the first clearly cannot be accepted and all editors regularly emend the word to *finitores*, for the law mentions their existence on other occasions. Each decemvir received twenty surveyors, for the phrase *vicenos singulorum stipatores corporis* should be understood as being in apposition to *finitores*.

48. Cic. *Agr.* 2.13.34. Cicero used *mittant* to describe the dispatch of a *finitor* by a decemvir and *renuntiaverit* to indicate the report of that surveyor to the magistrate who had sent him. Rudorff, "Gromatische Institutionen," p. 321 n. 236, noted that both *mittere* and *renuntiare* are technical words, and thus the actions they describe have both a legal force and the appropriate forms of action. The use of the singulars (*quod finitor uni illi a quo missus erit renuntiaverit*) indicates that each decemvir alone could send *finitores* and these surveyors could be dispatched individually. For a discussion of the operations these *finitores* were permitted to perform, see the following section.

49. See Cic. *Div.* 2.76; Mommsen, *Str.*, 1:101.

50. See North, "Diviners and Divination," p. 55.

51. Cic. *Phil.* 2.100–104; *Att.* 14.20, 14.21.

52. It is conceivable that Antony also accompanied the soldiers on their way to the site, since he and the settlers may have left Rome at about the same time. According to Appian (*BC* 2.120), at the time of Caesar's death, many soldiers, who had been waiting in temples and sacred precincts in Rome, were on the verge of departing to their colony under one standard and one leader; the description best fits a single unit, probably a legion, and because of the coincidence of dates, that leader may have been preparing to take his soldiers to Casilinum, where legion VIII was settled; thus, Keppie, *Colonisation and Veteran Settlement*, p. 96.

53. See Chapter 3, section II, and Chapter 5, section II.

54. Membership on the two colleges certainly overlapped. Cicero, who was offered a position to replace a member who had died, described the post both as a vigintivirate

and as a quinquevirate; see Cic. *Att.* 2.19, 9.2a.1; *Prov.* 41; Vell. Pat. 2.44.4; Quint. *Inst.* 12.1.16. For the judicial powers, see *CIL* I.2.1, p. 201.

55. Suet. *Aug.* 4.1; Dio 38.1.7; Plin. *Nat.* 7.176; Varro *R.* 1.2.10; Cic. *Att.* 2.12.1, 2.19.3. See Broughton, *MRR*, 2:191-92.

56. For Saxa, see Syme, "Who Was Decidius Saxa?," pp. 133-36.

57. For the rank of the supervisors, see Keppie, *Colonisation and Veteran Settlement*, pp. 50-51; Grant, *From Imperium to Auctoritas*, pp. 7-11; E. Kornemann, *RE* 4 (1901), col. 570, s.v. *coloniae*.

58. Ti. Nero: Suet. *Tib.* 4; Hortensius (his coins call him *praef(ectus) colon(iae) dedu(cendae)*: see Grant, *From Imperium to Auctoritas*, p. 10; Memmius: *CIL* XIV.2264 calls him *praef(ectus) legionum XXVI et VII Lucae ad agros dividundos*. The status of one of Cicero's correspondents, C. Cluvius, who founded settlements in Cisalpine Gaul (Cic. *Fam.* 13.7), is unclear. His coins carry the title *praef(ectus)*; see Crawford, *Roman Republican Coinage*, 1:486, no. 476; Grant, *From Imperium to Auctoritas*, pp. 7-11.

59. Cic. *Fam.* 13.4; *Att.* 14.12.1, 14.17.2, 14.20.3, 15.2.2, 15.15.1, 15.20.3, 15.19.3, 16.2.1, 16.4.3, 16a, 16b, 16c. See Broughton, *MRR*, 2:332.

60. Donatus *Vitae Vergilianae* p. 30 Diehl; Serv. *Ecl.* 11.1; Iunius Philargyrius II, *Ecl.* 6.7; Serv. Dan. *Ecl.* 6.6, 9.10. Bayet, "Virgile et les triumvirs 'agris dividundis,'" pp. 271-99, suggested that Pollio, Varus, and Gallus were *triumviri agris dividundis* on the traditional pattern, but all did not serve at the same time (Philargyrius and Servius Danielis held that Alfenus replaced Pollio in this role) and Servius Danielis (*Ecl.* 9.27) called them legates.

61. In some cases, different individuals may have prepared the land for settlement and led the colonists there. Cic. *Att.* 16.16a has the colonists for Buthrotum assembled in Rome waiting to go to an area in which land has already been confiscated by agents.

62. Thus App. *BC* 2.120. Appian (*BC* 2.141) represented Brutus as claiming that Caesar settled soldiers in colonies in their military units and under their standards. Tacitus (*Ann.* 14.27), while describing Nero's colonies, claimed that in the past tribunes and centurions had been installed in colonies along with the veterans.

63. For equestrian jurists, see Kunkel, *Herkunft und soziale Stellung*, pp. 50-53.

64. For the term *finitor*, see Chapter 4, section III.

65. Thus, Nicolet, "Les *finitores*," pp. 72-103.

66. Cic. *Agr.* 2.17.45, 2.19.53. Note also that Nicolet, "Les *finitores*," p. 74 n. 1, suggests that a fragment of one of Cicero's speeches against the law that mentions *imberba iuventute* (Charisius *Ars grammatica* 1.95 Keil) may refer to the *finitores*; Nicolet also notes that Cicero often used *iuventus* to indicate young men of the nobility and the more prominent families of the equestrian order.

67. For earlier practices in those matters, see Chapter 4, section III.

68. For the proper verbal forms of a *lex*, see Chapter 3, section I. Hinrichs, "Das legale Landversprechen," pp. 540-41, identified the text as an edict, but it does not conform to the proper wording of an edict; see Daube, *Forms*, pp. 37-49.

69. Hinrichs, *Gromatischen Institutionen*, pp. 77, 90, pointing to a provision in the agrarian law of 111, holds that magistrates put out a contract for the centuriation of the *ager Corinthus*, which he claims would have been the regular practice in civil projects (which he distinguishes strongly in personnel and in practice from military ones). Neither of those positions is likely to be correct; see Chapter 2, section VI, and Chapter 5, section II.

70. See Dilke, *Roman Land Surveyors*, pp. 37-46; Hinrichs, *Gromatischen Institutionen*, pp. 158-70; Nicolet, *Space, Geography, and Politics*, p. 150.

71. See Rudorff, "Gromatische Institutionen," pp. 320-23. Note that Cicero (*Agr.*

2.13.32) included the *finitores* with other functionaries — *scribae, librarii, praecones,* and *architecti* — among the necessary *apparitores,* and the holders of apparitorial posts received a regular, and fixed, pay. For the relationship between magistrates and imperial *agrimensores*, see Chapter 4, section III.

72. For "rationality" as a feature of governments deemed bureaucratic — and the limitations of the term — see section I of the Introduction.

BIBLIOGRAPHY

Abbott, F. F., and A. C. Johnson. *Municipal Administration in the Roman Empire*, Princeton, 1926.
Afzelius, A. "Das Ackerverteilungsgesetz des P. Servilius Rullus." *C & M* 3 (1940): 214–35.
Alexander, M. C. "*Praemia* in the *Quaestiones* of the Late Republic." *CPh* 80 (1985): 20–32.
Alföldi, A. "Hasta—Summa Imperii: The Spear as Embodiment of Sovereignty in Rome." *AJA* 63 (1959): 1–27.
———. "*Ager Romanus Antiquus*." *Hermes* 90 (1962): 187–213.
———. *Early Rome and the Latins*. Ann Arbor, 1965.
Allen, W. F. "Niese on the Licinian-Sextian Law." *CR* 3 (1889): 5–6.
Arthur, P. *Romans in Northern Campania*. London, 1991.
Astin, A. E. *The Lex Annalis before Sulla*. Brussels, 1958.
———. *Scipio Aemilianus*. Oxford, 1967.
Badian, E. *Foreign Clientelae, 264–70 B.C.* Oxford, 1958.
———. "From the Gracchi to Sulla." *Historia* 11 (1962): 197–245.
———. "The Early Historians." In *The Latin Historians*, ed. T. A. Dorey, pp. 1–38. New York, 1966.
———. "Roman Politics and the Italians (133–91 B.C.)." *Dialoghi di Archeologia* 4–5 (1970–71): 373–409.
———. "Tiberius Gracchus and the Beginning of the Roman Revolution." *ANRW* I.1 (1972): 668–731.
———. *Publicans and Sinners: Private Enterprise in the Service of the Roman Republic*. 2nd ed. Ithaca, 1983.
———. "The House of the Servilii Gemini: A Study in the Misuse of Occam's Razor." *PBSR* 52 (1984): 49–71.
Baltrusch, E. *Regimen morum: Die Reglementierung des Privatleben der Senatoren und Ritter in der römischen Republik und frühen Kaiserzeit*. Munich, 1989.
Bandelli, G. "La fondazione delle colonie di Piacenza e di Cremona: Alcuni problemi prosopografici." *Quaderni di storia antica ed epigrafia* 2 (1978): 39–57.
Baronowski, D. W. "The *Formula Togatorum*." *Historia* 33 (1984): 248–52.
Basanoff, V. *Evocatio. Étude d'un rituel militaire romain*. Paris, 1947.
Bauman, R. A. "Criminal Prosecutions by the Aediles." *Latomus* 33 (1974): 245–64.
———. "The Gracchan Agrarian Commission: Four Questions." *Historia* 28 (1979): 385–408.
———. *Lawyers in Roman Republican Politics: A Study of the Roman Jurists in Their Political Setting, 316–82 B.C.* Munich, 1983.
Bayet, J. "Virgile et les triumvirs 'agris dividundis.'" *REL* 6 (1928): 271–99.
Beard, M. "Priesthood in the Roman Republic." In *Pagan Priests: Religion and Power in the Ancient World*, ed. M. Beard and J. North, pp. 19–48. Ithaca, 1990.
Behrends, O. "Tiberius Gracchus und die Juristen seiner Zeit." In *Das Profil des Juristen in der europäischen Tradition*, ed. K. Luig and D. Liebs, pp. 25–121. Ebelsbach, 1980.
Beloch, K. J. *Der italische Bund unter Roms Hegemonie*. Leipzig, 1880.

———. *Römische Geschichte bis zum Beginn der punischen Kriege.* Berlin, 1926.
Bencivegna, C. "Un nuovo contributo alla conoscenza della centuriazione dell'ager Campanus." *RAAN* 51 (1976): 79–89.
Bernstein, A. *Tiberius Sempronius Gracchus: Tradition and Apostasy.* Ithaca, 1978.
Bleicken, J. "Kollisionen zwischen Sacrum und Publicum. Eine Studie zum Verfall der altrömischen Religion." *Hermes* 85 (1957): 446–80.
———. *Lex publica: Gesetz und Recht in der römischen Republik.* Berlin and New York, 1975.
Blume, F., K. Lachmann, and A. Rudorff (eds.). *Die Schriften der römischen Feldmesser.* Berlin, 1848–52. Reprint, Hildesheim, 1967.
Bonamente, M. "Legge suntuarie e loro motivazioni." In *Tra Grecia e Roma: Temi antichi e metodologie moderne,* ed. M. Pavan, pp. 67–92. Rome, 1980.
Bonfante Warren, L. "Roman Costumes. A Glossary and Some Etruscan Derivations." *ANRW* I.4 (1973): 584–614.
Bonnefond-Coudry, M. *Le sénat de la république romaine de la guerre d'Hannibal à Auguste: Pratiques délibératives et prise de décision.* Rome, 1989.
Boren, H. C. "Livius Drusus, t.p. 122, and His Anti-Gracchan Program." *CJ* 52 (1956–57): 27–36.
———. *The Gracchi.* New York, 1968.
Botsford, G. W. *The Roman Assemblies from Their Origin to the End of the Republic.* New York, 1909.
Bouché Leclerc, A. *Les pontifes de l'ancienne Rome.* Paris, 1871.
Boulvert, G. *Esclaves et affranchis impériaux sous le Haut-Empire romain: Rôle politique et administratif.* Naples, 1970.
Bozza, F. *La possessio dell'ager publicus.* Milan, 1939.
Bracco, V. "L'elogium di Polla." *RAAN* 29 (1954): 5–38.
———. "Un nuovo documento della centuriazione graccana: Il termine di Auletta." *RSA* 9 (1979): 29–37.
Briscoe, J. *Commentary on Livy Books XXXI–XXXIII.* Oxford, 1973.
———. *A Commentary on Livy Books XXXIV–XXXVII.* Oxford, 1981.
Broughton, T. R. S. "The *Elogia* of Julius Caesar's Father." *AJA* 52 (1948): 323–30.
Brown, F. E. "Cosa, I: History and Topography." Memoirs of the American Academy at Rome 20. Rome, 1951.
———. *Cosa: The Making of a Roman Town.* Ann Arbor, 1980.
Brown, F. E., E. H. Richardson, and L. Richardson, Jr. "Cosa II: The Temples of the Arx." Memoirs of the American Academy at Rome 26. Rome, 1960.
Brunt, P. A. "The Equites in the Late Republic." In *The Crisis of the Roman Republic,* ed. R. Seager. Cambridge, 1969.
———. "The Enfranchisement of the Sabines." In *Hommages à Marcel Renard,* ed. J. Bibauw, 2:121–29. Brussels, 1969.
———. *Italian Manpower, 225 B.C.–A.D. 14.* Oxford, 1971.
Buckland, W. W. *A Textbook of Roman Law from Augustus to Justinian.* 3rd ed., revised by P. Stein. Cambridge, 1975.
Burdese, A. *Studi sull'ager publicus.* Turin, 1952.
Carcopino, J. *La loi de Hiéron et les romains.* Paris, 1914.
———. *Autour des Gracques. études critiques.* Paris, 1928. Reprint, Paris, 1967.
Cardinali, G. *Studi graccani.* Genoa, 1912.
Càssola, F. *I gruppi politici romani nel III secolo a.C.* Trieste, 1962.
Castagnoli, F. "I più antichi esempi conservati di divisioni agrarie romane." *BCAR* 75 (1953–55): 3–9.

———. "La centuriazione di Cosa." *Memoirs of the American Academy at Rome* 24 (1956): 147–65.
———. *Le ricerche sui resti della centuriazione*. Rome, 1958.
———. *Orthogonal Town Planning in Antiquity*. Trans. V. Caliandro. Cambridge, Mass., 1971.
Catalano, P. "La divisione del potere in Roma. (A proposito di Polibio e Catone)." *Studi in onore di Giuseppe Grosso* 6 (1974): 667–91.
———. "Aspetti spaziali del sistema giuridico-religioso romano. Mundus, templum, urbs, ager, Latium, Italia." *ANRW* II.16.1 (1978): 440–553.
Chevallier, R. *Roman Roads*. Trans. N. H. Field. London, 1989.
Chouquer, G., and F. Favory. *Les paysages de l'antiquité. Terres et cadastres de l'Occident romain (IVe s. avant J.-C./IIIe s. après J.-C.)*. Paris, 1991.
———. *Les Arpenteurs romains. Théorie et Pratique*. Paris, 1992.
Cichorius, C. *Römische Studien: Historisches, epigraphisches, literargeschichtliches aus vier Jahrhunderten Roms*. Berlin, 1922.
Cimma, M. R. *Ricerche sulle società di publicani*. Milan, 1981.
Coarelli, F. *Il Foro Romano I. Periodo arcaico*. Rome, 1983.
Cohen, B. "Some Neglected *Ordines*: The Apparitorial Status-Groups." In *Des ordres a Rome*, ed. C. Nicolet, pp. 23–60. Paris, 1984.
Colonna, G. "Scriba cum rege sedens." In *L'Italie préromaine et la Rome républicaine: Mélanges offerts à Jacques Heurgon*, 1:187–95. Paris, 1976.
Corbett, J. H. "L. Metellus (cos. 251, 247), Agrarian Commissioner?" *CR* 20 (1970): 7–8.
Cornell, T. J. "The Recovery of Rome." In *The Cambridge Ancient History*, 2nd ed., vol. 7, pt. 2, ed. F. W. Walbank, A. E. Astin, M. W. Frederiksen, and R. M. Ogilvie, pp. 309–50. Cambridge, 1989.
Crawford, M. *Roman Republican Coinage*. 2 vols. Cambridge, 1974.
———. "Aut sacrom aut poublicom." In *New Perspectives in the Roman Law of Property: Essays for Barry Nicholas*, ed. P. Birks, pp. 93–98. Oxford, 1989.
———. "The Lex Iulia Agraria." *Athenaeum* 67 (1989): 179–90.
Dahlheim, W. *Struktur und Entwicklung des römischen Volkerrechts im 3. und 2. Jahrhundert v. Chr.* Munich, 1968.
Daube, D. "Two Early Patterns of Manumission." *JRS* 36 (1946): 68–72.
———. *Forms of Roman Legislation*. Oxford, 1956.
———. "Finium demonstratio." *JRS* 47 (1957): 39–52.
De Martino, F. "Riforme del IV secolo a.C." *BIDR* 17 (1975): 29–70.
———. *Storia economica di Roma antica*. Florence, 1979.
———. "Gromatici e questioni graccane." In *Sodalitas. Scritti in onore di Antonio Guarino*, 7:3125–50. Naples, 1984.
Degrassi, A. "Un nuovo miliario calabro della Via Popillia e la Via Annia del Veneto." *Philologus* 99 (1955): 259–65.
della Corte, M. "Groma." *MonAL* 28 (1922): 5–100.
Deniaux, E. "Le passage des citoyennetés locales à citoyenneté romaine." In *Les "bourgeoisies" municipales italiennes aux IIe et Ier siècles av. J.-C.*, pp. 267–77. Paris, 1983.
Dilke, O. A. W. *The Roman Land Surveyors: An Introduction to the Agrimensores*. New York, 1971.
———. "Archaeological and Epigraphic Evidence of Roman Land Surveys." *ANRW* II.1 (1974): 564–92.
———. "Varro and the Origins of Centuriation." *Atti del congresso internazionale di studi varroniani*, pp. 353–58. Rieti, 1976.

———. "Religious Mystique and the Training of Agrimensores." In *Hommages à Henri Le Bonniec: Res sacrae*, pp. 158–62. Brussels, 1988.
Dumézil, G. *Archaic Roman Religion*. Trans. P. Krapp. Chicago, 1970.
Earl, D. C. *Tiberius Gracchus: A Study in Politics*. Brussels, 1963.
———. "Appian B.C. 1.14 and *Professio*." *Historia* 14 (1965): 325–32.
Eck, W. "Senatorial Self-Representation: Developments in the Augustan Period." In *Caesar Augustus: Seven Aspects*, ed. F. Millar and E. Segal, pp. 129–67. Oxford, 1984.
Eckstein, A. M. "The Foundation Day of Roman *Coloniae*." *California Studies in Classical Antiquity* 12 (1979): 85–97.
———. *Senate and General: Individual Decision-Making and Foreign Relations, 264–194 B.C*. Berkeley, 1987.
Erskine, A. *The Hellenistic Stoa: Political Thought and Action*. Ithaca, 1990.
Ewins, U. "The Early Colonization of Cisalpine Gaul." *PBSR* (1952): 54–71.
Ferrary, J.-L. "Rogatio Servilia Agraria." *Athenaeum* 66 (1988): 141–64.
Forni, G. "Manio Curio Dentato uomo democratico." *Athenaeum* 31 (1953): 170–240.
Fraccaro, P. *Studi sull'età dei Gracchi. La tradizione storica sulla rivoluzione graccana*. Città del Castello, 1914. Reprint, Rome, 1967.
———. "Accensi." *Athenaeum* 15 (1927): 133–46.
———. "Polibio e l'accampamento romano." *Athenaeum* (1934): 154–61.
———. "La procedura del voto dei comizi tributi romani." *Opuscula* 2 (Pavia, 1958): 235–54.
Frank, T. *An Economic Survey of Ancient Rome*. 6 vols. Baltimore, 1933.
———. "The New Elogium of Julius Caesar's Father." *AJPh* 58 (1937): 90–93.
Frederiksen, M. *Campania*. Ed. N. Purcell. Rome, 1984.
Frier, B. *Libri Annales Pontificum Maximorum: The Origins of the Annalistic Tradition*. Rome, 1979.
Frothingham, A. L. "Circular Templum and Mundus: Was the Templum Only Rectangular?" *AJA* 18 (1914): 302–20.
Gabba, E. "Lex Plotia Agraria." *PP* 5 (1950): 66–68.
———. "Ricerche su alcuni punti di storia mariana." *Athenaeum* 29 (1951): 12–24.
———. *Appiano e la storia delle guerre civili*. Florence, 1956.
———. *Appiani bellorum civilium liber primus. Introduzione, testo critico e commento con traduzione e indici*. Florence, 1958.
———. *Esercito e società nella tarda repubblica romana*. Florence, 1973.
———. "Caio Flaminio e la sua legge sulla colonizzazione dell'agro gallico." *Athenaeum* 57 (1979): 159–63.
———. "Per un'interpretazione storica della centuriazione romana." *Athenaeum* 63 (1985): 265–84.
Galsterer, H. *Herrschaft und Verwaltung im republikanischen Italien. Die Beziehungen Roms zu den italischen Gemeinden vom Latinerfrieden 338 v. Chr. bis zum Bundesgenossenkrieg 91 v. Chr*. Munich, 1976.
Gargola, D. J. "The Colonial Commissioners of 218 B.C. and the Foundation of Cremona and Placentia." *Athenaeum* 78 (1990): 465–73.
Geertz, C. *Negara: The Theatre State in Nineteenth-Century Bali*. Princeton, 1980.
Gelzer, M. *The Roman Nobility*. Trans. R. Seager. Oxford, 1969.
Gluckman, M. *Politics, Law and Ritual in Tribal Society*. Oxford, 1965.
Göhler, J. *Rom und Italien*. Breslau, 1939.
Goody, J. "Religion and Ritual: The Definitional Problem." *British Journal of Sociology* 12 (1961): 143–64.
———. "Against Ritual: Loosely Structured Thoughts on a Loosely Defined Topic." In *Secular Ritual*, ed. Sally F. Moore and Barbara G. Myerhoff. Amsterdam, 1977.

Grant, M. *From Imperium to Auctoritas: A Historical Study of the Aes Coinage in the Roman Empire, 49 B.C.–A.D. 14.* Cambridge, 1946.
Grueber, H. A. *Coins of the Roman Republic in the British Museum.* London, 1910.
Gruen, E. *The Last Generation of the Roman Republic.* Berkeley, 1974.
Hall, U. "Voting Procedure in Roman Assemblies." *Historia* 13 (1964): 267–306.
———. "The 'IIIviri a.d.a.' of the 'Lex Bantina.'" In *Studi in onore di Edoardo Volterra,* 1:199–206. Milan, 1971.
Hardy, E. G. *Roman Laws and Charters.* Oxford, 1911.
———. *Three Spanish Charters and Other Documents.* Oxford, 1912.
Harris, W. V. *Rome in Etruria and Umbria.* Oxford, 1971.
———. *War and Imperialism in Republican Rome.* Oxford, 1979.
Harvey, P. "Cicero. *Leg. Agr.* 2.78 and the Sullan Colony at Praeneste." *Athenaeum* 53 (1975): 33–56.
———. "Cicero, Consius and Capua: II. Cicero and M. Brutus' Colony." *Athenaeum* 60 (1982): 145–71.
Hermon, E. "La loi agraire de Tiberius Gracchus." *Ktema* 1 (1976): 179–86.
Heurgon, J. "The Date of Vegoia's Prophecy." *JRS* 49 (1959): 41–45.
Hinard, F. "Spectacle des exécutions et espace urbaine." In *L' urbs. Espace urbain et histoire (Ier siècle av. J.-C.–IIIe siècle ap. J.-C.),* pp. 111–25. Rome, 1987.
Hinrichs, F. T. "Der römische Strassenbau zur Zeit der Gracchan." *Historia* 16 (1967): 162–76.
———. "Nochmals zur Inschrift von Polla." *Historia* 18 (1969): 251–55.
———. "Das legale Landversprechen im Bellum Civile." *Historia* 18 (1969): 521–44.
———. *Die Geschichte der gromatischen Institutionen: Untersuchungen zu Landverteilung, Landvermessung, Bodenverwaltung und Bodenrecht in römischen Recht.* Wiesbaden, 1974.
Hirschfeld, O. *Die kaiserlichen Verwaltungsbeamten bis auf Diokletian.* 2nd ed. Berlin, 1905.
Hopkins, K. *Conquerors and Slaves.* Cambridge, 1978.
———. *Death and Renewal.* Cambridge, 1983.
Humbert, M. *Municipium et civitas sine suffragio: L'organisation de la conquête jusqu'à la guerre sociale.* Rome, 1978.
Johannsen, K. "Die Lex Agraria des Jahres 111 v. Chr. Text und Kommentar." Ph.D. dissertation, Ludwig-Maximilians Universität, Munich, 1971.
Johnson, H. D. "The Roman Tribunal." Ph.D. dissertation, Johns Hopkins University, Baltimore, 1927.
Jolowicz, H. F., and B. Nicholas. *Historical Introduction to the Study of Roman Law.* 3rd ed. Cambridge, 1972.
Jonkers, E. J. *Social and Economic Commentary on Cicero's De Lege Agraria Orationes Tres.* Leiden, 1963.
Kain, R. J. P., and E. Baigent. *The Cadastral Map in the Service of the State.* Chicago, 1992.
Kaser, M. "Die Typen des römischen Bodenrechts in der späteren Republik." *ZRG* 62 (1941): 1–81.
———. *Das römisches Privatrecht.* 2nd ed. Munich, 1971.
Keppie, L. *Colonisation and Veteran Settlement in Italy, 47–14 B.C.* London, 1983.
Kertzer, D. I. *Rituals, Politics and Power.* New Haven, 1988.
Kunkel, W. "Zum römischen Königtum." In *Ius et Lex. Festgabe Max Gutzwiller,* pp. 1–22. Basel, 1959. Reprint, *Kleine Schriften.* Weimar, 1974.
———. *Herkunft und soziale Stellung der römischen Juristen.* 2nd ed. Graz, Vienna, and Cologne, 1967.

———. *An Introduction to Roman Legal and Constitutional History.* 2nd ed. Trans. J. M. Kelly. Oxford, 1973.
Kuper, A. *The Invention of Primitive Society.* London, 1988.
Labruna, L. *Vim fieri veto: Alle radice di una ideologia.* Naples, 1971.
Laffi, U. "I senati locali nell'Italia repubblicana." In *Les "bourgeoisies" municipales italiennes aux IIe et Ier siècles av. J.-C.*, pp. 59–74. Paris, 1983.
Latte, K. "The Origins of the Roman Quaestorship." *TAPhA* 67 (1936): 24–33.
———. "Augur und Templum in der varronischen Auguralformel." *Philologus* 97 (1948): 143–59. Reprint, *Kleine Schriften*, pp. 91–105. Munich, 1968.
———. *Römische Religionsgeschichte.* Munich, 1960.
Le Gall, J. "Les romaines et orientation solaire." *MEFRA* 87 (1975): 287–320.
———. "Evocatio." In *L'Italie préromaine et la Rome républicaine. Mélanges offerts à Jacques Heurgon*, pp. 519–24. Paris, 1976.
Levi, M. A. "Ricerche sulla genesi della *centuriatio* e dell'*ager vectigalis*." *PP* 23 (1968): 409–15.
———. "Sui confini dell'agro Campano." *AAT* 52 (1921–22): 604–16. Reprint, *Il tribunato della plebe e altri scritti su istituzioni pubbliche romane*, pp. 67–77. Milan, 1978.
———. "Una pagina di storia agraria romana." In *Il tribunato della plebe e altri scritti su istituzioni pubbliche romane*, pp. 53–65. Milan, 1978. Reprinted from *A & R*, n.s., 3 (1922).
———. Review of *Autour des Gracques*, by J. Carcopino. *RFIC* 57 (1929): 553–60.
Levick, B. *Roman Colonies in Southern Asia Minor.* Oxford, 1967.
Liebeschuetz, J. H. W. G. *Continuity and Change in Roman Religion.* Oxford, 1979.
Linderski, J. "Constitutional Aspects of the Consular Elections in 59 B.C." *Historia* 14 (1965): 423–42.
———. "Cicero and Roman Divination." *PP* 37 (1982): 12–38.
———. "The *Libri Reconditi*." *HSPh* 89 (1985): 207–34.
———. "The Augural Law." *ANRW* II.16.3 (1986): 2146–312.
———. "Roman Religion in Livy." *Xenia. Konstanzer Althistorische Vorträge und Forschungen* 31 (1993): 53–70.
Lintott, A. *Violence in Republican Rome.* Oxford, 1968.
———. "Le procès devant les *recuperatores* d'après les données épigraphiques jusqu'au règne d'Auguste." *RHD* 68 (1990): 1–11.
———. *Judicial Reform and Land Reform in the Roman Republic: A New Edition, with Translation and Commentary, of the Laws from Urbino.* Cambridge, 1992.
Liverani, P. "L'ager veientanus in età repubblicana." *PBSR* 52 (1984): 39–43.
Lübtow, U. von. "Catos leges venditioni et locationi dictae." *Eos* 48 (1956): 227–441.
MacBain, B. *Prodigy and Expiation: A Study in Religion and Politics in Republican Rome.* Brussels, 1982.
MacKendrick, P. "Roman Town Planning." *Archaeology* 9 (1956): 126–33.
MacMullen, R. "How Many Romans Voted?" *Athenaeum* 68 (1980): 454–57.
Madvig, J. N. *Disputationis de Q. Asconii Pediani et aliorum in Ciceronis orationes commentariis appendix critica, locorum Ciceronianorum et Asconianorum emendationes et indices continens.* Copenhagen, 1828.
Magdelain, A. *Recherches sur l'"imperium": La loi curiate et les auspices d'investiture.* Paris, 1968.
———. "L'auguraculum de l'arx à Rome et dans d'autres villes." *REL* 47 (1969): 253–69.
———. "Le pomerium archaïque et le mundus." *REL* 54 (1976): 71–109.
———. "L'inauguration de l'*urbs* et l'*imperium*." *MEFRA* 89 (1977): 11–29.
———. *La loi à Rome: Histoire d'un concept.* Paris, 1978.

Magie, D. *Roman Rule in Asia Minor to the End of the Third Century after Christ*. 2 vols. Princeton, 1950.
Marquardt, J. *Römische Staatsverwaltung*. 2nd ed. 2 vols. Berlin, 1885.
Marshall, A. J. "Symbols and Showmanship in Roman Public Life: The Fasces." *Phoenix* 38 (1984): 120–41.
Marshall, B. A. "The *Lex Plotia Agraria*." *Antichthon* 6 (1972): 43–52.
Maschke, R. *Zur Theorie und Geschichte der römischen Agrargesetze*. Tübingen, 1906. Reprint, Naples, 1980.
Michels, A. *The Calendar of the Roman Republic*. Princeton, 1967.
Millar, F. *The Emperor in the Roman World*. London, 1977.
Molthagen, J. "Die Durchführung der gracchischen Agrarreform." *Historia* 22 (1973): 423–58.
Momigliano, A. "An Interim Report on the Origins of Rome." *JRS* 53 (1963): 95–121.
Mommsen, T. "Die *Libri Coloniarum*." In *Die Schriften der römischen Feldmesser*, ed. F. Blume, K. Lachmann, and A. Rudorff, 2:143–226. Berlin, 1852. Reprint, Hildesheim, 1967.
———. "Die römische Anfänge von Kauf und Miethe." *ZRG* 6 (1885): 262ff.
Müller, K. O. *Die Etrusker*. 2nd ed. by W. Deecke. Stuttgart, 1877.
Münzer, F. *Römische Adelsparteien und Adelsfamilien*. Stuttgart, 1920.
Muzzioli, M. "Note sull'ager quaestorius nel territorio di Cures Sabini." *RAL* 30 (1975): 223–30.
Nagle, D. B. "The Failure of the Roman Political Process in 133 B.C." *Athenaeum* 48 (1970): 372–94.
———. "An Allied View of the Social War." *AJA* 77 (1973): 367–78.
Nap, J. M. *Die römische Republik und das Jahre 225 v. Chr.* Leiden, 1935.
Niccolini, G. *I fasti dei tribuni della plebe*. Milan, 1934.
Nicholas, B. *An Introduction to Roman Law*. Oxford, 1969.
Nicolet, C. "L'inspiration de Tiberius Gracchus." *REG* 67 (1965): 142–58.
———. *Les Gracques*. Paris, 1968.
———. "Les *finitores ex equestri loco* de la loi Servilia de 63 av. J.-C." *Latomus* 29 (1970): 72–103.
———. *Rome et la conquête du monde méditerranéen 264–27 avant J.-C.* Paris, 1977.
———. *The World of the Citizen in Republican Rome*. Trans. P. S. Falla. London, 1980.
———. *Space, Geography, and Politics in the Early Roman Empire*. Ann Arbor, 1991.
Niese, B. "Das sogennannte licinisch-sextische Ackergesetz." *Hermes* 23 (1888): 410–23.
Nissen, H. *Das Templum*. Berlin, 1869.
Norden, E. *Aus altrömischen Priesterbüchern*. Lund, 1939. Reprint, New York, 1975.
North, J. A. "Conservatism and Change in Roman Religion." *PBSR* 44 (1976): 1–12.
———. "Religion in Republican Rome." In *The Cambridge Ancient History*, 2nd ed., vol. 7, pt. 2, ed. F. W. Walbank, A. E. Astin, M. W. Frederiksen, and R. M. Ogilvie, pp. 573–624. Cambridge, 1989.
———. "Diviners and Divination at Rome." In *Pagan Priests*, ed. M. Beard and J. North, pp. 51–71. Ithaca, 1990.
Ogilvie, R. M. "Lustrum Condere." *JRS* 51 (1961): 31–39.
———. *Commentary on Livy Books 1–5*. Oxford, 1970.
Pais, E. "Il Liber Coloniarum." *MAL*, ser. 5, 16 (1920): 55–93, 377–411.
Palmer, R. E. A. *Roman Religion and Roman Empire: Five Essays*. Philadelphia, 1974.
Panerai, M. C. "Gli agrimensori romani: Studi e competenze." In *Misurare la terra: Centurazione e coloni nel mondo romano*, pp. 112–15. Modena, 1983.
Pani, M. "Potere di *iudicatio* e lavori della commissione agraria graccana dal 129 al 121 A.C." *AFLB* 19–20 (1976–77): 131–46.

———. "Il nuovo cippo graccano dauno." *RIL* 111 (1977): 389–400.
Peruzzi, E. "La formula augurale di Varrone LL VII 8." In *Atti del congresso internazionale di studi Varroniani*, 2:449–56. Rieti, 1976.
Pfiffig, A. J. "Eine etruskische Prophezeiung." *Gymnasium* 68 (1961): 55–64.
Pflaum, H.-G. *Les procurateurs équestres sous le Haut-Empire romain*. Paris, 1950.
———. *Les carrières procuratoriennes équestres sous le Haut-Empire romain*. Paris, 1960–61.
Piccaluga, G. *Terminus: I segni di confine nella religione romana*. Rome, 1974.
Piéri, G. *L'histoire du cens jusqu'à la fin de la république romaine*. Paris, 1968.
Pietilä-Castrén, L. *Magnificentia publica: The Victory Monuments of the Roman Generals in the Era of the Punic Wars*. Helsinki, 1987.
Piganiol, A. *Les documents cadastraux de la colonie romaine d'Orange*. Paris, 1962.
Piper, D. "Latins and the Roman Citizenship in Roman Colonies: Livy 34.42.5–6; Revisited." *Historia* 36 (1987): 38–50.
Polignac, F. de. *La naissance de la cité grecque*. Paris, 1984.
Price, S. R. F. *Rituals and Power: The Roman Imperial Cult in Asia Minor*. Cambridge, 1984.
Purcell, N. "The *Apparitores*: A Study in Social Mobility." *PBSR* 51 (1983): 125–73.
Quilici Gigli, S. "Considerazioni sui confini del territorio di Roma primitiva." *MEFRA* 90 (1978): 567–75.
Rauh, N. "Auctioneers and the Roman Economy." *Historia* 38 (1989): 451–71.
Rawson, E. "The Literary Sources for the Pre-Marian Army." *PBSR* 39 (1971): 13–31.
———. "Religion and Politics in the Late Second Century B.C. at Rome." *Phoenix* 28 (1974): 193–212.
———. *Intellectual Life in the Late Roman Republic*. Baltimore, 1985.
Regell, P. "Die Schautempla der Augurn." *Jahrbücher für classischen Philologie* 123 (1881): 597–637.
Regoli, E. "Centuriazione e strade." In *Misurare la terra: Centuriazione e coloni nel mondo romano*, pp. 106–7. Modena, 1984.
Rich, J. W. "The Supposed Manpower Shortage of the Second Century B.C." *Historia* 32 (1983): 287–331.
Richardson, L., Jr. "*Honos et Virtus* and the *Sacra Via*." *AJA* 82 (1978): 240–46.
Rostovtzeff, M. *Social and Economic History of the Roman Empire*. 2nd ed. Oxford, 1957.
Rudolph, H. *Stadt und Staat im römischen Italien. Untersuchungen über die Entwicklung des Munizipalwesens in der republikanischen Zeit*. Leipzig, 1935. Reprint, Göttingen, 1965.
Rudorff, A. "Gromatische Institutionen." In *Die Schriften der römischen Feldmesser*, ed. F. Blume, K. Lachmann, and A. Rudorff, 2:227–464. Berlin, 1852. Reprint, Hildesheim, 1967.
Ruoff-Väänänen, E. *Studies on the Italian Fora*. Wiesbaden, 1978.
Russi, A., and A. Valvo. "Note storiche sul nuovo termine graccana di Celenza Valforte." *MGR* 5 (1977): 225–49.
Sage, E. T., and A. J. Wegner. "Administrative Commissions and the Official Career, 218–167 B.C." *CPh* 31 (1936): 23–32.
Saller, R. *Personal Patronage under the Early Empire*. Cambridge, 1982.
Salmon, E. T. "The Last Latin Colony." *CQ* 27 (1933): 30–35.
———. "The *Coloniae Maritimae*." *Athenaeum* 41 (1963): 2–38.
———. *Samnium and the Samnites*. Cambridge, 1967.
———. *Roman Colonization under the Republic*. Ithaca, 1970.
———. *The Making of Roman Italy*. Ithaca, 1982.

Scardigli, B. *Grani Liciniani Reliquiae: Introduzione, commento storico e traduzione.* Florence, n.d.
Scheid, J. "Le prêtre et le magistrat: Réflexions sur les sacerdoces et le droit public à la fin de la République." In *Des ordres à Rome*, ed. C. Nicolet, pp. 243–81. Paris, 1984.
———. *Religion et piété à Rome.* Paris, 1985.
———. "Les sanctuaries de confins dans la Rome antique: Réalité et permanence d'une représentation idéale de l'espace romain." In *L'urbs: Espace urbain et histoire (Ier siècle av. J.-C.–IIIe siècle ap. J.-C.)*, pp. 583–95. Rome, 1987.
Schleussner, B. *Die Legaten der römischen Republik. Decem Legati und ständige Hilfsgesandte.* Munich, 1978.
Schulz, F. *History of Roman Legal Science.* Oxford, 1946.
Scuderi, R. "Decreti del senato per controversie di confine en età repubblicana." *Athenaeum* 79 (1991): 371–415.
Scullard, H. H. *Roman Politics.* 2nd ed. Oxford, 1973.
———. *Festivals and Ceremonies of the Roman Republic.* Ithaca, 1981.
Seibert, J. "IIIviri agris iudicandis adsignandis lege Sempronia." *RSA* 2 (1972): 53–86.
Sherwin-White, A. N. *The Roman Citizenship.* 2nd ed. Oxford, 1973.
Shochat, Y. "The Lex Agraria of 133 BC and the Italian Allies." *Athenaeum* 48 (1970): 25–45.
———. *Recruitment and the Programme of Tiberius Gracchus.* Brussels, 1980.
Slater, N. W. "Plautine Negotiations: The *Poenulus* Prologue Unpacked." *YClS* 29 (1992): 131–46.
Smith, R. E. "Latins and the Roman Citizenship in Roman Colonies: Livy 34.42.5–6." *JRS* 44 (1954): 18–20.
———. "The Lex Plotia Agraria and Pompey's Spanish Veterans." *CQ*, n.s., 7 (1957): 82–85.
Soltau, W. "Aechtheit des licinische Ackergesetze von 367 v. Chr." *Hermes* 30 (1895): 624–29.
Sterckx, C. "Appien, Plutarque et les premiers règlements *de modo agrorum*." *RIDA* 16 (1969): 309–35.
Stockton, D. *The Gracchi.* Oxford, 1979.
Sumner, G. V. "Cicero, Pompeius, and Rullus." *TAPhA* 97 (1966): 569–82.
———. *The Orators in Cicero's Brutus: Prosopography and Chronology.* Toronto, 1973.
———. Review of *A Commentary on Livy Books XXXI–XXXIII*, by J. Briscoe. *AJPh* 96 (1975): 317–22.
Suolahti, J. *The Junior Officers of the Roman Army in the Republican Period: A Study on Social Structure.* Helsinki, 1955.
Syme, R. "Who Was Decidius Saxa?" *JRS* 27 (1937): 127–37.
Szemler, G. J. *The Priests of the Roman Republic: A Study of the Interactions between Priesthoods and Magistracies.* Brussels, 1972.
———. "Priesthoods and Priestly Careers in Ancient Rome." *ANRW* II.16.3 (1986): 2314–31.
Talbert, R. J. A. *The Senate of Imperial Rome.* Princeton, 1984.
Tatum, W. J. "The *Lex Papiria de dedicationibus*." *CPh* 88 (1993): 319–28.
Taylor, L. R. "Symbols of the Augurate on Coins of the Caecilii Metelli." *AJA* 48 (1944): 352–56.
———. "On the Chronology of Caesar's First Consulship." *AJPh* 72 (1951): 254–68.
———. *Voting Districts of the Roman Republic.* Rome, 1960.
———. "Was Tiberius Gracchus' Last Assembly Electoral or Legislative?" *Athenaeum* 41 (1963): 51–69.

———. *Roman Voting Assemblies from the Hannibalic War to the Dictatorship of Caesar.* Ann Arbor, 1966.
Taylor, L. R., and R. T. Scott. "Seating Space in the Roman Senate and the *Senatores Pedarii.*" *TAPhA* 100 (1969): 529–82.
Thomasson, B. E. *Legatus. Beiträge zur römischen Verwaltungsgeschichte.* Stockholm, 1991.
Thomsen, R. *The Italic Regions from Augustus to the Lombard Invasions.* Copenhagen, 1947.
Thulin, C. *Die etruskische Disciplin.* 3 vols. Göteborg, 1905–9. Reprint, Darmstadt, 1968.
Tibiletti, G. "Il possesso dell'*ager publicus* e le norme *de modo agrorum* sino ai Gracchi." *Athenaeum* 26 (1948): 173–236; 27 (1949): 3–41.
———. "Ricerche di storia agraria romana: La politica agraria dalla guerra annibalica ai Gracchi." *Athenaeum* 28 (1950): 183–266.
———. "Les *treviri a.i.a. lege Sempronia.*" In *Hommage à la mémoire de Jérôme Carcopino*, pp. 277–81. Paris, 1977.
Torelli, M. "Un templum augurale d'età repubblicana a Bantia." *RAL* 21 (1966): 293–315.
———. "Contributi al supplemento del CIL IX." *RAL* 24 (1969): 39–48.
Toynbee, A. J. *Hannibal's Legacy.* Oxford, 1967.
Tozzi, P. *Storia padana antica.* Milan, 1971.
Triebel, C. "Ackergesetze und politischen Reformen: Eine Studie zur römischen Innenpolitik." Ph.D. dissertation, Bonn, 1980.
Turcan, R. "Encore la prophétie de Végoia." In *L'Italie préromaine et la Rome républicaine: Mélanges offerts à Jacques Heurgon*, 2:1009–19. Rome, 1976.
Turner, V. *The Forest of Symbols: Aspects of Ndembu Ritual.* Ithaca, 1967.
Ulrich, R. B. *The Roman Orator and the Sacred Stage: The Roman Templum Rostratum.* Brussels, 1994.
Ungern-Sternberg, J. von. *Capua im zweiten punischen Krieg: Untersuchungen zur römischen Annalistik.* Munich, 1975.
Valeton, I. M. J. "De modis auspicandi Romanorum." *Mnemosyne* 17 (1889): 275–325, 418–52; 18 (1890): 208–63, 406–56.
———. "De templis Romanis." *Mnemosyne* 20 (1892): 338–90; 21 (1893): 62–91, 397–440; 23 (1895): 15–79; 25 (1897): 93–144, 361–85; 26 (1898): 1–93.
Vallat, J.-P. "Statut juridique et statut réel des terres en Campanie du Nord (III–I av. J.C.)." *QS* 7 (1981): 87–96.
———. "*Ager publicus*, colonies et territoire agraire en Campanie du Nord à l'époque républicaine." In *Cadastres et espace rural: Approches et réalités antiques*, ed. M. Clavel-Lévêque, pp. 187–98. Paris, 1983.
Valvo, A. "Il modus agrorum e la legge agraria di C. Flaminio Nepote." *MGR* 5 (1977): 179–224.
Verbrugghe, G. P. "The Elogium from Polla and the First Slave War." *CPh* 68 (1973): 25–35.
Vittinghof, F. *Römische Kolonisation und Bürgerrechtspolitik unter Caesar und Augustus.* Wiesbaden, 1952.
Walbank, F. W. *Commentary on Polybius.* 3 vols. Oxford, 1957–79.
Ward-Perkins, J. B. "Early Roman Towns in Italy." *Town Planning Review* 26 (1955): 127–54.
———. "From Republic to Empire: Reflections on Early Provincial Architecture in the West." *JRS* 60 (1970): 1–19.
———. *Cities of Ancient Greece and Italy: Planning in Classical Antiquity.* New York, 1974.
Warde Fowler, W. *The Religious Experience of the Roman People.* London, 1911.

Watson, A. *Law Making in the Later Roman Republic.* Oxford, 1974.
———. *The State, Law and Religion: Pagan Rome.* Athens, Ga., 1992.
Weaver, P. R. C. *Familia Caesaris: A Social Study of the Emperor's Freedmen and Slaves.* Cambridge, 1972.
Weber, M. "Essay on Bureaucracy." In *From Max Weber: Essays in Sociology,* trans. H. H. Girth and C. Wright Mills, pp. 196–244. New York, 1946.
Weinstock, S. "Martianus Capella and the Cosmic System of the Etruscans." *JRS* 36 (1946): 101–29.
Wieacker, F. "Die römischen Juristen in der politischen Gesellschaft des zweiten Jahrhunderts." In *Sein und Werden im Recht: Festschrift für Ulrich von Lübtow,* pp. 183–214. Berlin, 1970.
Wightman, E. M. "The Plan of Roman Carthage: Practicalities and Politics." In *New Light on Ancient Carthage,* ed. J. Griffiths Pedley, pp. 29–46. Ann Arbor, 1980.
Willems, P. *Le sénat de la république romaine.* 2 vols. Paris, 1878–83.
Wiseman, T. P. "*Viae Anniae.*" *PBSR* 32 (1964): 21–37.
———. "*Viae Anniae* Again." *PBSR* 37 (1969): 82–91.
———. "The Census in the First Century." *JRS* 59 (1969): 59–75.
———. *Roman Studies.* Liverpool, 1987.
Wissowa, G. *Religion und Kultus der Römer.* 2nd ed. Munich, 1912. Reprint, Munich, 1971.
Zancan, L. "Sul possesso dell'ager publicus." *AAT* 67 (1931–32): 71–96.
———. *Ager publicus: Ricerche di storia e di diritto romano.* Florence, 1935.
———. "Il frammento di Vegoia e il novissimum saeculum." *A & R* 7 (1939): 203–19.
Ziolkowski, A. *The Temples of Mid-Republican Rome and Their Historical and Topographical Context.* Rome, 1992.
———. "Between Geese and the Auguraculum: The Origin of the Cult of Juno on the Arx." *CPh* 88 (1993): 206–19.

INDEX

Q. Aelius Tubero (tr. pl. 193). See *Lex Aelia*
Ager: verbal definition of an, 37–38, 81–82, 220 (n. 49); as complement to an *urbs*, 71, 81
Ager censorius, 117, 118–19, 141, 235 (n. 34); boundaries and, 120; in Campania, 124–25. See also *Ager quaestorius*; Auction
Ager Corinthus, 232 (n. 54)
Ager occupatorius, 120, 130–31, 139–40, 141, 233 (nn. 1, 2, 3), 236 (n. 41)
Ager quaestorius, 117, 118–19, 229 (n. 24), 231 (n. 51), 232 (n. 2), 235 (n. 34); in Campania, 122–23, 141. See also *Ager censorius*; Auction
Ager Romanus antiquus, 26, 33, 38, 84, 220 (n. 64)
Ager Thurinus. See *Lex Aelia*
Agrarian law: definition of, 2–3; of the elder Drusus (122), 165, 243 (n. 75); of Saturninus, 176, 177, 247 (n. 18); of the younger Drusus (91), 176, 246 (n. 2), 247 (n. 18); of L. Flavius (60), 246 (n. 4). See also *Lex Aelia*; *Lex Antonia*; *Lex Atinia*; *Lex Flaminia*; *Lex Iulia agraria*; *Lex Licinia agraria*; *Lex Rubria*; *Lex Saufeia*; *Lex Sempronia agraria*
Agrarian law of 111, 81–82, 127, 150–51, 166, 170, 181, 229 (n. 36), 232 (n. 54); titles of Gracchan commissioners in, 163, 242 (n. 67); and Carthage, 167, 170; sortition in, 226 (n. 31). See also *Duumviri*
Agrarian law of P. Servilius Rullus, 180, 209 (n. 36); delegates tasks to nonmagistrates, 183; and *finitores*, 183
Agrimensores, 9–10
T. Annius Rufus (cos. 128): and the inscription from Polla, 242 (n. 61). See also *Via Annia*
Antiquarianism, 8–9
M. Antonius (cos. 44): agrarian law of, 179, 180; performs *lustrum* and plows furrow, 180, 185; contracts with publicans for centuriation, 187–88
Apparitores: definition of, 18–19, 198 (n. 20); at Urso, 83; as surveyors, 94–95; in auctions, 117
L. Appuleius Saturninus (tr. pl. 103, 100). See Agrarian law: of Saturninus
Aquileia, 61–62, 69, 70, 212 (n. 64)
Assemblies, citizen, 13–14
Assembly, centuriate, 76; procedures in, 20, 209 (n. 41); trials by, 131–32, 133
Assembly, plebeian: meeting places, 53, procedures in, 53–55; trials by, 131–32
Assembly, tribal: election of colonial triumvirs, 56; meeting places, 58–59; procedures in, 58–59, 209 (n. 39); election of decemvirs, 103
C. Atinius Labeo (tr. pl. 196), 214 (n. 86). See also *Lex Atinia*
Attalus: bequest of, 152
Auction: magistrates and, 117; procedures of, 117–18
Auguraculum and *auguratorium*, 35, 36; in camps, 28; at Bantia, 36, 220 (n. 66). See also *Templum*; *Templum* (field of vision); *Templum* (tract of land)
Augurs and Augury, 43–46; number, status, and selection of, 14–16; and the definition of spaces, 26; categories of lands of, 26, 199 (nn. 3, 5); areas of responsibility of, 26–28, 166, 243 (n. 79); inauguration of officials, 35–36; at Urso and Capua, 82; and Carthage, 166, 243 (n. 79)
Augustus. See C. Iulius Caesar Octavianus
Auspices: as part of public acts, 16; at crossing of boundaries, 23, 200 (n. 11); types of auspices, 27, 44, 74; ritual form of, 35–36, 205 (nn. 97, 102); and *templa*, 35–36, 205 (nn. 97, 102); at start of centuriation, 46; and delegation, 184; of colonial foundation, 217 (n. 9), 218 (n. 10), 243 (n. 77)

Boundaries and boundary markers: symbolic significance of, 23, 32–33, 200 (n. 11); types of, 31; necessity of, 31, 38; violation of, 31–32; Gracchan markers, 34–35, 40, 156, 158, 159, 160; inscriptions on markers, 34–35, 202 (n. 52); ritual placement of, 37–38; of the *ager Romanus antiquus*, 84, 220 (n. 64); of colonial territory, 84–85. See also *Terminatio*

Bureaucracy: definition of, 3–4

Buxentum. See *Lex Atinia*

Calendar, 21, 33, 135

Campania, 116, 121–27, 137, 177, 179, 203 (n. 76), 229 (nn. 27, 31), 230 (nn. 39, 40, 43), 231 (nn. 46, 49, 50), 232 (n. 55). See also Capua

Camps: layout of, 28, 41, 200 (n. 17), 203 (n. 83), 222 (n. 88); construction of, 41, 93–94

Capua, 82, 83, 179; surrender of, 121–22, 230 (nn. 39, 40); *pomerium* at, 217 (n. 8). See also Campania

Carthage: Gracchan colony at, 164–67, 169–74, 203 (n. 76), 244 (n. 82) See also P. Cornelius Scipio Aemilianus; *Lex Rubria*; Triumvirs, Gracchan

Censors: lease of land by. See *Ager censorius*

Centuriation, 39–41; *per strigas et per scamna*, 38–39; instruments for, 41, 42; orientation of, 42–43, 47–48, 205 (n. 102), 206 (n. 104); augury and, 43–50, 88, 205 (n. 105); process of, 87–90; relation to town site, 87–88; triumvirs and, 89, 221 (n. 72); viritane assignments and, 108–9; centurions and, 222 (n. 89); *publicani* and, 232 (n. 54)

Ap. Claudius Pulcher (cos. 143): service on Gracchan commission, 150, 155; name inscribed on Gracchan markers, 159

Colonial commissioners. See Triumvirs

Colonial laws: and assemblies, 53, 207 (n. 4); and the senate, 53, 207 (n. 4); contents of, 55–58. See also Agrarian law: of the elder Drusus; Agrarian law: of the younger Drusus; *Lex Aelia*; *Lex Atinia*; *Lex Iulia agraria*; *Lex Rubria*; C. Sempronius Gracchus

Colonies: uses of, 51; distinction between citizen and Latin, 56; number of settlers, 56, 57, 165, 169, 208 (nn. 23, 24); subdivisions in, 76, 82, 96–97, 223 (n. 111); constitutions of, 80–81, 82–83; number of plots and size of fields, 89–90; relations to central government, 98–99; addition of new settlers, 99–100; Latins in citizen colonies, 213 (n. 75). See also Colonial laws; Foundation day of colonies; Triumvirs

Commentarii, 15, 20, 132, 222 (n. 88), 233 (n. 9)

Communities: types of, 17–18

Conciliabulum, 109–11, 226 (n. 32)

Contio: definition of, 54

Copia. See *Lex Aelia*

P. Cornelius Lentulus (cos. 162): in Campania, 125–27, 177

P. Cornelius Scipio Aemilianus (cos. 147, 134): and Carthage, 30, 169, 244 (n. 82); opposes Gracchan triumvirs, 151–52, 161–63

Cosa: centuriation of, 49; sacrificial pit at, 75; layout of, 83

Costumes and ritual paraphernalia, 19–20, 67, 117, 118

Cremona, 62, 68, 78–79; centuriation at, 40, 203 (n. 75), 215 (n. 90)

M'. Curius Dentatus (cos. 290): and assignments, 105, 108, 224 (n. 11); and *ager quaestorius*, 126, 231 (n. 51), 232 (n. 52)

Decemviri (viritane assignments), 105; of 173, 103, 106–7; of 201, 103, 106–7, 110–11; in the *lex Flaminia*, 105; membership in, 106–7; in law of Saturninus, 179, 247 (n. 18); in law of younger Drusus, 179, 247 (n. 18); in the law of Rullus, 179–80; *lege Livia*, 181; in law of the elder Drusus, 243 (n. 75)

L. Decidius Saxa: as *septemvir* under *lex Antonia*, 180, 185, 248 (n. 28). See also *Lex Antonia*

Decumanus, decumanus maximus, 39, 40–41, 42, 46, 47, 49, 86–88; in Campania, 203 (n. 76); at Carthage, 203 (n. 76)

Deditio (formal surrender of a city), 32–34

Delegation of tasks: importance in government of, 3–4; at Gracchan colony of Carthage, 173–74; in the law of Rullus, 183–84, 186–87; and the auspices, 184
Devotio (of a city), 244 (n. 82)
Dilectus, 65–66, 213 (n. 76), 214 (nn. 79, 80)
Disciplina Etrusca, 32, 42, 85
Domi et militiae, 26; governmental implications of, 27; ritualized transition between, 67
Duumviri: *aedibus locandi* and *aedibus dedicandae*, 22–23, 60; of the agrarian law of 111, 127, 232 (n. 54), 246 (n. 101)

Evocatio, 30, 244 (n. 82)
Exauguratio, 33

Finitor (Term), 46–47, 91–93, 183, 186–87, 205 (n. 99), 249 (nn. 47, 48). See also Surveyors
C. Flaminius (cos. 217): ritual failures leading to defeat, 24; land law of, 104–5, 224 (n. 7)
Forma, 40, 96, 126, 127, 229 (n. 31), 240 (n. 33), 249 (n. 42)
Forum (settlement), 109–12, 226 (n. 32)
Foundation day of colonies, 73–74, 217 (nn. 4, 7)
M. Fulvius Flaccus (cos. 125): service on the Gracchan commission, 155, 167; name inscribed on Gracchan markers, 160; at Carthage, 165–67, 169–71
Q. Fulvius Flaccus (cos. 212): in Campania, 121–22
L. Furius Philus (cos. 136), 201 (n. 29)

Genua, 38, 82, 87
Groma: description of, 41; range of uses of, 41; antecedents of, 42
Gromatici veteres. See *Agrimensores*
Groves, sacred, 30, 86

Haruspices, 42, 43, 45, 184, 243 (n. 79); at Urso, 83

Inauguration, 27, 35–36
Informers (*delatores*), 123, 134–35, 234 (n. 14)
Inlicium, 20

C. Iulius Caesar (cos. 59): colonies founded as dictator, 181–82. See also *Lex Iulia agraria*
C. Iulius Caesar Octavianus (Augustus): settles his veterans in colonies, 181–82; personally rewards recipients, 182–83; contracts with publicans for centuriation, 187–88
Iunonia. See Carthage; Triumvirs, Gracchan

Kardo, kardo maximus, 40–41, 42, 46, 47, 86–88; in Campania, 47, 203 (n. 76); at Carthage, 203 (n. 76)

Legates: and boundary disputes between cities, 34, 82, 98–99, 202 (n. 49); and land assignments, 185–86, 250 (n. 60)
Legis Actio, 21–22, 31–32, 199 (n. 29), 202 (n. 55)
Lex, leges: *lex templi*, 28–30, 200 (n. 22), 207 (n. 18); *leges datae* and *dictae*, 30, 35, 80–81, 201 (n. 31), 207 (n. 18); *lex luci*, 30, 86–87, 207 (n. 18); as a ritual text, 55; verbal forms of, 55, 207 (n. 18); *lex locationis* and *venditionis*, 118–19, 187–88, 207 (n. 18). See also Agrarian law
Lex Aelia, 57, 63, 73, 215 (n. 91); term of commissioners, 69; commissioners in the field, 69–70, 89; size of settlements, 209 (n. 33)
Lex Antonia, 179, 180
Lex Atinia, 63, 72–73; term of its commissioners, 56; the commissioners in the field, 67–68, 245 (n. 90); later modifications to, 209 (n. 34); prospective colonists and Roman citizenship, 213 (n. 75); date of, 214 (n. 86)
Lex coloniae Iuliae Genetivae (*lex Ursonensis*): proclamation of, 80–81; functionaries created by, 82–83; instructions to magistrates, 119, 181, 209 (n. 36)
Lex Flaminia, 104–5, 224 (n. 7)
Lex Hieronica, 140
Lex Iulia agraria, 177, 179, 185
Lex Licinia agraria, 136–37, 139, 144
Lex Mamilia Roscia Peducaea Alliena Fabia, 109, 111–12, 180–81, 248 (n. 31)
Lex Plotia agraria, 246 (n. 4)
Lex Rubria, 164–65, 166, 169
Lex Saufeia, 179

Lex Sempronia (123). *See* C. Sempronius Gracchus
Lex Sempronia agraria (133): magistrates created by, 149–50; provisions of, 149–51, 237 (nn. 6, 8); area covered by, 150–51; and judicial powers, 151–55. *See also* Ti. Sempronius Gracchus; Triumvirs, Gracchan
Liber coloniarum: value as a source, 158–59, 241 (n. 43)
Libri rituales, 85
P. Licinius Crassus Mucianus (cos. 131): advises Ti. Gracchus on law, 148–49; serves on Gracchan commission, 155, 167; name inscribed on Gracchan markers, 159
Lictors, 19, 21, 220 (n. 53); at Urso, 82
Limitation. *See* Centuriation
Liternum. See *Lex Atinia*
M. Livius Drusus (tr. pl. 91). *See* Agrarian law: of the younger Drusus
M. Livius Drusus (tr. pl. 122). *See* Agrarian law: of the elder Drusus
Luca, 63, 212 (n. 63), 216 (nn. 95, 96)
Ludi: at dedication of temples, 23; *Capitolini*, 117, 228 (n. 16)
Luna, 212 (n. 63), 216 (n. 95)
Lustrum, 16, 20, 76–80, 100, 112, 180, 185, 218 (nn. 26, 30), 219 (nn. 32, 41); at Rome, 20, 76–77, 79; ritual flaws in, 23, 78, 165–67; ritual form of, 28, 77; colonial, 77, 100, 165–67, 219 (nn. 32, 41, 42); military, 77–79; location of, 78–80; viritane assignments, 112; at Carthage, 165–67; colonial, on coins of Augustus and successors, 182

Magistrates, 12–13; and religion, 15–16; and the definition of spaces, 33–34. See also *Decemviri*; *Duumviri*; *Quinqueviri*; *Septemviri*; Triumvirs; *Vigintiviri*
P. Mucius Scaevola (cos. 133): advises Ti. Gracchus on law, 148–49
Mundus, 75, 80

Attus Navius, 44
Numa Pompilius: and boundaries, 31, 32; inauguration of, 35, 45

Occupatio. See *Ager occupatorius*
Olenus Calenus, 36–37, 45

Pali sacrificiales, 38, 85, 220 (n. 65)
C. Papirius Carbo (cos. 120): service on Gracchan commission, 155, 167; name inscribed on Gracchan markers, 160
Parilia, 73
Q. Petilius Spurinus (cos. 176): and ritual flaw, 24, 97
Placentia, 62, 68, 78–79, 215 (n. 90); layout of, 41
Plautus: on *finitores*, 46–47, 92
Pomerium, 27, 74, 79–80, 111–12, 131, 166–67, 184, 185, 200 (n. 13), 202 (n. 64), 205 (nn. 94, 102), 207 (nn. 8, 9), 244 (n. 81); extension of, 37; colonial, 165–67, 217 (nn. 7, 8, 9); at Carthage, 165–67, 244 (n. 81)
Cn. Pompeius Magnus: agrarian laws in the interest of, 176–77; serves on agrarian commission, 185
Pontiffs: numbers, status, and selection of, 14–15, as experts in private law, 14–15, 55; and dedication of temples, 28–29
Possessio, 130, 233 (nn. 2, 3)
Postliminium, 26
L. Postumius Albinus (cos. 173): in Campania, 120, 124–25
Praeco (herald), 19, 117, 132; at Urso, 83
Publicani, 13, 117, 119, 187–88, 235 (n. 27); and centuriation, 187–88, 232 (n. 54)
Puteoli. See *Lex Atinia*

Quinqueviri: *lege Saufeia*, 179; of the *lex Iulia* (59), 179, 185, 247 (n. 23); Sullan (?), 179, 247 (n. 20); legates mistaken for, 202 (n. 49); for the *ager Pomptinus*, 225 (n. 13)

Religion: and public life, 5–6
Ritual: significance of, 5–7; definition of, 5–7, 196 (n. 7)
Ritual faults: consequences of, 23–24; at Carthage, 165–67
Romulus: as dedicator of temple, 29, 36; as king and augur, 29, 184; as founder of city, 71, 217 (n. 9)

Salernum. See *Lex Atinia*
C. Sempronius Gracchus (tr. pl. 123, 122): service on triumvirate, 150, 155, 167; name inscribed on markers, 159, 160;

renews his brother's law, 163; colonial legislation of, 164–65, 242 (nn. 68, 69); at Carthage, 165–67, 169–71, 242 (n. 70)
Ti. Sempronius Gracchus (cos. 163): ritual fault of, 23
Ti. Sempronius Gracchus (tr. pl. 133): aided by others in drafting law, 148–49; serves on Gracchan commission, 150, 155; carries second agrarian law, 151–55. See also *Lex Sempronia agraria* (133)
P. Servilius Rullus (tr. pl. 63): law of, 178–79, 183, 186–88
Senate: and Roman government, 13–14; and colonization, 53; meeting places, 53
Septemviri: of the *lex Antonia agraria*, 179, 180, 185
Sortition, general principles of, 222 (n. 93), 223 (nn. 99, 100); to assign official tasks, 74, 95, 97, 169, 171–73; to assign lands, 95–98, 108–9, 180, 222 (n. 96), 226 (n. 31), 249 (n. 42); and augury, 97; and *templa*, 97
Stoicism, 154
Sulcus primigenius (primeval furrow), 80, 182, 217 (nn. 7, 8, 9), 218 (n. 14); creates and extends *pomerium*, 37, 74, 165–67; as founding act, 73–74, 165–67; ritual form of, 74–75; at Carthage, 165–67; on coins of Augustus and successors, 182
Sumptuary legislation, 144–45
Surveyors: role of, 46, 90–95, 183, 186, 249 (n. 48); status of, 90–95, 187, 222 (n. 89); as *apparitores*, 94–95; in the law of Rullus, 186–87; as *publicani*, 187–88. See also *Finitor*

Temple: as speakers' platform, 19, dedication of, 22–23, 28–30, 34, 36; as meeting places for the senate, 28, 53
Templum: and centuriation, 43–50; internal divisions in, 44–45; orientation of, 47–48, 205 (n. 102), 206 (nn. 104, 105); in colonies, 85–86
Templum (field of vision), 35–36, 43–45, 47, 204 (nn. 91, 93), 205 (n. 102); types of, 43–44
Templum (tract of land), 31, 36–37, 48, 53, 97, 204 (nn. 91, 93), 206 (n. 106); nature of, 27–28; uses of, 27–28, 53; visible boundaries of, 31; *minus*, 36, 38, 202 (n. 58); ritual establishment of, 36–37; stretches in front of auspiciant, 205 (n. 97)
Terminatio: definition of, 33; status of those who perform, 33–34; distinct from *limitatio*, 39, 203 (n. 71)
Terminus, Terminalia, 33, 201 (n. 40)
Towns: layout of, 41, 83–84; principles for placing, 72–73
Trials: *apud populum*, 20, 131–33, 135; in private law cases, 21–22
Tribunes, military: and the *dilectus*, 65–66; and camps, 93–94, 222 (n. 88); possible role in land assignments, 186; *commentarii* of, 222 (n. 88)
Triumvirs (colonial): terms in office, 56, 69; standardized form for the foundation of colonies, 56–57, 208 (nn. 23, 24, 26, 27); election of, 58–60; membership in, 60–63, 210 (n. 44), 212 (n. 64), 214 (n. 86); and centuriation, 90–92, 221 (n. 72); mode of operation, 215 (n. 93), 216 (n. 100). See also *Lex Aelia*; *Lex Atinia*
Triumvirs, Gracchan, 142: mode of election of, 150; members, 150, 155, 239 (nn. 28, 29); term in office, 150, 238 (n. 11), 244 (n. 88); judicial powers of, 151–55, 161–63, 238 (n. 22), 240 (nn. 33, 35); and centuriation, 156–58; strategy of, 156–58; and earlier assignments, 157–58; renewed by C. Gracchus, 163; relationship to college at Carthage, 164–65; at Carthage, 165–67, 169–71, 243 (n. 72); division of tasks among, 167–74; mode of operation, 172–73, 245 (n. 89); possible delegation of responsibilities, 173–74; possess auspices of colonial foundation, 243 (n. 77)
Twelve Tables, 22, 32

Urso: *pomerium* at, 217 (n. 8). See also *Lex coloniae Iuliae Genetivae*

Vegoia: prophecy of, 32, 201 (n. 39)
Via Aemilia, 47, 108; *Annia*, 159–60; *Appia*, 160; *Flaminia*, 160; *Aurelia*, 161; *Cassia*, 161
Viatores, 19; at Urso, 83
Vibo Valentia. See *Lex Aelia*

Vigintiviri: of *lex Iulia*, 179, 180, 185, 247 (n. 23)

Viritane assignments: where made, 103; assemblies and, 103, 104–5, 224 (n. 3); senate and, 103–4, 224 (n. 3); scale of, 108; sortition and, 108. See also *Decemviri*

Volturnum. See *Lex Atinia*

Vows, 22, 67

www.ingramcontent.com/pod-product-compliance
Lightning Source LLC
Chambersburg PA
CBHW021357290426
44108CB00010B/283